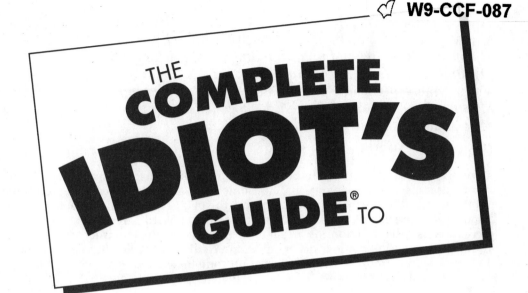

THE COMPLETE IDIOT'S GUIDE® TO

Learning Spanish
on Your Own

Second Edition

by Gail Stein

ALPHA

A Pearson Education Company

This book is dedicated to:
My tremendously patient and supportive husband, Douglas
My incredibly loving and understanding sons, Eric and Michael
My proud parents, Jack and Sara Bernstein
My extremely artistically gifted sister, Susan J. Opperman
My superior consultant and advisor, Roger Herz
My wonderful student, Alexandra Bernal

Copyright©1999 by Gail Stein

International Standard Book Number: 0-02-862743-1
Library of Congress Catalog Card Number: 95-083359

03   02   10   9   8

Interpretation of the printing code: the rightmost number of the first series of numbers is the year of the book's printing; the rightmost number of the second series of numbers is the number of the book's printing. For example, a printing code of 99-1 shows that the first printing occurred in 1999.

Printed in the United States of America

Alpha Development Team

Publisher
Kathy Nebenhaus

Editorial Director
Gary M. Krebs

Managing Editor
Bob Shuman

Marketing Brand Manager
Felice Primeau

Acquisitions Editor
Jessica Faust

Development Editors
Phil Kitchel
Amy Zavatto

Assistant Editor
Georgette Blau

Production Team

Development Editor
Mary Russell

Production Editor
Tammy Ahrens

Copy Editor
Amy Lepore

Cover Designer
Mike Freeland

Photo Editor
Richard H. Fox

Illustrator
Jody P. Schaeffer

Book Designers
Scott Cook and Amy Adams of DesignLab

Indexer
John Jefferson

Layout/Proofreading
Marie Kristine P. Leonardo
Ellen Considine
Laura Goetz
Carrie Allen

Contents at a Glance

Contents

Part 2: Traveling Around 69

8 Meetings and Greetings 71

9 Getting to Know You 83

Appendices

Foreword

The Complete Idiot's Guide to Learning Spanish on Your Own, Second Edition, is an easy-going, self-teaching guide that provides the student of Spanish with the necessary tools to learn and assimilate information that will enable the student to interact effectively in a Spanish-speaking context.

Each chapter deals dynamically with practical grammatical aspects that help build one's vocabulary and language structures. In addition, *Learning Spanish* focuses on the cultural nuances that are often neglected when learning a foreign language. Thus, the student will not only learn the linguistic system of Spanish but also the cultural subtleties, namely, common idiomatic expressions and body language pertinent to Spanish. All of these elements are essential to avoid being misunderstood or frustrated when visiting a Spanish-speaking country and communicating with native speakers.

Gregory D. Lagos-Montoya
Visiting professor of Spanish linguistics at Rutgers University
Prof. of Contrastive Ling. at Universidad de Los Lagos, Osorno-Chile.

Acknowledgments

The author would like to acknowledge the contributions, input, support, and interest of the following people: Tammy Ahrens; John Aliano; Trecia Ashman; Charles Bowles; Héctor Cardwood, head pastry chef of the San Juan Marriott; María Chin and Brenda Dávila of the San Juan Marriott; Nancy Chu; Micqual Coaxum; Gabriel Cruz; Trudy and Richard Edelman; Marc Einsohn; Raymond C. Elias; Angela Felipe; Barbara Gilson; Michelle and Stephen Gordon; Robert Grandt; Martin S. Hyman; Martin Leder; Amy Lepore; Christina Levy; Anne Marie Loffredo; Justin Mark; Marion Meitner; Robby Menke; Nancy Mikhail; Jennifer Nicholson; Violetta Ostafin; Liseth Prado; Catherine Ramai; Max Rechtman; Cynthia Reyes; Dr. Angel Rueda; Mary Russell; Barbara Shevrin; Maritza Trujillo; Herbert Waldren; Tywonne Wesley.

Special Thanks to the Technical Reviewer

The Complete Idiot's Guide to Learning Spanish on Your Own, Second Edition was reviewed by an expert who double-checked the accuracy of what you'll learn here, to help us ensure that this book gives you everything you need to know about learning Spanish. Special thanks are extended to Wigberto Rivera.

Introduction

Today, more than ever, knowledge of at least one foreign language is essential for both business-related and pleasurable pursuits. Sophisticated improvements in travel and communication have made the world our neighborhood. The world is now accessible to everyone: to you, to me, and to the generations that will follow.

Learn Spanish and you will enter a world that can provide you with endless opportunities, intriguing experiences, and exciting challenges. Learn Spanish and you will have the key to open the door to a different lifestyle, a distinctive culture, and a unique outlook on life. Learn Spanish and you will possess a valuable tool that will serve you well when you least expect it. Open your mind and immerse yourself in the beauty of the language and the culture. Study Spanish purposefully, with patience and love. You will be rewarded again and again.

Right from the start, you'll feel that this book was written with *you* in mind. It is extremely user-friendly and will make your language-learning experience pleasant, satisfying, and entertaining. You'll find the approach easygoing and clear-cut, enabling you to start communicating almost instantly with a reasonable amount of skill and an encouraging sense of achievement.

Why and How This Book Is Meant for You

This book takes you from basic material to a deeper understanding of the patterns of the Spanish language and finally to a higher level of expertise and accomplishment. This book is unique—it is a phrase book, a grammar book, a cultural guide, and a dictionary all wrapped up in one. Its goal is to enable you to handle common, everyday situations proficiently and competently. Whether you are a student, a traveler, a businessperson, or simply a lover of languages, this book will provide you with the knowledge and skills you need in a format that is simple to understand and easy to use. Thematically linked vocabulary, useful expressions, grammar, and practical activities for mastery and enrichment are presented in every chapter. Authentic materials will immerse you in the Spanish culture and will give you a thorough understanding of the people. Here's what you can expect to find in this book:

Part 1, "The Basics," shows you why Spanish is a language you should learn. The simple, phonetic pronunciation guide will have you pronouncing the language properly almost immediately. You'll also see how much Spanish you already know based on your knowledge of English. Don't fret over grammar—basic, elementary terms and rules are painlessly presented along with high-frequency idioms, slang, and gestures indigenous to the culture. Right from the start, you'll be asking and answering simple questions and even engaging in basic conversations.

Part 2, "Traveling Around," enables you to plan and take a trip to a Spanish-speaking country. When it's time to introduce yourself, you'll be able to use greetings and salutations, to describe yourself and others traveling with you, and to talk about your job. If you're the curious type, asking questions will prove easy. The chapters in this section can help you find your way to the airport, obtain necessary ground transportation, and even rent a car. Don't worry about giving or receiving directions; that will also be explained. Finally, this section will help you acquire a room with the creature comforts you prefer.

Part 3, "Having Fun," enables you to go out and have a great time in any Spanish-speaking country. Everything that makes for a superb experience is covered in this section: food, sports, museums, tourist attractions, musical events, and leisure activities. You'll learn to plan your daily activities around the weather, to offer suggestions, and to make your opinions and preferences known. The food chapters can help you stick to your diet or go all out. If you love to shop, one of the chapters can help you buy anything from typical native handicrafts to a tropical Guayabera shirt. Conversion charts for sizing clothes are provided to help you make correct selections.

Part 4, "Problem Solving," prepares you not only for simple, minor inconveniences but also for problems that are more serious in nature. Consult this section when you need a haircut, a stain removed, your camera fixed, a replacement contact lens, new heels on your shoes, prescription drugs, or a package sent.

Part 5, "Taking Care of Business," was written to meet the needs of people who want to conduct business transactions: making deposits and withdrawals, opening a checking account, and taking out a loan. A minidictionary of bank terms is included. There's also a section of computer terms and phrases as well as a section to help you rent or buy property and discuss your present and future needs.

If you persevere and study this book from cover to cover, you will learn and practice skills that will enable you to be confident in both social and business situations where Spanish is required. If you have the time and the patience and if you are willing to make the effort, you can successfully communicate in a new and beautiful language in a relatively short period of time.

Extras

In addition to grammatical explanations, useful phrases and expressions, and vocabulary lists, this book provides a wealth of interesting and informative facts formatted throughout the text as sidebars. Look for the following icons that set these tidbits apart:

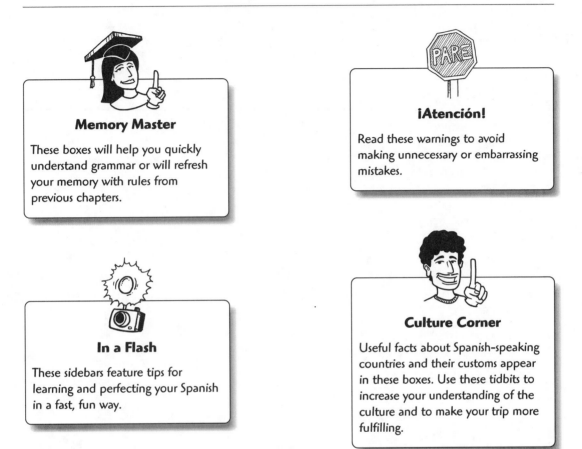

Memory Master

These boxes will help you quickly understand grammar or will refresh your memory with rules from previous chapters.

¡Atención!

Read these warnings to avoid making unnecessary or embarrassing mistakes.

In a Flash

These sidebars feature tips for learning and perfecting your Spanish in a fast, fun way.

Culture Corner

Useful facts about Spanish-speaking countries and their customs appear in these boxes. Use these tidbits to increase your understanding of the culture and to make your trip more fulfilling.

10 minutos al día

If you spend just 10 minutes each day reviewing these highlights of the most important information in the chapter, you'll be on the road to success.

Part 1
The Basics

Truth be told, the fastest, easiest, most efficient way to pick up Spanish is to start with basic grammar. Just learn a few simple rules—that's all it takes!

The thought of learning grammar probably sounds like an immediate turn-off. Nonsense! Don't let it be! The rules are quite simple, and I won't overtax your memorization skills. You'll also learn how to speak idiomatically so you don't sound like an inexperienced gringo. Take the plunge—you'll soon be able to understand and to communicate in Spanish with confidence and ease.

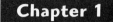

Chapter 1

The Top Ten Reasons You Should Study Spanish

In This Chapter

➤ What Spanish has to offer

➤ Where Spanish can be used

➤ Developing a learning strategy

➤ There is absolutely nothing to fear

If you haven't already purchased this book, you're probably leafing through it wondering, "Can I *really* do this?" No doubt you're deciding whether you'll have the time, whether you have what it takes to stick with it, and whether, indeed, it'll pay off in the end. Just like David Letterman on late-night television, I'm going to give my top 10 reasons why you should study Spanish:

Reason #10   You want to impress your date at a Spanish restaurant by ordering in Spanish.

Reason #9   You loved the movie *Man of La Mancha* so much that you want to read *Don Quijote* in its original language.

Reason #8   When you meet Paloma Picasso on the street, you want to be able to ask her questions she'll understand.

Reason #7   You want to buy time-share property on the beach in Puerto Rico.

Reason #6 When you get pulled over for speeding in Tijuana, you don't want to wind up in jail.

Reason #5 You want to study flamenco dancing in Madrid.

Reason #4 You can get a discount on Cuban cigars if you order them in español.

Reason #3 You want to sing along with Richie Valens when they play "La Bamba" on the oldies station.

Reason #2 You want to run with the bulls in Pamplona, but they don't understand English.

Reason #1 One word—Cancún.

Seriously Speaking

Now that we've had a little fun, it's time to seriously consider why you should study Spanish. Let's take a look at some more credible reasons:

Real Reason #10 You love music, especially music with a native beat. It just makes you want to move your feet. Although your friends are into more modern music, you have to admit you really find Casals's cello pieces and Segovia's guitar solos very relaxing.

Real Reason #9 You love to dance. The music starts to blare and you can't help it—your hips start to sway and your feet start to move. Let's face it, you've got rhythm. You want to mambo, cha-cha, salsa, even tango. Just reading this makes your feet start tapping.

Real Reason #8 You're an aficionado of Spanish movies, and you really would enjoy watching them without having to read the distracting, poorly translated, sometimes invisible subtitles.

Real Reason #7 You're an artist at heart. You long to spend time at El Prado admiring the works of Zurbarán, Velázquez, Murillo, and El Greco. Picasso's *Guernica* brings tears to your eyes, and Dalí's surrealistic paintings make you wonder what was going on in his mind. You truly are a cultured person, and the Spanish-speaking world has a lot to offer.

Real Reason #6 You definitely are not money-hungry, but you'd like to improve your chances in the job market. With so many fields open today, a knowledge of Spanish would be a real plus. Here's your opportunity to get that little extra knowledge that will put you above all the others who are competing for the job you want.

Real Reason #5 You want to live in a warm climate, and the countries in Spanish America have a lot to offer: The landscape is beautiful, the people are friendly, the food is delicious, and you won't need an expensive winter wardrobe.

Real Reason #4 Speaking of food, you love to cook. You want to learn how to make an authentic paella valenciana or a truly hot and spicy salsa picante. If you want to do it right, you have to go to the source. Besides, you probably won't be able to get all the spices and ingredients you need in your hometown.

Real Reason #3 You hate to cook but you love to eat, and you like everything hot and spicy. You're a fan of tropical fruits, and you dream of sipping an ice-cold piña colada on a white sandy beach in Mexico. You're tired of the same old fare, and you want to sample all the different types of food available in countries that are really quite close by. You can plan your next vacation accordingly.

Real Reason #2 You want to prove to yourself that you are smart. Foreign languages have always had the reputation of being impossible to learn. How many of your friends and acquaintances studied a language in school for two, three, or even four years and then claimed, "But I can't even speak a word!" That doesn't have to be the case. Learning a foreign language can be easy and fun. Try it. You'll be pleasantly surprised.

Real Reason #1 You're a traveler. You want to see the world and all it has to offer, so you make sure you never go to the same place twice on vacation. If that's the case, keep in mind that Spanish is spoken by more than 300 million people throughout the world in more than 20 countries. You have a lot of trips ahead of you! Look at the following maps to see all the countries in which Spanish is the primary language.

Go for It!

The best way to become proficient in a language is to plunge right in. Immerse yourself in anything and everything Spanish. Have a love affair with the language and culture. Follow these suggestions to ensure a long-lasting and fulfilling relationship with Spanish:

➤ Examine your goals honestly, evaluate your linguistic abilities, and pace yourself accordingly. Don't rush—take your time studying the language. Set aside a special time each day that you devote only to learning Spanish.

➤ Invest in or borrow a good bilingual dictionary. Keep in mind that pocket varieties might be too skimpy and might be inappropriate for learning a new language.

Carefully check what is available in your local bookstore or library before purchasing a dictionary. Current, popular, easy-to-use dictionaries that provide comprehensive listings of current, colloquial vocabulary words are published by a number of companies. (The best dictionaries include those by Simon & Schuster and Larousse.) They can be found in any bookstore to fit any size pocketbook.

➤ Take advantage of any opportunities to listen to the language. Rent Spanish movies and try not to read the English subtitles. If they broadcast in your area, listen to public service radio or television stations that provide Spanish programs. In addition, search bookstores and public or college libraries for language tapes that will help you hear and master spoken Spanish. Then try to create your own tapes and use them to perfect your accent. You can also ask to use the language laboratories and computer programs available in many high schools and universities.

➤ Read everything you can get your hands on, including fairy tales, children's books, and comic books. Try to read Spanish newspapers such as *El Diario/ La Prensa*. If you're not too bashful, read aloud to practice your pronunciation and comprehension at the same time.

➤ Set up *un rincón español* (a Spanish corner) in a convenient place in your home. Decorate it with posters or articles. Label any items whose names you want to learn and display them for easy viewing. Keep all your materials together and organized in this special Spanish spot.

10 minutos al día

Learn Spanish by immersing yourself in the language: buy a good bilingual dictionary; read, read, and then read some more; watch foreign films; tune in to Spanish programs on your TV or radio; make use of school language laboratories; surf the Internet; and use vocabulary labels throughout your home.

Fear Not!

Some people are truly afraid to study a foreign language. They think it will be too much work, too hard, and too time-consuming. In reality, however, if you take it slowly and don't allow yourself to become overly concerned with the grammar and the pronunciation, you'll manage very well. To help you feel more at ease as you begin your task, remember the following points:

➤ Don't be intimidated by grammar. Everyone makes mistakes, even in his or her native language. Besides, only one or two correctly used words (especially verbs) will often enable people to understand you.

➤ Don't be intimidated by pronunciation. Put on your best Spanish accent, don't be shy, and speak, speak, speak. All countries have different regional accents. Certainly yours will fit in somehow.

➤ Don't be intimidated by native speakers. They are usually helpful to anyone who makes a sincere attempt to communicate in their language.

➤ Don't be intimidated by the reputation foreign languages have for being difficult. As you will see right from the start, Spanish is fun and easy.

In a Flash

Buy a Spanish newspaper. Every day, choose one article that interests you. Underline and make a list of all the words whose meanings you don't recognize. Spend a few minutes each day studying these words. In a week's time, you'll develop an extensive Spanish vocabulary.

The Least You Need to Know

➤ Whether for business or pleasure, there are many reasons you should learn Spanish.

➤ The best way to learn a new language is to take your time and to read and listen to as much as you can in the language.

➤ There's nothing to fear when studying a language. Don't let grammar and pronunciation intimidate you. You'll be able to make yourself understood, even with limited vocabulary.

➤ You will become proficient in Spanish if you learn to love the language and immerse yourself in it as much as possible.

¡Hola!

Chapter 2

Say It Right!

In This Chapter

➤ The stress of it all

➤ Finding fluidity

➤ Getting the accent

➤ Phonetically yours

So you've decided you want to learn how to roll your *r*'s and how to purr like a wild *tigre*. You also want to learn how to make your *v*'s sound like *b*'s and how to silence some letters while emphasizing others. Lose your inhibitions, put on your best Spanish accent, and repeat and practice the sounds of the language. Remember, although Spanish is a foreign language to you, it is very phonetic; therefore, it is very easy to pronounce. That's right, just read what you see and pronounce it the way you think it should be pronounced. Chances are, you've got it right. Let's take a look at a few rules that will help you sound like a true Spanish-speaker. You'll be purrrrring away in no time at all!

Think of this lesson as a verbal workout. Like any other skill you might want to perfect, proper Spanish pronunciation requires a certain amount of practice and dedication. Don't hesitate to sit down and talk to yourself, read aloud, or sing along with your favorite Spanish singer. If you want to be successful, begin slowly at first and then gradually increase your efforts until you find yourself working at a comfortable pace. Avoid burning out by trying to accomplish too much too soon. Remember, practice makes perfect.

When There's Stress Involved

Pronounce each syllable of a word with equal emphasis unless it has a written accent. Unlike English, where words are often phonetically confusing, difficult to sound out, and contain syllables with varying amounts of stress, Spanish words are pronounced exactly as they are written. The songlike flow of Spanish is one of the reasons it is considered a romance language.

¡Atención!

If you want to sound like a native Spanish-speaker, remember to maintain an even keel by using an equal amount of stress for each syllable. Keep in mind that overemphasizing letters, syllables, or words will make you sound like a *gringo*.

In a Flash

Remember the articles from the newspaper in Chapter 1? Read aloud one paragraph from any article while sitting in front of a mirror. If possible, record yourself and then listen to the playback. Spend a few minutes each day watching your face and the movement of your lips and tongue. Move on to another article when you are pleased with how you sound.

Acceptable Accents

Don't worry that you'll have trouble sounding great. Spanish is a relatively simple language to pronounce. Sure, there are accent marks, but don't let them trouble or confuse you. Luckily, there are only three accents in the language.

➤ The most common accent (´) only requires that you put more stress on the syllable containing that letter. Examples include *mamá* (mah-mah), *interés*, (een-teh-rehs), *terrífico* (teh-rree-fee-koh), *avión* (ah-bee-yoHn), *único* (oo-nee-koh).

➤ The tilde (˜) only appears over an *n* (*ñ*, which is considered a separate letter). It produces the ny sound, as in the *ni* in onion. An example is *mañana* (mah-NYah-nah), which means "tomorrow" or "morning."

➤ The umlaut (¨) is used in diphthongs (combinations of two vowels). It indicates that each vowel should be pronounced separately. This last accent is very rarely seen and only occurs on the letter *u*. An example is *vergüenza* (behr-goowehn-sah), which means "shame."

As you can see, accents in Spanish really create no problems at all. You'll get more practice with them later in the chapter.

Perfecting Your Accent

Did you ever notice how some people can pick up another language and sound authentic with very little effort at all, but other people just can't seem to lose their native, hometown accent? If you are lucky, you can sound great by simply imitating the Spanish speakers you've heard on TV, in the movies, on the radio, or in your neighborhood. Right from the start, you'll be able to reproduce accentuation and pronunciation with minimal effort. Positive feedback will be immediate and a feeling of accomplishment will be yours with little practice.

How lucky for you. You probably have a "good ear" and also are somewhat musically talented. You probably could skip a large part of this chapter and maybe even ignore some of the phonetic spellings yet still manage quite well. There are people, however, who view foreign pronunciation with trepidation. If you were born with a "tin ear," chances are the words and phrases you speak just won't sound right at first. You'll need to spend a bit more time practicing your pronunciation. If you keep at it, however, eventually you'll get the hang of it.

Remember that, no matter how you sound, you'll be understood if you use the correct words. That should be your goal. Nobody is going to laugh at you. In the end, your level of competence in pronunciation is no big deal. Relax, try your best, and above all, don't be discouraged.

¡Atención!

Remember, if an accent is placed on one of the five vowels, you must stress that syllable for correct pronunciation.

Memory Master

The Spanish *r* is always rolled. At the beginning of a word or after the consonants *l* (*alrededor*—around), *n* (*honra*—honor), or *s* (*Israel*—Israel), the *r* requires two or three trills, just like the double *r* (*rr*).

Vowels Are Easy!

Unlike the English alphabet, the Spanish alphabet contains 28 letters. Five of these 28 letters are vowels: *a*, *e*, *i*, *o*, and *u*. The pronunciation of these vowels is shown in Table 2.1.

Table 2.1 Pronouncing Vowels Properly

Vowel	Sound	Example	Pronunciation
a	ah	artista	ahr-tees-tah
e	eh	egoísta	eh-goh-ees-tah
i	ee	isla	ees-lah
o	oh	objeto	ohb-heh-toh
u	oo	uno	oo-noh

The other 23 letters of the Spanish alphabet are consonants. Three letters not contained in the English alphabet are *ch*, *ll*, and *ñ*. (*Ch* and *ll* no longer are considered separate letters in the Spanish alphabet, but Spanish dictionaries have not yet noted this change.) The letter *w* is not considered part of the Spanish alphabet because it is only used in words of foreign origin, such as water closet, weekend, western, wharf, whisky, and wintergreen.

Table 2.2 illustrates the Spanish consonants. Note the sounds and the sample words with their phonetic spellings. After studying the chart, repeat the sample words aloud to practice your pronunciation.

Table 2.2   Pronouncing Consonants Properly

Letter	Sound	Example	Pronunciation
b	same as English	bebé	beh-beh
c	soft c (s) before e and i	centro	sehn-troh
	hard c (k) elsewhere	catedral	kah-teh-drahl
ch	ch	cheque	cheh-keh
d	d	dama	dah-mah
f	f	fiesta	fee-yehs-tah
g	soft h before e and i	general	heh-neh-rahl
	hard g elsewhere	gala	gah-lah
h	silent	hispano	ees-pah-noh
j	h	Julio	hoo-lee-yoh
k	k	kilo	kee-loh
l	l	libre	lee-breh
ll	y	llama	yah-mah
m	m	mamá	mah-mah
n	n	necesario	neh-seh-sah-ree-yoh
ñ	ny	niño	nee-nyoh
p	p	papá	pah-pah
q	k	Quito	kee-toh
r	r (slightly rolled)	libro	lee-broh
	rr (r rolled two or three times)	carro	kah-rroh
s	s	salsa	sahl-sah
t	t	toro	toh-roh
v	less explosive English b	vigor	bee-gohr
x	English ks (sinks)	exacto	ehk-sahk-toh
y	y	yoga	yoh-gah
z	s	zoo	soh

The Diphthong Dilemma

The Spanish language contains many diphthongs. A *diphthong* is a combination of two vowels—one weak and one strong—that appear in the same syllable. The strong vowels are *a*, *e*, and *o*. This means you should pronounce them with a lot of emphasis. The weak vowels, *i* and *u*, should be said more softly. Use Table 2.3 to practice pronouncing diphthongs.

Table 2.3 Spanish Diphthongs to Practice Aloud

Diphthong	Sound	Example	Pronunciation	Meaning
ai	ah-yee	aire	ah-yee-reh	air
au	ow	autor	ow-tohr	author
ay	ah-yee	hay	ah-yee	there is, there are
ei	eh-yee	seis	seh-yees	six
eu	eh-yoo	Europa	eh-yoo-roh-pah	Europe
ia	ee-yah	seria	seh-ree-yah	serious
ie	ee-yeh	siesta	see-yehs-tah	nap
io	ee-yoh	avión	ah-bee-yohn	airplane
iu	ee-yoo	ciudad	see-yoo-dahd	city
oi	oy	oigo	oy-goh	I hear
ua	wah	lengua	lehn-gwah	tongue, language
ue	weh	cuenta	kwehn-tah	check (bill)
ui	wee	cuidado	kwee-dah-doh	be careful
uo	oo-oh	continuo	kohn-tee-noo-oh	continuous

10 minutos al día

Spend 10 minutes each day reading aloud and taping yourself to perfect your Spanish accent. Give equal stress to all syllables unless they have an accented vowel (emphasize those syllables). Proceed at a steady pace. Remember that speaking in a natural, conversational tone requires moving steadily from one word to the next without hesitating.

Culture Corner

Even though Spanish is the common language spoken in Spain and in most Central American and South American countries (except Brazil, where Portuguese is spoken), people from different regions have their own individual speech and pronunciation patterns. In some countries, for example, the final *s* of a word is often not pronounced. One of the most commonly known speech pattern is that of the Castilians, who pronounce the *z* like *th*.

Don't Sound Like a Gringo!

Now that you are an expert on the Spanish alphabet and Spanish diphthongs, read each of the following sentences aloud to practice and improve your pronunciation.

El país es grande.
Ehl pah-yees ehs grahn-deh
The country is big.

Oiga, hay seis respuestas.
Oy-gah, ah-yee seh-yees rehs-pwehs-tahs
Listen, there are six answers.

Mi abuelo es viejo.
Mee ah-bweh-loh ehs bee-yeh-hoh
My grandfather is old.

Paula va al cine.
Pow-lah bah ahl see-neh
Paula goes to the movies.

El anciano tiene cien años.
Ehl ahn-see-yah-noh tee-yeh-neh see-yehn ahn-yohs
The old man is 100 years old.

The Least You Need to Know

➤ Although the Spanish alphabet differs slightly from the English one, Spanish words are easy to pronounce.

➤ Pronounce each Spanish word phonetically.

➤ Don't stress any syllable unless it includes an accented vowel.

➤ You must practice often if you want to improve your pronunciation.

➤ Remember that, even if your accent isn't great, you'll probably still be understood. Don't be afraid to try!

Chapter 3

The Spanish You Know

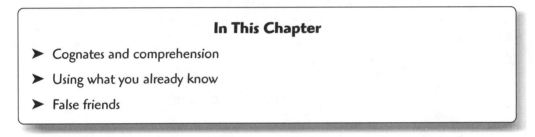

In This Chapter

➤ Cognates and comprehension

➤ Using what you already know

➤ False friends

Do you love chocolate? How about potatoes and tomatoes? Do you take a taxi often? When the weather is nice, do you sit on your patio? Can you play the piano? Perhaps you have a sweater made from the wool of an alpaca. And you've probably been stung by a mosquito more than once in your life. Well, look at that—you know some Spanish already! You're probably unaware that your vocabulary is filled with words and phrases borrowed from Spanish. Many other words and expressions are so similar to ours that you'll be able to use and understand them with very little trouble. By the time you finish this chapter, you'll be well on your way to creating simple, correct Spanish sentences that will enable you to express your ideas and opinions.

You Know This!

My husband makes frequent trips to the video store, especially in the summer when all the television stations show reruns. He takes his time and often spends an hour or more trying to pick out the perfect film for the evening. His taste is very eclectic: One night we'll watch a Japanese samurai warrior film, and the next night we'll watch a French romantic comedy. More often than not, he picks out foreign films. He thinks they are interesting and different from what we are used to. Although he only speaks English, he enjoys the experience of listening to native speakers.

One night he rented *Like Water for Chocolate,* a wonderful but sad Spanish love story. We sat in front of the TV for about two hours, totally involved in the tale being told. At one point, to my great astonishment, I noticed my husband wasn't reading the titles. I thought perhaps he was bored by the romance, but that wasn't the case. When I asked him why he wasn't reading, he said he understood what the people were saying. How could that be? He had never even studied Spanish. He replied that the words sounded just like English to him. I gave it some thought, and I understood his point. There is a logical explanation.

That explanation is cognates. Simply put, a *cognate* is a word that is spelled the same, or almost the same, in two different languages and that has the same definition. In many cases, we've borrowed a word from Spanish and have incorporated it into our vocabulary without giving much thought to the word's origin. Naturally, cognates are pronounced somewhat differently in each language, but the meaning of the Spanish word will be perfectly clear to an English speaker.

Let's take a closer look and see how much Spanish you already know.

A Perfect Match

Table 3.1 is a list of cognates with the same meaning in both Spanish and English. The first column is adjectives you can use to describe the nouns in the middle and last columns. Using the skills you've learned, pronounce the Spanish words and compare them to their English equivalents. Your goal is to sound Spanish.

When you look at the list of cognates, notice that the Spanish nouns are listed under a specific definite article, *el* or *la*. These articles both mean "the," and each indicates the gender of the noun (masculine or feminine, respectively). All Spanish nouns (people, places, things, ideas) have a gender. This might seem strange to you at first because we do not have anything similar in English. For now, just remember that if you want to express that Spanish is easy, you must say, *"El español es fácil."*

Memory Master

Although a noun's gender is often easily identifiable in Spanish, it is best to learn the noun with its corresponding article. See Chapter 6, "Sexually Speaking," for more details. For now, just remember that *el* is the article for masculine singular nouns and *la* is for feminine singular nouns.

Culture Corner

Many English words have infiltrated the Spanish language. We politely refer to these words as *spanglish*. Examples include los jeans, el bloque, el CD, la soda, el bistec, el rosbif, el champú, el cóctel, la hamburguesa, el sandwich, el béisbol, el fútbol, el básquetbol, and el boxeador.

Table 3.1   Perfect Cognates

Adjectives	Masculine Nouns El (ehl)	Feminine Nouns La (lah)
horrible (oh-rree-bleh)	color (koh-lohr)	banana (bah-nah-nah)
natural (nah-too-rahl)	chocolate (choh-koh-lah-teh)	fiesta (fee-yehs-tah)
popular (poh-poo-lahr)	doctor (dohk-tohr)	alpaca (ahl-pah-kah)
sociable (soh-see-yah-bleh)	hotel (oh-tehl)	plaza (plah-sah)
terrible (teh-rree-bleh)	soda (soh-dah)	radio (rrah-dee-yoh)
tropical (troh-pee-kahl)	motor (moh-tohr)	taxi (tahk-see)

Almost Perfect Partners

Near cognates are words that look so similar in both languages that their meanings are unmistakable. Perhaps a letter or two is different, or there might be an accent mark on the Spanish word; essentially, however, the words are the same. Look at Table 3.2 and see whether you can figure out the meanings of all the words. Are you up to the challenge?

Table 3.2   Near Cognates

Adjectives	Masculine Nouns El (ehl)	Feminine Nouns La (lah)
americano (ah-meh-ree-kah-noh)	aniversario (ah-nee-behr-sah-ree-yoh)	aspirina (ahs-pee-ree-nah)
confortable (kohn-fohr-tah-bleh)	automóvil (ow-toh-moh-beel)	bicicleta (bee-see-kleh-tah)
curioso (koo-ree-yoh-soh)	banco (bahn-koh)	blusa (bloo-sah)
delicioso (deh-lee-see-yoh-soh)	ciclismo (see-klees-moh)	catedral (kah-teh-drahl)
diferente (dee-feh-rehn-teh)	diccionario (deek-see-yoh-nah-ree-yoh)	computadora (kohm-poo-tah-doh-rah)
difícil (dee-fee-seel)	grupo (groo-poh)	dieta (dee-yeh-tah)
elegante (eh-leh-gahn-teh)	jardín (har-deen)	familia (fah-mee-lee-yah)
excelente (ehk-seh-lehn-teh)	limón (lee-mohn)	hamburguesa (ahm-boor-geh-sah)
famoso (fah-moh-soh)	mecánico (meh-kah-nee-koh)	lámpara (lahm-pah-rah)
grande (grahn-deh)	parque (pahr-keh)	medicina (meh-dee-see-nah)
importante (eem-pohr-tahn-teh)	plato (plah-toh)	guitarra (gee-tah-rrah)

continues

Table 3.2 Continued

Adjectives	Masculine Nouns El (ehl)	Feminine Nouns La (lah)
imposible (eem-poh-see-bleh)	presidente (preh-see-dehn-teh)	mansión (mahn-see-yohn)
interesante (een-teh-reh-sahn-teh)	programa (proh-grah-mah)	música (moo-see-kah)
magnífico (mahg-nee-fee-koh)	menú (meh-noo)	nacionalidad (nah-see-yoh-nah-lee-dahd)
moderno (moh-dehr-noh)	restaurante (rrehs-tow-rahn-teh)	opinión (oh-pee-nee-yohn)
necesario (neh-seh-sah-ree-yoh)	salario (sah-lah-ree-yoh)	persona (pehr-soh-nah)
ordinario (ohr-dee-nah-ree-yoh)	supermercado (soo-pehr-mehr-kah-doh)	región (rreh-hee-yohn)
posible (poh-see-bleh)	teatro (teh-yah-troh)	rosa (rroh-sah)
probable (proh-bah-bleh)	teléfono (teh-leh-foh-noh)	turista (too-rees-tah)

Spanish words that begin with *es-* are often near cognates. You can guess the meaning of many Spanish words beginning with *es-* by simply dropping the initial *e-*:

Word	Pronunciation	English Meaning
escarlata	ehs-kahr-lah-tah	scarlet
escéptico	ehs-kehp-tee-koh	skeptical
escultor	ehs-kool-tohr	sculptor
espacio	ehs-pah-see-yoh	space
España	ehs-pah-nyah	Spain
especial	ehs-peh-see-yahl	special
espectáculo	ehs-pehk-tah-koo-loh	spectacle, show
espía	ehs-pee-yah	spy
espiral	ehs-pee-rahl	spiral
espléndido	ehs-plehn-dee-doh	splendid
esquí	ehs-kee	ski
estudiar	ehs-too-dee-yahr	to study
estupendo	ehs-too-pehn-doh	stupendous

Practice Makes Perfect?

Practice reading the following Spanish sentences and then decipher what they mean. (The pronunciations of the Spanish phrases are provided below them.) Keep in mind that the Spanish word *es* means "is." (Answers can be found on page 405, in Appendix A.)

1. El piano es grande.
   Ehl pee-yah-noh ehs grahn-deh

   _____

2. El actor es horrible.
   Ehl ahk-tohr ehs oh-rree-bleh

   _____

3. La información es terrible.
   Lah een-fohr-mah-see-yohn ehs teh-rree-bleh

   _____

4. El profesor es sincero.
   Ehl proh-feh-sohr ehs seen-seh-roh

   _____

5. El tigre es cruel.
   El tee-greh ehs kroo-ehl

   _____

6. El cereal es delicioso.
   Ehl seh-reh-yahl ehs deh-lee-see-yoh-soh

   _____

It's Easy to Write!

Try writing and saying the following sentences in Spanish. You can peek back at the cognate list to make sure you are using the correct article (*el* or *la*) and to check your pronunciation. (Answers can be found on page 405, in Appendix A.)

1. The president is elegant.

   _____

2. The computer is interesting.

   _____

3. The information is important.

   _____

4. The hotel is large.

   _____

5. The color is magnificent.

   _____

Memory Master

In Spanish, adjectives must agree in number and gender with the nouns they describe. We'll cover this in detail in Chapter 9, "Getting to Know You." For now, just remember to use adjectives ending with *-o* to describe masculine nouns and adjectives ending with *-a* to describe feminine nouns. Adjectives ending in *-e* can describe either one.

In a Flash

Create five flash cards with a Spanish word on one side and the English cognate on the other. Practice looking at the English and giving the correct Spanish pronunciation.

Versatile Verbs

Many Spanish verbs (words that show action or a state of being) are so similar to their English counterparts that you should have no difficulty recognizing their meanings.

Spanish verbs are governed by certain rules that will be explained in Chapter 7, "Going Places." For now, look at the three major verb families—verbs ending in *-ar*, *-er*, and *-ir*. Any verbs belonging to a family are considered regular; those that do not belong to a family are irregular. Each family has its own set of rules that will also be explained in Chapter 7. (Irregular verbs don't follow the family rules. Think of them as the black sheep. More information about irregular verbs is available in later chapters.) Check out the following members of the three major families and see whether you can determine their meanings.

-ar Verbs

acompañar	entrar	negar	reparar
adorar	explicar	observar	reservar
celebrar	ignorar	pasar	terminar
comenzar	invitar	practicar	usar
declarar	marchar	preparar	verificar
eliminar	modificar	refusar	

-er Verbs

comprender	responder	vender

-ir Verbs

aplaudir	dividir	omitir
decidir	persuadir	recibir
describir	preferir	sufrir

You've Got the Swing of It!

The preceding section showed that you know a lot more Spanish than you realized. As a matter of fact, I'll bet you can easily read and understand the following sentences without any problems. (Answers can be found on page 405, in Appendix A.)

1. Juan prepara el menú.

   _____

2. El mecánico repara el carro.

   _____

3. El turista usa la información.

   _____

4. El programa termina.

   _____

5. Marta celebra su aniversario.

   _____

6. José adora el programa.

   _____

Give Your Opinions

Pretend you are a tourist in a Spanish-speaking country. Use what you have learned to express the following feelings to a fellow tourist. (Answers can be found on page 405, in Appendix A.)

1. The program is excellent.

   _____

2. The park is popular.

   _____

3. The dish is famous.

   _____

4. The restaurant is large.

   _____

5. The theater is modern.

   _____

6. The program is magnificent.

   _____

7. The actor is dynamic.

   _____

8. The hotel is comfortable.

   _____

False Amigos

Don't assume every Spanish word that looks like an English word is a cognate. Nothing is ever that simple. Although you might think you've mastered cognates, every rule has exceptions. In the case of cognates, exceptions are called *false friends*. False friends are words spelled exactly or almost the same in both Spanish and English, but they have different meanings in each language. They might even be different parts of speech. Beware of the false friends listed in Table 3.3. You want to use them correctly.

Table 3.3   False Friends

Spanish Word	English Meaning	Spanish Word	English Meaning
asistir	to attend	hay	there is (are)
caro	expensive	librería	bookstore
comer	to eat	joya	jewel
fábrica	factory	pan	bread
flor	flower	sopa	soup

Now You're a Pro!

A complimentary copy of a Spanish newspaper was delivered to your hotel room. Curiosity has gotten the best of you, and you've decided to see how much Spanish you already know. Identify the sections of the newspaper shown below and determine the contents of the articles. (Answers can be found on page 406, in Appendix A.)

DEPORTES
Bogotá, defiende su título

ECONOMICAS
Informe confirma vitalidad de la economía

INTERNACIONAL
China pone interés en restaurantes de comida rápida

INFORMACION
ATEROESCLEROSIS TIENE UNA SOLUCION

The Least You Need to Know

➤ You know more Spanish than you think because of words called cognates.

➤ Cognates are words that look exactly or almost the same in English and in Spanish and that have the same meaning in both languages.

➤ Watch out for false friends (words spelled the same in Spanish and in English that have different meanings in each language).

Chapter 4

Grappling with Grammar

In This Chapter

➤ An overview of basic grammar

➤ How to use a bilingual dictionary

There's more to speaking a foreign language than merely translating words from one language to another—despite what you might remember from high school. To communicate effectively, you cannot simply walk around with a dictionary and read from it. Instead, you must learn to use the language and its patterns the way native speakers do.

For any student of a foreign language, one of the most difficult concepts to grasp is that different languages follow different grammatical patterns. Trying to translate word for word from one language to the next often produces awkward results and, in many instances, becomes an exercise in futility. To truly sound like a native, a student must have not only a grammatical understanding of the language but also a colloquial, idiomatic command of it.

Grammar! Good Grief!

Does the word "grammar" send chills up your spine? Does it bring back bad memories of the days when you sat in school learning the parts of speech, conjugating verbs, and diagramming sentences? Well, that was then and this is now. To learn a foreign language, you don't have to become an expert grammarian. All you need is to know some of the simple parts of speech: nouns, verbs, adjectives, and adverbs. Don't panic—just follow along and see how simple it is.

Nouns

Nouns refer to people, places, things, or ideas. Unlike in English, all nouns in Spanish have a gender (masculine or feminine). Just like in English, however, they also have a quantity or number (singular or plural). Articles that serve as noun identifiers often help to indicate gender and number. You will learn more about this in Chapter 6, "Sexually Speaking." In Spanish, as in English, nouns can be replaced by pronouns.

Verbs

Verbs are words that show action or a state of being. In both English and Spanish, verbs are generally conjugated. In English, this is so automatic (because we've been doing it practically since birth) that we don't even realize we are doing it. *Conjugating* means using the correct form of the verb so it agrees with the subject. In English, for example, we say "I am," "you are," "he is," and so on; "I look" but "she looks."

It is improper to mix and match the subjects and verb forms, whether you are speaking in English or in Spanish. Imagine how strange it would sound to you if a Spanish speaker said, "I is from Cuba." You would understand the meaning, of course, which is what the person is striving for—to be understood. Never lose hope; you'll always be able to get your message across. The language, however, does have a much better ring to it when the subjects and verbs correspond. Verb conjugation will be explained in greater depth in Chapter 7, "Going Places."

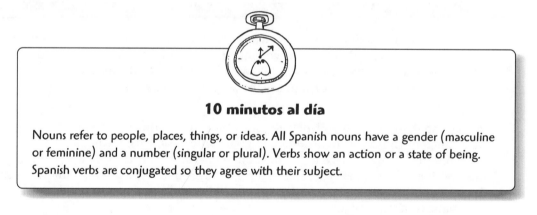

10 minutos al día

Nouns refer to people, places, things, or ideas. All Spanish nouns have a gender (masculine or feminine) and a number (singular or plural). Verbs show an action or a state of being. Spanish verbs are conjugated so they agree with their subject.

Adjectives

Adjectives are words that describe nouns. Unlike in English, all adjectives in Spanish agree in number and gender with the nouns they modify. If a noun is singular, you must describe it with a singular adjective. If the noun is feminine, be sure to use the correct feminine form of the adjective.

Another difference is that, in English, adjectives generally precede the nouns they modify, as in "the blue house." In Spanish, most adjectives come after the nouns they describe. Translated into Spanish, "the blue house" becomes *la casa azul*, in which *casa* means "house" and *azul* means "blue." You will find out more about adjectives in Chapter 9, "Getting to Know You."

Adverbs

Adverbs are words that describe verbs, adjectives, or other adverbs. Adverbs are used about the same way in both languages. In English, most adverbs end in -*ly*, such as *slowly*. In Spanish, most adverbs end in -*mente*, such as *lentamente* (slowly). We will discuss adverbs in greater detail in Chapter 18, "Play Time!"

10 minutos al día

Adjectives describe nouns or pronouns. In Spanish, they must agree in gender (masculine or feminine) and number (singular or plural) with the nouns they modify. Unlike in English, most Spanish adjectives follow the noun. Adverbs modify verbs, adjectives, or other adverbs. English adverbs generally end in -*ly*; in Spanish, adverbs generally end in -*mente*.

Just Look It Up

Using a bilingual dictionary requires a little more knowledge than using an English dictionary. That's right, we're talking grammar again. To use a bilingual dictionary effectively and correctly, you must know and be aware of the differences between the various parts of speech.

Bilingual Dictionaries—A Crash Course

Before looking up your first word, take time to study the abbreviations at the front of your dictionary. You probably will find a long, comprehensive list. Don't get discouraged. Only a handful of the abbreviations really require your attention:

➤ *adj*   Adjective.

➤ *adv*   Adverb.

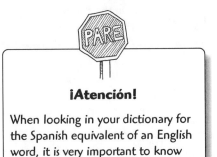

¡Atención!

When looking in your dictionary for the Spanish equivalent of an English word, it is very important to know which part of speech you need.

➤ *f* Feminine noun. (Gender will be explained further in Chapter 6, "Sexually Speaking.")

➤ *m* Masculine noun.

➤ *n* Noun. (Sometimes *s.* is used.) The *n.* designation generally is used only if the noun can be either masculine or feminine.

➤ *pl* Plural noun. (More information about plural nouns also is located in Chapter 6.)

➤ *vi* (or *v. intr.*) Intransitive verb. An intransitive verb can stand alone as a sentence, as in "I run."

➤ *vt* (or *v tr*) Transitive verb. A transitive verb can be followed by a direct object, as in "He puts on his coat." Unlike "run" in the preceding example, however, "puts on" cannot stand alone. A transitive verb also can be used in the passive tense, in which the subject is acted upon, as in "I was helped."

➤ *vr* Reflexive verb. When using a reflexive verb, the subject acts upon itself, as in "I comb my hair." Reflexive verbs will be discussed in Chapter 20, "Is There a Doctor in the House?"

In a Flash

Think quickly of the many different ways can you use: "record," "fire," "place," "stand," and "well." Now look them up in the dictionary and see what you find.

Learning how to use a bilingual dictionary requires a certain amount of grammatical expertise. You must know how to use the various parts of speech. Let's use the English word "mean" as an example. Consider the following sentences and how the meaning of the word "mean" changes:

That boy is *mean.* (adjective)

What can that *mean*? (verb)

What is the *mean* (average)? (noun)

If we change "mean" to its plural form, the meaning changes again:

What is the *means* of transportation? (noun)

Now look up the word "mean" in a bilingual dictionary. You might see the following:

mean [min] *vt* significar; *adj* (miserly) tacaño(ña), (unkind) mezquino(na), malo(a); *n* (average) promedio *m*, media *f*; see also *means*.

means [minz] *n* (method, way) medio *m*; *npl* (money) recursos.

Based on the Spanish definitions of "mean" provided here, look at the following English sentences, figure out which part of speech "mean" is in each, and complete the translated sentences in Spanish using the correct translation of "mean."

➤ *That boy is mean.*

Figure out the part of speech and complete the following Spanish sentence:

Ese muchacho es _____.

The correct answer is *mezquino*, an adjective.

➤ *What can that mean?*

The Spanish sentence would be:

¿Qué puede_____eso?

Did you use *significar*, a verb? Great!

➤ *What is the mean?*

This term refers to the average of two numbers. Because the correct word can be either masculine or feminine, you have to use *el* in front of the masculine word and *la* in front of the feminine word. (Articles will be discussed in more detail in Chapter 6, "Sexually Speaking.") The Spanish translation would be:

¿Cuál es_____?

Did you choose *el promedio* or *la media*? Both are correct.

➤ *What is the means of transportation?*

Means is plural in English but is masculine and singular in Spanish. Use *el* before the noun you choose.

Your Spanish sentence should be:

¿Cuál es _____ de transporte?

The answer is *el medio*.

Memory Master

In Spanish, an inverted question mark (¿) or exclamation point (¡) is placed at the beginning of a sentence to prepare you for what will follow. It's really a very clever idea.

In a Flash

Pick a common English word that can be used as different parts of speech (as a noun, as a verb, as an adjective, and/or as an adverb). Try the word "watch" or "tear," for example. Find as many Spanish equivalent words as you can and take note of how these words are used.

As you can see, to successfully look up the meaning of a word you want to use, you must do three things:

1. Verify the part of speech—noun, verb, adjective, or adverb—that you want to use.

2. Verify that you have found the right word by looking up the Spanish word you have chosen to see whether the English meaning is the one you want.

(Sometimes you might have to think of a synonym for the word you want to use to get the proper Spanish meaning.)

3. Make sure you are using the correct form of the word in number (singular or plural) and in gender (masculine or feminine).

Use your bilingual dictionary to find the correct word to complete each of the following Spanish sentences. (Answers can be found on page 406, in Appendix A.)

---

1. That boy dances *well*.
   Ese muchacho baila _____.

2. Where is the *well*?
   ¿Dónde está _____?

3. I heard *the cry* of the animal.
   Oí _____ del animal.

4. The child is going *to cry*.
   El niño va a _____.

5. I have *just* ten dollars.
   Tengo _____ diez dólares.

6. The punishment is *just*.
   El castigo es _____.

7. He is going *to check* the motor.
   Él va a _____ el motor.

8. I am going to cash my *check*.
   Voy a tocar mi _____.

The Least You Need to Know

➤ The Spanish language contains the same parts of speech as the English language.

➤ To use a bilingual dictionary effectively, you must know the differences between the various parts of speech.

Chapter 5

Idioms Aren't for Idiots

In This Chapter

➤ What are idioms?

➤ What is slang?

➤ How do I use them?

➤ Expressing yourself with gestures

A knowledge of idioms is important for a complete understanding of a language. Imagine you are shopping in one of Madrid's finest jewelry stores. You overhear a conversation between a couple as they examine the diamond necklaces. The woman selects one she likes, but her husband replies *"Este collar cuesta un ojo de la cara."* You interpret this to mean that the necklace costs an eye taken from your face. Sounds like a pretty drastic measure, wouldn't you say? In reality, the expression *costar un ojo de la cara* means "to cost a small fortune," although you'd never figure that out from the vocabulary and grammar in the sentence.

An Idiom? What's That?

In any language, an *idiom* is a particular word or expression whose meaning cannot be readily understood by analyzing its component words. It is, however, still considered an acceptable part of the standard vocabulary of the language. The following are some common English idioms:

Look on the bright side

Fall head over heels

On the other hand

To be down and out

Slang—Should I Use It?

What's the difference between an idiom and slang? *Slang* refers to colorful, popular, informal words or phrases that are *not* part of the standard vocabulary of a language. Slang is considered unconventional and has evolved to describe particular items or situations in street language. Slang vocabulary is composed of coinages, arbitrarily changed words, and extravagant, forced, or facetious figures of speech. The following are some examples of English slang:

Give me a break!

Get real!

Tough luck!

Get a life!

Idioms and Slang

Idioms are acceptable in oral and written phrases; slang, although freely used in informal conversations, is generally considered substandard in formal writing or speaking. Some slang is, at best, X-rated.

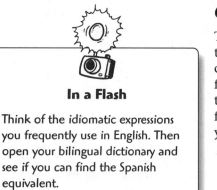

In a Flash

Think of the idiomatic expressions you frequently use in English. Then open your bilingual dictionary and see if you can find the Spanish equivalent.

Choose One

Take a look at the following popular expressions. Are they idioms or slang? Certainly, these expressions couldn't be translated word for word. Read them carefully and decide whether they are idioms (acceptable terms) or slang (street language). When you speak a foreign language, it's important to know what phrases you can use politely and which will be offensive.

You drive me crazy.

Keep your shirt on.

I'm always on the go.

He likes to play the field.

It's raining cats and dogs.

She got angry and lost it.

He's on his way up.

Did you fall for it?

Don't jump the gun.

Did you recognize that these sentences contain idiomatic expressions used in English all the time? Now compare the preceding sentences with the following:

Shucks!

What a cop out!

She just flipped out.

Don't dis my friend.

My son is a computer geek.

That's tacky!

Did you notice that the slang sentences used substandard English and were more offensive than those containing idiomatic expressions? Excellent! You probably won't use much Spanish slang, but the idioms will come in handy.

There are many idioms in Spanish. This chapter looks at six categories of idioms that you might find helpful: travel and transportation, time, location and direction, expressing opinions, physical conditions, and weather conditions. Other idiomatic expressions will appear in the appropriate chapters.

Taking Off

Let's say you are taking a trip. You might be asked, "Are you going on a plane or on a boat?" In Spanish, the word for "on" is *sobre*. If you say "Voy sobre el avión," you are telling people you are going to ride on the exterior of the plane. To avoid putting yourself in such an awkward position, you should learn the idiomatic expressions covered in Table 5.1.

Memory Master

The preposition *en* is usually used when one travels inside a means of ground transportation, such as a subway. Use *a* when traveling *on* something that allows you to safely feel the wind blowing in your hair.

Table 5.1   Travel and Transportation

Idiom	Pronunciation	Meaning
en bicicleta	ehn bee-see-kleh-tah	by bicycle
a caballo	ah kah-bah-yoh	by horseback
a pie	ah pee-yeh	by foot
en automóvil	ehn ow-toh-moh-beel	by car
por avión	pohr ah-bee-yohn	by plane
en barco	ehn bahr-koh	by boat
en autobús	ehn ow-toh-boos	by bus
en metro	ehn meh-troh	by subway
en taxi	ehn tahk-see	by taxi
en tren	ehn trehn	by train
en carro	ehn kah-rroh	by car

On the Go

Some people lead a quiet life and amble along the scenic route; others run here and there for business or pleasure. Which means of transportation would you choose to get to the following places? (Sample responses can be found on page 406, in Appendix A.)

1. work or school

_____

2. the movies

_____

3. your doctor

_____

4. the nearest hospital

_____

5. Europe

_____

6. the park

_____

7. a tropical island

_____

8. a fishing trip

_____

9. a museum

_____

10. the library

_____

Time Is on My Mind

How time conscious are you? Do you always wear your watch because time is of the essence? Are you up and at 'em at the crack of dawn so you get a head start on your day? Or are you the laid-back type who doesn't give time a second thought? Whatever your personality, the idioms in Table 5.2 will serve you well whenever time is on your mind.

Memory Master

Use *hasta* + time when you want to tell someone when you'll be seeing each other again: *Hasta el lunes* (ahs-tah ehl loo-nehs)—Until Monday.

Table 5.2   Time Expressions

Idiom	Pronunciation	Meaning
hasta la noche	ah-stah lah noh-cheh	See you this evening
hasta mañana	ah-stah mah-nyah-nah	See you tomorrow
a tiempo	ah tee-yehm-poh	on time
hasta el sábado	ah-stah ehl sah-bah-doh	until Saturday
hasta luego	ah-stah loo-eh-goh	see you later
adiós	ah-dee-yohs	good-bye
temprano	tehm-prah-noh	early
a veces	ah beh-sehs	from time to time
tarde	tahr-deh	late
hace que	ah-seh keh	ago (+ time)
por semana, día, mes	pohr seh-mah-nah, dee-yah, mehs	by week, day, month
inmediatamente	een-meh-dee-yah-tah-mehn-teh	immediately

What Time Is It?

Every day brings into your life new situations in which time counts. Imagine you become involved in the following activities. Choose the appropriate expression for each situation. (Sample responses can be found on page 406, in Appendix A.)

1. You are leaving work for the day. You say _____.

2. You miss the bus and arrive at 6:30 p.m. for a 6:00 p.m. movie. You arrive _____.

3. You have a date at 8 p.m. and you arrive at exactly 8 p.m. You arrive _____.

4. You are going to see a friend later in the day. When you leave now you say_____.

Follow the Leader

Among the most useful idioms are those that tell you how to get where you want to go. For example, I always have to know where the nearest rest room can be found—just in case. Is it upstairs, downstairs, next to someplace important, near, or far (heaven forbid)? If you haven't learned the proper terms, you could wind up at the baggage claim instead of the *baño* or, worse yet, at the wrong gender's *baño*. This is why the idioms of location and direction in Table 5.3 are worth studying.

Table 5.3 Idioms Showing Location and Direction

Idiom	Pronunciation	Meaning
al lado de	ahl lah-doh deh	next to
a la derecha de	ah lah deh-reh-chah deh	to the right of
a la izquierda de	ah lah ees-kee-yehr-dah deh	to the left of
en casa	ehn kah-sah	at home
al otro lado (de)	ahl oh-troh lah-doh (deh)	on the other side
dar a	dahr ah	to face
enfrente de	ehn-frehn-teh deh	in front of
hacia	ah-see-yah	toward
frente a	frehn-teh ah	facing, opposite
al centro	ahl sehn-troh	downtown
por aquí	pohr ah-kee	this way
por allá	pohr ah-yah	that way

Following Directions

You have just checked into your hotel, and you're eager to get your bearings. You go to the *recepción* to ask where you can find certain places. Someone gives you a map, but unfortunately, some of the buildings are not identified. Figure 5.1 is a map of a city street. Use the following Spanish directions to label the missing buildings. (Answers can be found on page 406, in Appendix A.)

La Calle Cristobal Colón

la panadería

la farmacia	el restaurante
el cine	el teatro
el café	el museo de arte

A la izquierda de la panadería hay un teatro. Al lado del teatro hay un café. Frente al café hay un restaurante. A la derecha de la panadería hay una farmacia. Al otro lado de la calle, frente a la farmacia, hay un cine. A la izquierda del cine, enfrente del teatro, hay un museo de arte moderno.

What's Your Opinion?

Everyone has opinions. Whether you're talking about your flight, the food you ate, the movie you watched, the people you met, or your life in general, you need to know how to properly express your feelings. Table 5.4 should help.

Table 5.4 Expressing Opinions with Idioms

Idiom	Pronunciation	Meaning
en mi opinión	ehn mee oh-pee-nee-yohn	in my opinion
a decir verdad	ah deh-seer behr-dahd	to tell the truth
al contrario	ahl kohn-trah-ree-yoh	on the contrary
en vez de	ehn behs deh	instead of
por supuesto	pohr soo-pwehs-toh	of course
claro	klah-roh	of course
está bien	eh-stah bee-yehn	all right
no importa	noh eem-pohr-tah	it doesn't matter
de acuerdo	deh ah-kwehr-doh	agreed
sin duda	seen doo-dah	without a doubt
es evidente	ehs eh-bee-dehn-teh	it is evident

In a Flash

To remember these useful expressions, write each one on a separate index card. Attach them to your refrigerator with magnets. Everytime you go for a snack, take one card and memorize it. Next time a friend makes a suggestion to you, think of the appropriate Spanish response.

Memory Master

Remember that the verb *tener* (to have) is used to describe physical conditions, whereas in English we use the verb "to be."

Sure, I'll Go!

It's a bright, sunny day. Your friend has just called to invite you out for a hearty breakfast and a tour of the city. Choose four expressions from the preceding list to indicate your willingness to go along. (Answers can be found on page 407, in Appendix A.)

How Are You?

If you've ever been to the Dominican Republic, you know it can get extremely hot, especially in the summertime. Suppose you are visiting a friend there in August. To express your discomfort, you say *"Estoy calor."* Your host, a very polite person, looks at you and has to refrain from laughing. Why? In English, we use adjectives to describe how we feel; thus, you've chosen (so you think) "I am hot." In Spanish, however, you must say "I have heat" (which doesn't mean you are sick and have a fever). Saying "I am hot" tells your Spanish host that you are hot to the touch. This sounds very strange to us, but *tengo calor* is the expression you need. Remember, our idioms don't always make sense either.

You will notice that all the idioms in Table 5.5 begin with the verb *tener*, which means "to have." Remember that the form of the verb changes as the subject of the sentence changes. (Conjugating verbs is covered in detail in Chapter 7, "Going Places.")

Table 5.5   Idiomatic Physical Conditions

Idiom	Pronunciation	Meaning
tener calor	teh-nehr kah-lohr	to be hot
tener hambre	teh-nehr ahm-breh	to be hungry
tener frío	teh-nehr free-yoh	to be cold
tener vergüenza	teh-nehr behr-goo-wehn-sah	to be ashamed
tener dolor de	teh-nehr doh-lohr deh	to have an ache in
tener miedo de	teh-nehr mee-yeh-doh deh	to be afraid of
tener razón	teh-nehr rrah-sohn	to be right
tener sed	teh-nehr sehd	to be thirsty
tener sueño	teh-nehr sweh-nyoh	to be sleepy
tener *xx* años	teh-nehr ah-nyohs	to be *xx* years old

Is Everything Okay?

Tell how you feel. Start by using *tengo* (I have) and then add the correct Spanish word to express the following. (Answers can be found on page 407, in Appendix A.)

1. sleepy	4. thirsty
_____	_____
2. hot	5. afraid
_____	_____
3. hungry	6. correct
_____	_____

How's the Weather?

It's always a good idea to stay on top of the weather when you travel because most of your plans are probably contingent upon it. Discussing weather in Spanish requires using a different verb than the one we use in English. If you said to your host, "*Está frío*," he or she would think you were talking about something you had touched. The Spanish use the verb *hacer* (to do or to make) to describe most weather conditions, as in "It makes cold." Study the common weather expressions in Table 5.6.

In a Flash

Look at the weather section of your newspaper. Give the weather reports for as many different cities as you can. Look out your window and give a report for your town.

Table 5.6 Idiomatic Weather Expressions

Idiom	Pronunciation	Meaning
hace buen tiempo	ah-seh bwehn tee-yehm-poh	to be nice weather
hace calor	ah-seh kah-lohr	to be hot
hace fresco	ah-seh frehs-koh	to be cool
hace sol	ah-seh sohl	to be sunny
hace viento	ah-seh bee-yehn-toh	to be windy
hace frío	ah-seh free-yoh	to be cold
hace mal tiempo	ah-seh mahl tee-yehm-poh	to be bad weather
¿Qué tiempo hace?	keh tee-yehm-poh ah-seh	What is the weather?

But never use *hacer* when discussing snow or rain. Use *nieva* (nee-eh-bah),which means "It's snowing," and *llueve* (yoo-eh-beh), which means "It's raining."

What's Happening in the World?

You're trying to decide where you would like to go on vacation. You have many places in mind, but what concerns you most is the weather. You want to make sure you don't plan your trip to Puerto Rico during the hurricane season or purchase a ski package for Argentina in December (when they have summer). Take a look at the weather for various cities and countries and express what it is like there today. (Answers can be found on page 407, in Appendix A.)

El tiempo en el mundo (*world*) hispano: El quince de enero

	TIEMPO	TEMPERATURA mínima	máxima
Madrid		5°	17°
Sevilla		-3°	4°
Barcelona		20°	27°
Córdoba		7°	17°
México		21°	31°
Panamá		6°	13°
Argentina		16°	26°
Colombia		25°	37°
Perú		2°	6°

1. En Madrid _____ .

2. En Sevilla _____ .

3. En Córdoba _____ .

4. En México _____ .

5. En Panamá _____ .

6. En Argentina _____ .

7. En Colombia _____ .

8. En Perú _____ .

9. En Barcelona _____ .

I Love Your Body (Language)

Spanish-speaking people, as a whole, tend to be very demonstrative. They frequently use body language to communicate various emotions and feelings. Many gestures enable the speaker to convey slang expressions without having to use words. These movements, of course, play an important role in the language and culture of the people.

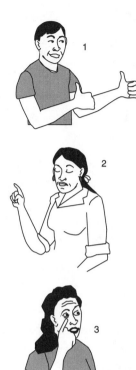

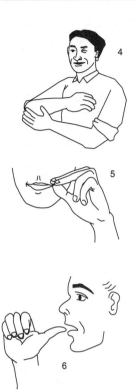

1. ¡Bien hecho!
   bee-yehn eh-choh
   Well done!

2. ¡No lo hagas!
   noh loh ah-gahs
   Don't do it!

3. ¡Ten cuidado!
   tehn kwee-dah-doh
   Be careful!

4. ¡Qué tacaño!
   keh tah-kah-nyoh
   What a cheapskate!

5. ¡Vamos a comer algo!
   bah-mohs ah koh-mehr ahl-goh
   Let's go eat something!

6. ¡Vamos a tomar (beber) algo!
   bah-mohs ah toh-mahr (beh-behr) ahl-goh
   Let's go get something to drink!

Remember, do not attempt to translate word for word from English to Spanish. This can backfire and cause embarrassment, especially in circumstances that call for specific idiomatic expressions that must be memorized. Although idioms are an accepted means of communication in any language, slang is not. When you can't think of the words you need, do not hesitate to use gestures and body language to convey your thoughts and feelings.

39

The Least You Need to Know

➤ Every language has its own idioms that can't be translated word for word.

➤ Every language also has slang. Be careful how you use it.

➤ Idioms can describe many thoughts and ideas, including time, opinions, directions, and the weather.

➤ With body language, you can communicate without saying anything at all.

Chapter 6

Sexually Speaking

In This Chapter

➤ How to determine gender

➤ Masculine and feminine nouns

➤ Changing from singular to plural

This chapter will help you better understand how the Spanish view gender. Unlike in English, every single noun (person, place, thing, or idea) in Spanish is designated as either masculine or feminine and either singular or plural. That's right, the taco you're consuming, the ball you're throwing, and the museum you're visiting all have a specific gender. How is the determination made? Sometimes it's obvious, sometimes there are clues, and sometimes it's just downright tricky. This chapter will teach you to make the right connections.

The Battle of the Sexes

Deciding which gender to use is obvious when you're speaking about a man or a woman. But what if you want to talk about a lovely store you passed the other day? Which gender do you use with *tienda* (store)? You don't know the rules yet, so do you assume it's feminine because women like to shop more than men? Better not—you could get into big trouble with that kind of sexist presumption.

Suppose you want to purchase a tie you saw in a store. You might assume that *corbata* is masculine because men wear ties more than women. But you would be wrong— *corbata* is a feminine word. How about a dress? It must be feminine; after all, dresses

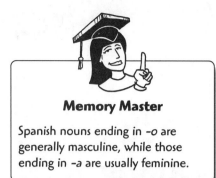

Memory Master

Spanish nouns ending in *-o* are generally masculine, while those ending in *-a* are usually feminine.

are not for men. Wrong again! The word for dress, *vestido*, is masculine. By now you're probably saying, "How can that be? It doesn't make sense!" You're absolutely correct. For the most part, it makes no sense.

Fortunately, there are clues to help you with these words and others like them. Should you come across a noun whose gender is a mystery to you, you can always resort to your trusty Spanish dictionary. Remember, even if you make a mistake in gender, as long as you have the correct vocabulary word, you'll be understood.

Noun Markers

All nouns in Spanish have a gender, either masculine (m) or feminine (f). They also are singular (sing) or plural (pl). Noun markers can help you identify these characteristics for any noun. The most common markers, shown in Table 6.1, are definite articles ("the") and indefinite articles ("a," "an," or "one").

Table 6.1   Singular Noun Markers

Article	Masculine	Feminine
the	el (ehl)	la (lah)
a, an, one	un (oon)	una (oo-nah)

Some nouns in Spanish, such as those shown in Table 6.2, are easy to categorize because they obviously refer to masculine or feminine people.

Table 6.2   Gender-Obvious Nouns

Masculine Noun	Pronunciation	English Meaning	Feminine Noun	Pronunciation	English Meaning
el padre	ehl pah-dreh	the father	la madre	lah mah-dreh	the mother
el abuelo	ehl ah-bweh-loh	the grand-father	la abuela	lah ah-bweh-lah	the grand-mother
el chico	ehl chee-koh	the boy	la chica	lah chee-kah	the girl
el amigo	ehl ah-mee-goh	the friend (m)	la amiga	lah ah-mee-gah	the friend (f)
el tío	ehl tee-yoh	the uncle	la tía	lah tee-yah	the aunt

Masculine Noun	Pronunciation	English Meaning	Feminine Noun	Pronunciation	English Meaning
el primo	ehl pree-moh	the cousin (m)	la prima	lah pree-mah	the cousin (f)
el hombre	ehl ohm-breh	the man	la mujer	lah moo-hehr	the woman

El or La?

Imagine you are having an animated conversation with a fellow traveler about people you've met, people in the news, or members of your family. Provide the definite article you would use when referring to the following people (the English translation of the word is in italics). (Answers can be found on page 407, in Appendix A.)

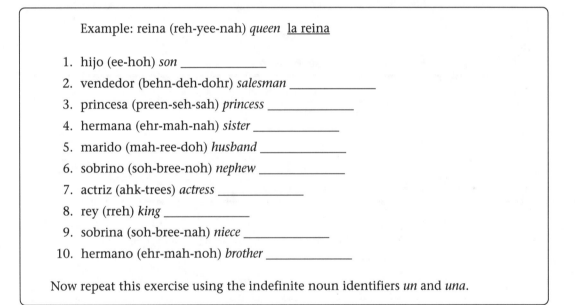

Example: reina (reh-yee-nah) *queen* <u>la reina</u>

1. hijo (ee-hoh) *son* _____

2. vendedor (behn-deh-dohr) *salesman* _____

3. princesa (preen-seh-sah) *princess* _____

4. hermana (ehr-mah-nah) *sister* _____

5. marido (mah-ree-doh) *husband* _____

6. sobrino (soh-bree-noh) *nephew* _____

7. actriz (ahk-trees) *actress* _____

8. rey (rreh) *king* _____

9. sobrina (soh-bree-nah) *niece* _____

10. hermano (ehr-mah-noh) *brother* _____

Now repeat this exercise using the indefinite noun identifiers *un* and *una*.

10 minutos al día

All nouns must be identified as either masculine or feminine. Use *el* to express the definite article (the) and *un* to express the indefinite article ("a," "an," or "one") before a masculine singular noun. Use *la* to express the definite article ("the") and *una* to express the indefinite article ("a," "an," or "one") before a feminine singular noun.

A few nouns can be either masculine or feminine. Just change the article to refer to either gender. Table 6.3 identifies some high-frequency nouns for which this rule applies.

Table 6.3   Either-Gender Nouns

Noun	Pronunciation	Meaning
artista	ahr-tees-tah	artist
dentista	dehn-tees-tah	dentist
estudiante	ehs-too-dee-yahn-teh	student
joven	hoh-behn	youth
modelo	moh-deh-loh	model

Some nouns are always masculine or always feminine despite the gender of the person to whom they refer. Observe the following nouns:

Always Masculine	Always Feminine
bebé (baby)	persona (person)
bombero (firefighter)	víctima (victim)

Some endings help determine the gender of the noun and make marking easier. You might have noticed in the preceding list that the masculine nouns ended in *-o* and *-e*, and the feminine nouns ended in *-a* (although a feminine nouns also can end in *-e*). If you don't know the gender of a Spanish word, you usually can make an accurate guess by looking at the vowel with which the word ends. Table 6.4 shows you the gender-identifying endings.

Table 6.4 Gender-Identifying Endings

Masculine Endings	Example	Feminine Endings	Example
-o	abrigo	*-a*	pluma
-ema	tema	*-ión*	lección
consonants (usually)	reloj	*-dad*	ciudad
		-tad	libertad
		-tud	juventud
		-umbre	costumbre
		-ie	serie

Gender Benders

Of course, there are always some exceptions to the rule, just to make sure you don't get overconfident. Keep the following in mind for future use.

Masculine nouns that end in *-a*:

> el clima (ehl klee-mah) *the climate*
>
> el día (ehl dee-yah) *the day*
>
> el drama (ehl drah-mah) *the drama*
>
> el problema (ehl proh-bleh-mah) *the problem*
>
> el programa (ehl proh-grah-mah) *the program*
>
> el telegrama (ehl teh-leh-grah-mah) *the telegram*

Feminine nouns that end in *-o*:

> la mano (lah mah-noh) *the hand*
>
> la foto (short for *fotografía*) (lah foh-toh) *the photo*
>
> la moto (short for *motocicleta*) (lah moh-toh) *the motorcycle*

In a Flash

When in doubt, always consult your dictionary for the gender of a word. An *m* or an *f* will appear if the gender isn't obvious or doesn't follow the rules.

¡Atención!

When you come across Spanish words that can be either masculine or feminine, your dictionary will show *m/f*.

Gender Changes

Masculine nouns that end in *-és, -r,* or *-n* add *-a* at the end to form the feminine equivalent. The following are examples:

el francés	la francesa
the Frenchman	*the French woman*
el autor	la autora
the author	*the authoress*
el alemán	la alemana
the German	*the German woman*

In the following two cases, none of these rules apply:

el actor	el emperador
the actor	*the emperor*
la actriz	la emperatriz
the actress	*the empress*

Note that any accent marks over the masculine nouns in the preceding examples are dropped for the feminine equivalent.

Identifying More Nouns

You are looking around a gift shop for some souvenirs to bring home to your family and friends. You have all kinds of requests for T-shirts, postcards, and posters. Tell the salesperson what you would like to see. Using the word endings as a clue, use the proper indefinite article, *un* or *una*, to ask for the item you want. (Answers can be found on page 407, in Appendix A.)

Example: reloj (rreh-loh) *watch*

Quisiera ver <u>un</u> reloj, por favor.
I'd like to see a watch, please.

1. bufanda (boo-fahn-dah) *scarf*

   _____

2. camiseta (kah-mee-seh-tah) *tee shirt*

   _____

3. sombrero (sohm-breh-roh) *hat*

   _____

4. libro (lee-broh) *book*

   _____

5. juguete (hoo-geh-teh) *toy*

   _____

6. cinta (seen-tah) *tape*

   _____

7. cinturón (seen-too-rohn) *belt*

   _____

8. vela (beh-lah) *candle*

   _____

9. chaleco (chah-leh-koh) *vest*

   _____

10. periódico (peh-ree-yoh-dee-koh) *newspaper*

    _____

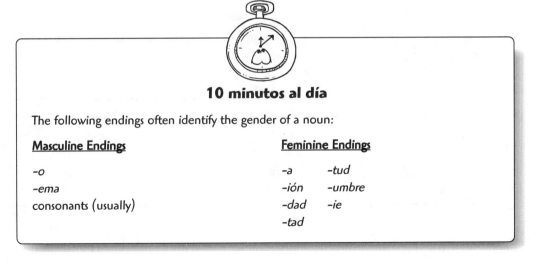

10 minutos al día

The following endings often identify the gender of a noun:

Masculine Endings	Feminine Endings	
-o	-a	-tud
-ema	-ión	-umbre
consonants (usually)	-dad	-ie
	-tad	

47

When There's More Than One

When a Spanish noun refers to more than one of something, it becomes plural. Just like in English, right? Not quite. As shown in Table 6.5, it is not enough to simply change the noun to its plural form in Spanish. The article must be made plural as well.

Table 6.5   Plural Noun Markers

English	Spanish	
	Masculine	*Feminine*
the	los	las
some	unos	unas

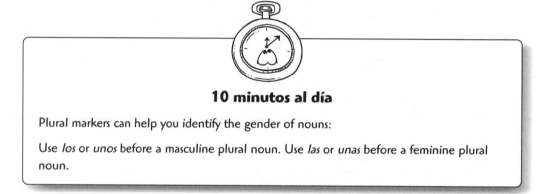

10 minutos al día

Plural markers can help you identify the gender of nouns:

Use *los* or *unos* before a masculine plural noun. Use *las* or *unas* before a feminine plural noun.

Plural Nouns

Forming plural nouns in Spanish is not difficult. Most Spanish nouns can be made plural by adding -*s* to the singular form, as follows:

Singular	Plural	Meaning
el libro	los libros	the books
un libro	unos libros	some books
la mesa	las mesas	the tables
una mesa	unas mesas	some tables

For Spanish nouns that end in a consonant (including -*y*), add -*es* to the noun to form the plural, as follows:

Singular	Plural	Meaning
el rey	los reyes	the kings
el mes	los meses	the months
un mes	unos meses	some months
la explicación	las explicaciones	the explanations
una explicación	unas explicaciones	some explanations

For Spanish nouns that end in -*z*, change the *z* to a *c* and then add -*es* to form the plural, as follows:

Singular	Plural	Meaning
el pez	los peces	the fish
un pez	unos peces	some fish
la actriz	las actrices	the actresses
una actriz	unas actrices	some actresses

It might be necessary to add or delete an accent mark to maintain the original stress, as follows:

Singular	Plural	Meaning
el joven	los jóvenes	the young people
el examen	los exámenes	the tests
el francés	los franceses	the French (people)
la reunión	las reuniones	the meetings

Except for nouns ending in *-és*, no ending is added for nouns ending in *-s*:

Singular	Plural	Meaning
el martes	los martes	Tuesdays
el paréntesis	los paréntesis	parentheses

In a Flash

Set up *un rincón español* (a Spanish corner) in your home where you study Spanish. Label the items you keep there: photos, stationery items, books, and so on. Practice identifying them using *el, la, los,* and *las*. Then switch to *un, una, unos,* and *unas*. Then change all the singular nouns to plural and vice versa.

Mixed Doubles

In a mixed group of males and females, the masculine plural form always prevails. *Los amigos*, for example, can refer to male friends or a group of male and female friends. If there are only females present, use *las amigas*. *Los hijos* can refer to sons or to children of both genders. If there are only daughters, however, use *las hijas*.

Some nouns are always plural:

las gafas (lahs gah-fahs) *eyeglasses*

las vacaciones (lahs bah-kah-see-yoh-nehs) *vacation*

las tijeras (lahs tee-heh-rahs) *scissors*

More Than One

Imagine you are describing what you saw on vacation to your friends back home. Although you try not to, you tend to exaggerate a little. Tell everyone you saw more than one of the following. (Answers can be found on page 407, in Appendix A.)

Example: almacén (ahl-mah-sehn) *department store*

Ví los almacenes.
I saw department stores.

1. tienda (tee-yehn-dah) *store* _____.
2. actriz (ahk-trees) *actress* _____.
3. restaurante (rrehs-tow-rahn-tay) *restaurant* _____.
4. palacio (pah-lah-see-yoh) *palace* _____.
5. automóvil (ow-toh-moh-beel) *automobile* _____.
6. flor (flohr) *flower* _____.
7. rey (rreh) *king* _____.
8. monumento (moh-noo-mehn-toh) *monument*_____.
9. francés (frahn-sehs) *Frenchman* _____.
10. autor (ow-tohr) *author* _____.

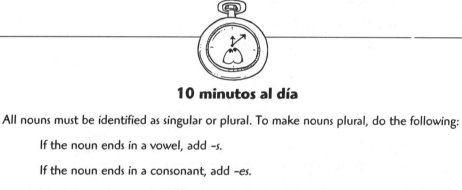

10 minutos al día

All nouns must be identified as singular or plural. To make nouns plural, do the following:

If the noun ends in a vowel, add *-s*.

If the noun ends in a consonant, add *-es*.

Note that *z* changes to *c* before adding *-es*, as in *el pez* but *los peces*.

Except for nouns ending in *-és*, no plural ending is added for nouns already ending in *-s*, as in *el francés* but *los franceses* and *el martes* but *los martes*. Practice with Plurals

Practice with Plurals

Imagine you've misplaced some items in your hotel room. You know how messy these places can get, especially when you're living out of a suitcase. You've found most of your missing items. Now you are looking for one more of each of the following. (Answers can be found on page 408, in Appendix A.)

Example: llaves (yah-behs) *keys*

Busco la llave.
I am looking for the key.

1. lápices (lah-pee-sehs) *pencils* _____ .
2. regalos (rreh-gah-lohs) *gifts* _____ .
3. collares (koh-yah-rehs) *necklaces* _____ .
4. paquetes (pah-keh-tehs) *packages* _____ .
5. revistas (rreh-bees-tahs) *magazines* _____ .
6. lociones (loh-see-yoh-nehs) *lotions* _____ .

The Least You Need to Know

➤ Certain endings are almost always masculine (*-o, -ema,* consonants); others are almost always feminine (*-a, -ión, -dad, -tad, -tud, -umbre, -ie*).

➤ Some nouns can be changed from masculine to feminine by adding the appropriate ending.

➤ Nouns ending in a vowel can be made plural by adding *-s.* Nouns ending in a consonant require *-es.* Nouns ending in *-s* (not *-és*) remain unchanged.

Going Places

In This Chapter

➤ Subject pronouns

➤ Conjugating verbs

➤ How to ask a question

➤ Common regular verbs

In the preceding chapter, you learned how easy it is to determine whether a Spanish noun is masculine or feminine and how simple it is to form plurals. This chapter shows you how to replace a noun with a pronoun and how to construct simple Spanish sentences by using verbs to talk about a variety of activities.

An excellent way to practice your Spanish is to use the language in everyday situations. Imagine you're on a trip in a Spanish-speaking country. What will you do there? There's probably something for everyone: cosmopolitan cities, ancient ruins, sandy beaches. What will you see? The choices are endless: cathedrals, museums, parks, bullfights. Who will you meet? How about the Spanish-speaking communities of South and Central America and Spain? You'll have countless opportunities to use your newfound skills. Let's go!

What's the Subject

Verbs are words that express an action, occurrence, or a state of being. To form a complete sentence, you also need to know who or what is the subject of the verb. The subject can be stated (as in "*I* would like to go to the Prado" or "*The tour bus* has just arrived"), or it can be understood in a command (as in "Visit the Alhambra," where the subject is understood to be *you*). The subject can be a noun or a pronoun that replaces the noun. In the sentence "The toreador is entering the arena," for example, *the toreador* can be replaced with the pronoun *he* to form the new sentence, "He is entering the arena."

Subject Pronouns

Just as in English, subject pronouns in Spanish, shown in Table 7.1, are given a person (first, second, or third) and a number (singular or plural). In Spanish, however, subject pronouns are used far less frequently than in English. This is because verbs have different endings depending on who is performing the action. If you listen carefully, you can usually determine the subject, even when it is not specified in the sentence. In general, Spanish only uses subject pronouns for the following:

➤ *Clarity:* To differentiate who is doing the action for cases in which verb forms are the same.

Él (or Ella or Ud.) habla bien.
He (or she or you) speak(s) well.

Él descansa mientras Ud. trabaja.
He rests while you work.

➤ *Emphasis:* To clearly underline the fact that the subject will be performing the action.

Voy a España.
I'm going to Spain.

Yo voy a España.
I'm going to Spain.

➤ *Politeness*: To be extremely formal and to show impeccable manners and deference to an individual.

¡Pase **Ud.**!
Enter!

¡Atención!

Although subject pronouns usually are omitted, you will notice that Spanish speakers regularly use the pronouns *usted* and *ustedes* in conversation. In writing, *usted* is abbreviated as *Ud.* and *ustedes* as *Uds.*

Ud. es muy inteligente.
You (singular) are very intelligent.

Uds. son amables.
You (plural) are very nice.

Table 7.1   Subject Pronouns

Person	Singular	Plural
first	yo (yoh) I	nosotros (noh-soh-trohs) we
second	tú (too) you	vosotros (boh-soh-trohs) you
third	él (ehl) he	ellos (eh-yohs) they
	ella (eh-yah) she	ellas (eh-yahs) they
	usted (oo-stehd) you	ustedes (oo-steh-dehs) you

Note that, in Spanish, distinctions are made to accommodate groups containing only females: *nosotros* becomes *nosotras*, *vosotros* becomes *vosotras,* and *ellos* becomes *ellas*. What happens when you want to refer to a mixed group? Nosotros, vosotros, and ellos are used, regardless of the number of males and females in the group.

Says You!

If you studied the subject pronoun chart carefully, you probably noticed that there are two singular and two plural forms for the English word *you*. *Tú* (singular) and *vosotros* (plural) are used when speaking to a friend, relative, child, or pet. *Tú* and *vosotros* are called familiar forms. *Usted* (singular) and *ustedes* (plural) are used to show respect to an older person or when speaking to someone you don't know very well. These are referred to as polite forms and generally are abbreviated as *Ud.* and *Uds*. The abbreviations are always capitalized.

Culture Corner

The plural *vosotros* form is used in Spain because the Spaniards tend to be purists about their language. In the Spanish–speaking countries of Central and South America and the Caribbean, only the *ustedes* form is used.

Formal or Informal?

Would you use *tú*, *usted*, *vosotros*, or *ustedes* when speaking to the following people? (Answers can be found on page 408, in Appendix A.)

1. A doctor? _____ .
2. Your cousin? _____ .
3. Your friend? _____ .
4. A salesman? _____ .
5. A woman waiting in line for a bus? _____ .
6. Two female friends? _____ .
7. Two male friends? _____ .
8. A policeman from whom you are asking directions? _____ .
9. Your friends? _____ .

55

¡Atención!

In English, the subject pronoun "I" is always capitalized, regardless of its position in the sentence. In Spanish, *yo* is only capitalized at the beginning of a sentence, just like any other word. But *usted* and *ustedes* are always capitalized when they are abbreviated (*Ud., Uds.*).

Pronouns are useful because they enable you to speak fluidly without having to constantly repeat the noun. Imagine how tedious it would be to hear "Jorge is Spanish. Jorge is from Madrid. Jorge really knows Jorge's way around the country." Subject pronouns can replace proper nouns as follows:

Noun	Pronoun
Ricardo	él
Marta	ella
Pedro y Carlos	ellos
Ana y Susana	ellas
Pablo y Carlota	ellos

Who's Who?

Which pronoun would you use when speaking about the following people? (Answers can be found on page 408, in Appendix A.)

1. Eduardo? _____
2. Anita? _____
3. Sara y Beatriz? _____
4. Gloria? _____
5. Arturo? _____
6. Juan y Miguel? _____
7. Roberto y Lupita? _____
8. Alba? _____
9. Blanca? _____
10. Cristina y Manuel? _____
11. Paco? _____
12. Julio y Amalia? _____

Just Keep Moving

You routinely use verbs to express action, motion, or a state of being. In Spanish, there are two types of verbs: regular and irregular. All regular verbs follow a set pattern of rules particular to the family to which the verb belongs (*-ar, -er,* or *-ir* family). These verbs are easy to use after you've learned the pattern. Irregular verbs, on the other hand, do not have a specific pattern; their conjugations must be memorized individually. Fortunately, regular verbs far outnumber irregular verbs. To get you off to a fast start, this chapter only covers regular verbs.

10 minutos al día

The Spanish subject pronouns are:

yo	*I*	nosotros(as)	*we*
tú	*you* (familiar)	vosotros(as)	*you* (used primarily in Spain)
él	*he*	ellos	*they*
ella	*she*	ellas	*they*
Ud. (usted)	*you* (polite)	Uds. (ustedes)	*you*

Always use the masculine plural subject pronoun when referring to a mixed group of people.

Use *tú* when speaking to a friend or relative. Use *Ud.* when speaking formally.

Regular Verbs

The basic "to" form of a verb is referred to as the *infinitive* (to live, to laugh, to love). In dictionaries (of any language), verbs are presented in the infinitive form, the form of the verb before it has been conjugated.

Most people are totally unaware that, when they speak in English, they conjugate verbs without giving this grammatical process a second thought. It just comes naturally as the result of copying speech patterns when you first learn to talk. *Conjugation*, quite simply, refers to changing the ending of a regular verb or changing the entire form of an irregular verb so it agrees

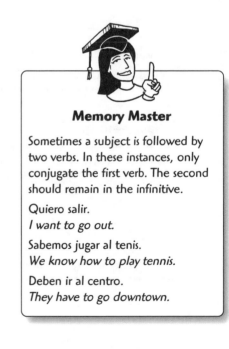

Memory Master

Sometimes a subject is followed by two verbs. In these instances, only conjugate the first verb. The second should remain in the infinitive.

Quiero salir.
I want to go out.

Sabemos jugar al tenis.
We know how to play tennis.

Deben ir al centro.
They have to go downtown.

with its subject. The following shows the infinitive verb "to sing" (a regular verb in English), for example, conjugated into three of its forms:

I sing You sing He sings

The verb "to be" is an irregular verb. Here it is conjugated the same way:

I am You are He is

In Spanish, there are three large families of regular verbs—verbs whose infinitives end in *-ar*, *-er*, or *-ir*. All verbs within a family are conjugated in exactly the same manner. After you learn the pattern for a family, you know how to conjugate all the verbs in that family.

The *-ar* Verb Family

Let's start by looking at the *-ar* verb family, which is by far the largest. Notice that the endings are really quite simple. To conjugate *-ar* verbs, drop *-ar* from the infinitive and add the following endings:

Pronoun	Verb Ending
yo	*-o*
tú	*-as*
él, ella, Ud.	*-a*
nosotros	*-amos*
vosotros	*-áis*
ellos, ellas, Uds.	*-an*

Hablar—to Speak

Singular Forms	Plural Forms
Yo hablo *I speak*	Nosotros hablamos *We speak*
Tú hablas *You (sing.) speak*	Vosotros habláis *You (pl.) speak*
Él, ella, Ud. habla *He, she, you (sing.) speak(s)*	Ellos, Ellas, Uds. hablan *They, you (pl.) speak*

Conjugation 101

Now you can conjugate any *-ar* verb.

Imagine you are traveling with a tour group to various countries in Central America. Practice the conjugation of *-ar* verbs to describe what everyone is doing. (Answers can be found on page 408, in Appendix A.)

> Example: mirar (to look at)
>> Yo <u>miro</u> el programa.

---

1. anunciar (to announce)

   Él _____ la partida del avión.

2. buscar (to look for)

   Ellos _____ la oficina.

3. observar (to observe)

   Nosotros _____ mucho.

4. andar (to walk)

   Yo _____ por el parque.

5. nadar (to swim)

   Vosotros _____ .

The -er Verb Family

Now let's look at another family that will also prove easy to manage. To conjugate *-er* verbs, drop *-er* from the infinitive and add the following endings:

Pronoun	Verb Ending
yo	*-o*
tú	*-es*
él, ella, Ud.	*-e*
nosotros	*-emos*
vosotros	*-éis*
ellos, ellas, Uds.	*-en*

Leer—To Read

Singular Forms	Plural Forms
Yo le**o**	Nosotros le**emos**
I read	*We read*
Tú le**es**	Vosotros le**éis**
You (sing.) read	*You (pl.) read*
Él, ella, Ud. le**e**	Ellos, Ellas, Uds. le**en**
He, she, you (sing.) read(s)	*They, you (pl.) read*

In a Flash

Thumb through a family album and use pronouns to identify the people you see. Try to describe in Spanish what the different people are doing.

Conjugation 102

In the summer, when there are lots of tourists, you'll see many people doing all kinds of things. Practice *-er* verb conjugation by choosing the verb that best completes the following sentences and then putting it in its correct form. (Answers can be found on page 408, in Appendix A.)

comer (to eat)	aprender (to learn)
correr (to run)	deber (to have to)
beber (to drink)	responder (to answer)

1. Tú _____ al centro.
2. Ellos _____ en el restaurante.
3. Nosotros _____ soda.
4. Ud. _____ a las preguntas.
5. Él _____ frases españolas.
6. Yo _____ firmar (to sign) muchos documentos.

The -ir Verb Family

If you've mastered the *-er* verb family, you will find the *-ir* family to be a snap. When you study the chart you'll understand why. To conjugate *-ir* verbs, drop *-ir* from the infinitive and add the following endings:

Pronoun	Verb Ending
yo	*-o*
tú	*-es*
él, ella, Ud.	*-e*
nosotros	*-imos*
vosotros	*-ís*
ellos, ellas, Uds.	*-en*

Decidir—To Decide

Singular Forms	Plural Forms
Yo decid**o** *I decide*	Nosotros decid**imos** *We decide*
Tú decid**es** *You (sing.) decide*	Vosotros decid**ís** *You (pl.) decide*
Él, ella, Ud. decid**e** *He, she, you (sing.) decide(s)*	Ellos, Ellas, Uds. decid**en** *They, you (pl.) decide*

Conjugation 103

When traveling in a group, some people want to break away and do their own thing. It's important to them to spend their time the way they want. Using the following *-ir* verbs, tell what each tourist does. (Answers can be found on page 408, in Appendix A.)

1. vivir (to live)
   Vosotros _____ rápidamente.

2. aplaudir (to applaud)
   Ella _____.

3. escribir (to write)
   Ellos _____ cartas.

Memory Master

Verbs whose infinitives end in *-er* or *-ir* have the same endings except for the *nosotros* and *vosotros* forms. In these forms, *-er* verbs use *-e* and *-ir* verbs use *-i* as the ending.

4. omitir (to omit)

   Tú _____ mucho.

5. asistir (to attend)

   Él _____ a la conferencia.

6. abrir (to open)

   Yo _____ una cuenta de banco.

7. descubrir (to discover)

   Nosotros _____ cosas interesantes.

8. recibir (to receive)

   Ana y Linda _____ paquetes.

10 minutos al día

The infinitives of regular verbs ending in *-ar*, *-er*, and *-ir* all follow the same pattern of conjugation. Simply drop the infinitive ending (*-ar*, *-er*, *-ir*) and add the ending that corresponds to the subject.

	-ar verbs	*-er* verbs	*-ir* verbs
yo	*-o*	*-o*	*-o*
tú	*-as*	*-es*	*-es*
él, ella, Ud.	*-a*	*-e*	*-e*
nosotros(as)	*-amos*	*-emos*	*-imos*
vosotros(as)	*-áis*	*-éis*	*-ís*
ellos, ellas, Uds.	*-an*	*-en*	*-en*

Subject pronouns can be omitted in Spanish when the verb ending clearly indicates the subject.

Go Ahead! Ask Me!

If you're planning a trip, you surely have loads of questions to ask. This section starts with the quick and easy ones—those that require a simple yes or no answer. In Spanish, there are three ways to ask a yes or no question: by intonation, by using the *¿verdad?* tag, and by inversion.

When to Raise Your Voice

The easiest way to signify that you're asking a question is simply to change your intonation and to raise your voice at the end of the sentence, just like in English. To do this, speak with a rising inflection.

> ¿(Tú) quieres ir a México?
> *Do you want to go to Mexico?*

Notice how your intonation starts out lower and gradually keeps rising until the end of the sentence.

The Tags ¿Verdad?, ¿No?, and ¿Está Bien?

Another way to ask a yes or no question is to simply add one of these tags: *¿verdad?* (behr-dahd), *¿no?* (noh), or *¿está bien?* (ehs-tah bee-yehn). These can mean "really?," "isn't that so?," "is it?," "isn't it?," "are you?," "aren't you?," "do you?," "don't you?," or "all right?" at the end of the phrase.

> ¿Tú quieres ir a México, verdad? (¿no?) (¿está bien?)
> *You want to go to Mexico, right? (isn't that so?) (no?) (don't you?)*

About Face

The third way to form a question is by inversion, in which the order of the subject (noun or pronoun) and the verb is simply reversed. Once again, you need to raise your voice at the end of the phrase to indicate that you are, in fact, asking a question.

> ¿Quieres (tú) ir a México?
> *Do you want to go to Mexico?*

> ¿Son Uds. españoles?
> *Are you Spanish?*

> ¿Es Juanita de Puerto Rico?
> *Is Juanita from Puerto Rico?*

Remember, whether you are using intonation or inversion, you are asking for exactly the same information: a *sí* or *no* answer.

Memory Master

When writing, Spanish speakers use two question marks: an upside down one (¿) at the beginning of the question and a standard one (?) at the end.

¿Quieres hacer un viaje conmigo?
Would you like to take a trip with me?

Ask Away

Is it in your nature to be inquisitive about everyone and everything? If you're anything like me, there's always a question on the tip of your tongue. Practice the art of asking questions by conjugating the following infinitives and using intonation, tags, or inversion to satisfy your curiosity. (Answers can be found on page 408, in Appendix A.)

1. nosotros/hablar demasiado _____ .
2. él/asistir a muchos conciertos _____ .
3. Uds./comprender mucho_____ .
4. María/escribir cartas en español_____ .

And the Answer Is...

To answer a question affirmatively, use *sí* (pronounced *see*) and give your response, as in the following example:

¿Fuma Ud.?	Sí, fumo.
Do you smoke?	*Yes, I smoke.*

To answer negatively, first say *no* and then repeat it before the conjugated verb. (Remember, if there are two verbs, only the first is conjugated.)

¿Fuma Ud.?	No, no fumo.
Do you smoke?	*No, I don't smoke.*
	or
	No, no quiero fumar.
	No, I don't want to smoke.

You can vary your negative responses by using one of the following negative expressions:

nunca (noon-kah) *never*   nada (nah-dah) *nothing*   nadie (nah-dee-eh) *no one*

Sentences can be made negative in Spanish in one of two ways:

➤ Put the negative word before the conjugated verb.

Nunca fumo.	Nada puedo ver.	Nadie llega.
I never smoke.	*I can't see anything.*	*No one is arriving.*

➤ Put *no* before the conjugated verb and place the negative expression after the entire verb phrase. Notice how this creates a double negative, which is perfectly acceptable in Spanish.

No fumo nunca.	No puedo ver nada.
I never smoke.	*I can't see anything.*

No llega nadie.
No one is arriving.

When answering a question, a triple negative might even be used.

¿Quieres comer algo?
Do you want to eat something?

No, no quiero comer nada.
No, I don't want to eat anything.

Tell Us About Yourself

What are your good or bad habits? Do you have hobbies? Are there activities you really enjoy doing to relax? Read the following list of activities and answer with a yes or no sentence. (Sample responses can be found on page 409, in Appendix A.)

¡Atención!

The negative construction with nada is most uncommon. To speak colloquially, use *no*.

In a Flash

Make a list of five questions in Spanish that you'd like to ask a friend. Then write what you think your friend's answers will be.

---

1. Fumar? (to smoke) _____ .

2. Gritar? (to shout) _____ .

3. Bailar bien? (to dance) _____ .

4. Cocinar bien? (to cook) _____ .

5. Hablar español? _____ .

6. Charlar con sus amigos? _____ .

7. Leer muchas revistas? _____ .

8. Escribir muchas cartas? _____ .

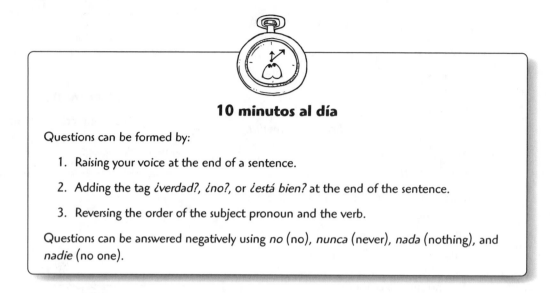

10 minutos al día

Questions can be formed by:

1. Raising your voice at the end of a sentence.

2. Adding the tag *¿verdad?*, *¿no?*, or *¿está bien?* at the end of the sentence.

3. Reversing the order of the subject pronoun and the verb.

Questions can be answered negatively using *no* (no), *nunca* (never), *nada* (nothing), and *nadie* (no one).

Verb Tables

If you want to increase your vocabulary quickly, you need to have as many verbs as possible on the tip of your tongue. The cognates in Chapter 3, "The Spanish You Know," and the lists of regular verbs in Tables 7.2, 7.3, and 7.4 should get you off to a flying start and can help you in many everyday situations.

Table 7.2　Common *-ar* Verbs

Verb	Pronunciation	Meaning
anunciar	ah-noon-see-yahr	to announce
ayudar	ah-yoo-dahr	to help
buscar	boos-kahr	to look for
caminar	kah-mee-nahr	to walk
comprar	kohm-prahr	to buy
desear	deh-seh-yahr	to desire
enviar	ehn-bee-yahr	to send
escuchar	ehs-koo-chahr	to listen (to)
estudiar	ehs-too-dee-yahr	to study
expresar	ehks-preh-sahr	to express
firmar	feer-mahr	to sign
funcionar	foonk-see-yoh-nahr	to function
gastar	gahs-tahr	to spend (money)
hablar	ah-blahr	to speak, to talk
hallar	ah-yahr	to find

Verb	Pronunciation	Meaning
lavar	lah-bahr	to wash
llegar	yeh-gahr	to arrive
mandar	mahn-dahr	to order
mirar	mee-rahr	to look at
necesitar	neh-seh-see-tahr	to need
olvidar	ohl-bee-dar	to forget
organizar	ohr-gah-nee-sahr	to organize
pagar	pah-gahr	to pay
preguntar	preh-goon-tahr	to ask
quitar	kee-tahr	to leave, to remove
regresar	rreh-greh-sahr	to return
reservar	rreh-sehr-bahr	to reserve
telefonear	teh-leh-foh-neh-yahr	to phone
tomar	toh-mahr	to take
viajar	bee-yah-hahr	to travel
visitar	bee-see-tahr	to visit

Table 7.3 Common *-er* Verbs

Verb	Pronunciation	Meaning
aprender	ah-prehn-dehr	to learn
beber	beh-behr	to drink
comer	koh-mehr	to eat
correr	koh-rrehr	to run
creer	kreh-yehr	to believe
deber	deh-behr	to have to, to owe
leer	leh-yehr	to read
prometer	proh-meh-tehr	to promise

Table 7.4 Common *-ir* Verbs

Verb	Pronunciation	Meaning
abrir	ah-breer	to open
asistir	ah-sees-teer	to attend
cubrir	koo-breer	to cover

continues

Table 7.4 Continued

Verb	Pronunciation	Meaning
decidir	deh-see-deer	to decide
escribir	ehs-kree-beer	to write
omitir	oh-mee-teer	to omit
partir	pahr-teer	to divide, to share
subir	soo-beer	to go up, to climb
vivir	bee-beer	to live

The Least You Need to Know

➤ Subject pronouns often are omitted in Spanish because the verb ending generally indicates who or what the subject is.

➤ Any verb that follows a subject noun or pronoun must be properly conjugated.

➤ There are three ways to ask a question in Spanish: intonation, ¿tags, and
inversion.

Part 2
Traveling Around

At some point in your life, no doubt, your travels will take you to a Spanish-speaking country. In a fast-paced world where people come and go at an ever-increasing rate, it is inevitable that one day your Spanish will come in handy and will prove to be a useful tool.

You'll want to be able to introduce yourself and your traveling companions, perhaps to glean some useful travel tips on the plane. Of no small significance will be the capability to maneuver your way around the airport so you can get to your destination in a timely fashion. Your comfort will also surely be of paramount importance to you.

The highlights of Part 2 include how to get where you're going with style and grace and how to get what you need after you've arrived.

Chapter 8

Meetings and Greetings

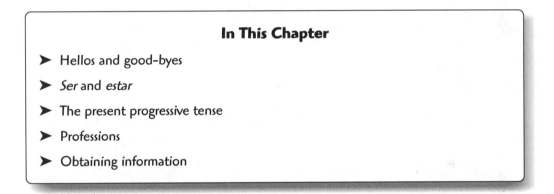

In This Chapter

➤ Hellos and good-byes

➤ *Ser* and *estar*

➤ The present progressive tense

➤ Professions

➤ Obtaining information

By now you should feel confident in your ability to combine nouns or pronouns with regular verbs to create simple sentences and to ask basic questions in Spanish. It's time to put your knowledge to work by engaging in a short conversation.

Imagine you're flying to Spain for the eagerly anticipated, well-deserved vacation about which you've always dreamed. You find yourself seated next to a Spanish-speaking person. Don't waste this golden opportunity. Introduce yourself. Get some pointers about places to visit, sights to see, and restaurants to sample. It's the perfect way to get your trip off to a great start.

Ask Your Friends

When you travel, do you get last minute jitters? Are you nervous about how you'll manage after you've arrived in a country where not everyone speaks your language? To relieve this anxiety, consult your travel agent and your friends. They'll be happy to share their experiences and to give you tips, hints, and recommendations on where to stay, eat, and go sight-seeing. If at all possible, speak to someone who has lived or spent considerable time in the country you plan to visit. If you find that person sitting next to you on the plane, don't be shy. Take the initiative and strike up a conversation.

Because your fellow traveler is still a stranger to you, good manners dictate that you employ a formal approach. Use some or all of the following phrases as an opening to your conversation:

Phrase	Pronunciation	Meaning
Buenos días	bweh-nohs dee-yahs	Hello
Buenas tardes	bweh-nahs tahr-dehs	Good afternoon
Buenas noches	bweh-nahs noh-chehs	Good evening
Señor	seh-nyohr	Mr., sir
Señorita	seh-nyoh-ree-tah	Miss, young woman
Señora	seh-nyoh-rah	Mrs., madam, woman
Me llamo	meh yah-moh	My name is
¿Cómo se llama?	koh-moh seh yah-mah	What is your name?
¿Cómo está Ud.?	koh-moh ehs-tah oo-stehd	How are you?
Muy bien	mwee bee-yehn	Very well
Regular	rreh-goo-lahr	So-so

An informal opening conversation (between young people or friends) might use the following phrases:

Phrase	Pronunciation	Meaning
¡Hola!	oh-lah	Hi!
Me llamo	meh yah-moh	My name is
¿Cómo te llamas?	koh-moh teh yah-mahs	What's your name?
¿Cómo estás?	koh-moh ehs-tahs	How are you?
¿Cómo te va?	koh-moh teh bah	How are you?
¿Qué tal?	keh tahl	How are things?
¿Qué pasa?	keh pah-sah	What's happening?
Nada de particular	nah-dah deh pahr-tee-koo-lahr	Nothing much

To Be or—to Be!

Many people respond favorably when asked questions about themselves. They like to be the center of attention and enjoy engaging in friendly conversation. If you'd like to get to know the person sitting next to you, ask him or her a few questions. What country or city is he from? How does she feel at the moment? You will need to use the verbs *ser* (to be) and *estar* (to be) to ask any of these questions.

No, you didn't misread that. In Spanish, there are two ways to express the verb "to be." Let's say your teenage son was born with blond hair. If someone asked about him, you'd use the verb *ser* to say "*Es rubio.*" ("He's blond.") If he's anything like my son's friend who has green hair one day and pink the next, you might be tempted to respond with the verb *estar* (even though it's not really correct), "Está rubio," to denote the impermanence of the hair-color situation. Sound strange? Don't worry. The differences between the two verbs will be clear by the end of this section.

Memory Master

Married women in Spanish-speaking countries are referred to and addressed as *señora* (Mrs.). Younger women are addressed as *señorita* (Miss, Ms.).

First, let's take a closer look at the conjugations of these two verbs. Just like the English verb "to be," *ser* and *estar* are irregular; all of their forms must be memorized. Because both verbs are used so frequently, learning them should be a top priority. Compare the conjugations in Table 8.1. As you will see, there are more irregular forms in Spanish than in English.

Table 8.1   The Verbs *Ser* and *Estar* (to Be)

Ser	Estar
yo *soy* (soy)	yo *estoy* (ehs-toy)
tú *eres* (eh-rehs)	tú *estás* (ehs-tahs)
él, ella, Ud. *es* (ehs)	él, ella, Ud. *está* (ehs-tah)
nosotros *somos* (soh-mohs)	nosotros *estamos* (ehs-tah-mohs)
vosotros *sois* (soy-ees)	vosotros *estáis* (ehs-tah-yees)
ellos, ellas, Uds. *son* (sohn)	ellos, ellas, Uds. *están* (ehs-tahn)

Determining the Difference

You should have little trouble distinguishing between the two verbs. What happens if you inadvertently use the wrong one? Nothing much. You'll still be understood.

Use *ser* in the following situations:

➤ To express origin, nationality, or an inherent characteristic or quality that will not change.

Ana es de Cuba.	Mi hijo es rubio.
Ana is from Cuba.	*My son is blond.*
Es cubana.	Es un anillo de oro.
She's Cuban.	*It's a gold ring.*

➤ To describe the subject of a sentence and any traits that will probably remain unchanged for an extended period of time.

Ricardo es alto.	El coche es nuevo.
Ricardo is tall.	*The car is new.*
Mi madre es profesora.	¿Quién es? Soy yo.
My mother is a teacher.	*Who is it? It's me.*

➤ To express time and dates.

Son las dos.	Es el once de julio.
It's two o'clock.	*It's July 11.*

➤ To express possession.

Es mi libro.	Esta cartera es de Juan.
It's my book.	*This is Juan's wallet.*

➤ The preposition *de* (of, from) is preceded by the verb *ser*.

Somos de México.	La casa es de madera.
We are from Mexico.	*The house is made of wood.*

➤ With certain impersonal expressions.

Es necesario practicar.	Es importante estudiar.
It's necessary to practice.	*It's important to study.*

Use *estar* in the following situations:

➤ To describe a temporary state or condition of the subject.

Yo estoy triste.	Las puertas están cerradas.
I am sad.	*The doors are closed.*
La casa está sucia.	
The house is dirty.	

➤ To express location.

El hotel está en la ciudad.	¿Dónde está el aeropuerto?
The hotel is in the city.	*Where's the airport?*

➤ To form the progressive tenses. (These are explained later in this chapter.)

Estoy cantando.　　　　　　　Está lloviendo.
I'm singing.　　　　　　　　*It's raining.*

Idioms with Estar

Imagine you are having a phone conversation with a Spanish friend who says *"Estoy a punto de salir."* Your Spanish is not quite up to snuff yet, so you get insulted. You hear the cognate *punto* (point), and you immediately jump to the conclusion that your friend is making a point of leaving because the phone call is boring. In fact, your friend was simply explaining to you that he or she was just about to leave when you called. If something doesn't sound right, it's probably because an idiomatic expression is being used. Table 8.2 contains some idioms using *estar*.

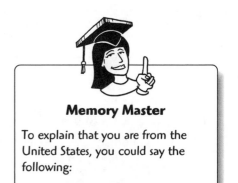

Memory Master

To explain that you are from the United States, you could say the following:

Soy de los Estados Unidos.
soh-ee deh lohs ehs-tah-dohs
oo-nee-dohs

Table 8.2　Idioms with *Estar*

Idiomatic Expression	Pronunciation	Meaning
estar a punto de + infinitive	ehs-tahr ah poon-toh deh	to be just about + infinitive
estar por	ehs-tahr pohr	to be in favor
estar por + infinitive	ehs-tahr pohr	to be inclined + infinitive
estar de acuerdo (con)	ehs-tahr deh ah-kwehr-doh (kohn)	to agree (with)
estar de vuelta	ehs-tahr deh bwehl-tah	to be back

You're now ready for a more extensive conversation with the person sitting next to you on the plane. Begin with one of the following phrases:

Formal:　　　　　　　¿De dónde es Ud.?
　　　　　　　　　　　Where are you from?

Informal:　　　　　　¿De dónde eres?
　　　　　　　　　　　Where are you from?

Ser vs. Estar

Imagine you are sitting on a plane having an informal conversation with your traveling companion. The verb "to be" seems to be repeated over and over again. Should you use *ser* or *estar*? Complete the following sentences with the correct form of the necessary verb. (Answers can be found on page 409, in Appendix A.)

1. Nosotros _____ de países diferentes.
2. Este vuelo _____ muy interesante.
3. Sus maletas (suitcases)_____ aquí (here).
4. Los pilotos _____ responsables.
5. El avión_____ cerca de (near) la ciudad.

10 minutos al día

The verbs *ser* and *estar* both express *to be*. Here are the forms of these verbs for different subjects.

	Ser	Estar
yo	soy	estoy
tú	eres	estás
él, ella, Ud.	es	está
nosotros	somos	estamos
vosotros	sois	estáis
ellos, ellas, Uds.	son	están

Use *ser* to express permanent characteristics: size, coloring, and height; nationality; possession; and time and date.

Use *estar* to express temporary conditions: emotions, feelings, and states of being; location; and what the subject is doing at this particular time (the present progressive tense).

What Are You Up To?

Imagine you're on a plane going to Costa Rica. What are you doing right now? Are you thinking about your jealous friends back home? Maybe you took my advice and are speaking to the person seated next to you. Are you watching a movie or listening to the music being piped through the airline headphones? Perhaps you're just relaxing and tuning out the world. To describe whatever you are doing at this moment (an action in progress), you must use the present progressive tense. Here's an English example to which we all can relate: "Right now, I'm soaking in the sun on Condado Beach in Puerto Rico."

To form the present progressive in Spanish, use the present-tense form of the verb *estar* that corresponds to the subject. *Estar* says that the subject is doing something. Next choose the verb that expresses the action. You will need the gerund (the -ing form) of this verb. To form the gerund, do the following:

Memory Master

In Spanish, the present tense expresses what generally happens in the present: Miro la televisión. I (generally) watch television. The present progressive, on the other hand, expresses what the subject is doing at this moment in time: Estoy mirando la televisión. I'm watching television (right now).

➤ For verbs whose infinitives end in *-ar*, drop *-ar* and add *-ando*.

Infinitive	Present Progressive	English
cant*ar*	cant*ando*	singing

➤ For verbs whose infinitives end in *-er* or *-ir*, drop *-er* or *-ir* and add *-iendo*.

Infinitive	Present Progressive	English
com*er*	com*iendo*	eating
escrib*ir*	escrib*iendo*	writing

➤ If a verb whose infinitive ends in *-er* or *-ir* has a stem ending in a vowel, add *-yendo* instead of *-iendo*.

Infinitive	Present Progressive	English
le*er*	le*yendo*	reading
o*ír*	o*yendo*	hearing

Some common irregular gerunds you might find useful include:

Infinitive	Present Progressive	English
decir	diciendo	saying, telling
dormir	durmiendo	sleeping
ir	yendo	going
pedir	pidiendo	asking
seguir	siguiendo	following
venir	viniendo	coming

In a Flash

Write down in Spanish what you are doing every hour on the hour for one entire day.

Now you can follow the simple formula for the formation of the present progressive tense—*estar* (conjugated) + gerund.

¿Qué estás haciendo?
keh ehs-tahs ah-see-yehn-doh
What are you doing?

Estoy escuchando música.
ehs-tohy ehs-koo-chahn-doh moo-see-kah
I'm listening to music.

What's Happening?

Use the present progressive tense to express what you are doing right now on your flight to Costa Rica. (Answers can be found on page 409, in Appendix A.)

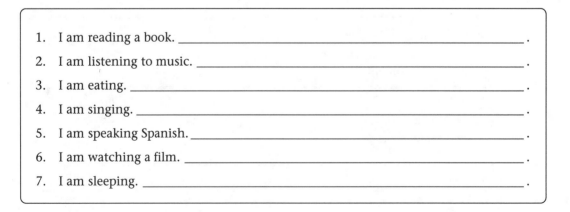

1. I am reading a book. _____ .

2. I am listening to music. _____ .

3. I am eating. _____ .

4. I am singing. _____ .

5. I am speaking Spanish. _____ .

6. I am watching a film. _____ .

7. I am sleeping. _____ .

10 minutos al día

To form the present progressive, conjugate the verb *estar*. Drop the *-ar*, *-er*, or *-ir* ending from the verb you are using. Add *-ando* for *-ar* verbs or *-iendo* for *-er* and *-ir* verbs to form the gerund (the *-ing* form of the verb).

Estar (conjugated) + gerund = present progressive.

Example: Yo estoy comiendo.
　　　　I am eating.

What's Your Line?

If you want to ask about someone's line of work or to talk about your own, you'll need the proper question and answer format. In a formal situation use the following:

> ¿Cuál es su profesión?
> *What is your profession?*

In an informal setting use the following:

> ¿Cuál es tu profesión?
> *What is your profession?*

The response to either of these questions would be the following:

> Soy + your profession.
> *I am* + your profession.

> Soy sastre.
> *I am a tailor.*

> Ella es camarera.
> *She is a waitress.*

¡Atención!

Do not use the indefinite article *un* (*una*) when talking about someone's profession. Simply place the profession after the conjugated form of the verb *ser* (to be).

In a Flash

Imagine you are going to meet a Spanish-speaking business associate for the first time. Prepare a brief speech to introduce yourself in Spanish.

Use *ser* to talk about the professions in Table 8.3. Unless otherwise indicated, change *-o* to *-a* or add *-a* to the final consonant to get the female counterpart for the jobs listed.

Mi hermana es secretaria.

La señora Rueda es profesora.

Mi tía es jueza.

Table 8.3   Professions

Profession	Spanish	Pronunciation
actor, actress	actor, actriz	ahk-tohr, ahk-trees
cashier	cajero	kah-heh-roh
dentist	dentista (m or f)	dehn-tees-tah
doctor	doctor (m)	dohk-tohr
	médico (m)	meh-dee-koh
electrician	electricista (m or f)	eh-lehk-tree-sees-tah
firefighter	bombero	bohm-beh-roh
hairdresser	barbero	bahr-beh-roh
jeweler	joyero	hoh-yeh-roh
judge	juez	hwehs
lawyer	abogado	ah-boh-gah-doh
manager	gerente (m or f)	heh-rehn-teh
mechanic	mecánico	meh-kah-nee-koh
musician	músico	moo-see-koh
nurse	enfermero	ehn-fehr-meh-roh
police officer	policía (m or f)	poh-lee-see-yah
postal worker	cartero	kahr-teh-roh
secretary	secretario	seh-kreh-tah-ree-yoh
student	estudiante (m or f)	ehs-too-dee-yahn-teh
teacher	profesor	proh-feh-sohr
waitress	camarera	kah-mah-reh-rah

Having a Conversation

You're sitting on the plane reading your traveler's guide to Spain when your seatmate finally gets talkative. How would you respond to him when he says the following? (Sample responses can be found on page 409, in Appendix A.)

1. Buenas tardes. _____ .
2. ¿Cómo se llama Ud? _____ .
3. ¿Cómo está Ud? _____ .
4. ¿De dónde es Ud.? _____ .
5. ¿Cuál es su profesión? _____ .

Tell Me All About It

The person on your other side seems rather nice. Perhaps she can give you some pointers about what to see when you arrive. You'll need more than simple yes or no answers, though. What you really want is information. The words and phrases in Table 8.4 will see you through.

In a Flash

Make a chart that lists the names of your friends and relatives, their relationships to you, their professions, and one question you would like to ask each of them.

Table 8.4   Gathering Information

Word/Phrase	Pronunciation	Meaning
adónde	ah-dohn-deh	to where
a qué hora	ah keh oh-rah	at what time
a quién	ah kee-yehn	to whom
a qué	ah keh	to what
cuál	kwahl	which
de quién	deh kee-yehn	of, about, from whom
cuánto	kwahn-toh	how much, how many
cómo	koh-moh	how
dónde	dohn-deh	where
de dónde	deh dohn-deh	from where
por qué	pohr keh	why
cuándo	kwahn-doh	when
quién*	kee-yehn	who, whom
qué	keh	what

Note that Spanish does not have separate words to distinguish between who (subject) and whom (object). The word quién serves as both.

Memory Master

All *interrogatives* (words that ask questions) in Spanish have accent marks. This distinguishes them from words that are spelled the same but that state a fact rather than ask for information.

Getting Information

The easiest way to get information is to ask for it. The easiest way to ask for information is to put the question word (or words) immediately before the verb. If you are using a subject pronoun or noun, put it after the verb. The following are some questions you might want to ask a traveling companion. Try them with the familiar tú form (in parentheses) as well.

¿Con quién viaja Ud.? (viajas)
With whom are you traveling?

¿Por qué viaja Ud.? (viajas)   ¿De dónde es Ud.? (eres)
Why are you traveling?   *Where are you from?*

¿Cómo viaja Ud.? (viajas)   ¿Qué mira Ud.? (miras)
How are you traveling?   *What are you looking at?*

Tell Me More

Read the following paragraphs. Ask as many questions as you can based on the information given in each selection. In Paragraph 1, you ask questions about Roberto. In Paragraph 2, you ask Ana questions about herself. (Sample responses can be found on page 409, in Appendix A.)

1. Roberto es de los Estados Unidos. Viaja en automóvil con su familia en España. Pasan un mes en España. Desean visitar todas las ciudades importantes. Regresan a Syracuse en septiembre.

2. Me llamo Ana. Soy de Quito. Busco a una amiga por correspondencia americana porque deseo practicar el inglés. Hablo inglés sólamente cuando estoy en clase. El inglés es una lengua muy interesante. Soy una estudiante muy seria.

The Least You Need to Know

➤ Different greetings are used depending on how well you know the other person.

➤ The verb *ser* expresses permanent traits, nationality, origin, time, and dates.

➤ The verb *estar* is used to express location and temporary conditions.

➤ Use the present progressive tense to explain what is going on right now.

➤ Learn to ask questions to get the information you need.

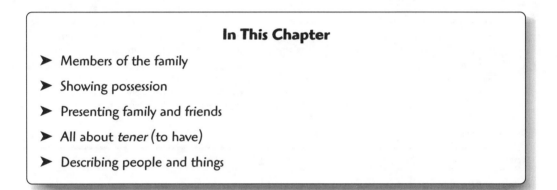

Chapter 9

Getting to Know You

> **In This Chapter**
>
> ➤ Members of the family
>
> ➤ Showing possession
>
> ➤ Presenting family and friends
>
> ➤ All about *tener* (to have)
>
> ➤ Describing people and things

Your conversations in the preceding chapter enabled you to make new friends and to introduce yourself. If you're traveling with family members, it's time to introduce them or to help them jump in and join the discussion. Perhaps you will be presented to family members of your newfound friend. Be prepared for any and all circumstances.

Meet the Clan!

While sitting on a tour bus to El Yunque (the rain forest in Puerto Rico), I struck up a conversation with a lovely older couple carrying an adorable young child. I went on and on, admiring and cootchie-cooing their grandson. In retrospect, I really didn't know when to stop. Imagine my overwhelming embarrassment when, at the end of the trip, the gentleman politely took me aside and explained that the child was their son. I learned some very important lessons that day: Keep your mouth shut, give the other person an opportunity to talk, and never, ever make assumptions when you meet someone. If you want to prevent a potentially mortifying situation such as this, consult Table 9.1.

Table 9.1   Family Members

Male	Pronunciation	Meaning	Female	Pronunciation	Meaning
abuelo	ah-bweh-loh	grandfather	abuela	ah-bweh-lah	grandmother
padrino	pah-dree-noh	godfather	madrina	mah-dree-nah	godmother
padre	pah-dreh	father	madre	mah-dreh	mother
padrastro	pah-drahs-troh	stepfather	madrastra	mah-drahs-trah	stepmother
hijo	ee-hoh	son, child	hija	ee-hah	daughter
hermano	ehr-mah-noh	brother	hermana	ehr-mah-nah	sister
hermanastro	ehr-mah-nahs-troh	stepbrother	hermanastra	ehr-mah-nahs-trah	stepsister
primo	pree-moh	cousin (male)	prima	pree-mah	cousin (female)
sobrino	soh-bree-noh	nephew	sobrina	soh-bree-nah	niece
tío	tee-yoh	uncle	tía	tee-yah	aunt
nieto	nee-yeh-toh	grandson	nieta	nee-yeh-tah	granddaughter
suegro	sweh-groh	father-in-law	suegra	sweh-grah	mother-in-law
yerno	yehr-noh	son-in-law	nuera	nweh-rah	daughter-in-law
cuñado	koo-nyah-doh	brother-in-law	cuñada	koo-nyah-dah	sister-in-law
novio	noh-bee-yoh	boyfriend	novia	noh-bee-yah	girlfriend

You Belong to Me

Don't fret, but you are probably possessed. That is, you're somebody's somebody: your parents' child, your friend's friend, your brother's sister, your sister's brother, and so on. There are two ways to show possession in Spanish: by using the preposition *de* or by using possessive adjectives.

Possession with De

In English, we use -'s or -s' after a noun to show possession. Apostrophes don't exist in Spanish. If you want to talk about Santiago's sister, you have to say *la hermana de Santiago*, which translates word-for-word to "the sister of Santiago." To express possession or relationship, the preposition *de* (of) is used and the word order is changed from what we are accustomed to in English.

> Es la madre de Enrique.
> *She's Enrique's mother.*

If the possessor is referred to by a common noun such as "the boy" ("He is the boy's father"), in Spanish, *de* contracts with the definite article *el* to become *del* (of the), as follows:

> Es el padre *del* muchacho.
> *He's the boy's father.*

Memory Master

No changes are necessary for *de* + *la*, *de* + *los*, or *de* + *las*.

Son los padres *de la* muchacha.
They are the girl's parents.

Es la abuela *de los* muchachos.
She is the boys' grandmother.

Es el tío *de las* muchachas.
He is the girls' uncle.

A Sense of Belonging

Now that you understand how to use *de* to express possession, tell how you would say the following. (Answers can be found on page 409, in Appendix A.)

1. Miguel's aunt

   _____

2. The boys' father

   _____

3. The girls' grandparents

   _____

4. Lupe's uncle

   _____

5. The family's cousins

   _____

6. The nephew's girlfriend

   _____

10 minutos al día

Spanish does not use the English possessive construction –'s or –s' to express possession. Instead, use the following formula:

thing or person possessed + de (of) + person to whom the thing or person belongs

> la madre de Juanita   el padre del (de + el) muchacho
> *Juanita's mother*   *the boy's father*

What's in an Apellido?

When you are introduced to Spanish-speaking people, it is important to understand how they use last names. Spanish speakers usually have more than one *apellido* (ah-peh-yee-doh), or last name. *El apellido paterno* (the first last name) comes from the father's last name. *El apellido materno* is the mother's maiden name. A person always identifies him- or herself by the paternal surname.

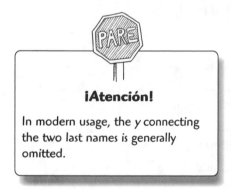

¡Atención!

In modern usage, the *y* connecting the two last names is generally omitted.

Let's take the example of Gabriel Cruz Rodríguez. Gabriel might also call himself Gabriel Cruz y Rodríguez (*y* means "and"). Gabriel's father's last name was Cruz, and his mother's maiden name was Rodríguez.

Suppose Gabriel marries Sarita Sánchez (father) González (mother). After the wedding, Sarita would normally drop her maternal last name (González) and add her husband's last name to that of her father. She would now be called Sarita Sánchez de (of) Cruz.

It might seem to be very unfair and the ultimate in *machismo*, but Spanish women remain forever linked to the men in their lives.

Let's say that, some time later, Gabriel and Sarita have a child, Alfredo. Alfredo's *apellidos* would be as follows: Alfredo Cruz (father's first *apellido*, which is considered to be his last name) Sánchez (his mother's maiden name). He might also call himself Alfredo Cruz y Sánchez.

Look carefully at the family tree, and answer the following questions. (Answers can be found on page 410, in Appendix A.)

Ramón Vega Pérez   Ana Fernández Rueda

Diego   María

1. What is the *apellido paterno* of Ramón Vega Pérez? _____

2. Of Ana Fernández Rueda? _____

3. What is the *apellido materno* of Ramón? _____

4. Of Ana? _____

5. What will Ana's married name be? _____

6. What name will she drop? _____

7. If Ramón and Ana have a son named Diego, what will his name be? _____

8. What about their daughter María? _____

What would your name be if you followed this tradition?

Possessive Adjectives

Possessive adjectives (my, your, his, her, and so on) are used to show that something belongs to someone. In Spanish, possessive adjectives agree with the nouns they describe (the person or thing possessed) rather than with the subject (the person possessing them). See how this compares with English:

English	Spanish
He speaks with his parents.	Habla con sus padres.
He speaks with their parents.	Habla con sus padres.
She speaks with our uncle.	Habla con nuestro tío.

¡Atención!

A possessive adjective agrees in number and gender with the noun it modifies, and not with the subject.

Sus padres (his or their parents) is used because *sus* agrees with the word *padres*, which is plural. *Sus* can mean his, her, its, your, or their. *Nuestro tío* (our uncle) is used because *nuestro* agrees with the word *tío*, which is masculine. This difference can make Spanish somewhat tricky for English speakers. Just remember that it is important to know the gender (masculine or feminine) of the item possessed. When in doubt, look it up. Table 9.2 summarizes the use of possessive adjectives.

Table 9.2   Possessive Adjectives

Used Before Masculine Nouns		Used Before Feminine Nouns		English
Singular	Plural	Singular	Plural	
mi	mis	mi	mis	my
tu	tus	tu	tus	your
su	sus	su	sus	his, her, your, its
nuestro	nuestros	nuestra	nuestras	our
vuestro	vuestros	vuestra	vuestras	your
su	sus	su	sus	their

What Are Your Preferences?

State your preference for each of the following items. Use the examples to learn how to structure your responses. (Sample responses can be found on page 410, in Appendix A.)

Mi actor favorito es _____.

Mis actores favoritos son _____.

1. actrices _____.

2. canción (song) _____.

3. restaurantes _____.

4. deporte (sport) _____.

5. color _____.

6. película (film) _____.

I'll Introduce You

When I travel, I like to speak to as many new and different people as I can. It's amazing how many great tips you can get and how much money you can save by listening to the experiences and advice of others. If you want to introduce yourself, here's the way to start:

To introduce yourself, you would say:

> Buenos días. Me llamo _____.
> bweh-nohs dee-yahs. meh yah-moh
> *Hello. My name is _____.*

You might ask about a companion:

> ¿Conoce Ud. (or Conoces tú) a mi primo, Paco?
> koh-noh-seh oo-stehd (koh-noh-sehs too) ah mee pree-moh pah-koh
> *Do you know my cousin, Paco?*

Memory Master

If *su* makes the meaning of the possessor unclear, you can clarify your thoughts by adding *de* + the name of the person, or *de + él, de + ella, de + Ud.*

Es su padre.   Es el padre de Marta. Es el padre de ella.

¡Atención!

Le is used in Spain while *lo* (when referring to a male) and *la* (when referring to a female) are used in South and Central American countries.

If the answer to this question is no, you then would say:

Quiero presentarle (or presentarte) a mi primo, Paco.
kee-yeh-roh preh-sehn-tahr-leh (preh-sehn-tahr-teh) ah mee pree-moh pah-koh
I'd like to introduce you to my cousin, Paco.

Or you might respond:

Le (or Te) presento a mi primo, Paco.
leh (teh) preh-sehn-toh ah mee pree-moh pah-koh
Let me present you to my cousin, Paco.

To express pleasure at having met someone in a formal situation, you might say:

Mucho gusto en conocerle.
moo-choh goo-stoh ehn koh-noh-sehr-leh
It's nice to meet (know) you.

If you are introduced to someone less formally, it is all right to say:

Encantado (masculine speaker)/Encantada (feminine speaker).
ehn-kahn-tah-doh/ehn-kahn-tah-dah
Delighted.

The correct reply to an introduction is:

El gusto es mío.
ehl goos-toh ehs mee-yoh
The pleasure is mine.

You're on Your Own

You have been sitting next to an interesting-looking traveler for some time now. Unfortunately, she has been engrossed in reading a magazine. You've decided to make your move and to strike up a conversation. You'll even try that tired old line of asking whether you know someone in common. Seize the moment and see whether you can do the following. (Sample responses can be found on page 410, in Appendix A.)

1. Introduce yourself.

2. Ask her whether she knows a member of your family.

3. Introduce a member of your family to her.

4. Express pleasure at having met her.

5. Respond to her after she says how glad she is to have met you.

More and More

That wasn't so difficult, was it? Now your curiosity has gotten the best of you, and you'd like to take the conversation a little further. Maybe you want to discuss your marital situation or your age or to ramble on about your family and friends. If you want to strike up a friendship, you have to keep the conversation flowing. The verb you will find most helpful is *tener* (to have). Like the verbs *ser* and *estar* (to be) *tener* is an irregular verb; all its forms (as seen in Table 9.3) must be memorized.

Table 9.3   Conjugating Tener (to Have)

Conjugated Form of Tener	Pronunciation	Meaning
Yo tengo	tehn-goh	I have
Tú tienes	tee-yeh-nehs	You have
Él, Ella, Ud. tiene	tee-yeh-neh	He, she, one has
Nosotros tenemos	teh-neh-mohs	We have
Vosotros tenéis	teh-neh-ees	You have
Ellos, Ellas, Uds. tienen	tee-yeh-nehn	They have

Idioms with Tener

Chapter 5, "Idioms Aren't for Idiots," showed you idioms with *tener* that describe physical conditions. (To refresh your memory, take a quick look back.) Now let's look at some different idioms with *tener*.

Imagine you finally have arrived at your destination after a long flight. You're tired and hungry, and all you want to do is get to your hotel and start your vacation. You want to find the exit, and you want to find it now. Spanish is an easy language; just add the letter *-o* and whatever you say will sound okay—right? You approach a distinguished-looking couple and ask, "*¿Tiene éxito?*" They look at you strangely and reply, "Sí," and walk away somewhat confused. You just asked them if they were successful, and you are no closer to your exit than you were a minute ago. To avoid this type of mistake, study the *tener* idioms in Table 9.4.

91

Table 9.4   Idioms with Tener

Idiom	Pronunciation	Expression
tener cuidado	teh-nehr kwee-dah-doh	to be careful
tener éxito	teh-nehr ehk-see-toh	to be successful
tener ganas de	teh-nehr gah-nahs deh	to feel like
tener lugar	teh-nehr loo-gahr	to take place
tener prisa	teh-nehr pree-sah	to be in a hurry
tener que + infinitive	teh-nehr keh	to have to + infinitive
tener suerte	teh-nehr swehr-teh	to be lucky

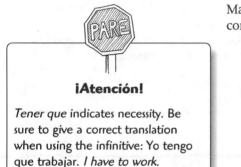

¡Atención!

Tener que indicates necessity. Be sure to give a correct translation when using the infinitive: Yo tengo que trabajar. *I have to work.*

Make sure to conjugate the verb when you use it in context, as in the following examples:

Yo siempre tengo cuidado.
I'm always careful.

Nosotros tenemos éxito.
We are successful.

¿Tú tienes ganas de salir?
Do you feel like going out?

Using Tener

Determine which of the following idioms goes with each of these sentences to appropriately complete the thought. Then conjugate *tener* so the verb agrees with the subject. (Answers can be found on page 410, in Appendix A.)

tener cuidado	tener éxito
tener suerte	tener lugar
tener prisa	tener dolor de estómago

1. Nosotros _____ cuando vamos a la playa (the beach).
2. La fiesta _____ el 6 de septiembre.
3. El doctor gana mucho dinero. Él _____.
4. Mis hermanos comen demasiado (too much). Ahora ellos _____.
5. Yo tengo un profesor de español excelente. Yo _____.
6. Ya es tarde (late) y tú tienes una cita (a date). Tú _____.

What's He/She Like?

Your conversation with the person sitting next to you is becoming increasingly intimate as the flight continues. If you were asked to describe yourself, what would you want to say? Are you a romantic? Do you consider yourself patient? Do your friends consider you to be introverted or extroverted?

If you want to describe a person, place, thing, or idea in detail, you must use adjectives. Spanish adjectives always agree in gender (masculine or feminine) and number (singular or plural) with the nouns or pronouns they modify. In other words, all the words in a Spanish sentence must conform. Notice the difference between the adjectives in the following examples:

> Su padre está contento.
> *Her father is happy.*

> Su madre está contenta.
> *Her mother is happy.*

Fortunately, adjectives follow the same (or similar) rules for gender and number formation as the nouns you studied in Chapter 6, "Sexually Speaking."

Adjectives Have Gender

Most adjectives can be made feminine by simply replacing the *-o* ending of the masculine singular form with an *-a*, as shown in Table 9.5. Remember that the sound changes as well; the final *-o* sound (oh) of the masculine changes to the *-a* sound (ah) of the feminine.

Table 9.5 Forming Feminine Adjectives

Masculine	Pronunciation	Feminine	Meaning
alto	ahl-toh	alta	tall
atractivo	ah-trahk-tee-boh	atractiva	attractive
bajo	bah-hoh	baja	short
bonito	boh-nee-toh	bonita	pretty
divertido	dee-behr-tee-doh	divertida	fun
enfermo	ehn-fehr-moh	enferma	sick
extrovertido	ehks-troh-behr-tee-doh	extrovertida	extroverted
feo	feh-yoh	fea	ugly
guapo	gwah-poh	guapa	pretty

continues

Table 9.5   Continued

Masculine	Pronunciation	Feminine	Meaning
impulsivo	eem-pool-see-boh	impulsiva	impulsive
introvertido	een-troh-behr-tee-doh	introvertida	introverted
listo	lees-toh	lista	ready
malo	mah-loh	mala	bad
moreno	moh-reh-noh	morena	dark-haired, dark-skinned
nuevo	nweh-boh	nueva	new
pequeño	peh-keh-nyoh	pequeña	small
rico	rree-koh	rica	rich
rubio	rroo-bee-yoh	rubia	blond
simpático	seem-pah-tee-koh	simpática	nice
tímido	tee-mee-doh	tímida	shy
viejo	bee-yeh-hoh	vieja	old

Refer to Chapter 3, "The Spanish You Know," for more adjectives.

If an adjective already ends in an -*e*, -*a*, or a consonant, it is not necessary to make any changes at all. Both the masculine and feminine forms are spelled and pronounced exactly the same as in Table 9.6.

Table 9.6   Adjectives Ending in -e, -a, or a Consonant

Adjectives Ending in -e

Adjective	Pronunciation	Meaning
alegre	ah-leh-greh	happy
amable	ah-mah-bleh	nice
eficiente	eh-fee-see-yehn-teh	efficient
independiente	een-deh-pehn-dee-yehn-teh	independent
inteligente	een-teh-lee-gehn-teh	intelligent
paciente	pah-see-yehn-tee	patient
pobre	poh-breh	poor
responsable	rrehs-pohn-sah-bleh	responsible
triste	trees-teh	sad
valiente	bah-lee-yehn-teh	brave

Adjectives Ending in -a

Adjective	Pronunciation	Meaning
egoísta	eh-goh-ees-tah	selfish
idealista	ee-deh-yah-lees-tah	idealistic
materialista	mah-teh-ree-yah-lees-tah	materialistic
optimista	ohp-tee-mees-tah	optimistic
pesimista	peh-see-mees-tah	pessimistic
realista	rreh-yah-lees-tah	realistic

Adjectives Ending in a Consonant

Adjective	Pronunciation	Meaning
cortés	kohr-tehs	courteous
cruel	kroo-wehl	cruel
emocional	eh-moh-see-yoh-nahl	emotional
fácil	fah-seel	easy
joven	hoh-behn	young
normal	nohr-mahl	normal
sentimental	sehn-tee-mehn-tahl	sentimental
tropical	troh-pee-kahl	tropical

Although they end in a consonant, adjectives describing nationality add -a to form the feminine, as follows:

> español   *española*
>
> francés   *francesa*
>
> alemán   *alemana*

Adjectives that end in -or add -a to form the feminine, as follows:

> trabajador   *trabajadora*
>
> hablador   *habladora*
>
> encantador   *encantadora*

In a Flash

Read the personal ads in a Spanish newspaper and circle all the adjectives. Now pick the one you find the most interesting.

When There's a Crowd

Adjectives are often made plural in the same way as nouns.

➤ When the singular form of the adjective ends in a vowel, simply add an -s.

Singular	Plural
alto	altos
alta	altas
egoísta	egoístas
grande	grandes

➤ If an adjective ends in a consonant, add *-es*.

Singular	Plural
fácil	fáciles
emocional	emocionales
sentimental	sentimentales
popular	populares

The Perfect Position

In Spanish, descriptive adjectives are generally placed after the nouns they modify. Compare this with English, in which the opposite is done.

In a Flash

Make a list of all the adjectives you would use to describe yourself. Then describe as many of your acquaintances as you can.

un hombre interesante
an interesting man

Adjectives of description can be placed before the noun to emphasize the quality of the characteristic being described:

Juan tiene malas notas.
Juan has bad grades.

Anita tiene bellos ojos.
Anita has beautiful eyes.

When used before a masculine, singular noun, *bueno* becomes *buen*, *grande* becomes *gran*, and *malo* becomes *mal*.

Esteban es un buen muchacho.
Stephen is a good boy.

Give Your Own Descriptions

Some people have an opinion about everything, and they're not at all shy about expressing it. Tell how you feel about the people and places in the following list. Remember that to use the verb *ser* you must be describing a permanent characteristic. (Sample responses can be found on page 410, in Appendix A.)

1. El Prado es un museo _____.

2. Las películas españolas son _____.

3. El presidente de los Estados Unidos es un hombre _____.

4. Las tiendas de Madrid son _____.

5. Las corridas de toros son _____.

10 minutos al día

In Spanish, adjectives must agree in gender (masculine or feminine) and number (singular or plural) with the nouns they modify. Change the *-o* at the end of a masculine, singular adjective to an *-a* to form the feminine singular version.

> Él es alto. *He is tall.*
> Ella es alta. *She is tall.*

If the adjective ends in *-e*, *-a*, or a consonant, both the masculine and feminine forms are spelled and pronounced exactly the same way.

> Él es triste. *He is sad.*
> Ella es triste. *She is sad.*

Check Out the Personal Ads

Read the following personal ads taken from Spanish magazines and newspapers.
Describe the person writing the ad and the type of person being sought. Translations
can be found on page 410, in Appendix A. No fair peeking!

---

1. Abogado norteamericano y director de
   galerías de arte; alto, atractivo,
   sofisticado, 47. Busca amorosa joven,
   educada, 28-42, cabello largo,
   preferiblemente que hable algo deú
   inglés. Para romance, matrimonio, y
   familia. Manhattan.

---

2. Chileno, 28, 6', 166 libras. Me gusta la
   música romántica, bailar, deportes, y
   estudiar. Deseo conocer dama, 25-35,
   comprensiva, buen humor, inteligente,
   honesta, para amistad.

---

3. Dama de 40, trabajadora, cariñosa,
   simpática, desea conocer caballero
   brasileño con las mismas cualidades,
   para una bonita amistad o fines serios.

---

4. Dominicana, 37, divorciada, 2 niños,
   busca compañero para la vida, 35-40,
   5'10" o más, trabajador, divertido,
   buen sentido del humor, que no fume.

The Least You Need to Know

➤ There are no apostrophes in the Spanish language. To show possession in
   Spanish, use *de* or a possessive adjective. The adjective must agree in gender and
   number with the person or item possessed.

➤ A Spanish-speaking person uses both his/her mother's and father's last name, but
   is always identified by the paternal surname.

➤ Always use formal Spanish to introduce yourself to someone new.

➤ *Tener* is an important irregular verb that has a number of idiomatic uses.

➤ Descriptive adjectives describe people and things. They must agree in number
   and gender with the nouns they describe and usually are placed after the nouns
   they modify.

Chapter 10

The Plane Has Landed

In This Chapter

➤ Getting around planes and airports

➤ The verb *ir* (to go)

➤ How to give and receive directions

➤ Getting help when you need it

Your dream vacation is off to a good start, and you're settled in for a long, smooth flight. You've really accomplished quite a bit already. You've planned your trip, introduced yourself to your seatmates, and struck up conversations with people about all kinds of topics. Perhaps you've been successful in obtaining the names of some fabulous restaurants, attractions you don't want to miss, or even the phone number of someone who would be thrilled to show off his or her hometown when you arrive.

Once you're on the ground and have deplaned, you'll discover there are many things to do before you can catch a ride to wherever you are staying. Your first stop might be the passport check. Then it's off to retrieve your bags so you can pass uneventfully through Customs. You'll certainly want to pick up some local currency before you choose a means of transportation to your destination. You will be able to achieve all this and more by the time you finish this chapter.

On the Plane

The person next to you on the plane is blowing smoke rings in your face, is carrying his pet lizard in his shirt pocket, and has his headset turned up to the max (and you don't like his taste in music). You *must* change your seat. While you have the stewardess's attention, you'd like to ask some questions about takeoff and landing. This section gives you the vocabulary you need to solve these problems and to get the information you need.

Culture Corner

In the airport, you'll often see a sign that says *Bienvenido*, which means "Welcome."

The Plane Plan

Once on board the airplane, you will hear safety announcements that refer to items in and around the plane. If you have any questions or doubts, the words in Table 10.1 will help you figure things out.

Table 10.1   Inside the Plane

Airport Term	Spanish Translation	Pronunciation
airplane	el avión	ehl ah-bee-yohn
aisle	el pasillo	ehl pah-see-yoh
by the window	cerca de la ventana	sehr-kah deh lah behn-tah-nah
crew	el equipo	ehl eh-kee-poh
to deboard, to exit	salir	sah-leer
emergency exit	la salida de emergencia	lah sah-lee-dah deh eh-mehr-hehn-see-yah
life vest	el chaleco salvavidas	ehl chah-leh-koh sahl-bah-bee-dahs
(no) smokers	(no) fumadores	noh foo-mah-doh-rehs
to smoke	fumar	foo-mahr
on the aisle	en el pasillo	ehn ehl pah-see-yoh
row	la fila	lah fee-lah
seat	el asiento	ehl ah-see-yehn-toh
seat belt	el cinturón de seguridad	ehl seen-too-rohn deh seh-goo-ree-dahd

Airline Advice

To make your flight more enjoyable and comfortable, airlines provide advice they would like their passengers to follow. Read some of the tips the airlines suggest. Can you tell what rules and regulations are being explained to you? (Translations can be found on page 411, in Appendix A.)

➤ **Reglas de la FAA**

La FAA exige que todo equipaje de mano que se traiga abordo de los aviones se guarde en un compartimiento alto especial para ello, debajo del asiento del pasajero, o bien en depósitos generales para guardar equipaje durante el despegue y el aterrizaje. Para su mayor conveniencia, en todos nuestros aviones hay compartimientos altos y muchos tienen también depósitos generales para guardar equipaje.

➤ **Artículos de valor en su equipaje**

No incluya en su equipaje artículos de valor (dinero, joyas, etc.) ni documentos como pasaportes.

Dichos artículos no están sujetos a indemnización en caso de pérdida o extravío.

➤ **Artículos Frágiles**

No debe incluir en su equipaje artículos frágiles o de fácil deterioro. Dichos artículos no están sujetos a indemnización en caso de daños.

Culture Corner

Every country has its own rules and regulations, so check with Customs beforehand to find out what you may and may not bring with you without having to pay a special duty or tax. In many areas, items made from endangered species are prohibited. Remember that if you're taking prescription drugs, it's a good idea to bring along a copy of your prescription. Fear of insect infestation explains why most countries do not allow fruits, vegetables, or plants to pass their borders.

Filling Out Forms

Passengers boarding a flight will need *una tarjeta de embarque* (oo-nah tahr-heh-tah day ehm-bahr-kay), a boarding pass, in order to board an aircraft. A disembarkation card, *una carta de desembarco* (oo-nah kahr-tah day dehs-ehm-bahr-koh), or an identification card, *una carta de identidad* (oo-nah kahr-tah day ee-dehn-tee-dahd), is filled out towards the end of the flight, before passengers leave the plane or at the airport. The information on this card will be reviewed by customs officers at the airport.

Imagine you are nearing the end of your trip and the stewardess hands you *una carta de desembarco*. See how successful you can be at filling in the information required. The only words that might be unfamiliar are *imprenta* (printing), *soltera* (unmarried, single), *lugar* (place), *fecha* (date), *nacimiento* (birth), and *expedido* (issued). Note that this card is not necessary for Spanish nationals. (The translations can be found on page 411, in Appendix A.)

101

CARTA DE DESEMBARCO

no concierne a los pasajeros de nacionalidad española (hispana)

1. Apellidos: _____
   (en caracteres de imprenta)

   Apellido de soltera: _____

   Nombre: _____

2. Dirección: _____
   (número)   (calle)

   _____
   (ciudad, pueblo)   (estado)   (área postal)

   _____
   (país)

3. Fecha de nacimiento: _____

4. Lugar de nacimiento: _____

5. Profesión: _____

6. Aeropuerto o puerto de desembarco: _____

7. Línea aérea: _____

8. Número del vuelo: _____

9. Pasaporte expedido en: _____

10. Firma del pasajero: _____

Culture Corner

If you want to bring your pet with you on vacation, Spain is one of the few countries that does not require a quarantine period. A veterinary certificate attesting to the fact that the animal is in good health and has been inoculated against rabies is sufficient.

At the Airport

The plane has landed, and everyone rushes to collect his carry-on luggage and disembark. Once you're in the airport, expect to find signs everywhere pointing you in various directions. Where should you go first? You don't have much choice here. You need to proceed to passport control and customs, where it will be established that you're not an international jewel thief. Next, you might want to stop at a money exchange. If you're anything like me, you'll probably head for the nearest *baños* (bathrooms). Table 10.2 provides all the words you need to know to get through the airport and on your way to your first destination!

Table 10.2   Inside the Airport

Airport Term	Spanish Translation	Pronunciation
airline	la aerolínea	lah ah-yee-roh-lee-neh-yah
airline terminal	la terminal	lah tehr-mee-nahl
airport	el aeropuerto	ehl ah-yee-roh-pwehr-toh
arrival	la llegada	lah yeh-gah-dah
baggage claim area	el reclamo de equipaje	ehl rreh-klah-moh deh eh-kee-pah-heh
bathrooms	los baños	lohs bah-nyohs
bus stop	la parada de autobús	lah pah-rah-dah deh ow-toh-boos
car rental	el alquiler de carros	ehl ahl-kee-lehr deh kah-rrohs
carry-on luggage	el equipaje de mano	ehl eh-kee-pah-heh deh mah-noh
cart	el carrito	ehl kah-rree-toh
Customs	la aduana	lah ah-doo-wah-nah
departure	la salida	lah sah-lee-dah
destination	la destinación	lah dehs-tee-nah-see-yohn
elevators	los ascensores	lohs ah-sehn-soh-rehs
entrance	la entrada	lah ehn-trah-dah
exit	la salida	lah sah-lee-dah
flight	el vuelo	ehl bweh-loh
gate	la puerta	lah pwehr-tah
information	la información	lah een-fohr-mah-see-yohn
landing	el aterrizaje	ehl ah-teh-rree-sah-heh
lost and found	la oficina de objetos perdidos	lah oh-fee-see-nah deh ohb-heh-tohs pehr-dee-dohs
to miss the flight	perder el vuelo	pehr-dehr ehl bweh-loh
money exchange	el cambio de dinero	ehl kahm-bee-yoh deh dee-neh-roh
passport control	el control de pasaportes	ehl kohn-trohl deh pah-sah-pohr-tehs
porter	el portero	eh pohr-teh-roh
security check	el control de seguridad	ehl kohn-trohl deh seh-goo-ree-dahd
stop-over	la escala	lah ehs-kah-lah
suitcase	la maleta	lah mah-leh-tah

continues

Table 10.2 Continued

Airport Term	Spanish Translation	Pronunciation
takeoff	el despegue	ehl dehs-peh-geh
taxis	los taxis	lohs tahk-sees
ticket	el boleto	ehl boh-leh-toh
trip	el viaje	ehl bee-yah-heh

Culture Corner

Mexico City's airport is one of the busiest in the world. Millions of tourists pass through this airport each year and are treated to a pictur–esque view of Mexico City. Because high mountains surround this capital, pilots are given special training to make the difficult landing.

Significant Signs

Bomb scares and terrorist threats have airline security on constant red alert. Don't even try joking about weapons with airline personnel; they'll immediately flag you for a search. Signs all over the airport list warnings, tips, and regulations that must be followed. It is of the utmost importance that you understand what is and isn't allowed. Should you break a rule unintentionally, it can be a mighty unpleasant experience to be approached by *policías* who speak a language you don't understand very well. You might see the following signs in any airport serving a large Spanish-speaking population. Read them carefully and match each sign with the correct bullet. (Answers can be found on page 411, in Appendix A.)

Which sign is telling you the following:

1. If you leave something behind it might be destroyed? ___
2. All of your baggage will be checked, even carry-on baggage? ___
3. You can be searched for hidden weapons? ___
4. You may carry a weapon if you declare it? ___
5. You can only use the baggage cart within the airport? ___
6. You shouldn't carry a suitcase for someone else? ___

A.

CONSEJOS A LOS PASAJEROS

Portar armas en el avión está terminantemente prohibido por ley.

Las reglas en vigor imponen la inspección de los pasajeros y de su equipaje al momento de pasar por seguridad.

Esta inspección puede ser rehusada. Los pasajeros que se rehusen a pasar por esta inspección no van a ser autorizados a pasar por el control de seguridad.

B.

Los carritos para cargar el equipaje están reservados para los pasajeros; su utilización fuera del aeropuerto está prohibida.

Por favor presente todo su equipaje al registro, incluyendo su equipaje de mano.

E.

C.

ATENCIÓN:

Para su seguridad, todo objeto abandonado puede ser destruído por la policía.

Le pedimos cordialmente a los pasajeros que conserven su equipaje consigo.

D.

ATENCIÓN:
No ponga su seguridad en peligro. No acepte ningún equipaje de otra persona.

TRANSPORTE DE ARMAS DE FUEGO

Las armas de fuego transportadas dentro de su equipaje deben estar descargadas y declaradas.

Los pasajeros que transporten una arma sin declarar o sin descargar son sujetos a una multa de mil dólares o su equivalente.

F.

105

What's the Message?

Perhaps you've chosen to travel to a Spanish-speaking country, and you want to make sure you're not bringing in anything that will be dangerous or offensive. Read the following restrictions to see what you should leave out when packing your suitcases. (Check page 411 in the Answer Key if you need help.)

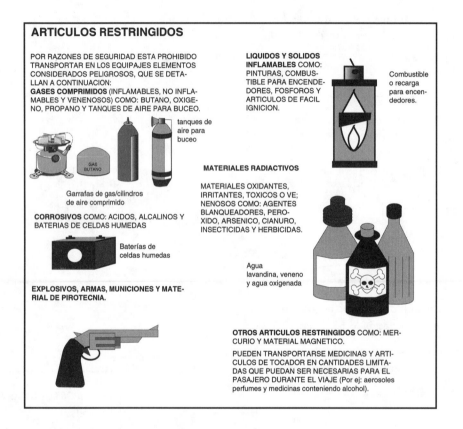

ARTICULOS RESTRINGIDOS

POR RAZONES DE SEGURIDAD ESTA PROHIBIDO TRANSPORTAR EN LOS EQUIPAJES ELEMENTOS CONSIDERADOS PELIGROSOS, QUE SE DETALLAN A CONTINUACION:
GASES COMPRIMIDOS (INFLAMABLES, NO INFLAMABLES Y VENENOSOS) COMO: BUTANO, OXIGENO, PROPANO Y TANQUES DE AIRE PARA BUCEO.

tanques de aire para buceo

GAS BUTANO

Garrafas de gas/cilindros de aire comprimido

CORROSIVOS COMO: ACIDOS, ALCALINOS Y BATERIAS DE CELDAS HUMEDAS

Baterías de celdas humedas

EXPLOSIVOS, ARMAS, MUNICIONES Y MATERIAL DE PIROTECNIA.

LIQUIDOS Y SOLIDOS INFLAMABLES COMO: PINTURAS, COMBUSTIBLE PARA ENCENDEDORES, FOSFOROS Y ARTICULOS DE FACIL IGNICION.

Combustible o recarga para encendedores.

MATERIALES RADIACTIVOS

MATERIALES OXIDANTES, IRRITANTES, TOXICOS O VE; NENOSOS COMO: AGENTES BLANQUEADORES, PEROXIDO, ARSENICO, CIANURO, INSECTICIDAS Y HERBICIDAS.

Agua lavandina, veneno y agua oxigenada

OTROS ARTICULOS RESTRINGIDOS COMO: MERCURIO Y MATERIAL MAGNETICO.

PUEDEN TRANSPORTARSE MEDICINAS Y ARTICULOS DE TOCADOR EN CANTIDADES LIMITADAS QUE PUEDAN SER NECESARIAS PARA EL PASAJERO DURANTE EL VIAJE (Por ej: aerosoles perfumes y medicinas conteniendo alcohol).

In a Flash

Make a list of the places to which you and your friends are going this weekend.

Going Places

The irregular verb *ir* (to go) will come in handy if you need directions at the airport or anywhere else. When you want to tell someone exactly where you want to go, refer to Table 10.3.

Table 10.3   Conjugating Ir (to Go)

Conjugated Form of Ir	Pronunciation	Meaning
yo voy	boy	I go
tú vas	bahs	you go
él, ella, Ud. va	bah	he, she, you, one goes
nosotros vamos	bah-mohs	we go
vosotros vais	bah-yees	you go
ellos, ellas, Uds. van	bahn	they go

Ir is generally followed by the preposition *a* (to). If the location to which the subject is going is masculine, *a* contracts with *el* (the) to become *al* (to the), as in the following example:

> Yo voy al aeropuerto.
> *I'm going to the airport.*

No changes are necessary with *a la, a los,* or *a las*:

> Vamos a la salida.　　　　　　　　¿Vas a las ventanas?
> *We're going to the exit.*　　　　　*Are you going to the windows?*

> Van a los ascensores.
> *They are going to the elevators.*

Use *ir + a* to express going to a city, a state, or a country:

> Voy a Nueva York.　　　　　　　　¿Van a México?
> *I'm going to New York.*　　　　　*Are they going to México?*

> Ana va a Florida.
> *Anna is going to Florida.*

Use *ir + en* to express the many different ways to go someplace.

> Yo voy a España en avión.
> *I'm going to Spain by plane.*

The only exception is when you decide to walk.

> ir a pie　　　　　　　　　　　　Vamos a casa a pie.
> *to go by foot*　　　　　　　　　*We walk home.*

107

Where To?

It's been a long flight. After two piña coladas, people tend to become rather friendly and chatty. Everyone is discussing where he or she is going. Complete their sentences by filling in the correct form of *ir*. (Answers can be found on page 411, in Appendix A.)

1. Nosotros _____ a Barcelona.
2. Marta _____ a Madrid.
3. Tú _____ a Sevilla.
4. Uds. _____ a Toledo.
5. Yo _____ a Granada.
6. Vosotros _____ a Cádiz.

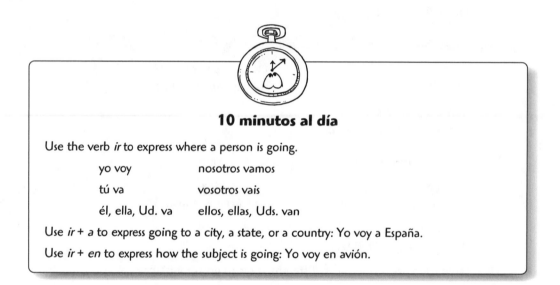

10 minutos al día

Use the verb *ir* to express where a person is going.

yo voy	nosotros vamos
tú va	vosotros vais
él, ella, Ud. va	ellos, ellas, Uds. van

Use *ir* + *a* to express going to a city, a state, or a country: Yo voy a España.

Use *ir* + *en* to express how the subject is going: Yo voy en avión.

How Do I Get to...?

It's easy to become disoriented in a large, bustling airport after a tiring journey. No doubt, you will need to ask for directions at some point. Here are some easy phrases to help you on your way.

¿Dónde está la salida?
dohn-deh ehs-tah lah sah-lee-dah
Where is the exit?

La salida, por favor.
lah sah-lee-dah pohr fah-bohr
The exit, please.

¿Dónde están los taxis?
dohn-deh ehs-tahn lohs tahk-sees
Where are the taxis?

Los taxis, por favor.
los tahk-sees pohr fah-bohr
The taxis, please.

In a Flash

Imagine you are in a familiar airport. Try to identify as many locations as you can in Spanish.

If you're not sure whether the airport has the facilities you are looking for, or if you just want to know if they are nearby, use the word *hay* (Is there?, Are there?, There is..., There are...). *Hay* probably is one of the most useful words in the Spanish language. Here is how it works to both ask and answer questions:

¿Hay baños por aquí?
ah-yee bah-nyohs pohr ah-kee
Are there bathrooms nearby?

Hay baños al lado de la entrada.
ah-yee bah-nyohs ahl lah-doh deh lah ehn-trah-dah
There are bathrooms next to the entrance.

Ask for It

Imagine you've just gotten off the plane, and you have a million things to do at once. Find the places you need by asking for them in two different ways: Los baños, por favor. ¿Dónde están los baños? Then try asking whether they are nearby: ¿Hay baños por aquí? (Sample responses can be found on page 411, in Appendix A.)

1. bathrooms _____
2. passport control _____
3. customs _____
4. elevators _____
5. taxis _____
6. money exchange _____
7. bus stop _____
8. lost and found _____
9. exit _____
10. car rental _____

Following Directions

Suppose the place you are looking for is out of pointing range. In this case, you'll need more specific directions. The verbs in Table 10.4 will help get you where you want to go.

Table 10.4 Verbs Giving Directions

Verb	Pronunciation	Meaning
bajar	bah-hahr	to go down
caminar	kah-mee-nahr	to walk
continuar	kohn-tee-noo-ahr	to continue
cruzar	kroo-sahr	to cross
doblar	doh-blahr	to turn
ir	eer	to go
pasar	pah-sahr	to pass
seguir	seh-geer	to follow, to continue
subir	soo-beer	to go up
tomar	toh-mahr	to take

In a Flash

Pretend you have a Spanish-speaking visitor staying at your house. Give directions in Spanish to the nearest movie theater, museum, library, and supermarket.

To give you directions, a person in the know has to give you a command. Because you are being told where to go or what to do, the subject of the command is "you." In English, the subject "you" is understood and is not spoken. In Spanish, although often omitted, the subject pronoun for "you" can be used in the command.

You have already learned that there are four ways to say "you" in Spanish: the familiar *tú* and *vosotros* forms and the polite *Ud.* and *Uds.* forms. In this book we'll concentrate only on the formal commands, the ones you'd give or get from someone you don't know well. (Chances are you'll be speaking to your loved ones in English.)

To form commands with regular verbs using *Ud.*:

1. Drop the *-o* ending from the *yo* form of the present tense of the verb you're using.

2. If the verb is an *-ar* infinitive verb, add an *-e*.

3. If the verb is an *-er* or *-ir* infinitive verb, add an *-a*.

To use *Uds.* as your subject, just add an *-n* to the *Ud.* form. Here's how it's done:

| | | Formal Commands | | |
Infinitive	Present Tense Yo Form	Singular (Ud.)	Plural (Uds.)	Meanings
tomar	tomo	tome	tomen	take
leer	leo	lea	lean	read
abrir	abro	abra	abran	open

Here are some examples:

¡Tome el autobús!
Take the bus.

¡Lea este folleto!
Read this brochure.

¡Abran sus maletas!
Open your suitcases.

Memory Master

Spanish requires an upside down exclamation mark (¡) at the beginning of an emphasized command and a regular exclamation mark (!) at the end.

Some Spanish verbs have an irregular *yo* form. You have already seen this with *tener,* and you'll come across others in later chapters. These verbs follow the same rules as regular verbs to form commands. Here is how it works with *tener:*

| | Present Tense Yo Form | Formal Commands Singular (Ud.) | Plural (Uds.) |
Infinitive			
tener	tengo	tenga	tengan

Here is an example of *tener* in a command:

¡Tengan cuidado!
Be careful.

111

The following three irregular verbs are useful in the command form:

Verb (Meaning)	Formal Commands Singular (Ud.)	Plural (Uds.)
dar (to give)	dé	den
ir (to go)	vaya	vayan
ser (to be)	sea	sean

Here is an example of using *ir* in a command:

¡Vaya al aeropuerto ahora!
Go to the airport now.

Giving Commands

Before you can receive or give commands, you'll need a little practice. Complete the following exercise by filling in the missing command forms as well as their meanings. (Answers responses can be found on page 412, in Appendix A.)

Verb	Ud.	Uds.	Meaning
ir	_____	_____	_____
continuar	_____	_____	_____
seguir*	siga	_____	_____
caminar	_____	_____	_____
subir	_____	_____	_____
pasar	_____	_____	_____
tomar	_____	_____	_____
doblar	_____	_____	_____
cruzar*	cruce	_____	_____

* These verbs, and others ending in -car, -gar, -zar, and -guir, have special spelling changes that will be explained in Chapter 11. Once you have learned the Ud. form, however, Uds. should be a snap for you.

10 minutos al día

To give directions, you must use the command form. Take the *yo* form of the present tense of the verb and then drop the final -*o*.

For -*ar* verbs, add -*e* to command one person and add -*en* to command more than one.

> Tome (Ud.)/Tomen (Uds.) el bús.

For -*er* and -*ir* verbs, add -*a* to command one person and add -*an* to command more than one.

> Lea (Ud.)/Lean (Uds.) en español.

> Abra (Ud.)/Abran (Uds.) la puerta.

It is not necessary to use the subject *Ud.* or *Uds.* when giving a command.

Prepositions

Prepositions show the relation of a noun to another word in a sentence. Take a look back at the idiomatic expressions for direction and location in Chapter 5, "Idioms Aren't for Idiots." These are, in fact, prepositional phrases. Study the simple prepositions in Table 10.5. These also will be useful for giving or receiving directions.

Table 10.5   Prepositions

Preposition	Pronunciation	Meaning
a	ah	to, at
alrededor (de)	ahl-reh-deh-dohr (deh)	around
antes (de)	ahn-tehs (deh)	before
cerca (de)	sehr-kah (deh)	near
contra	kohn-trah	against
de	deh	of, from, about
debajo (de)	deh-bah-hoh (deh)	under
delante (de)	deh-lahn-teh (deh)	in front (of)
después (de)	dehs-pwehs (deh)	after

continues

Table 10.5 Continued

Preposition	Pronunciation	Meaning
detrás (de)	deh-trahs (deh)	behind, in back (of)
en	ehn	in
encima (de)	ehn-see-mah (deh)	above
entre	ehn-treh	between, among
frente a	frehn-teh ah	opposite, facing
hacia	ah-see-yah	toward
lejos (de)	leh-hohs (deh)	far (from)
para	pah-rah	for, in order to
por	pohr	by, through
sin	seen	without
sobre	soh-breh	on, upon

Memory Master

There are no contractions with *la*, *los*, and *las*.

Contractions

In certain cases, contractions form with the prepositions *a* and *de*, whether they are used alone or as part of a longer expression. *A + el* becomes *al*, and *de + el* becomes *del*. For example:

Voy al teatro.   Hablo del teatro.
I go to the theater.   *I speak about the theater.*

Hablo a la muchacha, a los hombres, y a las mujeres.
I speak to the girl, the men, and the women.

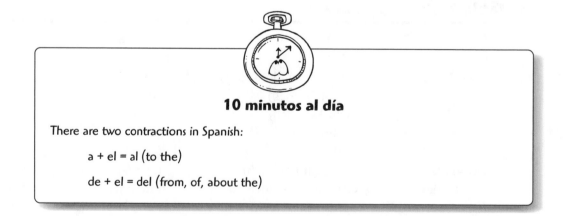

10 minutos al día

There are two contractions in Spanish:

   a + el = al (to the)

   de + el = del (from, of, about the)

Por vs. Para

Because both *por* and *para* can mean "for," there often is confusion about when to use these prepositions. Study the following chart to learn how to use them properly. Keep in mind, though, that even if you use the wrong word, you'll still be understood.

Por Indicates	Para Indicates
motion Paso por el aeropuerto. *I pass by the airport.*	**destination to a place** El avión sale para Madrid. *The airplane leaves for Madrid.*
means, manner Viajo por tren. *I travel by train.*	**destination to a recipient** Este regalo es para mi esposo. *This gift is for my husband.*
a period of time Trabajo por la noche. *I work at night*	**a time limit** La cita es para el lunes. *The appointment is for Monday.*
frequency; in exchange for Salgo una vez por semana. *I go out once a week.* Son dos libros por $20. *They are two books for $20.*	**purpose** Es un billete para entrar. *It's an admission ticket.*

What Did You Say?

Have you ever gotten directions from someone and nodded as if you understood where to go, but with so many rights and lefts and so much pointing you actually lost track halfway through? The phrases in Table 10.6 will be an invaluable aid if you need something repeated or need more information.

Table 10.6 Expressing Lack of Understanding and Confusion

Expression	Pronunciation	Meaning
Con permiso.	kohn pehr-mee-soh	Excuse me.
Yo no comprendo.	yoh noh kohm-prehn-doh	I don't understand.
Yo no le (lo, la) oigo.	yoh noh leh (loh, lah) oy-goh	I don't hear you.
Repita por favor.	rreh-pee-tah pohr fah-bohr	Please repeat it.

continues

Table 10.6   Continued

Expression	Pronunciation	Meaning
Hable más despacio.	hah-bleh mahs dehs-pah-see-yoh	Speak more slowly.
¿Qué dijó?	keh dee-hoh	What did you say?

Always be polite. After getting directions from a Spanish-speaking person, you should say *Muchas gracias* (moo-chahs grah-see-ahs), "Thank you." The answer you will probably receive is *De nada* (deh nah-dah), "You're welcome."

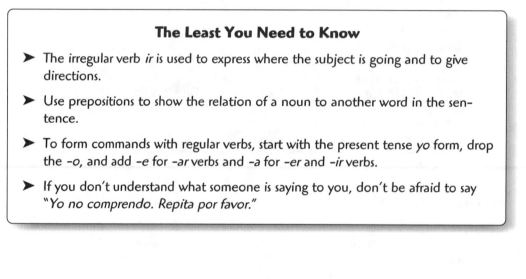

The Least You Need to Know

➤ The irregular verb *ir* is used to express where the subject is going and to give directions.

➤ Use prepositions to show the relation of a noun to another word in the sentence.

➤ To form commands with regular verbs, start with the present tense *yo* form, drop the *-o*, and add *-e* for *-ar* verbs and *-a* for *-er* and *-ir* verbs.

➤ If you don't understand what someone is saying to you, don't be afraid to say "*Yo no comprendo. Repita por favor.*"

Chapter 11

Getting There Is Half the Fun

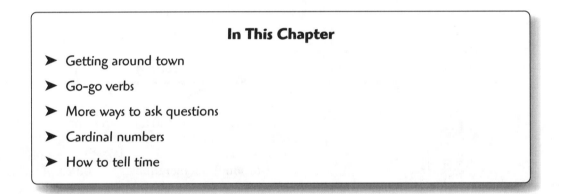

In This Chapter

➤ Getting around town

➤ Go-go verbs

➤ More ways to ask questions

➤ Cardinal numbers

➤ How to tell time

Maneuvering your way through passport control, baggage claim, and Customs can take a bit of time. Although you're probably tired and travel-worn, be patient. Despite your honest face and harried look, the people in charge have a job to do and really do need to unpack your suitcases. Really.

Maybe your travel agent has provided transfers (transportation to your final destination) as part of your travel package. If so, expect a bus, a car, or a taxi to be waiting to whisk you away. Look for a driver carrying a sign bearing your name or the name of your hotel. If not, it's up to you to find your own way. Some of your choices are presented in this chapter.

The Way to Go

You usually can find buses, subways, trains, taxis, and cars at the airport to get you where you want to go. Before making a choice, consider what is of foremost importance to you. If money is tight and you're traveling light, you might opt for a bus, subway, or train. If you're in a big hurry and money is no object, take a cab. If it's comfort you want and you're an experienced international driver, you might want to rent a car. Weigh all the pros and cons and make the decision that's best for you.

Method of Transportation	Pronunciation	Meaning
el coche	ehl koh-cheh	car
el automóvil	ehl ow-toh-moh-beel	car
el carro	ehl kah-rroh	car
el taxi	ehl tahk-see	taxi
el autobús	ehl ow-toh-boos	bus
el tren	ehl trehn	train
el metro	ehl meh-troh	subway

Culture Corner

If you take the bus in Madrid, you will find that it is inexpensive, efficient, and runs frequently. You must hail for the bus to stop; buses don't stop automatically at every stop on the route. Pick up a free bus map (*Plano de la Red*, plah-noh deh lah rehd) at designated kiosks.

The subway systems in Madrid and Barcelona can be proud of their cleanliness (no graffiti), comfort, safety, and economy. Maps (*el plano del Metro*, ehl plah-noh dehl meh-troh) indicate by numbers and different colors the various subway routes. These maps are available without charge at metro stops, hotels, department stores, tourist offices, and other convenient spots.

Transfers from one subway line to another are free, and connections are indicated by *correspondencia* (koh-rrehs-pohn-dehn-see-yah) signs. To navigate the *metro*, find the *línea* (lee-neh-yah) you need. Look in the direction you want to go and find the name of the last station. Follow the signs for that station. The *metro* is open seven days a week from 6 a.m. until 1:30 a.m.

You can buy single *metro* tickets (*un billete sencillo*, oon bee-yeh-teh sehn-see-yoh) or a pack of 10 (*un billete de diez viajes*, oon bee-yeh-teh deh dee-ehs bee-ah-hehs). Tourist tickets (*un metrotour de tres días* or *de cinco días*, oon meh-troh-toor deh trehs or deh seen-koh dee-ahs), which are available through travel agencies, tourist offices, and subway stations, enable you to choose unlimited bus, subway, and train travel for three or five consecutive days. A monthly commuter pass (*una tarjeta de abono transportes*, oo-nah tahr-heh-tah deh ah-boh-noh trahns-pohr-tehs) is another option.

Catching a Ride

Public transportation is convenient if you're going into Madrid or Mexico City from the airport. You also might decide to take a taxi. Taxis with meters impose surcharges for luggage, night fares, and holiday fares. Another option is public-service taxis, known as a *gran turismos* (grahn too-rees-mohs), which are unmetered and have higher rates than regular taxis. Should this be your choice, ask in advance for the fare to your destination.

Don't forget you can also travel very economically by taking *un colectivo* (oon koh-lehk-tee-boh), a car or van shared with others going to the same destination or in your general direction.

Spanish train fare is a best-buy—it's the most inexpensive train fare in Europe. *Una Tarjeta Turística* (oo-nah tahr-heh-tah too-rees-tee-kah, a Tourist Card), available only to non-residents, permits unrestricted train travel. The card can be for first- or second-class travel, and its price varies depending on the amount of travel time: 8, 15, or 22 days. A Eurail Pass can be purchased in the United States, and it also allows unlimited travel. Its price varies depending on how many days of travel you choose.

Culture Corner

In Mexico City, orange-colored taxis have the number of their taxi stand painted on their doors and can be called by phone. Yellow cabs, as in the United States, simply cruise for passengers. Due to inflation, taxis don't have set prices. It is best to fix the rate with the *chofér* (choh-fehr) before the trip.

Go-Go Verbs

You might decide to *hacer una excursión* (ah-sehr oo-nah ehks-koor-see-yohn, go on an outing) by subway, bus, train, or car. Whatever means of transportation you choose (*escoger*, ehs-koh-hehr), it's sure to be the right one for you. If you want to use the verbs in this paragraph (and other similar verbs) while planning a trip, you have to learn their idiosyncrasies and irregularities.

Go-go verbs are regular or irregular verbs whose *yo* form ends in *-go* instead of *-o*. Because these are all high-frequency verbs, it is best to spend a little time learning them. Let's start with verbs that are regular in all forms except *yo*.

Verb	Meaning	Yo Form	Remaining Conjugations
hacer	to make, to do	yo hago	haces, hace, hacemos, hacéis, hacen
poner	to put	yo pongo	pones, pone, ponemos, ponéis, ponen
salir	to leave, to go out	yo salgo	sales, sale, salimos, salís, salen
traer	to bring	yo traigo	traes, trae, traemos, traéis, traen
valer	to be worth	yo valgo	vales, vale, valemos, valéis, valen

Use *hacer* in the following phrases:

Phrase	Pronunciation	Meaning
hacer la maleta	ah-sehr lah mah-leh-tah	to pack
hacer una pregunta	ah-sehr oo-nah preh-goon-tah	to ask a question
hacer un viaje	ah-sehr oon bee-yah-heh	to take a trip
hacer una visita	ah-sehr oo-nah bee-see-tah	to pay a visit

For irregular go-go verbs, just concentrate on the *yo* form for the time being. You will see the complete conjugations of these verbs in later chapters.

Verb	Meaning	Yo Form
decir	to tell, to say	yo digo
oír	to hear	yo oigo
tener	to have	yo tengo
venir	to come	yo vengo

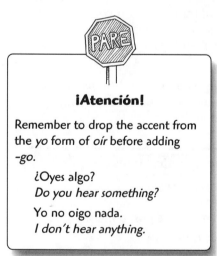

¡Atención!

Remember to drop the accent from the *yo* form of *oír* before adding *-go.*

¿Oyes algo?
Do you hear something?

Yo no oigo nada.
I don't hear anything.

Other spelling changes occur in regular verbs to preserve the original sound of the verb. These changes occur before an *o* or an *a* and enable the consonant to be pronounced correctly. Since all the verbs you will be looking at end in *-er*, *-ir*, or *-uir*, the only subject affected in the present tense is *yo*.

Why is that? Quite simply, it's because only *-ar* infinitives have verb forms that end in *-a*. All *yo* forms end in *-o*; therefore, all *yo* forms are affected. Verbs that end in *-er*, *-ir*, and *-uir* have an *-a* ending in the command form because opposite letters are used to form commands.

Take a closer look at some of these verbs you might want to use with regularity:

➤ Verbs ending in *-cer* and *-cir* change *c* to *z* before *o* or *a*, as follows:

Verb	Meaning	Affected Conjugation	Unaffected Conjugations	Command
convencer	to convince	yo convenzo	convences convence convencemos convencéis convencen	Convenza Ud. Convenzan Uds.

➤ Verbs ending in *-ger* and *-gir* change *g* to *j* before *o* or *a*, as follows:

Verb	Meaning	Affected Conjugation	Unaffected Conjugations	Command
escoger	to choose	yo escojo	escoges escoge escogemos escogéis escogen	Escoja Ud. Escojan Uds.
recoger	to pick up	yo recojo	recoges recoge recogemos recogéis recogen	Recoja Ud. Recojan Uds.
dirigir	to direct	yo dirijo	diriges dirige dirigimos dirigís dirigen	Dirija Ud. Dirijan Uds.

➤ Verbs ending in *-guir* change *gu* to *g* before *o* or *a*, as follows:

Verb	Meaning	Affected Conjugation	Unaffected Conjugations	Command
seguir	to follow, continue	yo sigo	sigues sigue seguimos seguís siguen	Siga Ud. Sigan Uds.

10 minutos al día

Go-go verbs have irregular *yo* forms that end in *-go* in the present tense. Here are some common ones:

Otherwise Regular Verbs		Otherwise Irregular Verbs	
hacer	hago	decir	digo
poner	pongo	oír	oigo
salir	salgo	tener	tengo
traer	traigo	venir	vengo
	valer	valgo

What's What?

When you're on a trip and you meet someone new, there are many questions you can ask, such as "What's your name? address? profession? What activities do you like?" The list is endless. In Spanish, two words can mean either which or what—*cuál* or *qué*. How do you know when to use each?

➤ *¿Qué?* asks "what" when referring to a description, a definition, or an explanation. It asks "which" when used before a noun.

¿Qué es esto?
What's that?

¿Qué estás haciendo?
What are you doing?

¿Qué libro lee Ud.?
Which book are you reading?

Memory Master

¿Cuál? becomes *¿cuáles?* when the noun to which you are referring is plural.

¿Cuál es la fecha?
What is the date?

¿Cuáles son los meses del año?
What are the months of the year?

➤ *¿Cuál? ¿Cuáles?* asks "what" before the verb *ser* (to be). It means "which (one[s])" before other verbs and the preposition *de.*

¿Cuál es su nombre?
What's your name?

¿Cuáles deseas?
Which (ones) do you want?

¿Cuál de los dos prefieres?
Which (one) of the two do you prefer?

If you want to go off on your own, expect to ask questions using *¿qué?* and *¿cuál?* to get you where you want to go. Do you feel confident enough to ask what bus you need to take and what its number is? These are the questions you would need:

¿Qué autobús tomo?
keh ow-toh-boos toh-moh
Which bus do I take?

¿Cuál es su número?
kwahl ehs soo noo-meh-roh
What is its number?

Using ¿Qué? and ¿Cuál?

Now that you've learned about *¿qué?* and *¿cuál?*, you can ask the nosy questions you didn't know how to ask before. Imagine you are speaking to the passenger next to you on the Customs line. Ask her for the following information. (Answers can be found on page 412, in Appendix A.)

1. name _____

2. address _____

3. what she is reading _____

4. what her nationality is _____

5. which subway line to take to Mexico City _____

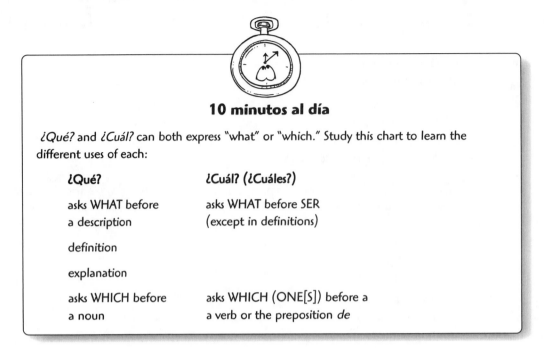

10 minutos al día

¿Qué? and *¿Cuál?* can both express "what" or "which." Study this chart to learn the different uses of each:

¿Qué?	¿Cuál? (¿Cuáles?)
asks WHAT before a description	asks WHAT before SER (except in definitions)
definition	
explanation	
asks WHICH before a noun	asks WHICH (ONE[S]) before a verb or the preposition *de*

Fill 'er Up

Do you feel daring enough to rent a car at *un alquiler de coches*? Make sure to compare the rates and models available at several rental agencies before making a final decision. Keep in mind that the cost of fuel in other countries is generally more than double the price in the United States. The following phrases will prove useful when renting a car:

Quiero alquilar un (make of car).
kee-yeh-roh ahl-kee-lahr oon
I'd like to rent a (make of car).

Prefiero el cambio automático.
preh-fee-yeh-roh ehl kahm-bee-yoh ow-toh-mah-tee-koh
I prefer automatic transmission.

¿Cuánto cuesta por día (por semana) (por kilómetro)?
kwahn-toh kwehs-tah pohr dee-yah (pohr seh-mah-nah) (por kee-loh-meh-troh)
How much does it cost per day (per week) (per kilometer)?

¿Cuánto es el seguro?
kwahn-toh ehs ehl seh-goo-roh
How much is the insurance?

¿Está incluída la gasolina?
ehs-tah een-kloo-wee-dah lah gah-soh-lee-nah
Is the gas included?

¿Acepta Ud. tarjetas de crédito? ¿Cuáles?
ah-sehp-tah oo-stehd tahr-heh-tahs deh kreh-dee-toh kwah-lehs
Do you accept credit cards? Which ones?

¡Atención!

Use the word *el semáforo* (*una luz de tráfico*) to refer to a traffic light. Don't forget to stop *al semáforo rojo* (at the red light) and to go *al semáforo verde* (at the green light).

So you've decided to rent a car. That's great, but take a tip from me—carefully inspect the car, inside and out. You never know what might go wrong once you're on the road. Make sure there is *un gato* (oon gah-toh), a jack, and *una goma de repuesto* (oo-nah goh-mah deh reh-pwehs-toh), a spare tire, in the trunk. It's no fun to get stuck on a road in the middle of nowhere.

Table 11.1   Car Parts

Car Part	Spanish Translation	Pronunciation
battery	la batería	lah bah-teh-ree-yah
bumper	el parachoques	ehl pah-rah-choh-kehs
carburetor	el carburador	ehl kahr-boo-rah-dohr
door handle	el tirador de puerta	ehl tee-rah-dohr deh pwehr-tah
fan	el ventilador	ehl behn-tee-lah-dohr
fender	el guardafango	ehl gwahr-dah-fahn-goh
gas tank	el tanque	ehl tahn-keh
headlight	el faro delantero	ehl fah-roh deh-lahn-teh-roh
hood	la capota	lah kah-poh-tah
license plate	la placa de matrícula	lah plah-kah deh mah-tree-koo-lah
motor	el motor	ehl moh-tohr
radiator	el radiador	ehl rah-dee-yah-dohr
tail light	el faro trasero	ehl fah-roh trah-seh-roh
tire	la goma, la llanta	lah goh-mah, lah yahn-tah

continues

Table 11.1 Continued

Car Part	Spanish Translation	Pronunciation
transmission	la transmisión	lah trahns-mee-see-yohn
trunk	el baúl	ehl bah-ool
wheel	la rueda	lah roo-weh-dah
windshield wiper	el limpia parabrisas	ehl leem-pee-yah pah-rah-bree-sahs

Table 11.2 Interior Car Parts

Car Part	Spanish Translation	Pronunciation
accelerator	el acelerador	ehl ah-seh-leh-rah-dohr
directional signal	el direccional	ehl dee-rehk-see-yoh-nahl
gear shift	el cambio de velocidades	ehl kahm-bee-yoh deh beh-loh-see-dah-dehs
horn	la bocina	lah boh-see-nah
ignition	el contacto	ehl kohn-tahk-toh
radio	la radio	lah rah-dee-yoh
steering wheel	el volante	ehl boh-lahn-teh
brakes	los frenos	lohs freh-nohs
clutch pedal	el embrague	ehl ehm-brah-geh
glove compartment	la guantera	lah gwahn-teh-rah
hand brake	el freno de mano	ehl freh-noh deh mah-noh
air bag	la bolsa de aire	lah bohl-sah deh ah-yee-reh
anti-lock brakes	los frenos anti-bloqueantes	lohs freh-nohs ahn-tee bloh-keh-yahn-tehs

In Europe, distance is measured by kilometers. Table 11.3 shows the approximate equivalents.

Table 11.3   Distance Measures (Approximate)

Miles	Kilometers
.62	1
3	5
6	10
12	20
31	50
62	100

Off You Go

If you decide to rent a car, you will be required to fill out a rental agreement. What will you do if it's in Spanish? Before renting, familiarize yourself with the terms and conditions of your rental contract. Read the fine print so there will be no misunderstandings when you return the car. You'll want everything to go smoothly. What do these terms spell out? (Translations appear on page 412, in Appendix A.)

In a Flash

Put labels on the interior parts of your car. Study these vocabulary words until you have them down pat. Remove your labels. Every time you enter your car, see whether you can name the parts. Then start on the exterior parts.

MÉTODO DE APLICACIÓN

RESERVACIÓN: Es recomendado hacer reservaciones con veinte y cuatro horas de adelanto.

CONDICIONES: El paquete económico MADRIDCAR es aplicable en todas las agencias MADRIDCAR en España. La duración del alquiler facturada (mínimo de un día) se calcula por un periodo de veinte y cuatro horas no fracturables. Le permiten a Ud. cincuenta y nueve minutos sin multa. Después de este tiempo, Ud. será multado por un día entero

KILOMERAJE: El kilometraje en el paquete económico MADRIDCAR es sin limites.

RENTE AQUÍ, DEJE ALLÍ: Este servicio permite la reinstitución de un vehículo en una agencia dferente a la agencia orignal. Está incluído en el paquete económico.

SEGUROS: En caso de daño, sólo una suma 1.500 pesos queda a cargo de la persona que alquila el carro.
En caso de robo, sólo un incremento monetario queda a cargo de la persona que alquila el carro.
Hay una garantía de asistencia técnica y médica veinte y cuatro horas al día.

GASOLINA: La gasolina no está incluída con nuestras tarifas y queda a cargo de la persona que alquila el carro.

VALIDEZ: Los precios indicados son expresandos en pesos . Estos son modificables sin previo aviso.

Show Me the Way to Go Home

Imagine you've rented a car but have failed to learn to translate the road signs. Now imagine you've received a traffic ticket while visiting a foreign country. Ouch. Take a moment to read these road signs. Some of them are trickier than they first seem.

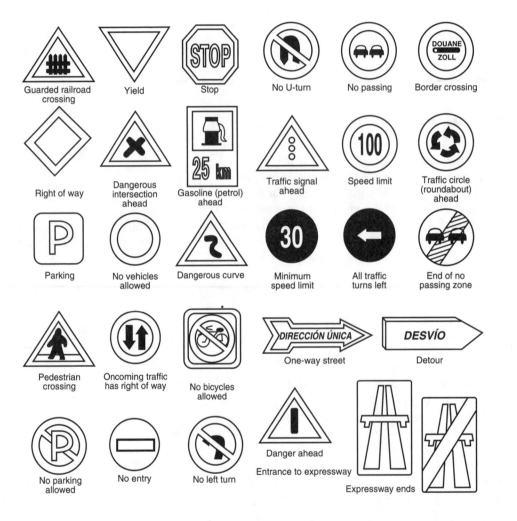

My husband and I, with kids in tow, were traveling from the city of Santo Domingo to the lovely Casa de Campo resort at the other side of the Dominican Republic. When we got to a fork in the road, which crept up on us a little too quickly, I screamed "Go this way!" He went that way. We got lost, of course. How much easier life would have been had I just said "Go north." Don't be like me, know your compass directions.

Direction	Pronunciation	Meaning
al norte	ahl nohr-teh	to the north
al este	ahl ehs-teh	to the east
al sur	ahl soor	to the south
al oeste	ahl oh-wehs-teh	to the west

What Did You Rent?

Imagine you saw the following ad in a Spanish newspaper and decided to rent this car. Read the ad carefully and see whether you can name the features it comes with. Translations can be found on page 412, in Appendix A. Drive safely!

> **Información y Reservaciones**
> **Tel.: (91) 322 45 00**
> **Avíos Acura Vigor**
>
> •*Aire acondicionado • Cinturón de seguridad delantero y trasero • Volante equipado de un saco inflable • Ventanas eléctricas • Cierre dentral de las puertas • Radio AM/FM*
>
> MADRIDCAR
> Para Uds. MADRIDCAR escoge Acura y otras marcas grandes.

How Much?

If you want to be able to say what number bus, subway, or flight you are taking or to find out just how big a dent that rent-a-car is going to make in your pocket, you need to know the Spanish numbers in Table 11.4. They also come in handy for other uses, such as asking what time the bank opens.

In a Flash

Tell a friend about the features of your car. Be specific and spare no details.

Table 11.4   Cardinal Numbers

Number	Spanish Translation	Pronunciation
0	cero	seh-roh
1	uno	oo-noh
2	dos	dohs
3	tres	trehs
4	cuatro	kwah-troh
5	cinco	seen-koh
6	seis	seh-yees
7	siete	see-yeh-teh
8	ocho	oh-choh
9	nueve	noo-weh-beh
10	diez	dee-yehs
11	once	ohn-seh
12	doce	doh-seh
13	trece	treh-seh
14	catorce	kah-tohr-seh
15	quince	keen-seh
16	dieciséis	dee-yehs-ee-seh-yees
17	diecisiete	dee-yehs-ee-see-yeh-teh
18	dieciocho	dee-yehs-ee-oh-choh
19	diecinueve	dee-yehs-ee-noo-weh-beh
20	veinte	behn-teh
21	veintiuno	behn-tee-oo-noh
22	veintidós	behn-tee-dohs
30	treinta	treh-een-tah
40	cuarenta	kwah-rehn-tah
50	cincuenta	seen-kwehn-tah
60	sesenta	seh-sehn-tah
70	setenta	seh-tehn-tah
80	ochenta	oh-chen-tah
90	noventa	noh-behn-tah
100	cien	see-yehn
101	ciento uno	see-yehn-toh oo-noh
200	doscientos	dohs see-yehn-tohs
500	quinientos	kee-nee-yehn-tohs

Number	Spanish Translation	Pronunciation
700	setecientos	seh-teh-see-yehn-tohs
900	novecientos	noh-beh-see-yehn-tohs
1,000	mil	meel
2,000	dos mil	dohs meel
100,000	cien mil	see-yehn meel
1,000,000	un millón	oon mee-yohn
2,000,000	dos millones	dohs mee-yoh-nehs

Spanish numbers are not too tricky. Look at Table 11.4 and then be aware of the following rules:

➤ The conjunction *y* (and) is used only for compound numbers between 30 and 99. Use of *y* with numbers between 16 and 29 is very rare.

dieciséis libros
16 books

veintiun días
21 days

BUT

treinta y nueve dólares
$39

➤ *Uno* (one) is used only when counting. It becomes *un* before masculine nouns and *una* before feminine nouns.

uno, dos, tres
one, two, three

un hombre y una mujer
a man and a woman

treinta y un muchachos
thirty-one boys

veintiuna muchachas
twenty-one girls

Culture Corner

The Spanish, as in many other European cultures, write the number 1 with a little hook on top. To distinguish a 1 from the number 7, put a line through the 7 when you write it.

In numerals and decimals, the Spanish use periods where we use commas, and vice versa:

ENGLISH	SPANISH
1,000	1.000
.25	0,25
$9.95	$9,95

➤ In compounds of *cien* (*doscientos, trescientos*), there must be agreement with a feminine noun.

> doscientos hombres
> *two hundred men*
>
> trescientas mujeres
> *three hundred women*

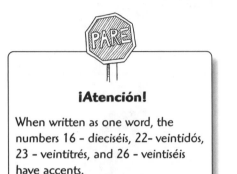

¡Atención!

When written as one word, the numbers 16 – dieciséis, 22– veintidós, 23 – veintitrés, and 26 – veintiséis have accents.

➤ Use *cien* before nouns and the numbers *mil* and *millones*. Before all other numbers, *ciento* is used.

> cien libros
> *one hundred books*
>
> ciento veinte carros
> *one hundred and twenty cars*
>
> cien mil personas
> *one hundred thousand people*
>
> cien millones de dólares
> *one billion dollars*

➤ *Un*, although not used before *ciento* or *mil*, is used before *millón*. If a noun follows *millón*, put *de* between *millón* and the noun.

> cien pesetas
> *one hundred pesetas*
>
> mil quinientos años
> *fifteen hundred years*
>
> un millón de habitantes
> *a million inhabitants*

In a Flash

When you go shopping or see prices in the newspaper, give the figures in Spanish. It takes a while to get accustomed to numbers in a foreign language.

Your Number's Up

Phone numbers in Madrid consist of seven numbers—one group of three and two pairs. The regional code for Madrid is (1). This number must be dialed before the phone number whenever you call from outside the city. In South American, Central American, and Caribbean countries, phone numbers are grouped in three pairs. How would you ask the operator for the following numbers? (Answers can be found on page 412, in Appendix A.)

45   67   89 _____

325   11   72 _____

What's the Time?

You will probably hear the following question often:

¿Qué hora es?
keh oh-rah ehs
What time is it?

Table 11.5 shows you how to answer it.

Table 11.5   Telling Time

The Time	Spanish Translation	Pronunciation
It is 1:00.	Es la una.	ehs lah oo-nah
It is 2:05.	Son las dos y cinco.	sohn lahs dohs ee seen-koh
It is 3:10.	Son las tres y diez.	sohn lahs trehs y dee-yehs
It is 4:15.	Son las cuatro y cuarto.	sohn lahs kwah-troh ee kwahr-toh
It is 5:20.	Son las cinco y veinte.	sohn lahs seen-koh ee behn-teh
It is 6:25.	Son las seis y veinticinco.	sohn lahs seh-yees ee behn-tee-seen-koh
It is 7:30.	Son las siete y media.	sohn lahs see-yeh-teh ee meh-dee-yah
It is 7:35. (25 min. to 8)	Son las ocho menos veinticinco.	sohn lahs oh-choh meh-nohs behn-tee-seen-koh
It is 8:40. (20 min. to 9)	Son las nueve menos veinte.	sohn lahs noo-weh-beh meh-nohs behn-teh
It is 9:45. (15 min. to 10)	Son las diez menos cuarto.	sohn lahs dee-yehs meh-nohs kwahr-toh
It is 10:50. (10 min. to 11)	Son las once menos diez.	sohn lahs ohn-seh meh-nohs dee-yehs
It is 11:55. (5 min. to noon)	Son las doce menos cinco.	sohn lahs doh-seh meh-nohs seen-koh
It is noon.	Es mediodía.	ehs meh-dee-yoh-dee-yah
It is midnight.	Es medianoche.	ehs meh-dee-yah-noh-cheh

In schedules and timetables, the official 24-hour system is commonly used. Midnight is the 0 hour:

0 h 15 = 12:15 a.m.

15 horas = 3:00 p.m.

21 h 50 = 9:50 p.m.

All numbers are expressed in full in the 24-hour system:

22 h 45 = veintidós horas cuarenta y cinco

Keep the following in mind when you tell time:

➤ Use *es* for "it is" when it's one o'clock. For other numbers, because they are plural, use *son*.

➤ To express the time after the hour, use *y* and the number of minutes past the hour.

➤ To express time before the next hour (after half past), use *menos* + the number of the following hour.

Son las tres menos cuarto.
It's 2:45.

You also might hear the time expressed as follows:

Son las dos y cuarenta y cinco.
It's 2:45.

Memory Master

Here's how to tell time:

Es la una.
It's 1:00.

Son las dos y cuarto.
It's 2:15.

Son las tres y media.
It's 3:30.

Son las cuatro menos cuarto
It's 4:45.

Use *y* to express the number of minutes after the hour (until half past) and *menos* to express the number of minutes before the hour.

In a Flash

Whenever you look at a clock or your watch, say the time to yourself in Spanish.

It's Movie Time

It's a gloomy and drizzly day, and you're in the mood for some quiet relaxation. Why not go to the movies? You call the following theaters and listen to the recordings. Tell what time the films start. (Sample responses can be found on page 413, in Appendix A.)

Example:

Trocadero—La lección de piano: 13h15, 16h20, 19h25

La lección de piano empieza a la una y cuarto, a las cuatro y veinte, y a las siete y veinticinco.

1. Cinemetro II—Mi querido presidente: 15h10, 17h35, 20h, 22h25

2. Metropol—Casino: 14h50, 16h35, 18h20, 20h05

3. San Marcos—Mi primo Vinnie: 13h30, 16h15, 18h45, 21h40

Knowing how to ask for and tell time is not enough if you want to schedule activities or find out when something is planned. Imagine you asked someone when a sporting event was taking place and the person responded *"Hace dos horas."* You might take this to mean "At 2 o'clock" or maybe "There are two hours before the match." Wrong. In fact, you've missed the match because it started two hours ago. The expressions in Table 11.6 will help you get there next time.

Table 11.6   Time Expressions

Time Expressions	Spanish Translation	Pronunciation
a second	un segundo	oon seh-goon-doh
a minute	un minuto	oon mee-noo-toh
an hour	una hora	oo-nah oh-rah
in the morning	de la mañana	deh lah mah-nyah-nah
in the afternoon (p.m.)	de la tarde	deh lah tahr-deh
in the evening	de la noche	deh lah noh-cheh
at what time?	¿a qué hora?	ah keh oh-rah
at exactly	a la(s) en punto	ah lah(s) ehn poon-toh
at about 2 o'clock	a eso de las dos	ah eh-soh deh lahs dohs
a quarter of an hour	un cuarto de hora	oon kwahr-toh deh oh-rah
a half hour	una media hora	oo-nah meh-dee-yah oh-rah
in an hour	en una hora	ehn oo-nah oh-rah
in a couple of hours	en un par de horas	ehn oon pahr deh oh-rahs
in a second (flash)	en un abrir y cerrar de ojos	ehn oon ah-breer ee seh-rrahr deh oh-hohs
in a while	dentro de un rato	dehn-troh deh oon rah-toh
often	a menudo	ah meh-noo-doh
until 2 o'clock	hasta las dos	ahs-tah lahs dohs
before 3 o'clock	antes de las tres	ahn-tehs deh lahs trehs
after 3 o'clock	después de las tres	dehs-pwehs deh lahs trehs
since what time?	¿desde qué hora?	dehs-deh keh oh-rah

continues

135

Table 11.6 Continued

Time Expressions	Spanish Translation	Pronunciation
since 6 o'clock	desde las seis	dehs-deh lahs seh-yees
an hour ago	hace una hora	ah-seh oo-nah oh-rah
per hour	por hora	pohr oh-rah
early	temprano	tehm-prah-noh
late	tarde	tahr-deh
late (in arriving)	en retraso	ehn rreh-trah-soh
on time	a tiempo	ah tee-yehm-poh
good-bye	adiós	ah-dee-yohs

The Least You Need to Know

➤ The verbs *hacer, poner, salir, traer,* and *valer* are regular in all forms except *yo*, in which they end in *-go*.

➤ The verbs *decir, oír, tener,* and *venir* are irregular verbs whose *yo* form also ends in *-go*.

➤ *¿Qué?* and *¿cuál? (¿cuáles?)* are used to ask what? and which? *¿Qué?* is used before nouns. *¿Cuál? (¿cuáles?)* is used before the preposition *de* and before the verb *ser,* except when giving a definition.

➤ Learning the cardinal numbers will help you in everyday situations like asking for prices, telling time, and determining flight information.

➤ Tell time easily by giving the hour and the number of minutes past the hour.

Chapter 12

Settling In

In This Chapter

➤ Hotel facilities

➤ Ordinal numbers

➤ Shoe verbs

Your plane has landed, you've cleared Customs, and you've found a mode of transportation that caters to your pocketbook and your needs. No matter how you've chosen to travel, remember to look out the window as you ride along. Taking in your surroundings right from the start will give you the lay of the land and will help you get your bearings. Before you know it, you'll be at your hotel.

For some people, the bare necessities are acceptable when it comes to travel accommodations. After all, why pay for luxurious décor when you plan to spend most of your time outside your room? You'd rather use the money for entertainment and souvenirs. Others prefer downright opulence. For them, vacation means being treated like royalty. Whatever your personal preferences might be, this chapter will teach you how to get the room and services you desire.

A Room with a View?

Before reserving a room anywhere, even here in the United States, make sure to verify with your travel agent or the hotel management that the facilities you need will be at your disposal. When you arrive, you want to be assured that your expectations will be met. Ask all important questions before you send a deposit. Use Table 12.1 to help you find out what hotel facilities are available.

Table 12.1   Hotel Facilities

Facilities	Spanish Translation	Pronunciation
bar	el bar	ehl bahr
business center	el centro de negocios	ehl sehn-troh deh neh-goh-see-yohs
cashier	el cajero	ehl kah-heh-roh
concierge (caretaker)	el conserje	ehl kohn-sehr-heh
doorman	el portero	ehl pohr-teh-roh
elevator	el ascensor	ehl ah-sehn-sohr
fitness center	el gimnasio	ehl heem-nah-see-yoh
gift shop	la tienda de regalos	lah tee-yehn-dah deh rreh-gah-lohs
laundry and dry-cleaning service	la lavandería	lah lah-bahn-deh-ree-yah
maid service	la gobernanta	lah goh-behr-nahn-tah
restaurant	el restaurante	ehl rrehs-tow-rahn-teh
swimming pool	la piscina	lah pee-see-nah
valet parking	la atendencia del garaje	lah ah-tehn-dehn-see-yah dehl gah-rah-heh

Do you want a great view when you book a hotel room? I never thought I did until I went to Dorado Beach in Puerto Rico. We booked a room facing the pool. What a mistake! Night and day all we heard were kids screaming and yelling. And we were trying to get away from ours! Next time I go, you can be sure I'll ask for *una habitación con vista al mar*. I'll also expect a lot of other amenities, too. Table 12.2 will help you get exactly what you want.

Table 12.2 Getting What You Want

Amenities	Spanish Translation	Pronunciation
a single room	una habitación con una sola cama	oo-nah ah-bee-tah-see-yohn kohn oo-nah soh-lah kah-mah
a double room	una habitación con dos camas	oo-nah ah-bee-tah-see-yohn kohn dohs kah-mahs
air-conditioning	el aire acondicionado	ehl ah-yee-reh ah-kohn-dee-see-yoh-nah-doh
alarm clock	el despertador	ehl dehs-pehr-tah-dohr
balcony	el balcón	ehl bahl-kohn
bathroom (private)	el baño privado	ehl bah-nyoh pree-bah-doh
on the courtyard	con vista al patio	kohn bees-tah ahl pah-tee-yoh
on the garden	con vista al jardín	kohn bees-tah ahl har-deen
on the sea	con vista al mar	kohn bees-tah ahl mahr
safe (deposit box)	la caja fuerte	lah kah-hah fwehr-teh
shower	la ducha	lah doo-chah
telephone (dial-direct)	el teléfono (directo)	ehl teh-leh-foh-noh (dee-rehk-toh)
television (color)	la televisión (en color)	lah teh-leh-bee-see-yohn (ehn koh-lohr)
toilet facilities	el W.C.	ehl doh-bleh-beh seh

In Spanish buildings, the ground floor is called la planta baja (lah plahn-tah bah-hah). On an elevator button, you can expect to see this abbreviated as PB or B. The basement is called el sótano. The "first floor" in Spain is on the second story.

In older establishments in some Spanish-speaking countries, toilet facilities are located in separate rooms. A sink and a bathtub (or shower) are located in what is called *el baño* (ehl bah-nyoh), the bathroom. The toilet and bidet are in the W.C., the water closet. Most bathrooms in modern buildings, however, are just like ours.

What Do You Need?

What if you need something for your room to make your stay more enjoyable? Any of the following phrases may help you:

Phrase	Pronunciation	Meaning
Quisiera	kee-see-yeh-rah	I would like
Me falta(n)	meh fahl-tah(n)	I need
Necesito	neh-seh-see-toh	I need

I have to have enough towels. That's one of my pet peeves. Unfortunately, hotels never seem to give you enough. If something you need or want is missing from your room, don't be shy. Ask for it! Remember, the management wants to please you and to make your stay enjoyable. Table 12.3 lists a few things you might need.

Table 12.3   Necessities

Necessity	Spanish Translation	Pronunciation
an ashtray	un cenicero	oon seh-nee-seh-roh
a bar of soap	una barra de jabón	oo-nah bah-rrah deh hah-bohn
a beach towel	una toalla de baño	oo-nah toh-wah-yah deh bah-nyoh
a blanket	una manta	oo-nah mahn-tah
hangers	unas perchas	oo-nahs pehr-chahs
ice cubes	cubitos de hielo	koo-bee-tohs deh yeh-loh
mineral water	agua mineral	ah-gwah mee-neh-rahl
a pillow	una almohada	oo-nah ahl-moh-ah-dah
a roll of toilet paper	un rollo de papel higiénico	oon rroh-yoh deh pah-pehl ee-hee-yeh-nee-koh
tissues	pañuelos de papel	pah-nyoo-weh-lohs deh pah-pehl
a towel	una toalla	oo-nah toh-wah-yah
a transformer (an electric adapter)	un transformador	oon trahns-fohr-mah-dohr

Remember that the verb *faltar* agrees with the number of items needed:

Me falta una toalla.   Me faltan seis perchas.
I need a towel.   *I need six hangers.*

Rate Your Hotel

Many hotels are curious to know whether you are happy with the services they provide. After all, they want you to return and would appreciate your recommendation to friends. How would you fill out their questionnaire?

¿Cómo estima...?

	Excelente	Bien	Mediano	Insuficiente
SU LLEGADA				
Portero	____	____	____	____
Recepción	____	____	____	____
Reservación	____	____	____	____
Seguridad	____	____	____	____
NUESTROS SERVICIOS				
Conserje	____	____	____	____
Teléfonos	____	____	____	____
Mensajes	____	____	____	____
Cajero	____	____	____	____
Centro de negocios	____	____	____	____
Gobernante	____	____	____	____
Lavandería	____	____	____	____
Minibar	____	____	____	____
Piscina	____	____	____	____
Gimnasio	____	____	____	____
SU HABITACIÓN				
Bien equipado	____	____	____	____
Adecuado espacio de trabajo	____	____	____	____
Suficients amenidades para invitados	____	____	____	____
Equipo en buenas condiciones	____	____	____	____

COMENTARIOS

_____

_____

_____

Just in Case

You've just walked into your room for the first time. If you're like me, you open every drawer to see if there's anything of interest inside, and you read all the notices and papers left for you on the dresser. You notice the following sign on the back of your door. What information is it giving you? Translations can be found on page 413, in Appendix A.

In a Flash

Pretend you are taking a trip to a Spanish-speaking country. Make a list in Spanish of everything you'd expect the hotel to provide.

CONDUCTA EN CASO DE INCENDIO

En caso de incendio en su habitación, si Ud. no puede controlar el fuego:

- Consiga la salida y cierre bien la puerta de su habitación al salir. Siga las luces en el piso.
- Avise a la recepción.

En caso de que Ud. oiga la alarma de fuego:

- Consiga la salida y cierre otra vez la puerta de su habitación al salir.
- Siga las luces en el piso.

Si el humo bloquea el pasillo o la escalera:

- Quédese en su habitación.
- Asómese a la ventana mientras espera la llegada de los bomberos.

Which Offers the Most?

Imagine your travel agent has sent you brochures for three hotels in Spain. Read what is available and use the following chart to check off the services offered in each. Then choose the one for you. Check your answers on page 413, in Appendix A.

	La Capilla	Plaza Central	Hotel España
bar	_____	_____	_____
color TV	_____	_____	_____
music	_____	_____	_____
laundry service	_____	_____	_____
dry-cleaning service	_____	_____	_____
air-conditioning	_____	_____	_____
in-room safe	_____	_____	_____
gym	_____	_____	_____
restaurant	_____	_____	_____
sauna	_____	_____	_____
Jacuzzi	_____	_____	_____
fitness center	_____	_____	_____
VIP room	_____	_____	_____
parking	_____	_____	_____
hair dryer in room	_____	_____	_____
terrace	_____	_____	_____
non-smoking room	_____	_____	_____
room service	_____	_____	_____
in the city	_____	_____	_____

La Capilla

Confortables y cálidas habitaciones, situadas en pleno centro de Madrid, ampliamente dotadas de las más modernas instalaciones como: TV Color - Hilo musical - teléfono directo - Minibar - Aire acondicionado - caja fuerte - toma de fax - baño de mármol. Construido en 1995, La Capilla tiene todo para los más exigentes: sala de convenciones - banquetes - restaurante - bar- cafetería - servicio de habiciones - gimnasio - zona de fitness - jacuzzi y sauna.

Plaza Central

Plaza Central dispone de 306 habitaciones, algunas con terraza y muchas con facilidades para no fumadores. Con aire acondicionado, mini-bar, teléfono automático directo, caja fuerte individual, TV color, hilo musical, baño completo con secador de pelo, y servicio de habitaciones de 24 horas.

Hotel España

Situado en plena corazón de la ciudad, el Hotel España dispone de 144 habitaciones con baño completo, teléfono, TV y aire acondicionado. Restaurante, salón de TV y salón social con TV y bar. Próximo al hotel existe un aparcamiento para 800 coches.

Going Up

When you get on an elevator in a Spanish-speaking country, someone will probably ask you, *"¿Qué piso, por favor?"* (keh pee-soh pohr fah-bohr) In this situation, you will be happy you studied the ordinal numbers in Table 12.4.

Table 12.4   Ordinal Numbers

Ordinal Number	Spanish Translation	Pronunciation
1st	primero	pree-meh-roh
2nd	segundo	seh-goon-doh
3rd	tercero	tehr-seh-roh
4th	cuarto	kwahr-toh
5th	quinto	keen-toh
6th	sexto	sehks-toh
7th	séptimo	sehp-tee-moh
8th	octavo	ohk-tah-boh
9th	noveno	noh-beh-noh
10th	décimo	deh-see-moh

The Spanish ordinal numbers can be abbreviated as follows. You will note that an 8 or superscript (^{er}) is used to denote a masculine ordinal number in a sequence. A superscript ($^{\circ}$) is used for the feminine.

Stands Alone (Masculine)	Stands Alone (Feminine)	Used Before a Masculine Noun	Used Before a Feminine Noun
primero 18	primera 1°	primer 1er	primera 1°
segundo 28	segunda 2°	segundo 28	segunda 2°
tercero 38	tercera 3°	tercer 3er	tercera 3°
cuarto 48	cuarta 4°	cuarto 48	cuarta 4°

Es el 1°.	Es la 4° vez.	Es el 3er día.
It's the first.	*It's the fourth time.*	*It's the third day.*

Keep the following in mind when using ordinal numbers:

➤ *Primero* and *tercero* drop their final *-o* before a masculine singular noun.

el primer día
the first day

la tercera mujer
the third woman

el tercer hombre
the third man

but

la primera semana
the first week

el siglo tercero
the third century

¡Atención!

The only cardinal number that has a masculine and feminine form is *un*, *una*. All ordinal numbers from 1 to 10 are masculine singular forms.

➤ Ordinal numbers can be made feminine by changing the final *-o* of the masculine form to *-a*, as in

el segundo acto
the second act

la segunda escena
the second scene

➤ The Spanish usually use ordinal numbers through the tenth. After that, cardinal numbers are used.

la tercera cuadra
the fourth block

la Sexta Avenida
Sixth Avenue

la página veinte
page 20

Using Ordinal Numbers

Imagine you are in El Corte Inglés, a large department store in Madrid. Look at the directory that shows what can be found on each floor. Where would you go to do the following? (Answers can be found on page 414, in Appendix A.)

Buy tobacco? _____

    flowers? _____

    records? _____

    toys? _____

    travel items? _____

Where can you park? _____

Where can you get the following services:

    an interpreter? _____

    a travel agency? _____

    photos? _____

    keys made? _____

10 minutos al día

Here's a quick fix on ordinal numbers:

1st	primero	2nd	segundo
3rd	tercero	4th	cuarto
5th	quinto	6th	sexto
7th	séptimo	8th	octavo
9th	noveno	10th	décimo

Only use ordinal numbers through ten. Remember that the ordinal number must agree with the masculine or feminine noun it modifies.

It's Time for a Change

Verbs are perhaps the most useful tool in any language because they help you express actions. You couldn't have a conversation without them. A few categories of regular *-ar*, *-er*, and *-ir* verbs in Spanish require spelling changes within the stem of the verb. Only the beginning of the verb is affected; the regular endings remain the same.

I like to call these verbs "shoe verbs" because the rules for the spelling changes work as if we put the subject pronouns that follow one set of rules within the shoe and the others outside the shoe. To make this more clear, let's look at the pronouns that go inside and outside the shoe.

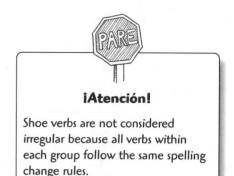

¡Atención!

Shoe verbs are not considered irregular because all verbs within each group follow the same spelling change rules.

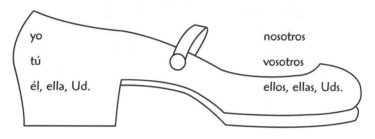

yo

tú

él, ella, Ud.

nosotros

vosotros

ellos, ellas, Uds.

In other words, the verb forms for *yo*, *tú*, *él*, *ella*, *Ud.*, *ellos*, *ellas*, and *Uds.* follow one set of rules. *Nosotros* and *vosotros* follow a different set of rules. Now let's look at the different categories.

Verbs Ending in -ar and -er

For verbs ending in *-ar* or *-er*, the stem vowel change takes place in the present tense. The *e* changes to *ie* and *o* changes to *ue* in all forms of the shoe except *nosotros* and *vosotros*.

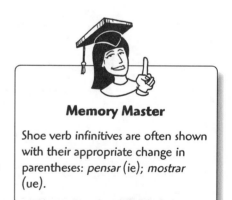

Memory Master

Shoe verb infinitives are often shown with their appropriate change in parentheses: *pensar* (ie); *mostrar* (ue).

pensar (to think)

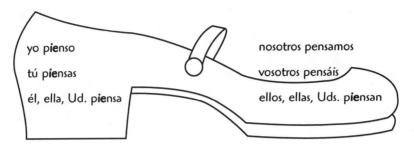

yo pienso   nosotros pensamos

tú piensas   vosotros pensáis

él, ella, Ud. piensa   ellos, ellas, Uds. piensan

Other verbs that can be conjugated just like *pensar* include the following:

Verb	Pronunciation	Meaning
atravesar	ah-trah-beh-sahr	to cross
cerrar	seh-rrahr	to close
comenzar	koh-mehn-sahr	to begin
empezar	ehm-peh-sahr	to begin
quebrar	keh-brahr	to break

querer (to want)

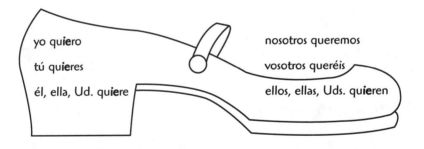

yo quiero   nosotros queremos

tú quieres   vosotros queréis

él, ella, Ud. quiere   ellos, ellas, Uds. quieren

Other verbs that can be conjugated just like *querer* include the following:

Verb	Pronunciation	Meaning
descender	deh-sehn-dehr	to descend
entender	ehn-tehn-dehr	to understand
perder	pehr-dehr	to lose

mostrar (to show)

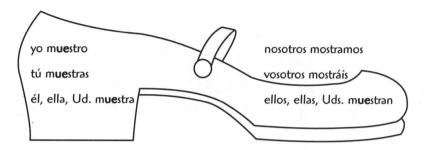

Other verbs that can be conjugated just like *mostrar* include the following:

Verb	Pronunciation	Meaning
almorzar	ahl-mohr-sahr	to eat lunch
contar	kohn-tahr	to tell
costar	kohs-tahr	to cost
encontrar	ehn-kohn-trahr	to meet, find
jugar(u to ue)	hoo-gahr	to play games, sports
recordar	reh-kohr-dahr	to remember

As you probably noticed in the list of verbs similar to *mostrar*, the *o* in the stem changes to *ue* in all the verbs except one—*jugar* (to play). There is no *o* in *jugar;* instead, the *u* changes to *ue*. It is a high-frequency verb, so pay special attention to this distinction.

The verb *jugar* changes *u* to *ue* as follows:

jugar (to play)

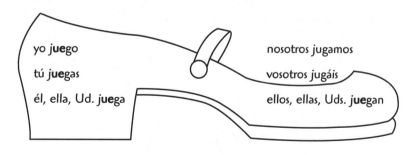

poder (to be able to, can)

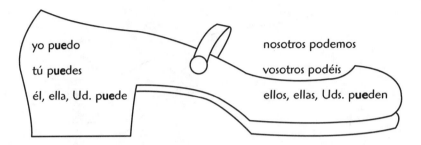

yo puedo

tú puedes

él, ella, Ud. puede

nosotros podemos

vosotros podéis

ellos, ellas, Uds. pueden

Other verbs that can be conjugated just like *poder* include the following:

Verb	Pronunciation	Meaning
doler	doh-lehr	to ache, pain
resolver	rreh-sohl-behr	to resolve
volver	bohl-behr	to return

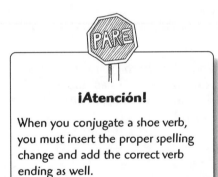

¡Atención!

When you conjugate a shoe verb, you must insert the proper spelling change and add the correct verb ending as well.

Using -ar and -er Verbs

You've finally settled into your hotel, and you are dozing off by the side of the pool. You hear bits and pieces of the conversations of other guests. Complete each of their sentences with the correct form of a verb from the following list. Answers can be found on page 414, in Appendix A.)

almorzar	costar
entender	poder
cerrar	descender
pensar	volver

1. ¿Qué _____ tú de esta idea?
2. Nosotros _____ al mediodía.
3. Yo _____ toda la conversación.
4. ¿A qué hora _____ Uds.?

5. Vosotros _____ jugar al parque.
6. ¿Cuánto _____ la blusa?
7. Nosotros _____ del autobús.
8. Vosotros siempre _____ las ventanas.

Verbs Ending in -ir

For verbs ending in *-ir*, the stem vowel change also takes place in the present tense. The *e* changes to *ie*, *o* changes to *ue*, and *e* changes to *i* in all forms of the shoe except *nosotros* and *vosotros*.

preferir (to prefer)

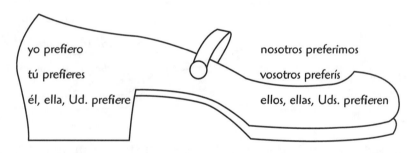

yo prefiero   nosotros preferimos
tú prefieres   vosotros preferís
él, ella, Ud. prefiere   ellos, ellas, Uds. prefieren

Other verbs that can be conjugated just like *preferir* include the following:

Verb	Pronunciation	Meaning
advertir	ahd-behr-teer	to notify, to warn
consentir	kohn-sehn-teer	to consent
mentir	mehn-teer	to lie
referir	rreh-feh-reer	to refer
sentir	sehn-teer	to regret

dormir (to sleep)

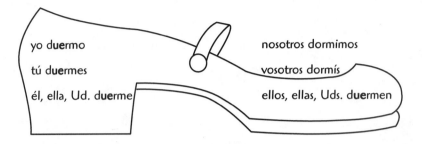

yo duermo

tú duermes

él, ella, Ud. duerme

nosotros dormimos

vosotros dormís

ellos, ellas, Uds. duermen

Another verb conjugated like *dormir* is the following:

Verb	Pronunciation	Meaning
morir	moh-reer	to die

repetir (to repeat)

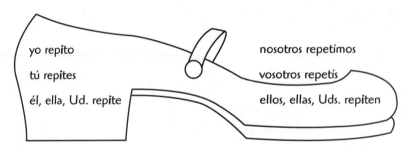

yo repito

tú repites

él, ella, Ud. repite

nosotros repetimos

vosotros repetís

ellos, ellas, Uds. repiten

Other verbs that can be conjugated just like *repetir* include the following:

Verb	Pronunciation	Meaning
impedir	eem-peh-deer	to prevent
medir	meh-deer	to measure
pedir	peh-deer	to ask
reír*	rreh-yeer	to laugh
servir	sehr-beer	to serve

* Reír keeps the accent over the i in all forms.

152

Using -ir Verbs

You are sitting in the lobby, and you hear the people all around you giving their opinions. Complete their sentences by giving the correct form of the verb in parentheses. (Answers can be found on page 414, in Appendix A.)

1. Yo (preferir) _____ ver el museo.

2. Nosotros no (dormir) _____ bastante.

3. Ellas (repetir) _____ muchas frases.

4. Vosotros (mentir) _____ todo el tiempo.

5. Él no (morir)_____.

6. Tú (reír) _____ mucho.

Verbs Ending in -uir

For verbs ending in *-uir* (except those ending in *-guir*, see Chapter 11, "Getting There Is Half the Fun"), insert a *y* after the *u* in all forms except *nosotros* and *vosotros*.

concluir (to conclude, end)

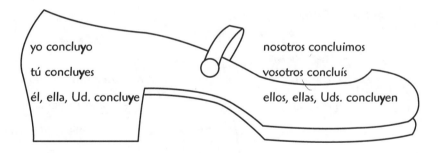

yo concluyo   nosotros concluimos

tú concluyes   vosotros concluís

él, ella, Ud. concluye   ellos, ellas, Uds. concluyen

Other verbs that can be conjugated just like *concluir* include the following:

Verb	Pronunciation	Meaning
construir	kohn-stroo-eer	to build
contribuir	kohn-tree-boo-eer	to contribute
destruir	dehs-troo-eer	to destroy
incluir	een-kloo-eer	to include
sustituir	soos-tee-too-eer	to substitute

Verbs Ending in -iar and -uar

Some verbs ending in *-iar* and *-uar* require an accent in all forms except *nosotros*.

guiar (to guide)

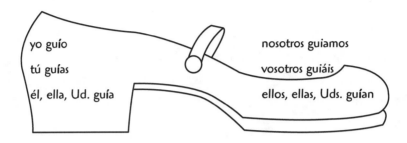

yo guío	nosotros guiamos
tú guías	vosotros guiáis
él, ella, Ud. guía	ellos, ellas, Uds. guían

Other verbs that can be conjugated just like *guiar* include the following:

Verb	Pronunciation	Meaning
confiar (en)	kohn-fee-yahr (ehn)	to confide (in), to rely (on)
enviar	ehn-bee-yahr	to send
variar	bah-ree-yahr	to vary

continuar (to continue)

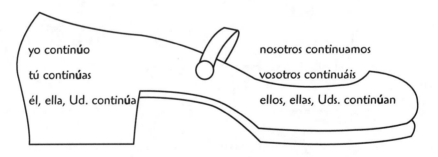

yo continúo	nosotros continuamos
tú continúas	vosotros continuáis
él, ella, Ud. continúa	ellos, ellas, Uds. continúan

Another verb that can be conjugated just like *continuar* is *actuar* (ahk-too-ahr), to act.

In the vosotros form of *-iar* and *-uar* verbs, make sure to put the accent on the *a*.

Vosotros confiáis en vuestros amigos.   Vosotros continuáis.
You confide in your friends.   *You continue.*

Some verbs in Spanish have both spelling changes and stem changes. The most common verb of this type is *seguir*. The *e* in the stem of *seguir* changes to *i*, except in the *nosotros* and *vosotros* forms. The *gu* changes to *g* in the *yo* form. The following is what the verb looks like when it is conjugated:

seguir (to continue, follow)

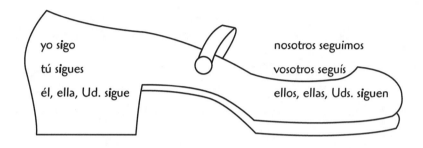

yo sigo   nosotros seguimos

tú sigues   vosotros seguís

él, ella, Ud. sigue   ellos, ellas, Uds. siguen

Using -uir, -iar, and -uar Verbs

You want to take a little *siesta* on the beach, but you are prevented from doing so by people merrily chatting away as they pass your chair. Complete what they say by giving the correct Spanish form of the English verb. (Answers can be found on page 414, in Appendix A.)

1. Yo (send) _____ una carta a mi familia.
2. Nosotras (include) _____ a todo el mundo.
3. Ud. (continue) _____ leyendo cuando yo hablo.
4. Ellos (contribute) _____ a esta conversación interesante.
5. Tú (act) _____ rápidamente.
6. Vosotros (guide) _____ a los otros al teatro.
7. Ella (continues) _____ hablando todo el tiempo.

10 minutos al día

Shoe verbs have changes in verb conjugation for all subjects except *nostotros* and *vosotros*. For verbs ending in *-ar* and *-er*, the vowel in the stem makes the following changes:

e	→	ie	pensar, querer
o	→	ue	mostrar, poder

For verbs ending in *-ir*, the vowel in the stem makes the following changes:

e	→	ie	preferir
o	→	ue	dormir
e	→	i	repetir

For verbs ending in *-uir*, insert *y* after *u* (as in *contribuir*). For some verbs ending in *-iar* and *-uar*, insert an accent on the vowel before the ending (as in *enviar* and *continuar*).

The Least You Need to Know

➤ Familiarize yourself with hotel vocabulary so that all your needs will be met.

➤ Ordinal numbers are used until ten. After that, use cardinal numbers.

➤ Shoe verbs follow a pattern of conjugation that resembles the outline of a shoe. Remember the shoe and you'll remember how to conjugate the verb.

Part 3
Having Fun

No trip is complete without some time for fun, games, amusements, and diversions. If it's a good time you're after, you've come to the right place.

Whatever the weather conditions, there's always something to do no matter where you are. Sight-seeing is often at the top of everyone's list. There are also exciting activities such as windsurfing, parasailing, scuba diving, and countless other sports. Cultural opportunities abound: museums, concerts, ballets, and operas. For some people, traveling is a shopping experience; for others, it's a gastronomic feast.

The six chapters in Part 3 cover the many ways to get the most out of the countries you visit. You'll learn how to do what you want when you want to do it and how to enjoy yourself to the fullest.

Chapter 13

How's the Weather?

In This Chapter

➤ Weather conditions

➤ Days and months

➤ The four seasons

➤ All about *dar* (to give)

Your hotel room is exactly what you'd hoped for and you're feeling great. Everything is in working condition, and there are even plenty of towels. Now you're eager to go out and have a wonderful time. When you look outside, however, you see clouds looming overhead. There's no sun in sight. What should you plan for the day?

Your first impulse will probably be to turn on the radio or TV to get the latest weather report. Unfortunately, all the forecasters are babbling away in rapid-fire Spanish, and your knowledge of cognates isn't helping you very much. No problem. This chapter will provide you with all the vocabulary you need to understand the forecast and plan your sightseeing.

It's 20 Degrees and They're Wearing String Bikinis!

You've opened your Spanish newspaper to the weather page. The weather forecaster has predicted a temperature of 20 degrees. You open your hotel window, and you're greeted with a balmy sea breeze and a view of a beach studded with bikini-clad bathers. Something must be amiss. Could *el pronóstico* (the forecast) be wrong? It's time to consult with someone in the know at *la recepción.* Phrases that will enable you to discuss the weather are listed in Table 13.1.

Table 13.1   Weather Expressions

Expression	Pronunciation	Meaning
¿Qué tiempo hace?	keh tee-yehm-poh ah-seh	What's the weather?
Hace buen tiempo.	ah-seh bwehn tee-yehm-poh	It's beautiful.
Hace calor.	ah-seh kah-lohr	It's hot.
Hace sol.	ah-seh sohl	It's sunny.
Hace mal tiempo.	ah-seh mahl tee-yehm-poh	It's nasty (bad).
Hace frío.	ah-seh free-yoh	It's cold.
Hace fresco.	ah-seh frehs-koh	It's cool.
Hace viento.	ah-seh bee-yehn-toh	It's windy.
Hay relámpagos.	ah-yee rreh-lahm-pah-gohs	It's lightning.
Truena.	troo-weh-nah	It's thundering.
Hay niebla (neblina).	ah-yee nee-yeh-blah (neh-blee-nah)	It's foggy.
Hay humedad.	ah-yee oo-meh-dahd	It's humid.
Hay nubes./ Está nublado.	ah-yee noo-behs/ ehs-tah noo-blah-doh	It's cloudy.
Está cubierto.	ehs-tah koo-bee-yehr-toh	It's overcast.
Llueve./ Está lloviendo.	yoo-weh-beh/ ehs-tah yoh-bee-yehn-doh	It's raining.
Hay lluvias torrenciales.	ahy yoo-bee-yahs toh-rrehn-see-yahl-ehs	It's pouring.
Nieva./ Está nevando.	nee-yeh-bah/ ehs-tah neh-bahn-doh	It's snowing.
Hay un vendaval.	ah-yee oon behn-dah-bahl	There's a windstorm.

Expression	Pronunciation	Meaning
Hay granizo.	ah-yee grah-nee-soh	There's hail.
Hay lloviznas.	ah-yee yoh-bees-nahs	There are showers.

If you want to use the present progressive tense (as discussed in Chapter 8, "Meetings and Greetings") to stress that a particular weather condition is in existence at the moment, conjugate the verb *estar*. Drop the *-ar* or *-er* infinitive ending from the verb and add *-ando* or *-iendo*, respectively: *Está lloviendo. Está nevando.*

So why *is* everyone wearing shorts and bikinis when it's 20 degrees out? The answer is really quite simple. Most of the Spanish-speaking world uses Celsius (centigrade) rather than Fahrenheit to tell the temperature (0°C = 32°F). Use these thermometers to help you:

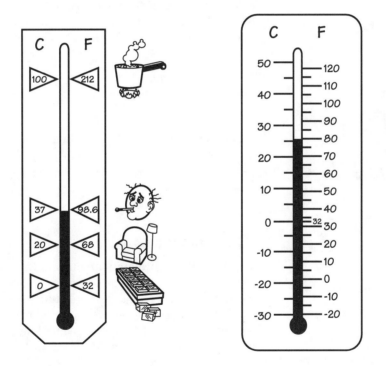

To change Fahrenheit to Centigrade, subtract 32 from the Fahrenheit temperature and multiply the remaining number by $5/9$. To change Centigrade to Fahrenheit, multiply the Centigrade temperature by $9/5$ and add 32 to the remaining number.

Culture Corner

The weather in Spain is much like the weather in the northeastern United States. It is temperate for much of the year, and the seasons change every three months. Autumn is probably the best time of the year to visit Spain because the climate is generally excellent. You can expect to have sunny days with blue skies most of the time.

Memory Master

The verbs llover (ue), tronar (ue), and nevar (ie) are stem–changing verbs. Remember to make the necessary changes when conjugating them:

Llueve.	*It's raining.*
Truena.	*It's thundering.*
Nieva.	*It's snowing.*

Baby It's Cold Outside

Should you bring along a sweater? Will you need a winter coat? How about your new bathing suit? If you want to dress appropriately and be comfortable, you'll want to know what the temperature is. To find out, you would ask:

¿Cuál es la temperatura?
kwahl ehs lah tehm-peh-rah-too-rah
What's the temperature?

To answer the question "What's the temperature?" simply give the number of degrees followed by the word *grados* (grah-dohs, degrees). To be more formal, you could say "Hay una temperatura de *xx* grados" (ahy oo-nah tehm-peh-rah-too-rah deh *xx* grah-dohs). If it's below zero, you need to add *menos* (meh-nohs, minus) before the number. If the temperature is one degree, make sure *grado* is used in the singular, *un grado*. For example:

Menos cinco grados.
meh-nohs seen-koh grah-dohs
It's five below.

Hay una temperatura de cuarenta grados.
ah-yee oo-nah tehm-peh-rah-too-rah deh kwah-rehn-tah grah-dohs
It's forty degrees.

The Forecast Is...

You are reading the complimentary newspaper available at your hotel in Uruguay. You're curious about the weather and turn to that section. Study the symbols in the following table to help you interpret the symbols on a weather map. Learn what each symbol means. If you ever want to know the weather in the countries you visit (and you will), you're going to love this visual vocabulary.

Symbol	Weather Expression	Pronunciation	Meaning
	cielo claro	see-yeh-loh klah-roh	clear sky
	algo nubloso	ahl-goh noo-bloh-soh	slightly cloudy
	nubloso	noo-bloh-soh	cloudy
	inestable	een-ehs-tah-bleh	changeable
	lluvioso	yoo-bee-yoh-soh	rainy
	tormenta eléctrica	tohr-mehn-tah eh-lehk-tree-kah	electrical storm
	frente frío	frehn-teh free-yoh	cold front
	frente cálido	frehn-teh kah-lee-doh	warm front
	frente estacionario	frehn-teh ehs-tah-see-yoh-nah-ree-yoh	stationary front
	temperatura máxima	tehm-peh-rah-too-rah mahk-see-mah	maximum temperature

What Day Is It?

In the midst of a glorious vacation, do you ever have to pause for a moment to remember what day it is? It happens to me all the time. For me, the best part of vacation—besides the rest and relaxation—is that time is not of the essence, and I don't have to scurry to get things done. I become totally caught up in having fun, and every day seems like a Saturday.

Occasionally, because I don't want to miss my flight home, I ask "What day is it, anyway?" You might also want to keep track of what day it is so you don't end up at the attraction you are dying to see on a day it's closed. Study the days of the week in Table 13.2 to ensure that you get to do everything you want.

To say that something is happening "on" a certain day, the Spanish use the definite article *el*.

> El martes yo voy al centro.
> ehl mahr-tehs yoh boy ahl sehn-troh
> *On Tuesday(s) I go downtown.*

On what days do you go to the movies? go to the supermarket? do laundry? go out with friends? eat out?

Table 13.2 Days of the Week

Day of the Week	Spanish Translation	Pronunciation
Monday	lunes	loo-nehs
Tuesday	martes	mahr-tehs
Wednesday	miércoles	mee-yehr-koh-lehs
Thursday	jueves	hweh-behs
Friday	viernes	bee-yehr-nehs
Saturday	sábado	sah-bah-doh
Sunday	domingo	doh-meen-goh

The Best Month for a Visit

If your travels or business take you to Latin America, you can see why it's important to know the names of the months. You wouldn't want to sit by a pool in Argentina in July, and you couldn't indulge in winter sports in Peru in December. Make sure you plan your trip wisely. With one slip of the tongue, you could wind up being in the wrong place at the wrong time. Table 13.3 will help you identify the months .

Table 13.3 Months of the Year

Month of the Year	Spanish Translation	Pronunciation
January	enero	eh-neh-roh
February	febrero	feh-breh-roh
March	marzo	mahr-soh
April	abril	ah-breel
May	mayo	mah-yoh
June	junio	hoo-nee-yoh
July	julio	hoo-lee-yoh
August	agosto	ah-gohs-toh
September	septiembre	sehp-tee-yehm-breh
October	octubre	ohk-too-breh
November	noviembre	noh-bee-yehm-breh
December	diciembre	dee-see-yehm-breh

To express "in" a certain month, the Spanish use the preposition *en*, as follows:

> Vamos a España en julio.
> bah-mohs ah ehs-pah-nyah ehn hoo-lee-yoh
> *We are going to Spain in July.*

The Four Seasons

Keep in mind that in countries south of the Equator, the seasons are opposite those in the United Sates. Now some like it hot. They go to Spain in the summer or to Chile in the winter. Some like it cold. They go to Argentina in the summer and to Costa Rica in the winter. Whatever you like, make sure you plan your trip when the weather will be perfect. You don't want to worry about hurricanes, storms, or other adverse weather conditions. Table 13.4 gives you the names of the seasons.

Culture Corner

In tropical climes, it is customary to take an afternoon nap, *una siesta* (oo-nah see-yehs-tah), to avoid the intense midday heat. In some countries, small businesses close for the hottest part of the day and stay open extra hours into the evening. The word *siesta* evolved from *la sexta hora* (lah sehk-stah oh-rah), or high noon.

Table 13.4   The Seasons of the Year

Season of the Year	Spanish Translation	Pronunciation
winter	el invierno	ehl een-bee-yehr-noh
spring	la primavera	lah pree-mah-beh-rah
summer	el verano	ehl beh-rah-noh
autumn, fall	el otoño	ehl oh-toh-nyoh

To express "in" with the seasons, the Spanish use the preposition *en* + the definite article for all the seasons. Here's some wishful thinking to show you how it's done:

Voy a Puerto Rico en el invierno, en la primavera, en el verano, y en el otoño.
boy ah pwehr-toh ree-koh ehn ehl een-bee-yehr-noh, ehn lah pree-mah-beh-rah, ehn ehl beh-rah-noh, ee ehn ehl oh-toh-nyoh
I go to Puerto Rico in the winter, in the spring, in the summer, and in the fall.

In which season do you go to the beach? watch a football game? go on outdoor picnics? watch the leaves turn colors?

Memory Master

The names of months and days are not capitalized in Spanish except when they begin a sentence or refer to a holiday:

Febrero es un mes importante.
February is an important month.

Voy a la iglesia el Viernes Santo.
I go to church on Good Friday.

When You Have a Date

When you have a lot on your mind, it's common to lose track of the date. That might be why so many of us have watches designed to help us remember. If you're traveling for pleasure, one day seems to run into the next, and somewhere along the line the date often gets lost. When you do get around it, dates are expressed as follows:

➤ day of week + *el* + cardinal number + *de* + month + *de* + year

➤ The first day of each month is called *el primero*. Cardinal numbers are used for all other days.

el primero de enero
January 1st

el dos de febrero
February 2nd

➤ In Spanish, the year is expressed in thousands and hundreds, not in just hundreds as in English. In Spanish, for example, 1996 is expressed as *mil novecientos noventa y seis*.

➤ To express "on" with dates, use the definite article *el*.

Salgo el tres de mayo.
I'm leaving on May 3.

¡Atención!

After the day of the week, the *el* is disappearing from use before the number; however, it is not incorrect to use it: *lunes (el) once de julio de 1999.*

When the Spanish write a date in numbers, the sequence is day + month + year. This is the reverse of the month + day + year sequence we use. Notice how different this looks:

Spanish	English
el 22 de abril de 1977	April 22, 1977
22.4.77	4/22/77
el cinco de febrero de 1995	February 5, 1995
5.2.95	2/5/95

To get information about the date, you can ask the following questions:

¿Cuál es la fecha de hoy?
kwahl ehs lah feh-chah deh oy
What is today's date?

¿A cuántos estamos hoy?
ah kwahn-tohs ehs-tah-mohs oy
What's today's date?

¿Qué día es hoy?
keh dee-yah ehs oy
What day is today?

In a Flash

The new year has just begun, and you are starting to fill out your date book. Of course, some dates are especially important to you. Give the day and dates for these important events of the year: your birthday, a friend's birthday, Thanksgiving, New Year's, Mother's Day, Valentine's Day, Father's Day, and Memorial Day.

The answer to your question would be one of the following:

Hoy es lunes (el) primero de abril.
oy ehs loo-nehs pree-meh-roh deh ah-breel
Today is Monday, April 1.

Estamos a lunes (el) primero de abril.
ehs-tah-mohs ah loo-nehs pree-meh-roh deh ah-breel
Today is Monday, April 1.

Words and expressions commonly used with days, weeks, and months will help you schedule your time. Keep the expressions in Table 13.5 in mind when you make your plans.

Table 13.5 Time Expressions

Expression	Pronunciation	Meaning
en	ehn	in
hace	ah-seh	ago
por	pohr	per
durante	doo-rahn-teh	during
próximo(a)	prohk-see-moh(mah)	next
último(a)	ool-tee-moh(mah)	last
pasado(a)	pah-sah-doh(dah)	last
la víspera	lah bees-peh-rah	eve
anteayer	ahn-teh-ah-yehr	day before yesterday
ayer	ah-yehr	yesterday
hoy	oy	today
mañana	mah-nyah-nah	tomorrow
pasado mañana	pah-sah-doh mah-nyah-nah	day after tomorrow
el día siguiente	ehl dee-yah see-gee-yehn-teh	the next day
desde	dehs-deh	from
de hoy en una semana	deh oy ehn oo-nah seh-mah-nah	a week from today
de mañana en dos semanas	deh mah-nyah-nah ehn dohs seh-mah-nahs	two weeks from tomorrow

The adjectives *próximo*, *último*, and *pasado* must agree with their noun in gender:

el próximo día	*the next day*
la próxima noche	*the next night*
el último año	*the last year*
la última hora	*the last hour*
el mes pasado	*the past month*
la semana pasada	*the past week*

Culture Corner

The word *mañana* can mean morning or tomorrow. It can also refer to an indefinite time in the future. Spanish speakers have a more relaxed attitude towards time than we do in the United States, and being on time is relative. Being late or doing something *mañana* is not considered rude; you're just allowing yourself a certain amount of luxury time.

What's the Date?

Imagine you are at an important business meeting in which you must use your Spanish to refer to certain past and future dates. If today is *el siete de agosto*, give the date for the following. (Answers can be found on page 414, in Appendix A.)

1. anteayer _____

2. de mañana en dos semanas _____

3. la víspera _____

4. mañana _____

5. de mañana en una semana _____

6. hace siete días _____

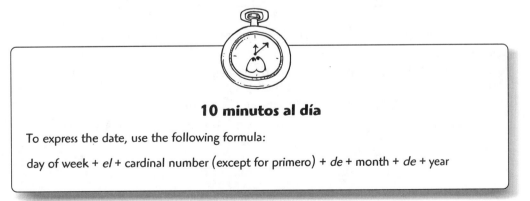

10 minutos al día

To express the date, use the following formula:

day of week + *el* + cardinal number (except for primero) + *de* + month + *de* + year

Give Me Good Weather

Don't you always pray for good weather when you travel? One time, when my husband and I were traveling, we found we were heading right into a potential hurricane. Luckily, we didn't give up and turn around, and the storm passed. Sometimes you have to go for it and give it your best shot. Study Table 13.6 to learn how to use the verb *dar* (dahr), which means "to give" and has an irregular *yo* form only.

Table 13.6   The Verb Dar (to Give)

The Conjugation of Dar	Pronunciation	Translation
yo doy	yoh doy	I give
tú das	too dahs	you give
él, ella, Ud. da	ehl, eh-yah, oo-stehd dah	he, she, you give(s)
nosotros damos	noh-soh-trohs dah-mohs	we give
vosotros dáis	boh-soh-trohs dah-yees	you give
ellos, ellas, Uds. dan	eh-yohs, eh-yahs, oo-stehd-ehs dahn	they, you give

Expressions with Dar

Imagine you are walking along the Paseo del Prado in Madrid. A young man approaches and says, "Quiero dar un paseo con Ud." Is this guy trying to make a pass at you? Before you give him *una bofetada* (oo-nah boh-feh-tah-dah), a slap, familiarize yourself with the following idioms with dar.

Table 13.7   Idioms with Dar

Idiom	Pronunciation	Meaning
dar a	dahr ah	to face
dar un abrazo	dahr oon ah-brah-soh	to hug
dar con	dahr kohn	to run into
dar de beber (comer)	dahr deh beh-behr (koh-mehr)	to give a drink (feed)
dar las gracias a	dahr lahs grah-see-yahs ah	to thank
dar un paseo	dahr oon pah-seh-yoh	to take a walk, to go for a ride

Idiom	Pronunciation	Meaning
dar recuerdos (a)	dahr rreh-kwehr-dohs (ah)	to give regards (to)
dar una vuelta	dahr oo-nah bwehl-tah	to take a stroll

Using Dar

Use the correct form of the verb *dar* to express what is going on with each of the following subjects. (Answers can be found on page 415, in Appendix A.)

1. (to take a stroll) Ellos

   _____.

2. (to give regards) Vosotros

   _____ a Ana.

3. (to thank) Nosotros_____ al hombre.

4. (to hug) Yo _____ a mi novio.

5. (to run into) Tú _____ con Julio en el parque.

Culture Corner

Part of the daily routine of Spanish life is the *paseo*, the stroll or walk, which usually takes place between the hours of 7 p.m. and 10 p.m. It provides an opportunity to socialize with family and friends.

During the *paseo*, it is common to stop for *tapas* (tah-pahs), or hors d'oeuvres. The snack is a necessity because work ends around 7:30 p.m. and dinner isn't served until 10 p.m.

10 minutos al día

The irregular verb *dar* is conjugated as follows:

yo doy	nosotros damos
tú das	vosotros dáis
él, ella, Ud. da	ellos, ellas, Uds. dan

The Least You Need to Know

➤ The names of the days, months, and seasons are generally not capitalized in Spanish.

➤ In Spanish, days and months are written in reverse order from what we are accustomed to (as in *el dos de enero*).

➤ The verb *dar*, to give, has an irregular *yo* form and is used in many different idiomatic expressions.

Chapter 14

Let's See the Sights

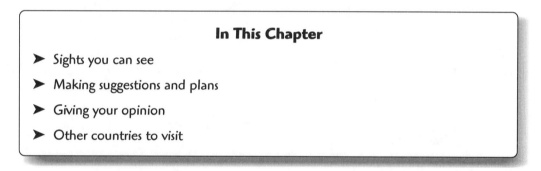

In This Chapter

➤ Sights you can see

➤ Making suggestions and plans

➤ Giving your opinion

➤ Other countries to visit

You've looked out the window and listened to the weather report for the day. You've consulted your guide book and decided what activities you'd like to have fun doing. The next step is to take out a map of the city and locate some important tourist attractions. Plan your itinerary so you don't have to run back and forth across town wasting time instead of having fun.

This chapter presents interesting places to visit and a wide variety of things to do in Spanish-speaking countries. In no time flat, you'll develop the proficiency you need to make suggestions and plans and to give your impressions and opinions. Because there are so many countries you might choose to visit, you'll also learn the Spanish names of the most popular ones.

Super Sights

Do you have a Type-A personality? Are you a super-active person who loves to fly from one activity to the next? Or are you the laid-back, mellow Type B, who just feels like relaxing and soaking up the sun? Whatever your preference, Spanish-speaking countries offer a variety of things to do and see. Travel brochures available at hotels and tourist offices propose countless suggestions. When you're ready to make a decision, consult Table 14.1, which lists common activities and sites.

Table 14.1 Where to Go and What to Do

El Lugar	The Place	La Actividad	The Activity
el acuario	the aquarium	ver los peces	see the fish
la arena	the ring	ver la corrida de toros	see the bullfights
el estadio	the stadium	ver la corrida de toros	see the bullfights
el carnaval	the carnival	mirar el desfile, las carrozas	look at the parade, floats
el castillo	the castle	ver los cuartos	see the rooms
la catedral	the cathedral	ver las vidrieras	see the stained glass windows
el circo	the circus	ver los espectáculos	see the shows
el club	the nightclub	ver un espectáculo	see a show
la feria	the fair	mirar las exposiciones	look at the exhibits
la fuente	the fountain	mirar el chorro de agua	look at the spray of water
la iglesia	the church	ver la arquitectura	see the architecture
el museo	the museum	ver las pinturas, las esculturas	see the paintings, sculptures
el parque de atracciones	amusement park	montar en los tiovivos	go on the rides

Culture Corner

Bullfighting is a colorful event that usually takes place in large Spanish cities on Sunday afternoons and on important holidays from March to October. You can purchase tickets through your hotel, at the *plaza de toros,* or at the official city box office in Madrid.

What Shall We See?

Are you off to the Prado to see the famous artwork? Or are you really curious about bullfighting? Perhaps you want to admire the stained glass windows of a famous church or the statues in a public square. To express what you would like to see, use the irregular verb *ver* (to see) presented in Table 14.2. *Ver* is an easy verb to learn because it is only irregular in the *yo* form (an extra *e* is added). All other forms follow the rules for regular -*er* verbs.

Table 14.2   The Verb Ver (to See)

Conjugated Form of Ver	Pronunciation	Meaning
yo veo	yoh beh-yoh	I see
tú ves	too behs	you see
él, ella, Ud. ve	ehl, eh-yah, oo-stehd beh	he, she, you see(s)
nosotros vemos	nohs-oh-trohs beh-mohs	we see
vosotros véis	bohs-oh-trohs beh-yees	you see
ellos, ellas, Uds. ven	eh-yohs, eh-yahs, oo-stehd-ehs behn	they see

10 minutos al día

The *irregular* verb *ver* is conjugated as follows:

yo veo	nosotros vemos
tú ves	vosotros véis
él, ella, Ud. ve	ellos, ellas, Uds. ven

Take Me to the Zoo!

Take a look at these ads for zoos and figure out the following. (Answers can be found on page 415, in Appendix A.)

1. Which one is in Madrid? _____
2. Which is closest to Madrid? _____
3. Which is farthest from Madrid? _____
4. Which is open all year? _____
5. Which are open every day? _____
6. In which can you have a picnic? _____
7. In which do the animals roam free? _____

PARQUE ZOOLÓGICO DEL BOSQUE

ABIERTO TODO EL AÑO

GRAN PARQUE NATURAL

PICNIC

25 KM DE MADRID

PARQUE ZOOLÓGICO DE MADRID

Abierto todos los días

Restaurante - Picnic

Autobús 46 - 86 - 92

Consúltenos por favor

PARQUE ZOOLÓGICO DEL CASTILLO

800 Animales en Libertad

Abierto todos los días

40 Km de Madrid

Consulte las páginas amarillas

Suggest Away!

Have you always had your heart set on a romantic second honeymoon in Cancún? The seductive brochures, the enticing ads, and your friends' pictures have convinced you that this is a vacation spot you'd really enjoy. How will your spouse feel about this? Will your enthusiasm be shared? Here's how to find out.

One way to make a suggestion in Spanish is to ask this simple question:

¿Por qué no? + a verb in the nosotros form

For example:

> ¿Por qué no vamos a Cancún?
> pohr keh noh bah-mohs ah kahn-koon
> *Why don't we go to Cancún?*

> ¿Por qué no partimos mañana?
> pohr keh noh pahr-tee-mohs mah-nyah-nah
> *Why don't we leave tomorrow?*

You can also tell someone what you'd like to do and then ask how he or she feels about the idea. Of course, they might think you're a little pushy. But what the heck. Go for it!

> Quiero ir a Cancún.
> kee-yeh-roh eer ah kahn-koon
> *I want to go to Cancún.*

> ¿Qué piensa(s)?
> keh pee-yehn-sah(s)
> *What do you think?*

> ¿Qué cree(s)?
> keh kreh-yeh(s)
> *What do you think?*

Memory Master

When using the command form that expresses "Let's," the subject pronoun *nosotros* never is used.

To express the English "Let's," use the *nosotros* form of the irregular verb *ir + a* + the infinitive of the activity you are suggesting. For example:

Vamos a viajar a Cancún.	Vamos a partir mañana.
bah-mohs ah bee-yah-hahr ah	bah-mohs ah pahr-teer
kahn-koon	mah-nyah-nah
Let's travel to Cancún.	*Let's leave tomorrow.*

The other way to make a polite suggestion is to use the *nosotros* form of the present subjunctive tense. Although this sounds complicated, it really is quite simple. Just insert the letter that is the opposite of the infinitive ending, like you did with commands using *Ud.* For regular *-ar* verbs, change the *-a* ending to *-e.* For regular *-er* and *-ir* verbs, change the *-e* or *-i* ending to *-a.*

Viajemos a Cancún.	Partamos mañana.
bee-yah-heh-mohs ah kahn-koon	pahr-tah-mohs mah-nyah-nah
Let's travel to Cancun.	*Let's leave tomorrow.*

Making Suggestions

The weather is simply beautiful, and you're itching to go out and have a great time. Suggest five things you and I can do together. (Sample responses can be found on page 415, in Appendix A.)

Example: ¿Por qué no vamos al parque?
Quiero nadar en el mar.
¿Qué piensas?

_____

_____

_____

_____

_____

In a Flash

Look at today's weather. Make as many suggestions as you can in Spanish for appropriate activities for the day.

Other Useful Phrases

I bet you're thinking that asking for what you want is pretty easy. Now that you're feeling good about your progress, let's try a more colloquial approach. You can use a number of phrases, as shown in the following table. To complete your thought, just tack on the infinitive of the verb and maybe an object for the verb.

The familiar forms are in parentheses. Note the use of the polite pronoun *le* (to you) and the familiar pronoun *te* (to you) in some of the following expressions. These pronouns are used to ask about "you" and are placed before the verb. A more detailed explanation of these pronouns appears in Chapter 15, "A Shopping Spree."

Phrase	Pronunciation	Meaning
¿Que le (te) parece...?	keh leh (teh) pah-reh-seh	Do you want...?
¿Le (te) gustaría...?	leh (teh) goos-tah-ree-yah	Would you like...?
¿Tiene(s) ganas de...?	tee-yeh-neh(s) gah-nahs deh	Do you feel like...?
¿Quiere(s)...?	kee-yeh-reh(s)	Do you want...?

For example:

>¿Le (te) parece salir?
>*Do you want to go out?*

>¿Le (te) gustaría ir al cine?
>*Would you like to go to the movies?*

>¿Tiene(s) ganas de ver una corrida de toros?
>*Do you feel like going to a bullfight?*

>¿Quiere(s) mirar las exposiciones?
>*Do you want to see the exhibits?*

All the phrases in the preceding list can be made
negative by using *no*.

>¿No le (te) parece nadar?
>*Don't you want to swim?*

>¿No le (te) gustaría ir al cine?
>*Wouldn't you like to go to the movies?*

>¿No quiere(s) mirar las exposiciones?
>*Don't you want to see the exhibits?*

>¿No tiene(s) ganas de ver una corrida de toros?
>*Don't you feel like seeing a bullfight?*

Culture Corner

Madrid's Prado museum, which houses over 6,000 works of art by such renowned Spanish artists as Goya, Velázquez, El Greco, Murillo, and Zurbarán, is considered one of the most important art museums in the world. It's a must-see. If you want to see Picasso's *Guérnica*, however, you'll have to stop at the Reina Sofía Art Center.

Are you acquainted with any grouchy-from-lack-of-sleep teenagers who give abrupt yes or no answers to questions? The rest of us are usually more polite and say "Yes, but…" or "No, because…" In Spanish, if you'd like to elaborate on your answer, here's what you have to do: If you see the pronoun *le* or *te* (to you) in the question, simply use *me* (to me) before the verb in your answer to express how *you* feel.

Sí, me parece nadar. Sí, me gustaría ir al cine.
No, no me parece nadar. No, no me gustaría ir al cine.

For the other sentences, you can give the *yo* form of the verb in the present.

Sí, tengo ganas de ver una corrida de toros.
No, no tengo ganas de ver una corrida de toros.

Sí, quiero mirar las exposiciones.
No, no quiero mirar las exposiciones.

Memory Master

Use *me gusta* and *me encanta* when referring to one thing you like or adore. If there's more than one, use *me gustan* and *me encantan*.

Me gusta la música.
Me encantan las óperas.

What Do You Think?

Someone suggested an activity to you. How do you feel about it? Are you interested in pursuing it further? Does it have appeal? If the answer is yes, you might say:

Me gusta la música clásica.
meh goos-tah lah moo-see-kah klah-see-kah
I like classical music.

Me encanta la ópera.
meh ehn-kahn-tah lah oh-peh-rah
I adore the opera.

Soy aficionado(a) al arte.
soy ah-fee-see-yoh-nah-doh(ah) ahl ahr-teh
I'm an art fan.

To express what you like or dislike, use *(no) me gusta (me encanta)* + the singular noun or infinitive:

Me gusta (encanta) el español.
I like (adore) Spanish.

Me gusta (encanta) hablar español.
I like to speak (adore speaking) Spanish.

You also can use *(no) me gustan (me encantan)* + the plural noun. Use (no) me gusta (me encanta) with infinitives.

No me gustan (encanta) los libros.
I don't like (adore) the books.

No me gusta (encanta) bailar y cantar.
I don't like (adore) dancing and singing.

10 minutos al día

To make a suggestion using the English "Let's," use the *nosotros* form of *ir* (*vamos*) + a + the infinitive of the action you're suggesting:

Vamos a ver una película.

You may also use the *nosotros* form of the subjunctive. This requires using the opposite letter from the infinitive ending: *-a* becomes *-e*, and *-e* and *-i* become *-a*:

Trabajemos.   Comamos.

Suppose you've tried something totally out of character. Chances are, you'll want to express what you think of the activity. Was it fun? Did you really enjoy it? You can give a positive opinion by using *es* (ehs) followed by an adjective, such as *Es excelente*, or "It's excellent." The following table provides a list of adjectives to help you describe the fun you can have in Spanish-speaking countries.

Adjective	Pronunciation	Meaning
estupendo	ehs-too-pehn-doh	stupendous
fenomenal	feh-noh-meh-nahl	phenomenal
excelente	ehk-seh-lehn-teh	excellent
magnífico	mag-nee-fee-koh	magnificent
fantástico	fahn-tahs-tee-koh	fantastic
terrífico	teh-rree-fee-koh	terrific
sensacional	sehn-sah-see-yoh-nahl	sensational
maravilloso	mah-rah-bee-yoh-soh	marvelous
divertido	dee-behr-tee-doh	fun
regio	rreh-hee-yoh	great
fabuloso	fah-boo-loh-soh	fabulous
de película	deh peh-lee-koo-lah	out of this world
bárbaro	bahr-bah-roh	awesome
extraordinario	ehks-trah-ohr-dee-nah-ree-yoh	extraordinary

Maybe the activity is totally unappealing to you. Perhaps you find it boring. Use the following phrases to express your dislikes.

Phrase	Pronunciation	Meaning
No me gusta...	noh meh goos-tah	I don't like...
Odio..., Detesto...	oh-dee-yoh, deh-tehs-toh	I hate...
No soy aficionado(a)...	noh soy ah-fee-see-yoh-nah-doh(ah)	I'm not a fan of...

Memory Master

Remember that, when you use the phrase *Soy aficionado(a) a...*, *a* contracts with *el* to become *al*.

Soy aficionada al ballet.

The following example sentences describe a few activities some people might not enjoy:

No me gusta la música clásica.

Odio (Detesto) la ópera.

No soy aficionado(a) al arte.

Are you the type of person who will try anything once? Maybe something you tried just wasn't your cup of tea. If you want to give a negative opinion about an activity, you might say *"Es aburrido,"* or "It's boring." Here is a list of adjectives you could use to describe something you don't like.

Adjective	Pronunciation	Meaning
aburrido	ah-boo-rree-doh	boring
asqueroso	ahs-keh-roh-soh	loathsome
feo	feh-yoh	ugly
un horror	oon oh-rrohr	a horror
un desastre	oon dehs-ahs-treh	a disaster
desagradable	dehs-ah-grah-dah-bleh	disgusting
terrible	teh-rree-bleh	terrible
tonto	tohn-toh	silly
horrible	oh-rree-bleh	horrible
ridículo	rree-dee-koo-loh	ridiculous

In a Flash

Look at the movies listed in your local newspaper. Give your opinion of as many as you can. Do the same for the television programs listed.

Your Sentiments, Exactly

Do you see things as either black or white or with shades of gray? Personally, I'm a very opinionated person—I love it or I hate it. Rarely is there an in-between. I love the ballet because I like to picture myself as one of the dancers—beautiful, lean, and in the best of shape. I hate the opera. It's just not my thing. The music's too loud, and I don't understand what they're saying. Tell how you feel about the following activities. Don't be afraid to speak up. (Sample responses can be found on page 415, in Appendix A.)

1. bullfight _____.
2. movies _____.
3. castles _____.
4. the circus _____.
5. aquarium _____.
6. museums _____.
7. amusement parks _____.

The World Beyond

You might be having a wonderful time in Spain and then, all of a sudden, decide you'd like to see other parts of the world. You'll need to know the names of the countries you want to visit to make your travel plans. If you can't distinguish *Suiza* (Switzerland) from *Suecia* (Sweden), you could wind up eating smorgasbord in Stockholm rather than chocolate fondue in the Alps. The Spanish names of various countries are listed in Table 14.3. The continents are in Table 14.4.

Table 14.3   Countries

Country	Spanish Translation	Pronunciation
Austria	Austria	ow-stree-yah
Belgium	Bélgica	behl-hee-kah
Belize	Belice	beh-lee-seh
Canada	Canadá	kah-nah-dah
Chile	Chile	chee-leh
China	China	chee-nah
Dominican Republic	la República Dominicana	lah reh-poo-blee-kah doh-mee-nee-kah-nah
England	Inglaterra	een-glah-teh-rrah
France	Francia	frahn-see-yah
Germany	Alemania	ah-leh-mah-nee-yah
Greece	Grecia	greh-see-yah
Haiti	Haití	ah-yee-tee
Italy	Italia	ee-tahl-ee-yah

continues

Table 14.3   Continued

Country	Spanish Translation	Pronunciation
Japan	Japón	hah-pohn
Mexico	México	meh-hee-koh
Netherlands	los Países Bajos	lohs pah-yee-sehs bah-hohs
Panama	Panamá	pah-nah-mah
Peru	Perú	peh-roo
Russia	Rusia	rroo-see-yah
Spain	España	ehs-pah-nyah
Sweden	Suecia	soo-weh-see-yah
Switzerland	Suiza	soo-wee-sah
United States	los Estados Unidos	lohs ehs-tah-dohs oo-nee-dohs

In Spanish, names of countries are not preceded by the definite article (*el, la, los,* or *las*). The exceptions are *El Salvador* and *La Républica Dominicana* because *El* and *La* are part of the countries' names. Do not make a contraction of *a* + *el* when speaking about El Salvador. For example:

Voy a Argentina.

Voy a El Salvador.

Table 14.4   The Continents

Continent	Spanish Translation	Pronunciation
Africa	África	ah-free-kah
Antarctica	Antártica	ahn-tahr-tee-kah
Asia	Asia	ah-see-yah
Australia	Australia	ow-strah-lee-yah
Europe	Europa	eh-yoo-roh-pah
North America	Norte América, América del Norte	nohr-teh ah-meh-ree-kah, ah-meh-ree-kah dehl nohr-teh
South America	Sud América, América del Sur	sood ah-meh-ree-kah, ah-meh-ree-kah dehl soor

Going Places

Do you plan to go to Puerto Rico for your next vacation? Will you be staying with relatives who have a beach house in the Condado area? To say that you are going "to" or staying "in" another country or city, use the preposition *a*.

> Voy a Puerto Rico.
> boy ah pwehr-toh rree-koh
> *I am going to Puerto Rico.*

Where Are You From?

Can you tell whether an American comes from the Northeast or the South? Of course you can. The different regional accents are a dead give-away. Sometimes, people who speak the same language have difficulty understanding each other. One time, I asked someone to translate what a fellow traveler was saying, only to find out he was speaking to me in English, my native tongue! Always play it safe and avoid embarrassing moments by asking from where a person hails. Use the preposition *de* to express "from."

> Soy de Nueva York.
> soy deh noo-weh-bah yohrk
> *I'm from New York.*

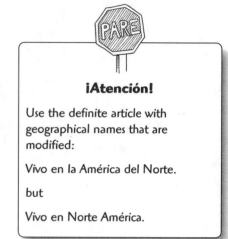

¡Atención!

Use the definite article with geographical names that are modified:

Vivo en la América del Norte.

but

Vivo en Norte América.

Where Are You Going?

Tell what country you are going to if you plan to see the following. Start your sentences with *Voy* (I'm going). (Answers can be found on page 415, in Appendix A.)

1. a bullfight _____
2. the Great Wall _____
3. Mexican jumping beans _____
4. the Moscow circus _____
5. the leaning Tower of Pisa _____
6. Big Ben _____
7. the Eiffel Tower _____
8. home _____

The Least You Need to Know

➤ There are several simple ways to suggest an activity in Spanish: *¿Por qué no?* + *nosotros; ¿Qué piensa(s)?* or *¿Qué cree(s)?;* and *ir a* + the infinitive.

➤ Simple phrases can express your likes (*¡Es fantástico!*) and dislikes (*¡Es horrible!*).

➤ It pays to learn your geography in the native language.

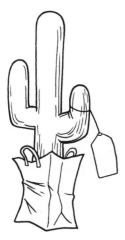

Chapter 15

A Shopping Spree

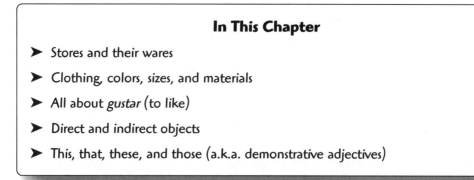

In This Chapter

➤ Stores and their wares

➤ Clothing, colors, sizes, and materials

➤ All about *gustar* (to like)

➤ Direct and indirect objects

➤ This, that, these, and those (a.k.a. demonstrative adjectives)

You've finally placed a check mark next to every tourist attraction on your "Don't Miss" list. It's time for a change. Why not concentrate on picking up some souvenirs for friends back home?

When I visit a foreign country, I try to bring back crafts that will remind me of my vacation for years to come. T-shirts, scarves, ashtrays, and wallets hold no appeal to me. Instead, give me a wide-brimmed Mexican sombrero and a multicolored serape, a set of ornate Spanish maracas, a painted mask from Puerto Rico, a carved stone statue from the Dominican Republic, or a simple doll made from hemp. No matter what your preference, this chapter can help you purchase items that will make you and your loved ones happy.

Stores Galore

It's been decided. Today you're going shopping. Will you join the crowds in the open markets, browse the small shops of local artisans, rub shoulders with the rich and famous in boutiques, or search out a large mall (*un centro comercial*, oon sehn-troh koh-mehr-see-yahl) where you can purchase anything and everything? Table 15.1 will help you find your way.

Table 15.1   Stores (Las Tiendas, lahs tee-yehn-dahs)

La Tienda	The Store	Las Mercancías	The Merchandise
la juguetería	toy store	los juguetes	toys
la librería	bookstore	los libros	books
la florería	florist	las flores	flowers
la tienda de ropa	clothing store	la ropa	clothing
el almacén	department store	por todo	almost everything
la tabaquería	tobacco store	el tabaco	tobacco
		los cigarillos	cigarettes
		los cigarros	cigars
		las pipas	pipes
		los fósforos	matches
		los encendedores	lighters
el quiosco de periódicos	newsstand	los periódicos	newspapers
		las revistas	magazines
la tienda de discos	record store	los discos	records
		los casetes	cassette tapes
		los CDs	compact discs
la joyería	jewelry store	las joyas	jewels
		los relojes	watches
		los collares	necklaces
		un anillo, una sortija	ring
		la pulsera	bracelet
		los aretes	earrings
la marroquinería	leather goods store	las carteras	wallets
		las bolsas	pocketbooks
		las maletas	suitcases
		las carteras	briefcases
la tienda de recuerdos	souvenir shop	las camisetas	T-shirts
		los carteles	posters
		los monumentos en miniatura	miniature monuments
		las máscaras	masks
		las pinturas	paintings

Gems and Jewels

You can get a good bargain on jewelry in some foreign countries because you can avoid local taxes and import duties. On our last trip to Puerto Rico, my husband purchased a beautiful gold necklace for me for my birthday. Before making our purchase, we went to several different stores to price gold by the ounce. When we found the best deal, we bargained with the sales clerk. It was, overall, a very friendly and amusing experience. Imagine how lucky I felt when I got home and saw a comparable piece in a discount store for almost twice the price. If you know your prices and are a good shopper, use Table 15.2 to get exactly what you want.

Memory Master

If you want to say that you are going to or will be at a store, remember to use *a* (to, at) + the definite article (*al*, *a la*), as in *al almacén*, *a la joyería*.

Table 15.2 Jewels (Las Joyas, lahs hoh–yahs)

Jewel	Spanish Translation	Pronunciation
amethyst	la amatista	lah ah-mah-tees-tah
aquamarine	el aguamarina	ehl ah-gwah-mah-ree-nah
diamond	el diamante	ehl dee-yah-mahn-teh
emerald	la esmeralda	lah ehs-meh-rahl-dah
ivory	el marfil	ehl mahr-feel
jade	el jade	ehl hah-deh
onyx	el ónix	ehl oh-neeks
pearls	las perlas	lahs pehr-lahs
ruby	el rubí	ehl rroo-bee
sapphire	el zafiro	ehl sah-fee-roh
topaz	el topacio	ehl toh-pah-see-yoh
turquoise	la turquesa	lah toor-keh-sah

If you are buying jewelry, you might want to ask the following questions:

¿Es oro macizo?　　　　　　　　¿Es plata?
ehs oh-roh mah-see-soh　　　　　ehs plah-tah
Is it solid gold?　　　　　　　　*Is it silver?*

Clothing

Maybe you're curious about Spanish fashions and have decided to try your luck at buying a typical item of clothing. Perhaps you'll choose a T-shirt, or maybe you've always craved a big sombrero to protect you from the sun. Whatever you decide to buy, Table 15.3 will help you in your quest for something *a la última moda* (ah lah ool-tee-mah moh-dah), in the latest style, or *tradicional* (trah-dee-see-oh-nahl), traditional.

Table 15.3   Clothing (La Ropa, lah roh–pah)

Piece of Clothing	Spanish Translation	Pronunciation
bathing suit	el traje de baño	ehl trah-heh deh bah-nyoh
bikini	el bikini	ehl bee-kee-nee
string bikini	la tanga	lah tahn-gah
belt	el cinturón	ehl seen-too-rohn
bikini briefs	los calzoncillos	lohs kahl-sohn-see-yohs
boots	las botas	lahs boh-tahs
gloves	los guantes	lohs gwahn-tehs
handkerchief	el pañuelo	ehl pah-nyoo-weh-loh
hat	el sombrero	ehl sohm-breh-roh
jacket	la chaqueta, el saco	lah chah-keh-tah, ehl sah-koh
jeans	los jeans, los vaqueros	lohs geens, lohs bah-keh-rohs
jogging suit	el traje de trotar la sudadera	ehl trah-heh deh troh-tahr lah soo-dah-deh-rah
overcoat	el abrigo	ehl ah-bree-goh
pajamas	las pijamas	lahs pee-hah-mahs
pants	los pantalones	lohs pahn-tah-loh-nehs
pullover	el jersey	ehl hehr-see
raincoat	el impermeable	ehl eem-pehr-meh-yah-bleh
robe	la bata	lah bah-tah
sandals	las sandalias	lahs sahn-dah-lee-yahs
scarf	la bufanda	lah boo-fahn-dah
shoes	los zapatos	lohs sah-pah-tohs
shorts	los pantalones cortos	lohs pahn-tah-loh-nehs kohr-tohs
sneakers	los tenis	lohs teh-nees
socks	los calcetines	lohs kahl-seh-tee-nehs
sweater	el suéter	ehl sweh-tehr

Piece of Clothing	Spanish Translation	Pronunciation
T-shirt	la camiseta, la playera	lah kah-mee-seh-tah, lah plah-yeh-rah
umbrella	el paraguas	ehl pah-rah-gwahs
underwear	la ropa interior	lah rroh-pah een-teh-ree-yohr
vest	el chaleco	ehl chah-leh-koh

Because most countries use the metric system, their sizes are different from ours. Look at the following conversion chart to determine the sizes you would wear.

CONVERSION TABLES FOR CLOTHING SIZES

WOMEN												
SHOES												
American	4	$4\frac{1}{2}$	5	$5\frac{1}{2}$	6	$6\frac{1}{2}$	7	$7\frac{1}{2}$	8	$8\frac{1}{2}$	9	$9\frac{1}{2}$	10
Continental	35	35	36	36	37	37	38	38	39	39	40	40	41
DRESSES, SUITS												
American	8	10	12	14	16	18						
Continental	36	38	40	42	44	46						
BLOUSES, SWEATERS												
American	32	34	36	38	40	42						
Continental	40	42	44	46	48	50						

MEN									
SHOES									
American	7	$7\frac{1}{2}$	8	$8\frac{1}{2}$	9	$9\frac{1}{2}$	10	$10\frac{1}{2}$	11	$11\frac{1}{2}$
Continental	39	40	41	42	43	43	44	44	45	45
SUITS, COATS									
American	34	36	38	40	42	44	46	48	
Continental	44	46	48	50	52	54	56	58	
SHIRTS									
American	14	$14\frac{1}{2}$	15	$15\frac{1}{2}$	16	$16\frac{1}{2}$	17	$17\frac{1}{2}$	
Continental	36	37	38	39	40	41	42	43	

In Spanish-speaking countries, there is a much more formal relationship between a sales person and a customer than we are accustomed to in the United States. Sales people are always courteous, respectful, and attentive, but they are more reserved. In smaller neighborhood stores, of course, the atmosphere is more friendly. If you are shopping and want to make sure you get the right size shoes or clothing, use one of the following phrases:

In a Flash

Look in your closet. Give the sizes for all your clothes and shoes in Spanish.

Llevo el tamaño...
yeh-boh ehl tah-mah-nyoh
I wear...

Mi talla es...
mee tah-yah ehs
My size is...

pequeño
peh-keh-nyoh
small

pequeña
peh-keh-nyah
small

mediano
meh-dee-yah-noh
medium

mediana
meh-dee-yah-nah
medium

grande
grahn-deh
large

grande
grahn-deh
large

When you make purchases in a foreign country, remember to save your receipts. Some countries refund sales tax, or value-added tax (VAT), to foreign visitors. In Spain, a seven percent VAT is added to the rates for all restaurants and hotel rooms. Look for rebate information in stores or at the airport before you leave the country.

Colors

When I look at the world, I usually describe things as red, yellow, green, blue, and so on. My sister Susan, on the other hand, *una artista*, talks about tangerine, burnt sienna, aubergine, and turquoise, and I rarely understand the shade she means. Let's keep things simple. Table 15.4 will help you with the basic colors you'll need in everyday situations.

Table 15.4   Colors (Los Colores, los koh-lohr-ehs)

Color	Spanish Translation	Pronunciation
beige	beige	beh-heh
black	negro	neh-groh
blue	azul	ah-sool
brown	marrón, pardo	mah-rrohn, pahr-doh
gray	gris	grees
green	verde	behr-deh
orange	anaranjado	ah-nah-rahn-hah-doh
pink	rosado	rroh-sah-doh
purple	púrpura, morado	poor-poo-rah, moh-rah-doh
red	rojo	rroh-hoh
white	blanco	blahn-koh
yellow	amarillo	ah-mah-ree-yoh

To describe a color as light, add the word *claro* (klah-roh) after the color. To describe a color as dark, add the word *oscuro* (oh-skoo-roh).

azul claro	verde oscuro
light blue	*dark green*

Colors are adjectives and must agree with the noun they are describing. Remember to change the ending from masculine to feminine as necessary if the adjective ends in -o. No change is necessary when the adjective ends in an -e or a consonant. All adjectives can be made plural by adding an -s, unless they already end in -s. If an adjective ends in a consonant, add -es to get the plural.

In a Flash

Make a list of all the new clothes you need. Be sure to include the color and material you prefer.

Materials

Do you bring along a travel iron, or do you hang your travel-wrinkled clothes in a steamy bathroom and hope for the best? Do you insist on permanent press, or do you prefer more exotic materials? If you plan to make a clothing purchase while on vacation, Table 15.5 will help you pick the right fabric.

Table 15.5 Materials (Las Telas, lahs teh-lahs)

Material	Spanish Translation	Pronunciation
cashmere	casimir	kah-see-meer
chiffon	gasa	gah-sah
corduroy	pana	pah-nah
cotton	algodón	ahl-goh-dohn
denim	tela tejana	teh-lah teh-hah-nah
flannel	franela	frah-neh-lah
gabardine	gabardina	gah-bahr-dee-nah
knit	tejido de punto	teh-hee-doh deh poon-toh
lace	encaje	ehn-kah-heh
leather	cuero	kweh-roh
linen	hilo	ee-loh
satin	raso	rrah-soh
silk	seda	seh-dah
suede	gamuza	gah-moo-sah
taffeta	tafetán	tah-feh-tahn
velvet	terciopelo	tehr-see-yoh-peh-loh
wool	lana	lah-nah

You're Putting Me On

Are you a clotheshorse, always making sure you appear in the latest styles? Or do you tend to stick to your comfy old jeans and T-shirts? Imagine you've found yourself in the following situations. Describe in detail (including jewelry) what you'd wear. (Sample responses can be found on page 416, Appendix A.)

1. to work: _____

    _____

2. to the beach: _____

    _____

3. to a formal dinner party: _____

    _____

4. to your friend's house: _____

    _____

5. to go skiing: _____

    _____

¡Atención!

Be careful! Some verbs such as *escuchar* (to listen to), *buscar* (to look for), *pagar* (to pay for), and *mirar* (to look at) take direct objects in Spanish because the English prepositions are built directly into the meaning of the Spanish verbs.

The Object of My Affection

I have an absolutely fabulous black dress. Imagine I am telling you about it: "I wear my black dress often. I put on my black dress to go to parties. I love my black dress." How tedious! It would be much easier to say: "I wear my black dress often. I put it on to go to parties. I love it."

What did I do to improve my conversation? I stopped repeating "my black dress" (a direct object noun) and replaced it with "it" (a direct object pronoun). What exactly are direct objects? Let's take a closer look.

Direct objects (which can be nouns or pronouns) answer the question "Whom or what is the subject of the sentence acting upon?" They can refer to people, places, things, or ideas, as follows:

I see the boy.   I like the dress.   He pays Jane, Mike, and me.
I see him.   I like it.   He pays us.

Direct object nouns can be replaced by the following direct object pronouns:

Direct Object Pronoun	Meaning
me (meh)	me
te (teh)	you (familiar)
le (leh)	you, him (used primarily in Spain)
lo (loh)	you, him, it (used primarily in Spanish America)
la (lah)	you, her, it
nos (nohs)	us
os (ohs)	you (familiar)
los (lohs)	them, you
las (lahs)	them, you (feminine)

Indirect objects can be replaced by indirect object pronouns. Take the story of my friend Marta, who is crazy about her new boyfriend, Paco. This is what she told me: "I write to Paco. Then I read my love letters to Paco. I buy presents for Paco. I bake cookies for Paco. I cook dinners for Paco." To get to the point more efficiently, all she had to say was: "I write to Paco and then I read him (to him) my love letters. I buy him (for him) presents. I bake him cookies (for him), and I cook him dinners (for him)."

How do indirect objects differ from direct objects? Take a closer look. Indirect objects answer the question: "To whom is the subject doing something?" or "For whom is the subject acting?"

I speak to the boys.
I speak to them.

I buy a gift for Mary.
I buy a gift for her.
I buy her a gift.

He gives (to) me a tie every Christmas.

Indirect objects only refer to people. Indirect object nouns can be replaced by indirect object pronouns. The Spanish preposition *a* (and the forms *al, a la, a los, a las*), meaning "to" or "for," indicates that an indirect object is needed.

Memory Master

In Spanish America, *lo* generally is used instead of *le* as the direct object to express "him" and "you."

Lo veo.
I see him (it).

Indirect Object Pronoun	Meaning
me (meh)	(to) me
te (teh)	(to) you (familiar)
le (leh)	(to) him, her, you, it
nos (nohs)	(to) us
os (ohs)	(to) you
les (lehs)	(to) them

The Personal A

The clue to the correct usage of an indirect object is the Spanish preposition *a* (and the forms *al, a la, a los, a las*) followed by the name of or reference to a person. The verb *telefonear* is always followed by *a* + indirect object. It, therefore, always takes an indirect object pronoun.

¿Le telefonea a Paco?
Are you calling Paco?

¿Le tefefonea?
Are you calling him?

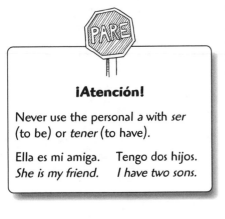

¡Atención!

Never use the personal *a* with *ser* (to be) or *tener* (to have).

Ella es mi amiga.   Tengo dos hijos.
She is my friend.   I have two sons.

This rule can be somewhat tricky because of the personal *a*. What is the personal *a*? It's the preposition *a* used before the direct object of the verb, if the direct object is a person, a pet, or a pronoun referring to a person. The personal *a* has no meaning and merely indicates a reference to a person.

Visito a mis amigos.
I visit my friends.

Queremos al perro.
We love the dog.

¿Ves a alguien?
Do you see someone?

Choose Your Words

To correctly choose between a direct or indirect pronoun, remember to see whether adding the word "to" or "for" makes sense in your sentence. If it does, choose an indirect object pronoun. If not, you must use the direct object pronoun. Look at the following English sentences:

I write (to) him love letters.

I buy (for) him presents.

Notice that the "to" or "for" often is understood but not used in English. Be careful in Spanish when choosing a direct or indirect object pronoun. If the words "to" or "for" make sense in the sentence even though they do not actually appear, use an indirect object pronoun.

You should have little problem using the direct or indirect object pronouns for "me"/ "to me" (*me*), "you"/"to you" (*te, nos*), or "us"/"to us" (*nos*) because these pronouns are exactly the same. You must be careful, however, when differentiating between "him" (her, it, you, them) and "to (for) him" (her, it, you, them) because there are now two sets of pronouns:

him (it, you)	*lo,le*	to him (it, you)	*le*
her (it, you)	*la*	to her (it, you)	*le*
them	*los, las*	to them	*les*

Sometimes this gets a bit tricky. Remember to choose the pronoun that reflects the number and gender of the noun to which you are referring.

Ella lleva el vestido rojo.	Él le habla a Ana.
Ella lo lleva.	Él le habla.
Él lleva la camisa blanca.	Él le habla a Pablo.
Él la lleva.	Él le habla.
Llevo mis zapatos negros.	Él les habla a Ana y Pablo.
Los llevo.	Él les habla.
Ellas llevan sandalias amarillas.	
Las llevan.	

The Position of Object Pronouns

Although we can automatically put object pronouns in their proper place in English, correct placement in Spanish does not follow English rules and requires some practice. Let's take a closer look:

➤ Object pronouns are normally placed before the verb.

Yo lo llevo.	Yo le hablo.
Yo no lo llevo.	Yo no le hablo.
¡No lo lleve!	¡No le hable!

➤ When direct and indirect object pronouns are used with an infinitive or a gerund (estar + *-ando, -iendo* endings), they can be placed before the verb or after it and attached to it.

Quiero llevarla.
La quiero llevar.

➤ When the gerund is followed by the object pronoun, count back three vowels and add an accent to obtain the proper stress.

Estoy llevándola.
La estoy llevando.

➤ In an affirmative command, the object pronoun follows the verb form and is attached to it. Again, count back three vowels and add an accent for proper stress. Note in the preceding example that, in a negative command, the object pronoun precedes the verb, as follows:

¡No lo (la) lleve!   ¡Llévela!

10 minutos al día

Direct and indirect object pronouns generally are placed before the conjugated verb.

With infinitives or gerunds (*estar* + *-ando* or *-iendo* endings), the pronoun can be placed either before the conjugated verb or after and attached to the infinitive or gerund. When the object pronoun is placed after the gerund, count back three vowels and add an accent mark.

For affirmative commands only, the object pronoun is placed after the command and attached to it. Again, count back three vowels and add an accent.

I Like It Like That

When you go on vacation, I hope you will enjoy everything, from the food you eat to your accommodations to the places you visit. To express that something is pleasing to you, use the verb *gustar*.

Translated literally, *gustar* means "to be pleasing to." You can't simply say "I like…" in Spanish. You must say "_____ is pleasing to me." The word "to" is very important. It instructs you to use an indirect object pronoun to get your point across. The verb *gustar* must agree with the noun because that word is the subject of the sentence. In general, the noun will be in either the third person singular (*él, ella, Ud.*) or plural (*ellos, ellas, Uds.*) form.

Les gusta el sombrero.
The hat is pleasing to them.
They like the hat.

In this example, *gusta* agrees with *sombrero*, which is the subject of the sentence.

> Le gustan las camisas.
> *The shirts are pleasing to him.*
> *He likes the shirts.*

Gustan agrees with *camisas*, which is the subject of the sentence.

Let's say you've gone shopping and have picked out some shirts you really love. The following sentences show how to express your likes:

> Me gusta la camisa.
> *I like the shirt.*
> *The shirt is pleasing to me.*

> Me gustan las camisas.
> *I like the shirts.*
> *The shirts are pleasing to me.*

Memory Master

If you want to specify who likes what, use the preposition *a* + the person's name before the *gustar* construction.

A Marta le gustan los casetes.
Marta likes the cassettes.

A Roberto y a Juan no les gusta la música.
Roberto and Juan don't like the music.

Don't let the reverse word order trick you. Pick the indirect object that expresses the person to whom the noun is pleasing. If you remember that the subject follows the verb *gustar*, you'll have little trouble. Let's take a look at a few more sentences to see how *gustar* works.

> ¿Te gusta el sombrero?
> *Do you like the hat?*

> Le gustan los zapatos.
> *He (She, You) likes (like) the shoes.*

> Nos gusta la falda.
> *We like the skirt.*

> No os gusta el traje.
> *You don't like the suit.*

> Les gusta la blusa.
> *They like the blouse.*

Two other verbs that work exactly like *gustar* are *encantar* (ehn-kahn-tahr), to like very much, and *faltar* (fahl-tahr), to lack, to need.

> Les encanta el abrigo.
> *They love the coat.*

> Me falta un vestido.
> *I need a dress.*

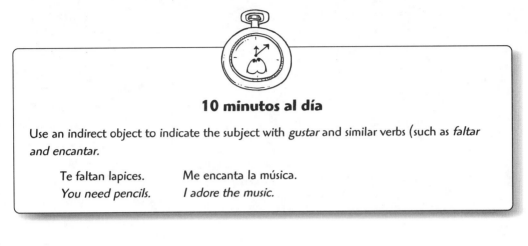

10 minutos al día

Use an indirect object to indicate the subject with *gustar* and similar verbs (such as *faltar* and *encantar*.

Te faltan lapices.   Me encanta la música.
You need pencils.   *I adore the music.*

I've Got It!

You and your friends have received many graduation gifts. Express how you feel about each one using the correct form of the verb in parenthesis. (Answers can be found on page 416, in Appendix A.)

1.   (encantar) Me _____ las joyas.

2.   (gustar) Nos _____ el reloj.

3.   (gustar) Te _____ los casetes.

4.   (encantar) Les _____ la ropa.

5.   (gustar) Le _____ los aretes.

6.   (gustar) Me _____ la cartera.

Putting Gustar to Work

Imagine your traveling companion has spent the day alone shopping. Upon arriving home, he unwraps all his purchases to get your opinion. If you don't like it, it's going back. Tell whether you like or dislike the following items. (Answers can be found on page 416, in Appendix A.)

1. The red hat _____ .
2. The small shirt _____ .
3. The big T-shirt _____ .
4. The green shoes _____ .

Using Direct Object Pronouns

Imagine you are on a shopping spree in the Galerías Preciadas department store in Spain, and your arms are loaded with all your finds. Your friend joins you and questions your choices. Answer all his questions using a direct object pronoun. (Answers can be found on page 416, in Appendix A.)

1. ¿Compras el pantalón azul? _____ .
2. ¿Quieres los guantes negros? _____ .
3. ¿Escoges la corbata roja? _____ .
4. ¿Tomas las camisas blancas? _____ .
5. ¿Consideras el traje de baño verde? _____ .
6. ¿Detestas los zapatos amarillos? _____ .

Using Indirect Object Pronouns

Your friend doesn't know what to buy her friends and family members as gifts. Offer some advice. (Sample responses can be found on page 416, in Appendix A.)

Example: Pablo/un radio/un libro
Cómprele un radio.
No le compre un libro.

sus hijos/camisas/corbatas
Cómpreles una camisa.
No les compre corbatas.

1. Roberto/abrigo/chaqueta

   _____

   _____

2. sus hermanas/vestidos/faldas

   _____

   _____

3. sus padres/sombreros/guantes

   _____

   _____

4. su amiga/una camiseta/una bolsa

   _____

   _____

5. sus amigos/casetas/discos

   _____

   _____

6. su abuela/una pulsera/un reloj

   _____

   _____

You Want It? Ask for It!

Do you get annoyed when a sales clerk hovers over your shoulder as you examine the merchandise? Or do you crave the assistance of someone in the know? Here are some phrases to help you deal with common shopping situations. Upon entering a store, an employee might ask you the following:

¿En qué puedo servirle?
ehn keh pweh-doh sehr-beer-leh
How may I help you?

¿Qué desea?
keh deh-seh-yah
What would you like?

¿Los están atendiendo?
lohs ehs-tahn ah-tehn-dee-yehn-doh
Is someone helping you?

If you are just browsing, you would answer:

No, gracias. Simplemente estoy buscando.
noh grah-see-yahs seem-pleh-mehn-teh ehs-toy boos-kahn-doh
No, thank you, I am (just) looking.

If you want to see or buy something, you would answer:

Sí, estoy buscando un (una) _____ por favor.
see ehs-toy boos-kahn-doh oon (oo-nah) _____ pohr fah-bohr
Yes, I'm looking for a _____ please.

Of course, if you're a shopper like me, you'd want to know:

¿Hay ventas (gangas)?
ah-yee behn-tahs (gahn-gahs)
Are there any sales?

¿Hay rebajas (descuentos)?
ah-yee rreh-bah-hahs (dehs-kwehn-tohs)
Are there any discounts?

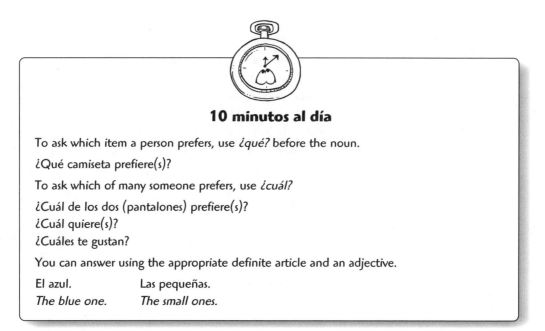

10 minutos al día

To ask which item a person prefers, use *¿qué?* before the noun.

¿Qué camiseta prefiere(s)?

To ask which of many someone prefers, use *¿cuál?*

¿Cuál de los dos (pantalones) prefiere(s)?
¿Cuál quiere(s)?
¿Cuáles te gustan?

You can answer using the appropriate definite article and an adjective.

El azul.   *Las pequeñas.*
The blue one.   *The small ones.*

Expressing Opinions

That shirt is you. You just love those pants. What a perfect jacket! If you are happy with an item, you can express your pleasure using one of the following phrases:

Phrase	Pronunciation	Meaning
Me gusta(n) (mucho).	meh goos-tah(n) (moo-choh)	I like it (them) (a lot).
Me queda muy bien.	meh keh-dah mwee bee-yehn	It suits (fits) me very well.
Me queda perfectamente.	meh keh-dah pehr-fehk-tah-mehn-teh	It suits (fits) me perfectly.
Está(n) bien.	ehs-tah(n) bee-yehn	It's nice.
Es elegante.	ehs eh-leh-gahn-teh	It's elegant.
Es práctico(a).	ehs prahk-tee-koh(kah)	It's practical.
Siempre es bonito(a).	see-yehm-preh ehs boh-nee-toh(tah)	It's always attractive.

Face it! The cookies you ate all winter are showing on your hips. This is, of course, the fault of your clothing. If you are disappointed with the way you look, you might use one of the following comments:

Phrase	Pronunciation	Meaning
No me gusta(n).	noh meh goos-tah(n)	I don't like it (them).
No me queda bien.	noh meh keh-dah bee-yehn	It doesn't suit (fit) me.
Es horrible.	ehs oh-rree-bleh	It's horrible.
Es pequeño(a).	ehs peh-keh-nyoh(nyah)	It's small.
Es apretado(a).	ehs ah-preh-tah-doh(dah)	It's tight.
Es corto(a).	ehs kohr-toh(tah)	It's short.
Es largo(a).	ehs lahr-goh(gah)	It's long.
Es chillón(ona).	ehs chee-yohn(yoh-nah)	It's loud.
Es estrecho(a).	ehs ehs-treh-choh(chah)	It's narrow.

If you're not satisfied and you want something else, use the following:

> Estoy buscando algo más (menos) + *adjective*
> ehs-toy boos-kahn-doh ahl-goh mahs (meh-nohs)
> *I'm looking for something more (less)…*

If something is "too" long or short, simply add the adverb *demasiado* (deh-mah-see-yah-doh) before the adjective:

> Es demasiado corto.
> *It's too small.*

Remember to change verbs and adjectives to accommodate plural subjects. Adverbs do not need to agree in Spanish; therefore, the adverb *demasiado* (too) does not change.

Los pantalones son demasiado cortos.
La blusa es demasiado apretada.

I'll Take This, That, and Some of Those

When I go shopping, I want a consultant. I either bring along a friend or I rely on the opinion of a well-put-together salesperson. It's common practice to ask how this shirt, that blouse, these pants, or those skirts look on the person buying them. A demonstrative adjective points out someone or something being referred to and allows you to be specific by expressing this, that, these, and those, as shown in Table 15.7.

Table 15.7 Demonstrative Adjectives

Demonstrative Adjective	Masculine	Feminine
this	este	esta
these	estos	estas
that (near speaker)	ese	esa
those (near speaker)	esos	esas
that (away from speaker)	aquel	aquella
those (away from speaker)	aquellos	aquellas

Notice that the demonstrative adjective you choose depends on how close the noun is to the subject.

➤ *Este* (*esta*, and so on) refers to someone or something near or directly concerning the speaker.

> Este vestido es bonito.
> *This dress is pretty.*

> Estos relojes son caros.
> *These watches are expensive.*

➤ *Ese* (*esa*, and so on) refers to someone or something not particularly near or not directly concerning the person being addressed.

> Ese hombre es guapo.
> *That man is handsome.*

> Esas bufandas son baratas.
> *Those scarves are inexpensive.*

Memory Master

The tags *aquí* (here), *ahí* or *allí* (there), and *allá* (over there) are used respectively with *este*, *ese*, and *aquel*.

Me gusta esta falda aquí.
I like this skirt here.

No le encantan esos zapatos allí.
He doesn't love those shoes there.

Nos falta aquel libro allá.
We need that book (over) there.

➤ *Aquel* (*aquella*, and so on) refers to someone or something quite remote from both the speaker and the person being addressed and that concerns neither of them directly.

> Aquel país es grande.   Aquella ciudad es bella.
> *That country is big.*   *That city is beautiful.*

What Do You Think?

Look at the gifts your friends bought. Using the demonstrative adjectives you've just learned, express how you feel about them. Give as much detail as possible. (Sample responses can be found on page 416, in Appendix A.)

The Least You Need to Know

➤ To shop successfully in a Spanish-speaking country, you must use the local system for sizing and measuring.

➤ Use object pronouns to replace object nouns. Object pronouns are usually placed before the conjugated verb, except in affirmative commands when they come after the verb.

➤ Use an indirect object pronoun with *gustar* to express who is doing the liking. The object that pleases is the subject of the sentence, and *gustar* must agree with it.

➤ Demonstrative adjectives (*este, ese, aquel*) must agree in number and gender with the nouns they describe. Use *este* for nouns that are closest, *ese* for nouns that are farther, and *aquel* for nouns that are the farthest from the speaker and the person being addressed.

Chapter 16

A Home-Cooked Meal

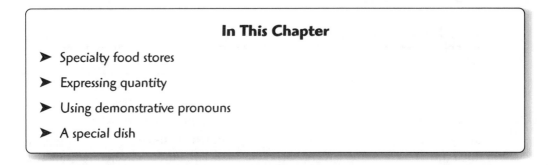

In This Chapter

➤ Specialty food stores

➤ Expressing quantity

➤ Using demonstrative pronouns

➤ A special dish

You've been shopping all day, and you've picked up some great souvenirs. Armed with your metric conversion charts, you even were able to select some fabulous native fashions in the correct sizes. Shopping 'til you drop really works up a voracious appetite. Dinner's not until after 7 p.m., and it's only 4:30 p.m. now. How should you proceed to ease that rumbling in your stomach?

One great idea is to drop into a local grocery store or specialty food store and grab something yummy to tide you over until your next meal. Why not try *un taco* filled with meat, *una tortilla* topped with *salsa verde*, or a pastry. Many different food choices are presented in this chapter. You'll also learn how to get the quantity you desire. This is important because the Spanish system of weights differs from ours. There's something special, too, at the end of the chapter.

Culture Corner

Although supermercados (soo-pehr-mehr-kah-dohs) and even hípermercados (ee-pehr-mehr-kah-dohs)—large specialty stores that sell food and other items—exist in Spain and Latin America, many shoppers still prefer to buy fresh produce in smaller specialty stores. They feel the quality is superior.

Shopping Around

When I travel, the height of luxury for me is having a refrigerator stocked with drinks and snacks in my room. No matter where I'm traveling, after I reach my destination and unpack, the first thing I do is scout out the nearest food supply and stock up. If you get the midnight munchies, come to my room. I'm always well supplied with native drinks and delicacies. If there's a stove in my room, however, I usually ignore it. I don't cook on vacation, but perhaps this is something you enjoy doing. Purchase your favorite culinary delights from the shops listed in Table 16.1.

Table 16.1   Food Shops

The Store	La Tienda	Pronunciation
bakery	la panadería	lah pah-nah-deh-ree-yah
butcher shop	la carnicería	lah kahr-nee-seh-ree-yah
candy store	la confitería	lah kohn-fee-teh-ree-yah
dairy store	la lechería	lah leh-cheh-ree-yah
delicatessen	la salchichonería	lah sahl-chee-choh-neh-ree-yah
fish store	la pescadería	lah pehs-kah-deh-ree-yah
fruit store	la frutería	lah froo-teh-ree-yah
grocery store	la abacería	lah ah-bah-seh-ree-yah
liquor store	la tienda de licores	lah tee-yehn-dah deh lee-koh-rehs
pastry shop	la pastelería	lah pahs-teh-leh-ree-yah
supermarket	el supermercado	ehl soo-pehr-mehr-kah-doh

Depending on the country you're in, the word for grocery store can vary. You might see *una tienda de comestibles, una tienda de abarrotes, una aborrotería, una pulpería, una tienda de ultramarinos,* or *una bodega.* In Spain, a *bodega* is a store that sells only wine from barrels, so you won't be able to purchase any food there. When in doubt, go to the local *supermercado!*

Going Places

You've decided to purchase some goodies for your room so you can spend some quiet time snacking and relaxing. Off you go to the local stores. To tell someone where you're going, use the verb *ir* and the preposition *a* + the appropriate definite article (*al*, *a la*) to give the correct information.

Voy a la pastelería.   Voy a la salchichonería.
I'm going to the pastry shop.   *I'm going to the deli.*

Try it. Tell your traveling companion where you are going to buy the following. (Answers can be found on page 417, in Appendix A.)

1. vegetables _____ .

2. pastries _____ .

3. meat _____ .

4. fruits _____ .

5. fish _____ .

6. wine _____ .

7. candy _____ .

8. milk _____ .

Are you ready to try something new? It's always interesting to taste a specialty that's new to your palate. If you wanted to savor a typical food, would you try a fruit? a vegetable? a dessert? Do you prefer meat? fish? poultry? game? What foods (*alimientos*) tempt you? Tables 16.2 through 16.9 can help you select something you'll enjoy.

Table 16.2   At the Grocery Store

Vegetables	Las Legumbres	Pronunciation
asparagus	los espárragos	lohs ehs-pah-rrah-gohs
broccoli	el brécol	ehl breh-kohl
carrot	la zanahoriía	lah sah-nah-oh-ree-yah
corn	el maíz	ehl mah-yees
eggplant	la berenjena	lah beh-rehn-heh-nah
lettuce	le lechuga	lah leh-choo-gah

continues

Table 16.2   Continued

Vegetables	Las Legumbres	Pronunciation
mushroom	el champiñón	ehl chahm-pee-nyohn
onion	la cebolla	lah seh-boh-yah
pepper	la pimienta	lah pee-mee-yehn-tah
potato	la papa, la patata	lah pah-pah, lah pah-tah-tah
rice	el arroz	ehl ah-rrohs
spinach	la espinaca	lah ehs-pee-nah-kah
sweet potato	la papa dulce	lah pah-pah dool-seh
tomato	el tomate	ehl toh-mah-teh

Table 16.3   At the Fruit Store

Fruits	Las Frutas	Pronunciation
apple	la manzana	lah mahn-sah-nah
apricot	el albaricoque	ehl ahl-bah-ree-koh-keh
banana	la banana	lah bah-nah-nah
blueberry	el mirtilo	ehl meer-tee-loh
cherry	la cereza	lah seh-reh-sah
date	el dátil	ehl dah-teel
fig	el higo	ehl ee-goh
grape	la uva	lah oo-bah
grapefruit	la toronja	lah toh-rohn-hah
guava	la guayaba	lah gwah-yah-bah
lemon	el limón	ehl lee-mohn
mango	el mango	ehl mahn-goh
melon	el melón	ehl meh-lohn
orange	la naranja	lah nah-rahn-hah
peach	el melocotón	ehl meh-loh-koh-tohn
pear	la pera	lah peh-rah
pineapple	la piña	lah pee-nyah
raisin	la pasa	lah pah-sah
raspberry	la frambuesa, la mora	lah frahm-bweh-sah, lah moh-rah
strawberry	la fresa	lah freh-sah

Nuts	Las Nueces	Pronunciation
almond	la almendra	lah ahl-mehn-drah
chestnut	la castaña	lah kahs-tah-nyah
hazelnut	la avellana	lah ah-beh-yah-nah
walnut	la nuez	lah nwehs

Table 16.4 At the Butcher or Delicatessen

Meats	Las Carnes	Pronunciation
bacon	el tocino	ehl toh-see-noh
beef	la carne de vaca (res)	lah kahr-neh deh bah-kah (rehs)
ham	el jamón	ehl hah-mohn
lamb	la carne de cordero	lah kahr-neh deh kohr-deh-roh
liver	el hígado	ehl ee-gah-doh
pork	la carne de cerdo	lah kahr-neh deh sehr-doh
roast beef	el rosbíf	ehl rohs-beef
sausage	las salchichas	lahs sahl-chee-chahs
sweetbreads	las criadillas	lahs kree-yah-dee-yahs
veal	la carne de ternera	lah kahr-neh deh tehr-neh-rah

Fowl and Game	La Carne de Ave y de Caza	Pronunciation
chicken	el pollo	ehl poh-yoh
duck	el pato	ehl pah-toh
goose	el ganso	ehl gahn-soh
pigeon	la paloma	lah pah-loh-mah
quail	la codorniz	lah koh-dohr-nees
rabbit	el conejo	ehl koh-neh-hoh
turkey	el pavo	ehl pah-boh

Table 16.5 At the Fish Store

Fish and Seafood	El Pescado y los Mariscos	Pronunciation
clam	la almeja	lah ahl-meh-hah
crab	el cangrejo	ehl kahn-greh-hoh

continues

Table 16.5   Continued

Fish and Seafood	El Pescado y los Mariscos	Pronunciation
crawfish	la cigala	lah see-gah-lah
flounder	el lenguado	ehl lehn-gwah-doh
halibut	el halibut	ehl ah-lee-boot
herring	el arenque	ehl ah-rehn-keh
lobster	la langosta	lah lahn-gohs-tah
mussel	el mejillón	lah meh-hee-yohn
oyster	la ostra	lah ohs-trah
red snapper	el pargo colorado	ehl pahr-goh koh-loh-rah-doh
salmon	el salmón	ehl sahl-mohn
sardine	la sardina	lah sahr-dee-nah
scallops	las conchas de peregrino	lahs kohn-chahs deh peh-reh-gree-noh
shrimp	los camarones, las gambas	lohs kah-mah-roh-nehs, lahs gahm-bahs
sole	el lenguado	ehl lehn-gwah-doh
squid	el calamar	ehl kah-lah-mahr
swordfish	el pez espada	ehl pehs ehs-pah-dah
trout	la trucha	lah troo-chah
tuna	el atún	ehl ah-toon

Table 16.6   At the Dairy

Dairy Products	Productos Lácteos	Pronunciation
butter	la mantequilla	lah mahn-teh-kee-yah
cheese	el queso	ehl keh-soh
cream	la crema	lah kreh-mah
eggs	los huevos	lohs hweh-bohs
yogurt	el yogur	ehl yoh-goor

Table 16.7   At the Bakery and Pastry Shop

Breads and Desserts	Pan y Postres	Pronunciation
biscuit	el bizcocho	ehl bees-koh-choh
bread	el pan	ehl pahn

Breads and Desserts	Pan y Postres	Pronunciation
cake	el pastel	ehl pahs-tehl
cookie	la galletita	lah gah-yeh-tee-tah
custard (caramel)	la crema catalana (el flan)	lah kreh-mah kah-tah-lah-nah (ehl flahn)
marzipan	el marzapán	ehl mahr-sah-pahn
meringue	el merengue	ehl meh-rehn-geh
pie	el pastel	ehl pahs-tehl
pudding (cream)	la natilla	lah nah-tee-yah
rice pudding	el arroz con leche	ehl ah-rrohs kohn leh-cheh
rolls (sweet)	los panecillos (dulces)	lohs pah-neh-see-yohs (dool-sehs)
tart	la torta	lah tohr-tah

Table 16.8   At the Candy Store

Sweets	Los Dulces	Pronunciation
candy	los dulces	lohs dool-sehs
chocolate	el chocolate	ehl choh-koh-lah-teh
gum	el chicle	ehl chee-kleh

Serious Shopping

Tell where you would go to purchase the following items. (Answers can be found on page 417, in Appendix A.)

1. _____   2. _____   3. _____   4. _____   5. _____

213

Table 16.9   At the Supermarket

Drinks	Las Bebidas	Pronunciation
cider	la sidra	lah see-drah
coffee (iced)	el café (helado)	ehl kah-feh (eh-lah-doh)
hot chocolate	el chocolate	ehl choh-koh-lah-teh
juice	el jugo	ehl hoo-goh
lemonade	la limonada	lah lee-moh-nah-dah
milk	la leche	lah leh-cheh
milk shake	el batido de leche	ehl bah-tee-doh deh leh-cheh
milk, malted	la leche malteada	lah leh-cheh mahl-teh-yah-dah
orangeade	la naranjada	lah nah-rahn-hah-dah
punch	el ponche	ehl pohn-cheh
soda	la gaseosa	lah gah-seh-yoh-sah
tea (iced)	el té (helado)	ehl teh (eh-lah-doh)
tonic water	el tónico	ehl toh-nee-koh
water	el agua	ehl ah-gwah
mineral	mineral	mee-neh-rahl
carbonated	con gas	kohn gahs
non-carbonated	sin gas	seen gahs
wine	el vino	ehl bee-noh

In a Flash

Label the foods in your refrigerator. Keep the labels on until you learn the names of your favorite foods. Remove the labels and practice naming what's on hand.

Take a Break

You've done some serious food shopping, and you deserve a break. Maybe you'll stop for a nice cup of coffee, a popular drink in Spanish-speaking countries throughout the world. Try a *café con leche* (kah-feh kohn leh-cheh), a cup of coffee topped with heated milk. American coffee, with just a little milk, is called *un cortado* (oon kohr-tah-doh).

On a hot day, sip *un blanco y negro* (oon blahn-koh ee neh-groh), a glass of iced coffee sweetened with sugar and topped with a scoop of vanilla ice cream. You also could try *un granizado de café* (ooh grah-nee-sah-doh deh kah-feh), iced coffee served over crushed ice. Maybe you'd like *un café solo* (oon kah-feh soh-loh) or *un exprés* (oon ehks-prehs), very strong black coffee served in a demitasse cup (what we refer to as *espresso*).

Also popular in Latin American countries are ice cold shakes made with tropical fruits. These are called *batidos* (bah-tee-dohs), *batidas* (bah-tee-dahs), or *licuados* (lee-kwah-dohs). All day and night, on the streets of every city and town, stands dispense these refreshing shakes. The main ingredients are fruit, milk, sugar, and crushed ice. If you want a really thick drink, a raw egg is added.

If you want to be specific about a type of juice, use *jugo de* + the name of the fruit.

jugo de naranja
orange juice

jugo de manzana
apple juice

Culture Corner

Chocolate is made from the beans of the cacao tree, which is native to Central and South America. In the sixteenth century, the Spanish conquistadors saw how fond the Aztecs were of a drink called *xocoatl*. The Spaniards added sugar and water to this bitter brew to make hot chocolate and introduced the drink to Europe.

Your Likes and Dislikes

Do you cringe at the sight of spinach but start to drool when you pick up the scent of a hamburger cooking on a grill? Are you picky when you have to choose what you like to eat? Or will you eat just about anything to stop your stomach from growling? For each group listed here, tell what you love (*me encanta[n]*), like (*me gusta[n]*), and dislike (*me disgusta[n]*). (Sample responses can be found on page 417, in Appendix A.).

1. Fish _____
2. Meat _____
3. Dairy _____
4. Fruits _____

5. Vegetables _____
6. Drinks _____
7. Dessert _____

Quantity Counts

Because most of us are used to dealing with ounces, pounds, pints, quarts, and gallons, I've included a conversion chart to help you out until the metric system becomes second nature.

Table 16.10   Measuring Quantities of Food*

Solid Measures		Liquid Measures	
U.S. System Customary	Metric Equivalent	U.S. Customary System	Metric Equivalent
1 oz.	28 grams	1 oz.	30 milliliters
1/4 lb.	125 grams	16 oz. (1 pint)	475 milliliters
1/2 lb.	250 grams	32 oz. (1 quart)	950 milliliters (approximately 1 liter)
3/4 lb.	375 grams	1 gallon	3.75 liters
1.1 lb.	500 grams		
2.2 lb.	1,000 grams (1 kilogram)		

All weight and measurement comparisons are approximate

When I was a kid, no one ever told us about the metric system. If you're a bit confused as to how it works, trust me, I understand perfectly. You can make measurements easier by simply asking for a box, a bag, or a can or by memorizing the amounts you think you'll need: a pound, a quart, or whatever. Consult Table 16.11 to help you get the right amount.

Table 16.11   Getting the Amount You Want

Amount	Spanish Translation	Pronunciation
a bag of	un saco de	oon sah-koh deh
a bar of	una barra de	oo-nah bah-rrah deh
a bottle of	una botella de	oo-nah boh-teh-yah deh
a box of	una caja de	oo-nah kah-hah deh
a bunch of	un atado de	oon ah-tah-doh deh
a can of	una lata de	oo-nah lah-tah deh
a dozen	una docena de	oo-nah doh-seh-nah deh
a half pound of	una media libra de	oo-nah meh-dee-yah lee-brah deh
a jar of	un pomo de	oon poh-moh deh
a package of	un paquete de	oon pah-keh-teh deh
a piece of	un pedazo de	oon peh-dah-soh deh
a pound of	una libra de	oo-nah lee-brah deh

Amount	Spanish Translation	Pronunciation
a quart of	un litro de	oon lee-troh deh
a slice of	un trozo de	oon troh-soh deh

If you want to get a true feel for Spanish culture, you have to go off your diet every now and then. You know you want to taste the *dulce de zapote* (dool-seh deh sah-poh-teh) that your Mexican friend has prepared for you. Never mind the caloric content of the zapote pulp, orange juice, and sugar. Taste it and savor its creamy texture and tangy flavor. Your friend offers you more. Don't allow yourself to completely blow your diet. Use the following expressions to limit the quantity you receive:

In a Flash

Write your shopping list in Spanish. Include the amounts you need.

Quantity	Spanish Translation	Pronunciation
a little	un poco de	oon poh-koh deh
a lot	mucho(a)	moo-choh(ah)
enough	bastante, suficiente	bahs-tahn-teh soo-fee-see-yehn-teh
too much	demasiado	deh-mah-see-yah-doh

What's in the Fridge?

Happiness is checking into your hotel room and discovering it is equipped with a small refrigerator. After unpacking, why not take a quick walk down to the nearest grocery store to stock up on some items you'd like to have on hand. What snacks would you purchase for that occasional craving? (Sample responses can be found on page 417, in Appendix A.)

¡Atención!

It is not customary to receive a shopping bag in neighborhood stores. Spanish shoppers usually bring along *un saco* (oon sah-koh), a bag in which they pack and carry their purchases.

What Would You Like?

When you go into a store, do you sometimes drive the clerk crazy by pointing to this item and that one? Do you make demands because you must have that brand and not this one? When you finally think you've made the best choice, do you notice that one over there and then spend several minutes debating your judgment? If this is the case, you'll certainly need demonstrative pronouns.

These nifty little words are extremely useful and are easy to learn. In fact, except for an accent mark, they are exactly the same as the demonstrative adjectives studied in Chapter 15, "A Shopping Spree." Table 16.12 will help you make your selections.

Table 16.12 Demonstrative Pronouns

Demonstrative Pronoun	Masculine	Feminine
this one	éste	ésta
these	éstos	éstas
that one (near speaker)	ése	ésa
those (near speaker)	ésos	ésas
that one (away from speaker, over there)	aquél	aquélla
those (away from speaker, over there)	aquéllos	aquéllas

➤ Demonstrative pronouns indicate a person, place, or thing when the noun itself is not mentioned.

Prefiero ésta.
I prefer this one.

➤ Demonstrative pronouns agree in number and gender with the nouns they replace.

esta botella y aquélla
this bottle and that (one)

Este vino es rojo, ése blanco, y aquél rosado.
This wine is red, that one white, and that one (over there) rosé.

Getting What You Want

In a small, neighborhood store, someone always is eager to help you. Be prepared for the questions you might be asked and have the proper answer ready so you get what you want.

¿Qué desea?
keh deh-seh-yah
What would you like?

¿En qué puedo servirle?
ehn keh pweh-doh sehr-beer-leh
May I help you?

Your answer might begin one of these ways:

Deseo…	¿Podría darme…?	Por favor.
deh-seh-yoh	poh-dree-yah dahr-meh	pohr fah-bohr
I would like…	*Could you give me…?*	*Please.*

You might then be asked one of the following:

¿Y con éso?	¿Es todo?
ee kohn eh-soh	ehs toh-doh
And with that?	*Is that all?*

The appropriate response is either to name additional items you want or to answer as follows:

Sí, es todo, gracias.
see ehs toh-doh grah-see-yahs
Yes, that's all, thank you.

Okay, you're on your own. Tell a shopkeeper you would like the following items. (Answers can be found on page 417, in Appendix A.)

1. A pound of ham _____ .

2. A liter of soda _____ .

3. A chocolate bar _____ .

4. A box of cookies _____ .

5. A bag of candy _____ .

6. A half pound of turkey _____ .

The Treat's on Alexandra

Alexandra Bernal, a lovely student of mine from Colombia, prepared a delicious *flan* for our Foreign Language Day celebration. Although I usually prefer something chocolate, I found her recipe for this caramel custard to be extremely tasty. You, too, can impress your friends with this wonderful treat. It's even easy to prepare. You need the following:

> 2 12 oz. cans of evaporated milk
>
> 2 eggs
>
> 1 14 oz. can of sweetened condensed milk
>
> 3 tablespoons of sugar

Mix the evaporated milk, the condensed milk, and the two eggs in a blender. In the meantime, melt the sugar in a pan set over a low flame. The sugar will caramelize and turn to a honey-brown color. Put the sugar on the bottom of an 8" or 9" diameter mold. Add the mixed ingredients on top of the sugar. Put the mold in a water bath (a shallow pan containing water). Bake in a 350° oven for one hour. Allow to cool. Refrigerate for at least 24 hours. Invert the mold to serve the flan. Enjoy!

The Least You Need to Know

➤ Use the verb *ir* + *a* + the definite article to say which store you are going to.

➤ Purchasing the correct amount of food in Spanish-speaking countries requires knowledge of the metric system.

➤ Demonstrative pronouns (*éste, ése, aquél*) must agree in number and gender with the nouns they replace. Use *éste* to replace nouns that are close, use *ése* to replace nouns that are farther away, and use *aquél* for nouns that are farthest from the speaker and the person being addressed.

Chapter 17

Dining Out

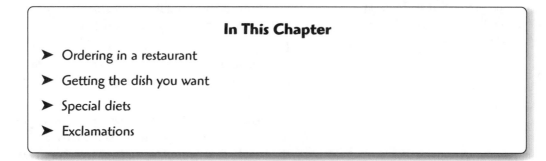

In This Chapter

➤ Ordering in a restaurant

➤ Getting the dish you want

➤ Special diets

➤ Exclamations

Let's say you're in Madrid. You shopped all morning and then stopped at a local store to pick up some snacks. You used what you learned about the metric system in Chapter 16, "A Home-Cooked Meal," to purchase appropriate quantities of all your favorite goodies. Before you took your *siesta*, you lounged around your room munching on *tacos* and *tortillas* and sipping *piña coladas*.

Now you've awakened and your stomach is growling again. It's time to venture out and find an enjoyable eating spot. Perhaps you'll stop at a *tapas* bar for some appetizers and a drink before your main meal, or maybe it's late and you're ready for dinner. This chapter will teach you how to order food from a Spanish menu, even if your diet is limited and requires certain restrictions. If you are not perfectly satisfied with every aspect of your meal, you will be able to send food back and get exactly what you want.

Pick a Place You Like

Whether you are just a little hungry and crave a small bite or you're ravenous and in search of a quality meal, a variety of establishments will cater to your needs and your pocketbook. If you want an informal setting, try one of the options in the following list. If you prefer a more formal meal, head for the nearest *restaurante* (rehs-tow-rahn-teh).

Culture Corner

In the Spanish-speaking world the cafe is an important meeting place for young and old alike. Found in every neighborhood, each cafe caters to its own crowd and has its own particular atmosphere. When the weather is warm, tables are set outside on *la terraza* (lah teh-rrah-sah).

➤ *Un café (oon kah-feh).* A small neighborhood restaurant where residents socialize.

➤ *Una cafetería (oo-nah kah-feh-teh-ree-yah).* Not at all the self-service type of establishment you would expect. A small, informal café serving snacks and drinks.

➤ *Un bar, una tasca, una taberna (oon bahr, oo-nah tahs-kah, oo-nah tah-behr-nah).* Pubs or bars in which drinks and small snacks known as *tapas* (tah-pahs) or *pinchos* (peen-chohs) are served.

➤ *Una fonda, una hostería, una venta, una posada (oo-nah fohn-dah, oo-nah ohs-teh-ree-yah, oo-nah behn-tah, oo-nah poh-sah-dah).* Inns specializing in regional dishes.

➤ *Un merendero, un chiringuito (oon meh-rehn-deh-roh, oon chee-reen-gee-toh).* Outdoor stands, usually at the beach, that sell seafood, drinks, and ice cream.

➤ *Una cervecería (oo-nah sehr-beh-seh-ree-yah).* A pub that specializes in German beer in the barrel as well as wine.

➤ *Una hacienda (oo-nah ah-see-yehn-dah).* A ranch-style restaurant found in Spanish America.

➤ *Una cantina (oo-nah kahn-tee-nah).* A men's bar found in Spanish America. (Sorry ladies. There's nothing illicit going on, though; the men simply want their privacy.)

Which Restaurant Do You Prefer?

Every country puts together a tourist guide that advertises a wide variety of restaurants from which to choose. Imagine you have to pick the place where you and your traveling companion are going to eat. What will it be? Explore the ads and determine what each restaurant has to offer. Check your translations on page 417, in Appendix A .

When Do We Eat?

El desayuno (ehl deh-sah-yoo-noh), Spanish breakfast, is usually served between 7 a.m. and 9 a.m. It is generally quite light and consists of coffee with milk and bread with butter, jam, or cheese.

A special breakfast favorite is *churros y chocolate* (choo-rrohs ee choh-koh-lah-teh). *Churros* (fritters) are made by frying long skinny strips of dough in very hot oil, cutting the strips into small pieces, and then sprinkling them with sugar. Hot chocolate is generally served with this treat.

Between 10:30 a.m. and noon, a mid-morning snack—referred to as *el almuerzo* (ehl ahl-mwehr-soh) in Mexico—is customary. People generally have a *batido* or *licuado* (fruit shake) or a regional snack at this time.

¡Atención!

In the Caribbean, *el almuerzo* means lunch, and it is not the main meal, which is called *la comida* dinner.

Culture Corner

Spanish cuisine is quite different from that of Mexico and Spanish America. Spanish cooking is Mediterranean style and uses many of the ingredients found in Greek and Italian cooking. In Spanish America, expect to experience flavors produced by the condiments and spices used there.

Lunch is eaten much later in the Spanish-speaking world than in the United States, and it is considered the main meal of the day. Generally eaten between 1:30 p.m. and 3 p.m., lunch is referred to as *la comida* (lah koh-mee-dah) in Spain and Mexico and as *el almuerzo* (ehl ahl-mwehr-soh) in South America and the Caribbean. Expect a full meal that includes soup, meat or fish, vegetables, salad, and dessert.

A late afternoon snack, *la merienda* (lah meh-ree-yehn-dah), referred to as *once* in Chile, is usually served between 5 and 6 p.m. in the evening. This usually consists of coffee or tea and pastry.

Supper is called *la cena* (lah seh-nah) in Spain and Mexico and *la comida* in Spanish America. Eaten rather late, sometimes not until 9 p.m., this meal tends to be very light.

Making a Reservation

Should you decide to eat in a popular restaurant, you might find it necessary to reserve a table. When you call, you will be asked for a lot of information. Make sure you know what to say.

Quisiera hacer una reservación.
kee-see-yeh-rah ah-sehr
oo-nah reh-sehr-bah-see-yohn
I would like to reserve a table.

para esta noche
pah-rah ehs-tah noh-cheh
for this evening

para mañana (el sábado) por la noche
pah-rah mah-nyah-nah
(ehl sah-bah-doh) pohr lah noh-cheh
for tomorrow (Saturday) evening

para dos personas
pah-rah dohs pehr-soh-nahs
for two people

para las ocho y media
pah-rah lahs oh-choh ee meh-dee-yah
for 8:30 p.m.

en la terraza (el rincón), por favor
ehn lah teh-rrah-sah (ehl reen-kohn)
pohr fah-bohr
on the terrace (in the corner), please

cerca de la ventana
sehr-kah deh lah behn-tah-nah
near the window

Memory Master

Refer back to Chapter 11, "Getting There Is Half the Fun," for help with time expressions.

Let's Eat Out

Practice what you've just learned by reserving a table for Friday evening at 9:30 p.m. for two people. Also request a table outdoors. (Check your answer on page 418, in Appendix A.)

Culture Corner

In the Spanish-speaking world it is customary to stop off at a bar before dinner. In Spain, a tapas bar serves a variety of appetizers: stuffed olives, artichokes, clams, fried eel, boiled squid, snails, grilled shrimp, cheese, ham on toast, salami, kebabs, spicy sausage, stuffed hard–boiled eggs, and pieces of tortilla.

At the Restaurant

Let's say you did not reserve a table, and you show up at a restaurant unannounced. *El jefe del comedor* (ehl heh-feh dehl koh-meh-dohr), the headwaiter, will most certainly ask the following:

> ¿Una mesa para cuántas personas?
> oo-nah meh-sah pah-rah kwahn-tahs
> pehr-soh-nahs
> *A table for how many?*

You respond:

> Una mesa para tres, por favor.
> oo-nah meh-sah pah-rah trehs pohr fah-bohr
> *A table for three, please.*

In a Flash

Label everything you put on your table when you set it. Practice this new vocabulary until you have it down pat. Remove the labels and test yourself.

Setting a Place

It's just been one of those days. You dropped your fork, and as you bent down to retrieve it, you spilled water on your suit and had to mop it up with your napkin. Your elbow hit your empty plate, which is now on the floor. After all this, a new place setting is needed. Table 17.1 gives you the vocabulary you need to ask the waiter for cutlery or other items.

Table 17.1   A Table Setting

Tableware	Spanish Translation	Pronunciation
bowl	el tazón	ehl tah-sohn
carafe	la garrafa	lah gah-rrah-fah
cup	la taza	lah tah-sah
dinner plate	el plato	ehl plah-toh
fork	el tenedor	ehl teh-neh-dohr
glass	el vaso	ehl bah-soh
knife	el cuchillo	ehl koo-chee-yoh
menu	el menú	ehl meh-noo
napkin	la servilleta	lah sehr-bee-yeh-tah
pepper shaker	el pimentero	ehl pee-mehn-teh-roh
place setting	el cubierto	ehl koo-bee-yehr-toh
salt shaker	el salero	ehl sah-leh-roh
saucer	el platillo	ehl plah-tee-yoh
soup dish	el sopero	ehl soh-peh-roh
soup spoon	la cuchara	lah koo-chah-rah
tablecloth	el mantel	ehl mahn-tehl
teaspoon	la cucharita	lah koo-chah-ree-tah
waiter	el camarero	ehl kah-mah-reh-roh
waitress	la camarera	lah kah-mah-reh-rah
wine glass	la copa	lah koh-pah

How May I Help You?

Is something missing from your table? Do you want to make a request of the head waiter, waiter, or wine steward? If you do, the following information and phrases will help you get want you want.

➤ Use an indirect object pronoun. Remember that the verb *faltar* must agree with the number of items lacking. If it's just one, use *falta*. For more than one, use *faltan*.

Showing Need	Pronunciation	Translation
Me falta(n)…	meh fahl-tah(n)	I need…
Te falta(n)…	teh fahl-tah(n)	You need…
Le falta(n)…	leh fahl-tah(n)	He, she, you need(s)…

Showing Need	Pronunciation	Translation
Nos falta(n)...	nohs fahl-tah(n)	We need...
Os falta(n)...	ohs fahl-tah(n)	You need...
Les falta(n)...	lehs fahl-tah(n)	They, you need...

➤ You also can use the verb *necesitar* (to need).

Showing Need	Pronunciation	Translation
Necesito...	neh-seh-see-toh	I need...
Necesitas	neh-seh-see-tahs	You need
Él necesita...	ehl neh-seh-see-tah	He needs...
Ella necesita...	eh-yah neh-seh-see-tah	She needs...
Necesitamos...	neh-seh-see-tah-mohs	We need...
Necesitáis...	neh-seh-see-tah-yees	You need...
Ellos necesitan...	eh-yohs neh-seh-see-tahn	They need...
Ellas necesitan...	eh-yahs neh-seh-see-tahn	They need...

Oh, Waiter!

Use what you've learned to tell your server you need the following items. (Answers can be found on page 418, in Appendix A.)

1. salt shaker _____ .
2. napkin _____ .
3. fork _____ .
4. knife _____ .
5. plate _____ .
6. spoon _____ .

Memory Master

Remember to use the appropriate direct object pronoun to refer to the noun you are using.

¿Ud. recomienda la paella?
¿Ud. *la* recomienda?

¿Ud. toma el lomillo?
Sí, *lo* tomo.

Camarero, What Do You Recommend?

Let's assume you've had a drink at a pub or bar before arriving at the restaurant. You'll probably want to order right away. The following phrases will help you ask the waiter for the specials of the day or for his own personal recommendations:

¿Cuál es el plato del día?
kwahl ehs ehl plah-toh dehl dee-yah
What is today's specialty?

¿Cuál es la especialidad de la casa?
kwahl ehs lah ehs-peh-see-yah-lee-dahd deh
lah kah-sah
What is the house specialty?

¿Qué recomienda Ud.?
keh rreh-koh-mee-yehn-dah oo-stehd
What do you recommend?

Culture Corner

When your meal arrives, good manners dictate that you should wish your fellow diners *buen provecho* (bwehn proh-beh-choh), a hearty appetite.

This Menu Is Greek to Me

A Spanish menu could prove a bit difficult to understand unless you are acquainted with certain culinary terms. If your waiter is too busy or speaks too fast, you might wind up with something you didn't really want or don't particularly like. Table 17.2 gives you the terms you need to interpret what's being offered.

Table 17.2   What's on the Menu?

Salsas (Sauces)	Pronunciation	Description
ají de queso	ah-hee deh keh-soh	cheese sauce
adobo	ah-doh-boh	chili sauce made with sesame seeds, nuts, and spices
mole	moh-leh	chili sauce made with sesame seeds, cocoa, and spices
pipián	pee-pee-yahn	chili and pumpkin seed sauce spiced with coriander and served with bread crumbs

Salsas (Sauces)	Pronunciation	Description
salsa cruda	sahl-sah kroo-dah	an uncooked tomato sauce dip
salsa de perejil	sahl-sah deh peh-reh-heel	parsley sauce
salsa de tomatillo verde	sahl-sah deh toh-mah-tee-yoh behr-deh	Mexican green tomato sauce

Chiles (Chilies)	Pronunciation	Description
ancho	ahn-choh	medium hot
chipotle	chee-poht-leh	hot, smokey-flavored
jalapeño	hah-lah-peh-nyoh	hot, meaty-flavored
pasilla	pah-see-yah	hot, rich, sweet-flavored
pequín	peh-keen	hot
pimiento	pee-mee-yehn-toh	peppery
poblano	poh-blah-noh	medium hot, rich-flavored
serrano	seh-rrah-noh	hot

Tortillas (Tortillas)	Pronunciation	Description
burrito	boo-rree-toh	flour tortilla with a cheese and meat filling served with salsa
chalupas	chah-loo-pahs	cheese or ground pork filling served with a green chili sauce
chilaquiles	chee-lah-kee-lehs	baked layers of tortillas filled alternately with beans, meat, chicken, and cheese
enchiladas	ehn-chee-lah-dahs	soft corn tortillas filled with meat, rice, and cheese and topped with spicy sauce
flautas	flow-tahs	rolled, flute-shaped, deep-fried tortilla sandwich
quesadillas	keh-sah-dee-yahs	deep-fried tortillas covered with cheese, tomato, and pepper
tacos	tah-kohs	crisp toasted tortillas filled with meat, poultry, or beans and topped with shredded lettuce, cheese, and sauce
tamal	tah-mahl	cooked corn husks stuffed with meat, chicken, and chile peppers (known as *tamales* in English)
tostada	tohs-tah-dah	tortilla chip with different pepper and cheese toppings

Let's Eat!

The *tortilla mexicana*, a flat pancake made of corn meal, is the *tortilla* with which most of us are familiar. In Mexico, the *tortilla* is served in place of bread and is an important part of every meal. In Spain, the *tortilla española* is a type of thick omelet made with potatoes, eggs, and onions. It also can be cut into pieces and served as an appetizer.

In Spain, salads are often served as appetizers and may contain a mixture of vegetables and seafood. In Spanish America, the salad is often served with the main course. Your *ensalada* (ehn-sah-lah-dah) might come with lettuce (*lechuga*, leh-choo-gah), tomato (*tomate*, toh-mah-teh), olives (*aceitunas*, ah-seh-yee-too-nahs), and cucumber (*pepino*, peh-pee-noh).

Parrillada refers to grilled meat; the expression *a la parrillada* means the meat is grilled or barbecued. This term is very popular in Latin American countries such as Argentina, where the beef is locally raised and, therefore, is plentiful.

Rice is a very important staple in Spain and is used as the base for the ever-popular paella. This dish varies from region to region throughout the country, but always contains saffron-flavored rice. The different types of paella can be made with meat, seafood, poultry, game, and vegetables.

You might choose to sample an appetizer from the restaurant before beginning your meal. Then it's on to the soup and the main course. Tables 17.3 to 17.5 list the interesting prospects awaiting you.

Table 17.3 Appetizers
(Los Aperetivos, lohs ah-peh-reh-tee-bohs)

Appetizer	Spanish Translation	Pronunciation
artichokes	alcachofas	ahl-kah-choh-fahs
avocado spread	guacamole	gwah-kah-moh-leh
clams	almejas	ahl-meh-hahs
crayfish	cigales	see-gah-lehs
eggs	huevos	weh-bohs
melon	melón	meh-lohn
mushrooms	champiñones	chahm-pee-nyoh-nehs
mussels	moluscos	moh-loos-kohs
oysters	ostras	ohs-trahs
sardines	sardinas	sahr-dee-nahs
shrimp	camarones	kah-mah-roh-nehs
smoked eels	anguilas ahumadas	ahn-gee-lahs ah-oo-mah-dahs
snails	caracoles	kah-rah-koh-lehs

Appetizer	Spanish Translation	Pronunciation
spicy sausage	chorizo	choh-ree-soh
squid	calamares	kah-lah-mah-rehs
tortilla chips	tostadas	tohs-tah-dahs

Table 17.4   Soups (Las Sopas, lahs soh-pahs)

Soup	Pronunciation	Description
gazpacho	gahs-pah-choh	puréed, uncooked tomatoes, served cold
potaje madrileño	poh-tah-heh mah-dree-leh-nyoh	thick, puréed cod, spinach, and chickpeas
sopa de ajo	soh-pah deh ah-hoh	garlic soup
sopa de albóndigas	soh-pah deh ahl-bohn-dee-gahs	meatball soup
sopa de cebolla	soh-pah deh seh-boh-yah	onion soup
sopa de fideos	soh-pah deh fee-deh-yohs	noodle soup
sopa de gambas	soh-pah deh gahm-bahs	shrimp soup
sopa de mariscos	soh-pah deh mah-rees-kohs	seafood soup
sopa de pescado	soh-pah deh pehs-kah-doh	fish soup
sopa de verduras	soh-pah deh behr-doo-rahs	soup made from puréed green vegetables

Table 17.5   Meats (Las Carnes, lahs kahr-nehs)

Meat	Spanish Translation	Pronunciation
bacon	el tocino	ehl toh-see-noh
beef	la carne de vaca	lah kahr-neh deh bah-kah
blood pudding	la morcilla	lah mohr-see-yah
chop, cutlet	la chuleta	lah choo-leh-tah
filet mignon	el lomo fino	ehl loh-moh fee-noh

continues

Table 17.5 Continued

Meat	Spanish Translation	Pronunciation
goat	el cabrito	ehl kah-bree-toh
ham	el jamón	ehl hah-mohn
hamburger	la hamburguesa	lah ahm-boor-geh-sah
lamb	el cordero	ehl kohr-deh-roh
pork	el cerdo	ehl sehr-doh
roast	el asado	ehl ah-sah-doh
roast beef	el rosbif	ehl rrohs-beef
sausage	la salchicha	lah sahl-chee-chah
sirloin	el lomillo	ehl loh-mee-yoh
steak	el bistec	ehl bees-tehk
steak, charcoal-grilled	el churrasco	ehl chuh-rrahs-koh
stew	el estofado, el guisado	ehl ehs-toh-fah-doh, ehl gee-sah-doh
veal	la ternera	lah tehr-neh-rah

Culture Corner

If you enjoy a meaty sandwich, try *un sándwich cubano,* made from a long, crusty bread called *pan de flauta* (pahn day flow-tah). Slice the bread and add *jamón* (hah-mohn, ham), *mortadela* (mohr-tah-deh-lah, a meat like bologna), *pierna de puerco* (pee-yehr-nah day pwehr-koh, pork), *queso* (keh-soh, cheese), and *pepinillos* (peh-pee-nee-yohs, pickles). Then heat until the cheese melts.

That's the Way I Like It

Even if you know how to order your hamburger or veal chops, you want to be certain your entree is cooked to your specifications. The waiter might ask the following question:

¿Comó lo (la, los, las) quiere?
koh-moh loh (lah, lohs, lahs) kee-yeh-reh
How do you want it (them)?

Do you prefer your fish baked or broiled? Do you want your meat medium-rare or well-done? If you want to make sure your food is prepared to your liking, use Table 17.6 to express your wants and needs.

Table 17.6 Proper Preparation

Meats and Vegetables		
Preparation	Spanish Translation	Pronunciation
baked	asado	ah-sah-doh
boiled	cocido	koh-see-doh
breaded	empanado	ehm-pah-nah-doh
broiled	a la parrilla	ah lah pah-rree-yah
fried	frito	free-toh
grilled	asado a la parrilla	ah-sah-doh ah lah pah-rree-yah
marinated	escabechado	ehs-kah-beh-chah-doh
medium	término medio	tehr-mee-noh meh-dee-yoh
medium-rare	un poco rojo pero no crudo	oon poh-koh rroh-hoh peh-roh noh kroo-doh
poached	escalfado	ehs-kahl-fah-doh
rare	poco asado	poh-koh ah-sah-doh
roasted	asado	ah-sah-doh
steamed	al vapor	ahl bah-pohr
very rare	casi crudo	kah-see kroo-doh
well-done	bien asado (hecho, cocido)	bee-yehn ah-sah-doh (eh-choh, koh-see-doh)
Eggs		
fried	fritos	free-tohs
hard-boiled	duros	doo-rohs
poached	escalfados	ehs-kahl-fah-dohs
scrambled	revueltos	rreh-bwehl-tohs
soft-boiled	pasados por agua	pah-sah-dohs pohr ah-gwah
omelette	una tortilla	oo-nah tohr-tee-yah
plain omelette	una tortilla a la francesa	oo-nah tohr-tee-yah ah lah frahn-seh-sah
herb omelette	una tortilla con hierbas	oo-nah tohr-tee-yah kohn yehr-bahs

Hot and Spicy

You should expect a variety of spices to be used in Spain and in the Spanish American countries. Menu descriptions or your waiter can usually help you determine whether the dish will be to your liking—whether you prefer bland or spicy. Table 17.7 will help you become acquainted with many of the spices you might encounter.

Table 17.7 Herbs, Spices, and Condiments

Spice	Spanish Translation	Pronunciation
basil	la albahaca	lah ahl-bah-ah-kah
bay leaf	la hoja de laurel	lah oh-hah deh low-rehl
butter	la mantequilla	lah mahn-teh-kee-yah
caper	el alcaparrón	ehl ahl-kah-pah-rrohn
chives	el cebollino	ehl seh-boh-yee-noh
dill	el eneldo	ehl eh-nehl-doh
garlic	el ajo	ehl ah-hoh
ginger	el jenjibre	ehl hehn-hee-breh
honey	la miel	lah mee-yehl
ketchup	la salsa de tomate	lah sahl-sah deh toh-mah-teh
mint	la menta	lah mehn-tah
mustard	la mostaza	lah mohs-tah-sah
nutmeg	la nuez moscada	lah nwehs mohs-kah-dah
oil	el aceite	ehl ah-seh-yee-teh
oregano	el orégano	ehl oh-reh-gah-noh
paprika	el pimentón dulce	ehl pee-mehn-tohn dool-seh
parsley	el perejil	ehl peh-reh-heel
pepper	la pimienta	lah pee-mee-yehn-tah
rosemary	el romero	ehl rroh-meh-roh
saffron	el azafrán	ehl ah-sah-frahn
salt	la sal	lah sahl
sesame	el ajonjolí	ehl ah-hohn-hoh-lee
sugar	el azúcar	ehl ah-soo-kahr

Diet Do's and Don'ts

Does your diet require certain restrictions? Are you a person with specific likes and dislikes of which your server should be aware? If so, you'll want to remember the following phrases:

Phrase	Spanish Translation	Pronunciation
I am on a diet.	Estoy a régimen.	ehs-toy ah rreh-hee-mehn
I'm a vegetarian.	Soy vegetariano(a).	soy beh-heh-tah-ree-yah-noh(ah)

Phrase	Spanish Translation	Pronunciation
Do you serve kosher food?	¿Sirven Uds. comida permitida por la religión judia?	seer-behn oo-steh-dehs koh-mee-dah pehr-mee-tee-dah pohr lah rreh-lee-hee-yohn hoo-dee-yah
I can't eat anything made with...	No puedo comer nada con...	noh pweh-doh koh-mehr nah-dah kohn
I can't have any...	No puedo tomar...	noh pweh-doh toh-mahr
dairy products	productos lácteos	proh-dook-tohs lahk-teh-yohs
alcohol	alcohol	ahl-koh-ohl
saturated fats	grasas saturadas	grah-sahs sah-too-rah-dahs
shellfish	mariscos	mah-rees-kohs
I'm looking for a dish...	Estoy buscando un plato...	ehs-toy boos-kahn-doh oon plah-toh
high in fiber	con mucha fibra	kohn moo-chah fee-brah
low in cholesterol	con poco colesterol	kohn poh-koh koh-lehs-teh-rohl
low in fat	con poca grasa	kohn poh-kah grah-sah
low in sodium	con poca sal	kohn poh-kah sahl
non-dairy	no lácteo	noh lahk-teh-yoh
salt-free	sin sal	seen sahl
sugar-free	sin azúcar	seen ah-soo-kahr
without artificial coloring	sin colorantes artificiales	seen koh-loh-rahn-tehs ahr-tee-fee-see-yah-lehs
without preservatives	sin preservativos	seen preh-sehr-bah-tee-bohs

I'm Sending It Back

The dish you ordered just doesn't seem right. Perhaps something is missing. Maybe you ordered it rare, but it looks and tastes like shoe leather. The waiter said it wouldn't be too hot, but you can't seem to get enough water to cool your palate. If there's a problem, you'll want to be able to communicate exactly what it is. Table 17.8 will help you send back that disappointing dish and get something more to your liking.

Table 17.8 Possible Problems with Your Food

Problem	Spanish Translation	Pronunciation
...is cold	está frío	ehs-tah free-yoh
...is too rare	está demasiado crudo	ehs-tah deh-mah-see-yah-doh kroo-doh
...is over-cooked	está sobrecocido	ehs-tah soh-breh-koh-see-doh
...is tough	está duro	ehs-tah doo-roh
...is burned	está quemado	ehs-tah keh-mah-doh
...is too salty	está muy salado	ehs-tah mwee sah-lah-doh
...is too sweet	está muy dulce	ehs-tah mwee dool-seh
...is too spicy	está demasiado picante	ehs-tah deh-mah-see-yah-doh pee-kahn-teh
...is spoiled	está pasado	ehs-tah pah-sah-doh
...is bitter (sour)	está agrio (cortado)	ehs-tah ah-gree-yoh (kohr-tah-doh)
...is dirty	está sucio	ehs-tah soo-see-yoh

Fancy Finales

Finally, it's time for dessert. There are some interesting specialties from which to choose. Table 17.9 will help you make your decision.

Table 17.9 Divine Desserts

Dessert	Spanish Translation	Pronunciation
caramel custard	el flan	ehl flahn
cookies	las galletitas	lahs gah-yeh-tee-tahs
gelatin	la gelatina	lah heh-lah-tee-nah
ice cream	el helado	ehl eh-lah-doh
pie	el pastel	ehl pahs-tehl
rice pudding	el arroz con leche	ehl ah-rrohs kohn leh-cheh
sponge cake	el bizcocho	ehl bees-koh-choh
tart	la tarta	lah tahr-tah
yogurt	el yogur	ehl yoh-goor

Here's an important distinction to make: If you are eating ensalada (salad), be sure to order *galletas saladas* (crackers). For dessert, order *galletitas* (cookies) because they are sweet.

If you'd rather have ice cream, the following terms will help you get the serving and flavor, *el sabor* (ehl sah-bohr), you prefer:

Ice Cream	Spanish Translation	Pronunciation
cone	un barquillo	oon bahr-kee-yoh
cup	una taza	oo-nah tah-sah
chocolate	de chocolate	deh choh-koh-lah-teh
vanilla	de vainilla	deh bah-yee-nee-yah
strawberry	de fresa	deh freh-sah
pistachio	de pistacho	deh pees-tah-choh
walnut	de nueces	deh nweh-sehs

Drink to Me Only

Spain is one of the top wine producers in the world. *Rioja,* a premier Burgundy and Bordeaux-type red table wine, is one of the world's finest, with an unmistakable bouquet and flavor. Its quality is protected by strict official regulations governing the seal of origin.

Sherry is the most international Spanish wine due to the high volume exported. The four different kinds of this Andalusian wine are *Manzanilla, Amontillado, Fino*, and *Los Dulces*. *Fino* and *Manzanilla* are dry aperitifs. The others are served with dessert or as after-dinner drinks.

Sangria, the popular fruit punch made from red wine, brandy, sugar, and soda, is not served at dinner. It is a popular picnic or afternoon wine. *Catalán cava* is an excellent sparkling wine grown in Catalonia. Beer (*cerveza*), although not traditionally Spanish, is currently popular in Spain. It is not generally served with meals, but it is quite popular in *tapas* bars.

Spaniards usually drink wine with dinner. The wines you might order include:

Wine	Spanish Translation	Pronunciation
red wine	el vino tinto	ehl bee-noh teen-toh
rosé wine	el vino rosado	ehl bee-noh rroh-sah-doh
white wine	el vino blanco	ehl bee-noh blahn-koh
dry wine	el vino seco	ehl bee-noh seh-koh
sweet wine	el vino dulce	ehl bee-noh dool-seh
sparkling wine	el vino espumoso	ehl bee-noh ehs-poo-moh-soh
champagne	el champán	ehl chahm-pahn

If you do not choose to have wine with your meal, you will, of course, want to order something else. You might even want to order different drinks with different courses. Table 17.10 lists other beverages you might enjoy with or after dinner.

Table 17.10   Beverages

Beverage	Spanish Translation	Pronunciation
coffee	un café	oon kah-feh
with milk	con leche	kohn leh-cheh
espresso	exprés	ehks-prehs
with cream	con crema	kohn kreh-mah
black	solo	soh-loh
iced	helado	eh-lah-doh
decaffeinated	descafeinado	dehs-kah-feh-yee-nah-doh
tea	un té	oon teh
with lemon	con limón	kohn lee-mohn
with sugar	con azúcar	kohn ah-soo-kahr
herbal	herbario	ehr-bah-ree-yoh
soda	una soda	oo-nah soh-dah
	una gaseosa	oo-nah gah-seh-yoh-sah
mineral water	un agua mineral	oon ah-gwah mee-neh-rahl
carbonated	con gas	kohn gahs
non-carbonated	sin gas	seen gahs
juice	un jugo	oon hoo-goh
milk	una leche	oo-nah leh-cheh
skim milk	desnatada	dehs-nah-tah-dah

You Can't Have It All

De is used after nouns of quantity, as follows:

un vaso de leche   una botella de agua
a glass of milk   *a bottle of water*

There is no Spanish equivalent for "some" when the noun can't be counted. To express what you want, simply use the word *quisiera* (kee-see-eh-rah), which means "I would like," and a noun. In general, "some" is understood when a noun is used.

Quisiera carne, por favor.
I'd like some meat, please.

When the noun can be counted, use *unos* or *unas* before the noun:

> Quisiera unos huevos, por favor.
> *I'd like some eggs, please.*

10 minutos al día

Use *de* after nouns of quantity, as in *un vaso de agua*. If the noun can't be counted, there is no Spanish equivalent for the English word "some." Simply use the noun without any article (*el, la, un, una*), as in "*Necesito agua.*" If the noun can be counted, use *unos* or *unas*, as in *Necesito unas tazas*.

¡Delicioso!

How was your meal? Would you tell your friends about it and recommend it highly? Or would you rate it as just so-so? If you are really happy with your meal and the food was exceptional, you might want to express your pleasure using the word *¡Qué...!* to say "What a...!"

¡Qué comida!	¡Qué servicio!
What a meal!	*What service!*

To make the exclamation more intense, add an adjective that agrees with the noun and place the word *tan* (tahn) or *más* (mahs) before the adjective. (Both words mean "so" in this context, although we do not use "so" in our English translation of the phrase.)

> ¡Qué comida tan rica!
> *What a rich meal!*

> ¡Qué servicio más excelente!
> *What excellent service!*

> ¡Qué platos tan sabrosos!
> *What tasty dishes!*

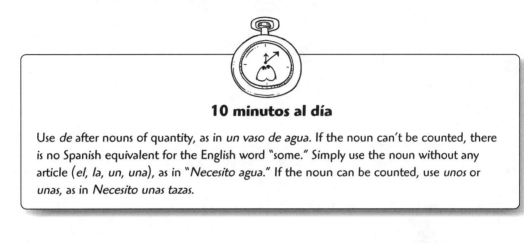

Culture Corner

Many Spanish restaurants offer a fixed-price menu that might be referred to as any of the following: *Menú Turístico, Menú del Día,* or *Plato Combinado.* The dinner consists of an appetizer, soup, main course, salad, dessert, and drink for a predetermined price. Your choice of dishes might be restricted, but this still offers an excellent value for the money.

Muchas Gracias

The meal was great. Tell the person who recommended the restaurant how much you enjoyed it. Use *que* + noun + *tan (más)* + adjective to express how you felt about what you ate and drank. (Sample responses can be found on page 418, in Appendix A.)

1. soup _____ .
2. steak _____ .
3. wine _____ .
4. salad _____ .
5. dessert _____ .

Don't forget to ask for the check at the end of your meal.

La cuenta, por favor.
lah kwehn-tah pohr fah-bohr
The check, please.

On many occasions, the tip is included in the bill. Look for the words *servicio incluído*.

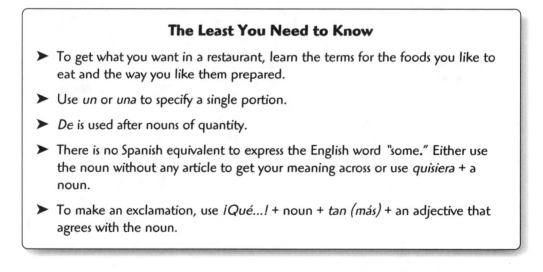

The Least You Need to Know

➤ To get what you want in a restaurant, learn the terms for the foods you like to eat and the way you like them prepared.

➤ Use *un* or *una* to specify a single portion.

➤ *De* is used after nouns of quantity.

➤ There is no Spanish equivalent to express the English word "some." Either use the noun without any article to get your meaning across or use *quisiera* + a noun.

➤ To make an exclamation, use *¡Qué...!* + noun + *tan (más)* + an adjective that agrees with the noun.

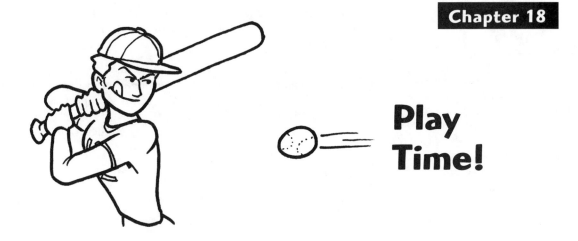

Chapter 18

Play Time!

In This Chapter

➤ Things to do to have fun

➤ Extending, accepting, and refusing invitations

➤ Using adverbs to describe abilities

You have visited countless tourist attractions, collected souvenirs, and purchased gifts for people you love. The meals you've eaten have been superb, and your appetite is truly sated. Now you want to have some fun, engage in your favorite sport, or simply lay back and relax.

You can go off to the sea to swim, snorkel, parasail, or windsurf. Or would you prefer to ski or hike on snow-covered mountains? Are you drawn to the links for a round of golf or to the courts for a friendly tennis match? Are you a film *aficionado* or a theater buff? An opera lover or a fan of the ballet? Would you like to gamble and spend some time in a Dominican casino? After studying this chapter, you'll be able to discuss any of these activities, invite someone to join you, and even brag about your skills and talents.

Sports Are My Life

I love a challenging tennis match, and my racquet has seen nearly as many countries as I have. My husband prefers the pool and likes nothing better than trying to surpass his daily record of laps. Whether you're into sports or you'd rather spend some

Culture Corner

Every four years, the *Campeonato Mundial de Fútbol* (World Soccer Championship) attracts several billion TV viewers around the world. No other sporting event is as popular. Half the championships have been won by European teams, but the rest have been won by teams from Latin America.

relaxing time at the pool or the beach, you'll need certain words and expressions to discuss your preferences.

Outdoor activities and sports are listed in Table 18.1. The verbs *hacer* and *jugar* + *a* + definite article are commonly used to describe participation in a sport. Words with one star (*) use *hacer*; those with two (**) use *jugar*. The verbs in parentheses are used in place of *jugar* or *hacer*.

Ella hace el ciclismo.	*She goes cycling.*
Juego al tenis.	*I play tennis.*
Vamos de pesca.	*We go fishing.*

If you want to say you like or dislike a sport, use the phrase *(no) me gusta* + definite article (*el, la, los, las*) + sport.

When using the verb *jugar* + *a* + definite article, remember that *a* contracts with *el* to form *al*.

Juego al tenis.	*I play tennis.*

Table 18.1 Sports

Sport	Spanish Translation	Pronunciation
aerobics	los aeróbicos*	lohs ah-yee-roh-bee-kohs
baseball	el béisbol**	ehl beh-yees-bohl
basketball	el baloncesto,** el básquetbol**	ehl bah-lohn-sehs-toh, ehl bahs-keht-bohl
bicycling	el ciclismo* (montar en bicicleta)	ehl see-klees-moh (mohn-tahr ehn bee-see-kleh-tah)
boating	(dar) un paseo en barco	(dahr) oon pah-seh-yoh ehn bahr-koh
bodybuilding	el fisiculturismo*	ehl fee-see-kool-too-rees-moh
canoeing	el piragüismo*	ehl pee-rah-gwees-moh
cycling	el ciclismo*	ehl see-klees-moh
diving	el clavado	ehl klah-bah-doh
fishing	la pesca (ir de pesca)	lah pehs-kah (eer deh pehs-kah)

Sport	Spanish Translation	Pronunciation
football	el fútbol americano**	ehl foot-bohl ah-meh-ree-kah-noh
golf	el golf**	ehl gohlf
horseback riding	la equitación*	lah eh-kee-tah-see-yohn
ice-skating	el patinaje sobre hielo* (patinar)	ehl pah-tee-nah-heh soh-breh yeh-loh (pah-tee-nahr)
jai alai	el jai alai**	ehl ah-yee ah-lah-yee
jogging	el footing* (trotar)	ehl foo-teeng (troh-tahr)
mountain climbing	el alpinismo*	ehl ahl-pee-nees-moh
Ping-Pong	el ping-pong**	ehl peeng-pohng
sailing	la navegación* (navegar)	lah nah-beh-gah-see-yohn (nah-beh-gahr)
scuba (skin) diving	el buceo	ehl boo-seh-yoh
skating	el patinaje*	ehl pah-tee-nah-heh
ski	el esquí* (esquiar)	ehl ehs-kee (ehs-kee-yahr)
soccer	el fútbol**	ehl foot-bohl
surfing	el surf* (surfear)	ehl soorf (soor-feh-yahr)
swimming	la natación* (nadar)	lah nah-tah-see-yohn (nah-dahr)
tennis	el tenis**	ehl teh-nees
volleyball	el volibol**	ehl boh-lee-bohl
waterskiing	el esquí acuático*	ehl ehs-kee ah-kwah-tee-koh

Shall We Play?

Are you the type of person who likes sports that involve team competition? Or do you prefer to engage in a one-person activity that affords lots of exercise? Using *me encanta*, *me gusta*, and *detesto*, express how you feel about the following sports. (Sample responses can be found on page 418, in Appendix A.)

1. horseback riding _____.
2. sailing _____.
3. swimming _____.
4. skiing _____.
5. soccer _____.
6. golf _____.
7. tennis _____.

Memory Master

To speak about more than one sport that you like, use *me gustan* (meh goos-tahn).

Me gustan el volibol y el tenis.

Please Join Us

If you prefer to play with a partner, you might find it necessary to extend an invitation to someone you don't know very well. To ask someone to join you, you can use the stem-changing verbs *querer* (ie), to want, or *poder* (ue), to be able to, plus the infinitive of the verb *jugar* (ue), to play. Remember that these verbs change in the shape of the shoe—within the stem of the verb, *e* changes to *ie* and *o* changes to *ue* in all present-tense forms except *nosotros* and *vosotros*. Here's a quick memory refresher from Chapter 12, "Settling In."

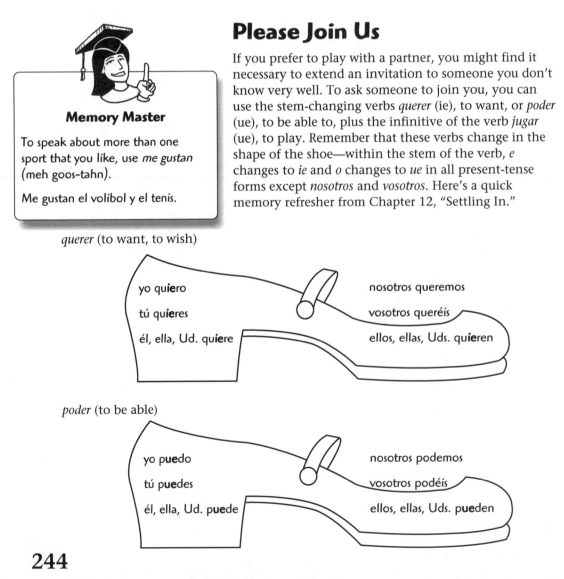

querer (to want, to wish)

yo quiero	nosotros queremos
tú quieres	vosotros queréis
él, ella, Ud. quiere	ellos, ellas, Uds. quieren

poder (to be able)

yo puedo	nosotros podemos
tú puedes	vosotros podéis
él, ella, Ud. puede	ellos, ellas, Uds. pueden

Now you are ready to ask someone to join you. First you have to find out whether he or she plays or enjoys the same activity as you. If the answer is yes, go ahead and extend an invitation using the following structure:

¿Le (Te) gusta + jugar + definite article + sport?

The following are some examples:

¿Le (Te) gusta jugar al tenis?
Do you like to play tennis?

¿Le (Te) gusta el alpinismo?
Do you like to go mountain climbing?

You also could ask something like:

¿Quiere (Quieres) acompañarme (acompañarnos)?
Do you want to join me (us)?

¿Puede (Puedes) acompañarme (acompañarnos)?
Can you accompany me (us)?

Let's Play

If you are going to play a sport in which there is a match, you would say:

Voy a jugar un partido de…
boy ah hoo-gahr oon pahr-tee-doh deh
I'm going to play a game of…

If you want to say you are going to engage in an activity, refer to Table 18.1 and use *ir + a +* the infinitive of the verb in parentheses. You also could use *ir + a + hacer +* a sport. Here are some examples:

Voy a nadar.
boy ah nah-dahr
I'm going to go swimming.

Voy a hacer la equitación.
boy ah ah-sehr lah eh-kee-tah-see-yohn
I'm going to go horseback riding.

Culture Corner

Want to work off the huge dinner you ate last night? Why not run with the bulls in Pamplona, Spain? Once a year, from July 6th through the 14th, the *Feria de San Fermín* is celebrated. Six bulls chase fleeing participants as spectators scream enthusiastically. The object is to survive the run so you can join the subsequent partying.

Culture Corner

Mexico City boasts one of the largest stadiums in the world. The *Estadio Azteca* holds more than 100,000 spectators.

Note the following irregularities:

> Voy de pesca.
> boy deh pehs-kah.
> *I'm going fishing.*

> Voy a jugar al ping-pong.
> boy ah hoo-gahr ahl peeng-pohng
> *I'm going to play Ping-Pong.*

It's time to get some exercise. Remember that each sport is played in a particular environment: a court, a field, a course, a rink, and so on. Table 18.2 will help you choose the proper venue for the sport that interests you.

10 minutos al día

Here's how the irregular verb *querer* is conjugated in the present tense: quiero, quieres, quiere, queremos, queréis, quieren.

Here's how the irregular verb *poder* is conjugated in the present tense: puedo, puedes, puede, podemos, podéis, pueden.

Table 18.2   Where to Go

Sports Venue	Spanish Translation	Pronunciation
beach	la playa	lah plah-yah
course (golf)	el campo	ehl kahm-poh
court	la cancha	lah kahn-chah
court (jai alai)	el frontón	ehl frohn-tohn
field	el campo	ehl kahm-poh
gymnasium	el gimnasio	ehl heem-nah-see-yoh
mountain	la montaña	lah mohn-tah-nyah
ocean	el océano	ehl oh-seh-yah-noh
park	el parque	ehl pahr-keh
path	el camino	ehl kah-mee-noh

Sports Venue	Spanish Translation	Pronunciation
pool	la piscina	lah pee-see-nah
rink	la pista	lah pees-tah
sea	el mar	ehl mahr
slope	la pista	lah pees-tah
stadium	el estadio	ehl ehs-tah-dee-yoh
track	la pista	lah pees-tah

See You There!

Various members of your group have received invitations and want to participate. Say that the given subjects can engage in the following sports, and tell where they will go. (Sample responses can be found on page 418, in Appendix A.)

> Example: yo (swim)
> Yo puedo nadar.
> Yo quiero ir a la playa.

1. tú (tennis) _____ .
2. nosotros (golf) _____ .
3. Uds. (fishing) _____ .
4. ella (baseball) _____ .
5. yo (skating) _____ .

Play by the Rules

When a sentence contains one subject noun or pronoun, be sure to conjugate the verb that immediately follows it. Any verb or verbs after that should remain in the infinitive. Express "at," "in," and "to the" by using *a* + definite article (*al, a la*).

> Yo quiero jugar al golf.
> yoh kee-yeh-roh hoo-gahr ahl gohlf
> *I want to play golf.*

Culture Corner

Baseball is also a popular pastime in Latin America, especially in those countries bordering the Caribbean. Many of the top U.S. ball players come from Spanish-speaking countries or are Hispanic born Americans.

Culture Corner

The national parks in Costa Rica are known for their wide variety of vegetation and wildlife: rain forest, tropical forests, caves, lagoons, marshes, volcanos, springs, mountains, beaches, and flora and fauna of all types.

If the sentence contains two subject nouns or pronouns, a verb must be conjugated after each.

> Susana va a la playa pero ella no quiere nadar.
> soo-sah-nah bah ah lah plah-yah peh-roh eh-yah noh kee-yeh-reh nah-dar
> *Susana is going to the beach but she doesn't want to swim.*

> ¿Quiere (Quieres) ir al parque a jugar un partido de fútbol?
> kee-yeh-reh (kee-yeh-rehs) eer ahl pahr-keh ah hoo-gahr oon pahr-tee-doh deh foot-bohl
> *Do you want to go to the park to play soccer?*

> ¿Puede (puedes) acompañarme a la playa?
> pweh-deh (pweh-dehs) ah-kohm-pah-nyahr-meh ah lah plah-yah
> *Can you go with me to the beach?*

Invite Your Friends Along

Today is a beautiful day, and you're in the mood to get some exercise. Phone a friend and invite her to go with you to the best place for the following activities. (Sample responses can be found on page 419, in Appendix A.)

Example: ¿Quieres ir al parque jugar al tenis?
Would you like to go to the park to play tennis?

1. hiking _____ .

2. skiing _____ .

3. swimming _____ .

4. skating _____ .

5. mountain climbing _____ .

6. golfing _____ .

Accepting the Invitation

It's always a friendly gesture to graciously accept an invitation offered to you. Perhaps you've been asked to play doubles tennis, to accompany someone on a sight-seeing trip, or to eat dinner at someone's house. Whatever the situation, the following phrases will help you in your social encounters:

Phrase	Pronunciation	Meaning
Con mucho gusto.	kohn moo-choh goos-toh	With pleasure.
Por supuesto.	pohr soo-pwehs-toh	Of course.
Claro.	klah-roh	Of course.
Es una buena idea.	ehs oo-nah bweh-nah ee-deh-yah	That's a good idea.
Magnífico.	mahg-nee-fee-koh	Great!
De acuerdo.	deh ah-kwehr-doh	O.K. (I agree.)
Sin duda.	seen doo-dah	There's no doubt about it.
¿Por qué no?	pohr keh noh	Why not?
Si tú quieres (Ud. quiere).	see too kee-yeh-rehs (oo-stehd kee-yeh-reh)	If you want to.
Con placer.	kohn plah-sehr	Gladly.

A Polite Refusal

There are times when you would like to accept an invitation but truly cannot. Maybe you have a previous appointment. Perhaps you're tired and would like to be alone for a while. Of course, you wouldn't want to offend anyone, so you need to turn down the invitation politely. Here's how to do just that:

Phrase	Pronunciation	Meaning
Es imposible.	ehs eem-poh-see-bleh	It's impossible.
No tengo ganas.	noh tehn-goh gah-nahs	I don't feel like it.
No puedo.	noh pweh-doh	I can't.
No estoy libre.	noh ehs-toy lee-breh	I'm not free.
No quiero.	noh kee-yeh-roh	I don't want to.
Lo siento.	loh see-yehn-toh	I'm sorry.
Estoy cansado.	ehs-toy kahn-sah-doh	I'm tired.
Estoy ocupado.	ehs-toy oh-koo-pah-doh	I'm busy.

I Don't Care

We've all received invitations that we can't decide whether to accept. If you can't make up your mind or are feeling indifferent towards an idea, use one of the following phrases:

Phrase	Pronunciation	Meaning
Depende.	deh-pehn-deh	It depends.
No me importa.	noh meh eem-pohr-tah	I don't care.
Me da lo mismo	meh dah loh mees-moh	It's all the same to me.
Lo que Ud. prefiera (tú prefieras).	loh keh oo-stehd preh-fee-yeh-rah (too preh-fee- yeh-rahs)	Whatever you want.
Lo que Ud. quiera (tú quieras).	loh keh oo-stehd kee-yeh-rah (too kee-yeh-rahs)	Whatever you want.
No tengo preferencia.	noh tehn-goh preh-feh-rehn-see-yah	I don't have any preference.
Yo no sé.	yoh noh seh	I don't know.
Tal vez.	tahl behs	Perhaps. (Maybe.)

Other Diversions

You like sports, and you're a cultured, refined person. Now it's time for a change of pace. Why not try some of the activities listed in Table 18.3? If you choose to see an opera, a ballet, or a concert, don't forget to bring along *los gemelos*, binoculars.

Table 18.3   Places to Go and Things to Do

El Lugar	The Place	La Actividad	The Activity
ir a la opera	go to the opera	escuchar a los cantantes	listen to the singers
ir a la playa	go to the beach	nadar, tomar sol	swim, sunbathe
ir a una discoteca	go to the disco	bailar	dance
ir a un ballet	go to the ballet	ver a los bailadores	see the dancers
ir a un casino	go to the casino	jugar	play, gamble
ir al centro comercial	go to the mall	mirar los escaparates	window-shop

El Lugar	The Place	La Actividad	The Activity
ir al cine	go to the movies	ver una película	see a film
ir a un concierto	go to a concert	escuchar a la orquesta	listen to the orchestra
ir al teatro	go to the theater	ver un drama	see a play
ir de excursión	go on an excursion	ver los sitios	see the sights
quedarse en su habitación (casa)	stay in one's room (home)	jugar a los naipes	play cards
		jugar a las damas	play checkers
		jugar al ajedrez	play chess
		leer una novela	read a novel

Won't You Join Us?

Imagine you're on a cruise, and your winning personality has attracted many new friends. You're about to land at your first port, and you've received a number of invitations. One person wants you to go shopping in town; another has suggested visiting famous ruins outside the city. Your traveling companion would like to go to a movie, but someone special has asked you to a famous (and expensive) restaurant and a trendy disco. Use the phrases you've learned in this chapter to give suitable replies. (Sample responses can be found on page 419, in Appendix A.)

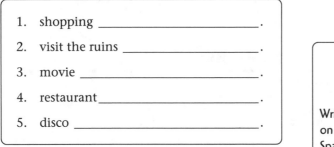

1. shopping _____.
2. visit the ruins _____.
3. movie _____.
4. restaurant_____.
5. disco _____.

In a Flash

Write a list of things you would do on your dream vacation to a Spanish-speaking country.

At the Shore

Have you ever been so excited to finally see the sea that you jumped into the ocean without a second thought? When you finally came out, you might have realized you forgot to get a towel. You're standing there dripping wet. If you want to have a pleasant day at the beach or the pool, remember to take along the following items:

Beach Items	Spanish Translation	Pronunciation
beach ball	una pelota de playa	oo-nah peh-loh-tah deh plah-yah
beach chair	un sillón de playa	oon see-yohn deh plah-yah
beach towel	una toalla de playa	oo-nah toh-wah-yah deh plah-yah
cooler	una nevera portátil	oo-nah neh-beh-rah pohr-tah-teel
radio	una radio	oo-nah rrah-dee-yoh
sunglasses	las gafas de sol	lahs gah-fahs deh sohl

Culture Corner

A *telenovela* (teh-lay-noh-beh-lah) is similar to our American soap operas. It is generally shown 5 times a week and runs for about a year. In Spanish-speaking households, watching these dramas is often a family affair.

Film at Eleven

You're all played out, you're all walked out, and your belly is full. If you're a film buff, you might want to catch the latest film or even your favorite show on TV. If you want some quiet entertainment, ask the following questions and consult Table 18.4.

¿Qué tipo de película están pasando?
keh tee-poh deh peh-lee-koo-lah ehs-tahn pah-sahn-doh
What kind of film are they showing?

¿Qué hay en la televisión?
keh ah-yee ehn lah teh-leh-bee-see-yohn
What's on TV?

Table 18.4 Movies and Television Programs

Type of Program	Spanish Translation	Pronunciation
adventure film	una película de aventura	oo-nah peh-lee-koo-lah deh ah-behn-too-rah
cartoon	los dibujos animados	lohs dee-boo-hohs ah-nee-mah-dohs
comedy	una comedia	oo-nah koh-meh-dee-yah
documentary	un documental	oon doh-koo-mehn-tahl
drama	un drama	oon drah-mah
game show	un juego	oon hweh-goh
horror movie	una película de horror	oo-nah peh-lee-koo-lah deh oh-rrohr
love story	una película de amor	oo-nah peh-lee-koo-lah deh ah-mohr
mystery	un misterio	oon mees-teh-ree-yoh

Type of Program	Spanish Translation	Pronunciation
news	las noticias	lahs noh-tee-see-yahs
police story	una película policíaca	oo-nah peh-lee-koo-lah poh-lee-see-yah-kah
science fiction film	una película de ciencia ficción	oo-nah peh-lee-koo-lah deh see-yehn-see-yah feek-see-yohn
soap opera	una telenovela	oo-nah teh-leh-noh-beh-lah
spy movie	una película de espionaje	oo-nah peh-lee-koo-lah deh ehs-pee-yoh-nah-heh
talk show	un programa de entrevistas	oon proh-grah-mah deh ehn-treh-bees-tahs
weather	el parte meteorológico, el pronóstico	ehl pahr-teh meh-teh-yoh-roh-loh-hee-koh, ehl proh-nohs-tee-koh
western	una película del oeste, un western	oo-nah peh-lee-koo-lah dehl oh-wehs-teh, oon wehs-tehrn

At the Movies

In Spanish movie theaters, an usher, *un(a) guía* (oon [oo-nah] gee-ah), will help you select a seat to your liking. Don't worry, no tip is necessary; it's their job. Don't be surprised to see commercials (which could collectively last as long as 15 minutes) before the main feature. And just like back home, there's an ample selection of candy, drinks, ice cream, and popcorn. The following will help you choose a suitable movie:

Prohibida para menores de 18 años (a menos de que esté acompañado por un adulto).
Forbidden for those under 18 (unless accompanied by an adult).

Mayores de 13 años.
You must be older than 13.

Versión original.
Original version, subtitled.

Versión doblada (doh-blah-dah) al español.
Dubbed in Spanish.

Culture Corner

Many American movies are shown in Spanish-speaking countries, and they usually are dubbed in Spanish. In some countries, such as Mexico, the government controls box office prices to make sure almost everyone can afford a movie ticket.

Tarifa reducida.
Reduced rate.

How Did You Like It?

Use the following phrases to express your enjoyment of a film or program:

Positive Review	Spanish Translation	Pronunciation
I love it!	¡Me encanta!	meh ehn-kahn-tah
It's a good movie.	¡Es una buena película!	ehs oo-nah bweh-nah peh-lee-koo-lah
It's amusing!	¡Es divertida!	ehs dee-behr-tee-dah
It's great!	¡Es fantástica!	ehs fahn-tahs-tee-kah
It's moving!	¡Me conmueve!	meh kohn-mweh-beh
It's original!	¡Es original!	ehs oh-ree-hee-nahl

If you are less than thrilled with the show, try the following phrases:

Negative Review	Spanish Translation	Pronunciation
I hate it!	¡La odio!	lah oh-dee-yoh
It's a bad movie!	¡Es una película mala!	ehs oo-nah peh-lee-koo-lah mah-lah
It's a loser!	¡Es un desastre!	ehs oon deh-sahs-treh
It's garbage!	¡Es una porquería!	ehs oo-nah pohr-keh-ree-yah
It's the same old thing!	¡Es lo mismo de siempre!	ehs loh mees-moh deh see-yehm-preh
It's too violent!	¡Es demasiado violenta!	ehs deh-mah-see-yah-doh bee-yoh-lehn-tah

I Think...

What exactly do you think? Use the phrases you learned to tell how you feel about the following types of movies. (Sample responses can be found on page 419, in Appendix A.)

a love story _____ .   a police film _____ .

a science fiction film _____ .   a mystery _____ .

a horror film _____ .   cartoons _____ .

At a Concert

On a trip to Spain, you discover your favorite rock group will be performing there during your visit. Or maybe you're more into classical guitar or chamber music. One young student of mine received an all-expense-paid trip to Europe to sing opera with a choir. Whatever your taste in music, Table 18.5 will help you with the names of the musical instruments you will hear.

Table 18.5   Musical Instruments

Instrument	Spanish Translation	Pronunciation
accordion	el acordeón	ehl ah-kohr-deh-yohn
cello	el violoncelo	ehl bee-yoh-lohn-seh-loh
clarinet	el clarinete	ehl klah-ree-neh-teh
drum	el tambor	ehl tahm-bohr
drum set	la batería	lah bah-teh-ree-yah
flute	la flauta	lah flow-tah
guitar	la guitarra	lah gee-tah-rrah
harp	el arpa	ehl ahr-pah
horn	el cuerno	ehl kwehr-noh
oboe	el oboe	ehl oh-boh-weh
piano	el piano	ehl pee-yah-noh
piccolo	el piccolo	ehl pee-koh-loh
saxophone	el saxofón	ehl sahk-soh-fohn
trombone	el trombón	ehl trohm-bohn
trumpet	la trompeta	lah trohm-peh-tah
violin	el violín	ehl bee-yoh-leen

Jugar vs. Tocar

In English, whether we're talking about engaging in a sport or playing an instrument, we use the verb "to play." In Spanish, however, a distinction is made. The verb *jugar* + *a* + definite article *(al, a la, a los, a las)* is used before the name of a sport or game. *Jugar* is a stem-changing shoe verb that changes *u* to *ue* in all forms except *nosotros* and *vosotros*. Here's a quick refresher course (or refer to Chapter 12, "Settling In").

jugar (to play)

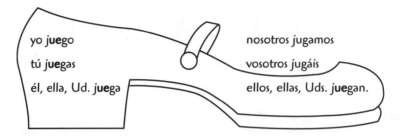

yo **juego**	nosotros **jugamos**
tú **juegas**	vosotros **jugáis**
él, ella, Ud. **juega**	ellos, ellas, Uds. **juegan.**

Jugamos a los naipes.   Juego al tenis.
hoo-gah-mohs ah lohs nah-yee-pehs   hweh-goh ahl teh-nees
We play cards.   *I play tennis.*

Use the verb *tocar* when you are talking about playing a musical instrument.

Me gusta tocar el piano.
meh goos-tah toh-kahr ehl pee-yah-noh
I like to play the piano.

10 minutos al día

Jugar (to play) + *a* is used when speaking about a sport or a game.

Tocar (to play) is used when speaking about playing a musical instrument.

Let's Play

Would you use *jugar* or *tocar*? Complete each of the following sentences with the correct form of the appropriate verb. Answers can be found on p.419, in Appendix A.

1. Nosotos _____ al fútbol.
2. Ellos _____ la guitarra.
3. Yo _____ a batería.
4. Tú _____ al tenis.
5. Ella _____ al beísbol.
6. Uds. _____ la flauta.

How Good Are You?

Adverbs are often used to describe how well someone does something, as in "He plays the classical guitar beautifully." (In English, most adverbs end in -ly.) In Spanish, adverbs are used for the same purpose, and they generally end in *-mente*.

To form most adverbs in Spanish, add *-mente* to the feminine singular form of the adjective. This works well as long as you look for the proper letter at the end of the adjective and know the feminine forms. (Refer to Chapter 9, "Getting to Know You," if you need a refresher.) Table 18.6 shows you how easy this is.

Table 18.6   Adverbs Formed from Feminine Adjectives

Feminine Adjective	Adverb	Meaning
atenta	atentamente	attentively
cariñosa	cariñosamente	affectionately
completa	completamente	completely
especial	especialmente	especially
fácil	fácilmente	easily
final	finalmente	finally
frecuente	frecuentemente	frequently
inteligente	inteligentemente	intelligently
lenta	lentamente	slowly
rápida	rápidamente	quickly
triste	tristemente	sadly

When you find it necessary to describe an action with two or more adverbs, add *-mente* only to the last one. The other adverbs should be in the feminine singular adjective form, to which it is assumed that *-mente* would be added had they stood alone. Here's an example:

> Enrique habla clara, lenta, fácil, y elocuentemente.
> *Henry speaks clearly, slowly, easily, and eloquently.*

If you can't think of the adverb or if one does not exist, use the preposition *con* + the noun, as follows:

Memory Master

To form the feminine of adjectives that end in -*o*, change the -*o* to -*a*; for adjectives that end in -*a*, -*e*, or a consonant, add nothing.

Con + Noun	Adverb	Meaning
con alegría	alegremente	happily
con cortesía	cortésmente	courteously
con cuidado	cuidadosamente	carefully
con habilidad	hábilmente	skillfully
con paciencia	pacientemente	patiently

Is your Spanish good? Do you speak the language well? How about your accent, is it good or bad? (Of course it's good—you're using the pronunciation guide.) Be careful with the adverbs "well" and "badly." They have distinctively different forms from the adjectives "good" and "bad."

Adjective	Meaning	Adverb	Meaning
bueno	good	bien	well
malo	bad	mal	badly

> Ella es buena y habla bien el español.
> eh-yah ehs bweh-nah ee ah-blah byehn ehl ehs-pah-nyohl
> *She is good, and she speaks Spanish well.*

Adverbs usually are placed after the verb they modify. Sometimes, however, the adverb is placed exactly where we would put it in English.

> Son malos músicos y tocan mal la guitarra.
> sohn mah-lohs moo-see-kohs ee toh-kahn mahl lah gee-tah-rrah
> *They are bad musicians, and they play the guitar poorly.*

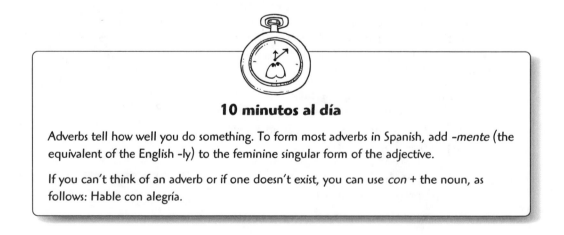

10 minutos al día

Adverbs tell how well you do something. To form most adverbs in Spanish, add *-mente* (the equivalent of the English -ly) to the feminine singular form of the adjective.

If you can't think of an adverb or if one doesn't exist, you can use *con* + the noun, as follows: Hable con alegría.

Some adverbs and adverbial expressions are not formed from adjectives at all; therefore, they do not end in *-mente*. Table 18.7 provides some of the most common adverbs that follow this rule.

Table 18.7 Adverbs and Adverbial Expressions Not Formed from Adjectives

Adverb/Adverbial Expression	Pronunciation	Meaning
ahora	ah-oh-rah	now
allá	ah-yah	there
aquí	ah-kee	here
peor	peh-yohr	worse
mejor	meh-hohr	better
más	mahs	more
menos	meh-nohs	less
a menudo	ah meh-noo-doh	often
muy	mwee	very
siempre	see-yehm-preh	always
también	tahm-bee-yehn	also, too
tan	tahn	as, so
tarde	tahr-deh	late
temprano	tehm-prah-noh	soon, early
todavía	toh-dah-bee-yah	still, yet
ya	yah	already

Position of Adverbs

Adverbs are generally placed after the verb they modify. Sometimes, however, the position of the adverb is variable, and it is placed where we would logically put an English adverb. Notice the position of the adverbs in the following examples:

Juega bien al fútbol.
hweh-gah bee-yehn ahl foot-bohl
He plays soccer well.

Juega muy bien al fútbol.
hweh-gah mwee bee-yehn ahl foot-bohl
He plays soccer very well.

Generalmente juega bien.
geh-neh-rahl-mehn-teh hweh-gah bee-yehn
Usually he plays well.

Do You Do It Well?

How's your flamenco dancing? Do you make a perfect flan? Can you sing like a nightingale? Or do you wail like a sick cat? Naturally, everyone's abilities differ. We're all good at some things and awful at others. How do you think you measure up? Use adverbs to express how you feel you perform the following activities. (Sample responses can be found on page 419, in Appendix A.)

    Example: hablar español
                        Hablo español lentamente.

1. hablar español (speak Spanish) _____ .

2. cocinar (cook) _____ .

3. pensar (think) _____ .

4. trabajar (work) _____ .

5. bailar (dance) _____ .

6. nadar (swim) _____ .

The Least You Need to Know

➤ The verbs *hacer* + noun, *ir* + *a* + infinitive, and *jugar un partido de* + noun can be used to describe participation in a sport.

➤ *Querer* and *poder* + infinitive can be used to propose, to accept, and to refuse invitations. Don't forget, both verbs are shoe verbs.

➤ *Jugar* + *a* + definite article (*al, a la, a los, a las*) is used to discuss playing a game. *Tocar* is used to discuss playing a musical instrument.

➤ Many adverbs can be formed by adding *-mente* to adjectives ending in a vowel.

Part 4
Problem Solving

Traveling is perfect when everything goes the way it should. Unfortunately, sometimes problems arise through no fault of your own. In Part 4, you'll learn how to deal with annoying inconveniences that can interfere with your daily routines. You certainly wouldn't want them to ruin your good time.

Some situations are relatively minor such as forgetting your toothpaste, staining your clothing, running out of film, breaking the heel on your shoe, or having to make a phone call or send a letter or package. Other situations are more serious and require immediate attention: an injury, a lost contact lens, broken glasses, or a forgotten prescription.

Part 4 covers a wide range of problems that might arise when you least expect them. The good news is that you'll be able to deal with any or all of them quite expeditiously.

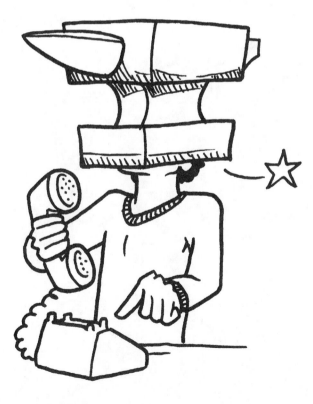

Getting Great Service

You're having the time of your life traveling throughout the Spanish-speaking world. You've been gone so long, however, that little by little, problems are starting to surface. First, have you looked at yourself in the mirror lately? It's time for a change. Your new tweed jacket has a hole in it, and you just dropped your glasses and broke the frames. And if that isn't enough, your shoes need resoling and the flash in your camera no longer works. Don't fret! Ask around or consult *las páginas amarillas* (lahs pah-hee-nahs ah-mah-ree-yahs), the Yellow Pages. Just explain your problems and expert technicians will see to all of them. This chapter will help you get the job done.

Dealing with a Bad Hair Day

Imagine you've spent the day relaxing in the sun. Now it's time to prepare for an important conference, meeting, or date that you've planned for this evening. Upon returning to your room, you cast a quick glance at yourself in the mirror. Good grief! You have terminal hat head, and your beautiful curls are as flat as a board. For a quick fix-me-up, run to the nearest *peinador* (peh-yee-nah-dohr), or hair stylist.

Gone are the days when men were treated solely *a la barbería* (ah lah bahr-beh-ree-ah), at the barbershop, while women went *al salón de belleza* (ahl sah-lohn deh beh-yeh-sah), to the beauty parlor. Thanks to the modern unisex trend, many establishments cater to the needs of everyone because both men and women frequently demand the same services. Use the following sentences when your hair needs help:

Puede darme
pweh-deh dahr-meh
Can you give me...

Por favor
pohr fah-bohr
Please

Quisiera...
kee-see-yeh-rah
I would like...

Do you want a quick fix-up or a whole new look? Check out the services listed in Table 19.1.

Table 19.1   Hair Care

Type of Service	Spanish Translation	Pronunciation
a blunt cut	un corto en cuadrado	oon kohr-toh ehn kwah-drah-doh
a coloring (vegetable)	un tinte (vegetal)	oon teen-teh (beh-heh-tahl)
a facial	un masaje facial	oon mah-sah-heh fah-see-yahl
a haircut	un corte de pelo	oon kohr-teh deh peh-loh
a manicure	una manicura	oo-nah mah-nee-koo-rah
a pedicure	una pedicura	oo-nah peh-dee-koo-rah
a permanent	una permanente	oo-nah pehr-mah-nehn-teh
a set	un marcado	oon mahr-kah-doh
a shampoo	un champú	oon chahm-poo
a trim	un recorte	oon rreh-kohr-teh
a waxing	una depilación	oo-nah deh-pee-lah-see-yohn
highlights	reflejos	rreh-fleh-hohs
layers	un corte en degradación	oon kohr-teh ehn deh-grah-dah-see-yohn

Do you need other services? Table 19.2 provides the phrases you need to explain exactly what you want. Use the following phrase to preface your request:

Podría _____ por favor.
poh-dree-yah _____ pohr fah-bohr
Could you _____ please.

Table 19.2   Other Services

Type of Service	Spanish Translation	Pronunciation
blow-dry my hair	secarme el pelo	seh-kahr-meh ehl peh-loh
curl my hair	rizarme el pelo	rree-sahr-meh ehl peh-loh
shave	afeitarme	ah-feh-yee-tahr-meh
my beard	la barba	lah bahr-bah
my mustache	el bigote	ehl bee-goh-teh
my head	la cabeza	lah kah-beh-sah
straighten my hair	estirarme el pelo	ehs-tee-rahr-meh ehl peh-loh
trim my bangs	recortarme el flequillo	rreh-kohr-tahr-meh ehl fleh-kee-yoh
trim	recortarme	rreh-kohr-tahr-meh
my beard	la barba	lah bahr-bah
my mustache	el bigote	ehl bee-goh-teh
my sideburns	las patillas	lahs pah-tee-yahs

Just a Trim?

We all know what it's like to go to a hair salon and explain in very clear English exactly what we want. A half hour later when the hair stylist is done, however, we end up shrieking at the mirror. That was *not* what we asked for. Imagine the same situation with a language barrier. Tables 19.3 and 19.4 can help.

Quisiera un peinado _____.
kee-see-yeh-rah oon peh-yee-nah-doh
I'd like a _____ style.

In a Flash

Imagine you are having your hair done in a Spanish-speaking country. Tell the stylist what you would like to have done.

Prefiero mi pelo _____.
preh-fee-yeh-roh mee peh-loh
I prefer my hair _____.

Table 19.3 Hairstyles

Hairstyle	Spanish Translation	Pronunciation
long	largo	lahr-goh
medium	mediano	meh-dee-yah-noh
short	corto	kohr-toh
wavy	ondulado	ohn-doo-lah-doh
curly	rizado	rree-sah-doh
straight	lacio (liso)	lah-see-yoh (lee-soh)

Table 19.4 Asking for the Perfect Hair Color

Haircolor	Spanish Translation	Pronunciation
auburn	rojizo	rroh-hee-soh
black	negro	neh-groh
blond	rubio	rroo-bee-yoh
brunette	castaño	kahs-tah-nyoh
chestnut brown	pardo	pahr-doh
red	pelirrojo	peh-lee-rroh-hoh
a darker color	un color más oscuro	oon koh-lohr mahs oh-skoo-roh
a lighter color	un color más claro	oon koh-lohr mahs klah-roh
the same color	el mismo color	ehl mees-moh koh-lohr

Problems and More Problems

When you need to have certain services performed or when something you own needs repair, you should have some key phrases on hand. Make use of the following sentences when you go to the dry cleaner, the shoemaker, the optometrist, the jeweler, or the camera store.

¿A qué hora abre Ud.?
ah keh oh-rah ah-breh oo-stehd
At what time do you open?

¿A qué hora cierra Ud.?
ah keh oh-rah see-yeh-rrah oo-stehd
At what time do you close?

¿Qué días abre (cierra) Ud.?
keh dee-yahs ah-breh (see-yeh-rrah)
oo-stehd
What days are you open? closed?

¿Puede arreglarme _____.
pweh-deh ah-rreh-glahr-meh _____.
Can you fix _____ for me?

¿Puede arreglármelo (la, los, las) hoy?
pweh-deh ah-rreh-glahr-meh-loh (lah, lohs,
lahs) oy
Can you fix it (them) today?

¿Puede arreglármelo (la, los, las)
temporalmente (mientras yo espero)?
pweh-deh ah-rreh-glahr-meh-loh (lah, lohs,
lahs) tehm-poh-rahl-mehn-teh (mee-yehn-
trahs yoh ehs-peh-roh)
Can you fix it (them) temporarily (while I wait)?

¿Me puede dar un recibo?
meh pweh-deh dahr oon reh-see-boh
May I have a receipt?

Memory Master

You may use both a direct and an indirect object in the same sentence. The indirect object (a person) precedes the direct object (usually a thing):

¿Puede Ud. arreglármelo?
Can you fix it for me?

Memory Master

The indirect object pronouns *le* and *les* become *se* before the direct objects *lo, la, los,* and *las:*

¿Puede Ud. arreglárselo?
Can you fix it for him?

At the Dry Cleaner's (En la Tintorería)

My friends think I'm crazy, but I like to travel with a compact travel iron. I can't stand that rumpled look. My husband believes that hanging anything in a damp bathroom will do the trick just fine. When you unpack, do you hate the way your clothes come

Memory Master

If you'd like a service performed for someone else, use the appropriate indirect object pronoun: *te* (for you), *le* (for him, her, you), *nos* (for us), *os* (for you), *les* (for them).

¿Puede tejerle este abrigo?
Can you please weave this coat for him?

out? Did you spill sangria on your favorite shirt? No problem. Every country has dry cleaning and laundry establishments that can deal with all your spots, stains, wrinkles, and tears. Here's how to explain your problem:

Tengo un problema.
tehn-goh oon proh-bleh-mah
I have a problem.

¿Cuál es el problema?
kwahl ehs ehl proh-bleh-mah
What's the problem?

Hay...
ah-yee
There is (are)...

Problem	Spanish Translation	Pronunciation
a hole	un roto	oon rroh-toh
a missing button	(le falta) un botón	(leh fahl-tah) oon boh-tohn
a spot, stain	una mancha	oo-nah mahn-chah
a tear	un desgarrón	oon dehs-gah-rrohn

Memory Master

Use the verb *remendar*, to repair, when referring to clothing or shoes.

Puede remendarme este vestido?
¿Puede remendarme estos zapatos?

Congratulations, you've successfully explained your problem. Now you're ready to state what you'd like done about it.

¿Puede lavarme en seco este (esta, estos, estas) _____ ?
pweh-deh lah-bahr-meh ehn seh-koh ehs-teh (ehs-tah, ehs-tohs, ehs-tahs)
Can you (dry) clean this (these) _____ for me?

¿Puede remendarme este (esta, estos, estas) _____ ?
pweh-deh rreh-mehn-dahr-meh ehs-teh (ehs-tah, ehs-tohs, ehs-tahs)
Can you please mend this (these) _____ for me?

¿Puede plancharme este (esta, estos, estas)
_____ ?

pweh-deh plahn-chahr-meh ehs-teh (ehs-tah,
ehs-tohs, ehs-tahs)

Can you please press this (these) _____ for me?

¿Puede almidonarme este (esta, estos, estas)
_____ ?

pweh-deh ahl-mee-doh-nahr-meh ehs-teh
(ehs-tah, ehs-tohs, ehs-tahs)

Can you please starch this (these) _____ for me?

¿Puede tejerme este (esta, estos, estas) _____ ?
pweh-deh teh-hehr-meh ehs-teh (ehs-tah,
ehs-tohs, ehs-tahs)

Can you please weave this (these) _____ for me?

Culture Corner

Don't expect to find as many dry cleaners and Laundromats in the Spanish–speaking world as in the United States. And don't expect same–day service. Plan on waiting a few days, or perhaps even a week, to get your clothes cleaned. If you're lucky, you might find dry cleaners in bigger cities who can have your laundry ready in a day.

At the Laundry (En la Lavandería)

Whether you're on the road or enjoying a leisurely vacation in a hotel, your laundry will pile up. If it can't wait until you get home, the following phrases will help you get started:

Quiero lavarme la ropa.
kee-yeh-roh lah-bahr-meh lah rroh-pah
I'd like to wash my clothes.

Quisiera que me laven la ropa.
kee-see-yeh-rah keh meh lah-behn lah
rroh-pah
I'd like to have my clothes washed.

¡Atención!

When traveling, you can make your life easy if you pack only wash and wear clothing. If you just need a quick touch up, use the sink and some soap. Remember, though, the bidet is not for doing your wash!

You don't want anyone to see that ring around your collar, or perhaps you're embarrassed by that tomato-sauce stain on your white shirt. Maybe you think no one does a better job washing clothes than you, or you're afraid that your new wool sweater will shrink. If you're intent on doing the job yourself, here are some phrases that might prove useful:

¿Hay una lavadora (secadora) libre?
ah-yee oo-nah lah-bah-doh-rah (seh-kah-doh-rah) lee-breh
Is there a free washing machine (dryer)?

¿Dónde puedo comprar jabón en polvo?
dohn-deh pweh-doh kohm-prahr hah-bohn ehn pohl-boh
Where can I can buy soap powder?

No Starch

If you're not up to washing your own clothes, you can fill out a laundry slip, which is usually left in every hotel room. After you complete the form, leave your clothes in the sack provided. Imagine you've let your dirty clothes pile up and you have to fill out a laundry slip. Read the following notice that accompanies your laundry slip. What does it tell you? (Check your translation on page 419 in the Answer Key.)

HABITACIÓN

NOTA: Su ropa será aceptada bajo las siguientes condiciones:

No somos responsables por botones o adornos que no resistan el lavado o aplanchado.

En caso de pérdida o daño, el hotel responderá hasta diez veces el valor del servicio encomendado a la lavandería.

No nos hacemos responsables por materiales sintéticos, ni por articulos dejados por más de 3 meses.

Cerrado los sábados, domingos y días de fiesta.

Servicios urgentes serán cargados con 50% sobre costo.

At the Shoemaker's (En la Zapatería)

Have you walked so much that your shoes need new soles? Perhaps you're going out on the town, and it's time for a shine. If you're a jeans and sneakers type of person, maybe it's time for some new laces. Use the following phrases to help you:

¿Puede remendarme...?
pweh-deh rreh-mehn-dahr-meh
Can you repair _____ for me?

In a Flash

Go to your closet and look at your shoes. Describe what you'd like the shoemaker to fix on each worn pair.

estos zapatos
ehs-tohs sah-pah-tohs
these shoes

este tacón
ehs-teh tah-kohn
this heel

estas botas
ehs-tahs boh-tahs
these boots

¿Vende cordones de zapatos?
behn-deh kohr-doh-nehs deh sah-pah-tohs
Do you sell shoelaces?

esta suela
ehs-tah sweh-lah
this sole

Quisiera que me lustre los zapatos.
kee-see-yeh-rah keh meh loos-treh lohs
sah-pah-tohs
I'd like a shoe shine.

Traveling Shoes

You just looked at the dress shoes you're planning to wear for a very important engagement. They are in serious need of repair, and you need them for tomorrow night. You look in the Yellow Pages and come across the following ad. What service does this *zapatería* provide? (For a translation see page 419, in Appendix A.)

ZAPATERÍA

BERNAL

Buscamos y Llevamos

Calle de la Cruz 154

Viejo San Juan

¡Atención!

If you wear glasses or contact lenses, make sure to take along a spare pair when traveling.

At the Optician's (En la Óptica)

People who wear contact lenses know that they tend to disappear or rip at the most inopportune moments. For people who rely on glasses, a broken lens or frame while on vacation could be a real disaster. Familiarize yourself with the following useful phrases:

¿Puede arreglarme estos lentes (estas gafas)?
pweh-deh ah-rreh-glahr-meh ehs-tohs lehn-tehs (ehs-tahs gah-fahs)
Can you repair these glasses for me?

El lente (la montura) está roto(a).
ehl lehn-teh (lah mohn-too-rah) ehs-tah rroh-toh(tah)
The lens (the frame) is broken.

¿Puede darme otra lentilla (otro lente) de contacto?
pweh-deh dahr-meh oh-trah lehn-tee-yah (oh-troh lehn-teh) deh kohn-tahk-toh
Can you replace this contact lens?

¿Tiene lentes progresivos?
tee-yeh-neh lehn-tehs proh-greh-see-bohs
Do you have progressive lenses?

¿Vende lentes (gafas) de sol?
behn-deh lehn-tehs (gah-fahs) deh sohl
Do you sell sunglasses?

Seeing About Glasses

If you have a problem, you'll probably turn to *las páginas amarillas*, the Yellow Pages, pretty quickly. No doubt there'll be plenty of ads to help you find the services you need. Read the following ad to find out what this optical service has to offer. (Check your translation on page 420 in the Answer Key.)

ÓPTICA

MUNDIAL

- Servicio el mismo día
- Gafas de sol con o sin prescripción
- Precios competitivos
- Gran selección
- Ajustes y reparaciones
- Lentes de contacto

Una promesa a nuestros clientes:

Cortesía, buen servicio y tratamiento experto de parte de
un personal
constituído por profesionales certificados

At the Jeweler's (En la Joyería)

What bad luck! The battery of your watch just went dead right in the middle of your trip. You'll have to stop in a jewelry store or a watchmaker's (*la relojería,* la rreh-loh-heh-ree-yah) for a quick repair.

¿Puede arreglarme este reloj?
pweh-deh ah-rreh-glahr-meh ehs-teh rreh-loh
Can you repair this watch?

Mi reloj no funciona.
mee rreh-loh noh foon-see-yoh-nah
My watch doesn't work.

Mi reloj está parado.
mee rreh-loh ehs-tah pah-rah-doh
My watch has stopped.

¿Vende pulsos (baterías)?
behn-deh pool-sohs (bah-teh-ree-yahs)
Do you sell bands (batteries)?

Cultural Corner

One of the most interesting and avant-garde jewelry designers today is Paloma Picasso, daughter of the famous Spanish–born painter, Pablo. Best known for her chic, exotic, and often-times colorful jewelry designs, Paloma (Spanish for dove) has also created a famous perfume bearing her name.

Time for Repairs

You're going to be late for an important date because your watch's battery died. Fortunately, there's a jewelry shop right outside your hotel. You decide to stop by for a quick repair, you hope. Write a quick note to explain the problem you're having and what you'd like done. (Sample responses can be found on page 420, in Appendix A.)

¡Atención!

If you forgot your camera at home, you can purchase a disposable one at most drugstores, stationery stores, or camera stores.

At the Camera Shop (En la Tienda del Fotógrafo)

If you're like me, you take your camera and a huge supply of film on every trip. You wouldn't want to miss any precious moments. Besides, when you get back, you like to look at the shots you snapped. In a way, this enables you to relive the vacation many times. If you need more supplies, a repair, or simply want to develop your film, the following words will help you:

Photo Supply	Spanish Translation	Pronunciation
a camera	una cámara	oo-nah kah-mah-rah
film	una película	oo-nah peh-lee-koo-lah
slides	las diapositivas	lahs dee-yah-poh-see-tee-bahs
a video camera	una videocámara	oo-nah bee-deh-yoh-kah-mah-rah

If you have special needs, you might ask the following:

¿Vende películas a color (en blanco y negro) de 20 (36) exposiciones?
behn-deh peh-lee-koo-lahs ah koh-lohr (ehn blahn-koh ee neh-groh) deh behn-teh (treh-een-tah ee seh-yees) ehks-poh-see-see-yoh-nehs
Do you sell rolls of 20 (36) exposure film in color (black-and-white)?

¿Vende películas para diapositivas?
behn-deh peh-lee-koo-lahs pah-rah dee-yah-poh-see-tee-bahs
Do you sell film for slides?

Quisiera que me revele este carrete (rollo).
kee-see-yeh-rah keh meh rreh-beh-leh ehs-teh kah-rreh-teh (roh-yoh)
I would like to have this film developed.

Getting the Picture

You took some great shots, and you want to see them right away. You read an ad in the paper and decided to bring your film in for developing. What did the ad promise you? (See page 420 of the Answer Key to check your translation.)

Finding Help

In addition to needing repairs, you might find that you need other services. Should you lose important papers or documents or need special assistance, you might find yourself in need of the police or the American embassy. Don't be afraid to ask for a translator, if necessary. Although you've become quite good at this, if you're nervous or upset, you might not be able to get your thoughts across in any language. The following phrases should help you get started:

¿Dónde está...?
dohn-deh ehs-tah
Where is...

> la comisaría de policía
> lah koh-mee-sah-ree-yah deh poh-lee-see-yah
> *the police station?*

> el consulado americano
> ehl kohn-soo-lah-doh ah-meh-ree-kah-noh
> *the American consulate?*

> la embajada americana
> lah ehm-bah-hah-dah ah-meh-ree-kah-nah
> *the American embassy?*

Yo perdí...
yoh pehr-dee
I lost...

> mi pasaporte
> mee pah-sah-pohr-teh
> *my passport*

> mi cartera
> mee kahr-teh-rah
> *my wallet*

Ayúdeme, por favor.
ah-yoo-deh-meh pohr fah-bohr
Help me, please.

Necesito un intérprete.
neh-seh-see-toh oon een-tehr-preh-teh
I need an interpreter.

Hay alguien aquí que hable inglés?
ah-yee ahl-gee-yehn ah-kee keh ah-bleh een-glehs
Does anyone here speak English?

Prepositional Pronouns

To get the services you need, you'll have to use prepositions. What are prepositions? They are words that are used to show the relation of a noun to another word in the sentence.

A prepositional pronoun replaces a noun as the object of a preposition. This pronoun always follows the preposition. Table 19.5 shows subject pronouns with their corresponding prepositional pronouns.

Table 19.5   Prepositional Pronouns

Subject	Prepositional Pronoun	Meaning
yo	mí	me
tú	ti	you (familiar)
él	él	him, it
ella	ella	her, it
Ud.	Ud.	you (formal)
nosotros (as)	nosotros (as)	us
vosotros (as)	vosotros (as)	you (familiar)
ellos	ellos	them
ellas	ellas	them
Uds.	Uds.	you (formal)

Make sure to use the correct pronoun in a prepositional phrase. The only prepositional pronouns that differ from subject pronouns are *mí* and *ti*, so this is fairly simple.

Este regalo no es para ti, es para mí.
ehs-teh rreh-gah-loh ehs pah-rah tee (ehs pah-rah mee)
This present isn't for you, it's for me.

No podemos partir sin ellos.
noh poh-deh-mohs pahr-teer seen eh-yohs
We can't leave without them.

Memory Master

Mí and *ti* combine with the preposition *con* (kohn), which means "with," as follows:

Él va al centro conmigo.
He's going downtown with me.

No puedo ir contigo.
I can't go with you.

Because indirect object pronouns often need clarification in Spanish, it is common to add the preposition *a* + a prepositional pronoun to avoid confusion.

Le doy a él la respuesta.
I give him the answer.

Le doy a ella la respuesta.
I give her the answer.

Le doy a Ud. la respuesta.
I give you the answer.

A + a prepositional pronoun can be added to stress to whom an action has importance:

A mí me gusta el chocolate.
I like chocolate.

A él no le encantan los deportes.
He doesn't adore sports.

Using These Pronouns

You are talking about some of the activities you and your friends do together. Use prepositions to complete the following sentences. (Answers can be found on page 420, in Appendix A.)

1. (you/fam.) Yo voy al cine con _____ .
2. (you/pl.) Nosotros estudiamos sin _____ .
3. (me) Tú vives cerca de _____ .
4. (them/m.) Ella trabaja lejos de _____ .
5. (us) Ellos siempre llegan depués de _____ .
6. (him) Este regalo es para _____ .

10 minutos al día

Prepositional pronouns replace a noun that is the object of a preposition:

> Este regalo no es para ti, es para mí.
> *This present isn't for you, it's for me.*

See Table 19.5 for a quick review. Remember, the only prepositional pronouns that differ from subject pronouns are *mi* and *ti*.

Making Comparisons

Which airline company has the best airfare to a Spanish-speaking country? Which hotel has the best facilities? Which car rental gives you the best deal? Who is the most reliable tour guide in the city? Every day, we make comparisons. Sometimes we're looking for the most, sometimes the least. Use Table 19.6 to help you with comparisons.

Table 19.6   Comparison of Adjectives: Inequality

	Adjective	Pronunciation	Meaning
Positive	triste	trees-teh	sad
Comparative	más triste	mahs trees-teh	sadder
	menos triste	meh-nohs trees-teh	less sad
Superlative	el (la, los, las) _____ más triste(s)	ehl (lah, lohs, lahs) mahs trees-teh(s)	the saddest _____
	el (la, los, las) _____ menos triste(s)	ehl (lah, lohs, lahs) meh-nohs trees-teh(s)	the least sad _____

Memory Master

The comparative and superlative forms of adjectives must agree in gender and number with the nouns they describe.

Julio es menos fuerte que su amigo.

Juanita es más linda que su hermana.

Estas camisetas son las menos caras.

Esos coches son los más deportivos.

The word *que* may or may not be used after the comparative. When used, *que* expresses "than."

¿Quién es más sincero?
Who is more sincere?

Roberto es más sincero (que Rafael).
Roberto is more sincere (than Rafael).

Amalia es menos sincera (que Ana).
Amalia is less sincere (than Ana).

The preposition *de* + a definite article *(del, de la, de los, de las)* can be used to express *in (of) the.*

Este hombre es simpático.
This man is nice.

Este hombre es más simpático que él.
This man is nicer than he.

Este hombre es el más simpático del pueblo.
This man is the nicest in the city.

Esas mujeres son ricas.
Those women are rich.

Esas mujeres son las más ricas.
Those women are the richest.

Aquellas mujeres son las menos ricas de la cuidad.
Those women are the least rich in the city.

That's Highly Irregular

Beware of irregular comparisons. Never use *más* or *menos* with the adjectives *bueno* and *malo*. Special comparative forms are used to express *better* and *best.*

Positive		Comparative		Superlative	
Spanish	English	Spanish	English	Spanish	English
bueno (-a, -os, -as)	good	mejor (-es)	better	el (la) mejor, los (las) mejores	best
malo (-a, -os, -as)	bad	peor (-es)	worse	el (la) peor, los (las) peores	worst

When *grande* and *pequeño* refer to age (older or younger), do not use *más* or *menos*. Use the following comparative forms instead:

Positive		Comparative		Superlative	
Spanish	English	Spanish	English	Spanish	English
grande	big	mayor (-es)	older	el (la) mayor, los (las) mayores	oldest
pequeño	small	menor (-es)	younger	el (la) menor, los (las) menores	youngest

Comparisons of Inequality

Each person in my family has different levels of artistic talent. When my husband picks up a pencil and a piece of paper, his drawings are quite good. My son, Michael, has the second-best genes and seems rather talented. I have the worst ability, which I passed on to my other son, Eric. He also draws horribly. No one can ever tell exactly what it is I've put on the paper. At least I make everyone laugh. Not only can people be compared, but the ways in which they do things can also be compared. Table 19.7 shows how to make comparisons using adverbs (to describe actions).

Table 19.7   Comparison of Adverbs: Inequality

	Adverb	Pronunciation	Meaning
Positive	rápidamente	rrah-pee-dah-mehn-teh	rapidly
Comparative	más rápidamente	mahs rrah-pee-dah-mehn-teh	more rapidly
	menos rápidamente	meh-nohs rrah-pee-dah-mehn-teh	less rapidly
Superlative	más rápidamente (que)	mahs rrah-pee-dah-mehn-teh (keh)	more rapidly (than)
	menos rápidamente (que)	meh-nohs rrah-pee-dah-mehn-teh (keh)	less rapidly (than)

No distinction is made between the comparative and superlative forms of adverbs. For the comparative and superlative, use *que* to express "than," as follows:

Yo camino rápidamente.
I walk fast.

Carlos camina más rápidamente.
Carlos walks faster.

Carlos camina más rápidamente que yo.
Carlos walks faster than I.

Comparisons of Equality

You've done a lot of sight-seeing on your trip. Did you find the modern museums as entertaining as museums that hold the treasures of antiquity? Did you spend as much time visiting the Picasso exhibits as you did those of Velázquez? If all things are equal, it becomes necessary to form a comparison of equality using either adjectives or adverbs. To do this, use the following formula:

tan + adjective or adverb + *como* ("as...as")

Él es tan elegante como su amigo.
He is as elegant as his friend.

Ella trabaja tan diligentemente como él.
She works as hard as he does.

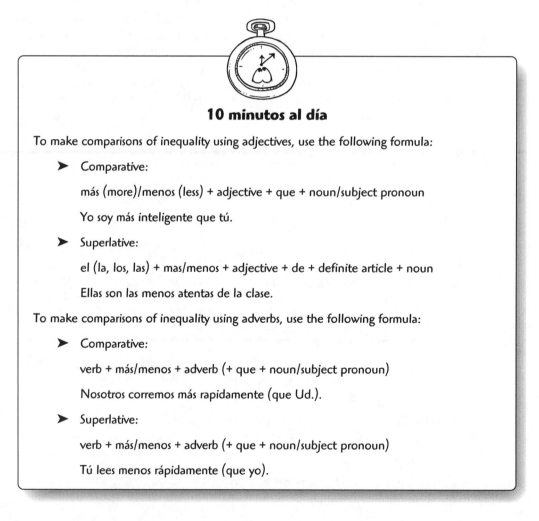

10 minutos al día

To make comparisons of inequality using adjectives, use the following formula:

➤ Comparative:

más (more)/menos (less) + adjective + que + noun/subject pronoun

Yo soy más inteligente que tú.

➤ Superlative:

el (la, los, las) + mas/menos + adjective + de + definite article + noun

Ellas son las menos atentas de la clase.

To make comparisons of inequality using adverbs, use the following formula:

➤ Comparative:

verb + más/menos + adverb (+ que + noun/subject pronoun)

Nosotros corremos más rapidamente (que Ud.).

➤ Superlative:

verb + más/menos + adverb (+ que + noun/subject pronoun)

Tú lees menos rápidamente (que yo).

Absolutely Superlative

When no comparison is involved and you want to express that something is absolutely superlative, you can attach *-ísimo*, *-ísima*, *-ísimos*, or *-ísimas* to the adjective (according to the number and gender of the noun being described). If the adjective ends in a vowel, drop the vowel before adding the superlative ending. The *-ísimo* ending means the same as using *muy* + adjective. In the following sentence pairs, both sentences have the same meaninge:

El hotel es muy grande.   Esta película es muy popular.
Es un hotel grandísimo.   Es una película popularísima.

Adjectives with certain endings make the following changes: *c* changes to *qu*, *g* changes to *gu*, and *z* becomes *c* before adding *-ísimo*. Notice these changes in the following, equivalent sentences:

Es un postre muy rico.   Es una avenida muy larga.
Es un postre riquísimo.   Es una avenida larguísima.

El tigre es muy feroz.
El tigre es ferocísimo.

Adverbs also can be made absolutely superlative, but you probably won't be hearing or saying this often because the words seem to be tongue twisters. If you'd like to give it a shot, add *-mente* to the feminine form of the adjective to which you are adding *-ísima*:

Él trabaja lentísimamente.
He works very slowly.

How Do You Measure Up?

How do you compare to people you know? Are you shorter? Thinner? More charming? Do you dance better? Work more seriously? Listen more patiently? Use what you've learned to compare yourself to friends or family members. (Sample responses can be found on page 420, in Appendix A.)

In a Flash

Describe as many things as you can that are absolutely superlative.

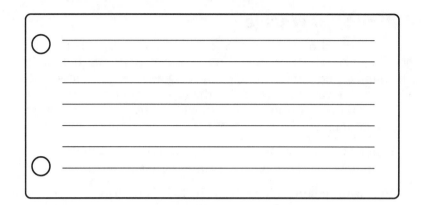

10 minutos al día

When there is no comparison and you want to express an absolute superlative, you can attach *-ísimo, -ísima, -ísimos,* or *-ísimas* to the adjective, according to the number and gender of the noun being described. If the adjective ends in a vowel, drop the vowel before adding the superlative ending.

Ella es bella.
Ella es bellísima.

The Least You Need to Know

➤ Prepositional pronouns are used after prepositions and for emphasis. They also can help clarify the identity of the indirect object pronoun.

➤ Use *más* (more) or *menos* (less) before adjectives or adverbs to make comparisons or to state the superlative.

➤ Use *tan* (as) before adjectives and adverbs + *como* to express that two things are equal.

➤ Use *-ísimo* (*-ísima, -ísimos, -ísimas*) to form the absolute superlative of adjectives and adverbs.

Chapter 20

Is There a Doctor in the House?

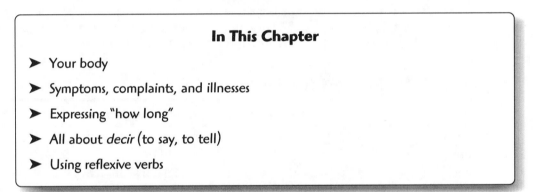

In This Chapter

➤ Your body

➤ Symptoms, complaints, and illnesses

➤ Expressing "how long"

➤ All about *decir* (to say, to tell)

➤ Using reflexive verbs

In the preceding chapter, you learned to cope with minor, everyday hassles. You should now feel assured that you can make yourself look presentable and obtain necessary repairs with a fair amount of expediency. In this chapter, you'll learn the words and expressions to help you deal with a more serious problem—an illness.

Of course, you probably think it can't happen to you. People travel far and wide all the time without ever having to visit a doctor. But let's face it. At the most inopportune moments, people can get sick or have freak accidents. My best friend passed a kidney stone in France, my son shattered a tooth in the Dominican Republic, my mother fell and fractured her wrist in Puerto Rico, and I got violently seasick on a two-day cruise to nowhere.

Life's medical annoyances really can bring us down when all we want to do is relax and have a good time. The situation can become even more frustrating if we can't communicate what is wrong. In this chapter, you will learn to describe what ails you and how long you've had your symptoms.

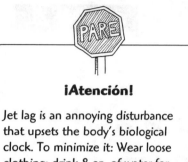

Love Your Body!

My Aunt Harriet drools over the sexy ads for Cancún, and she covets a genuine turquoise jewelry collection. Why hasn't she flown the coop and jumped on an Aeronaves de México flight during the winter snows? The answer is simple—Montezuma's Revenge (severe diarrhea). She's convinced that if she just looks at a glass of water, she'll wind up in *un consultorio* (oon kohn-sool-toh-ree-yoh), a doctor's office, or worse yet, she'll spend the entire week in *el baño* (ehl bah-nyoh), the bathroom.

Logically, she knows she can travel with a bottle of Lomotil and always keep mineral water on hand. But she's heard too many horror stories from friends who ate salad (washed in tap water) or had drinks on the rocks (with ice cubes made from local water). Everyone says that, with today's modern technology and advanced hygienic conditions, the curse of Montezuma is a thing of the past. Perhaps one day you'll see my aunt on that flight. If you go, however, you'll want to learn the words in Table 20.1 so that you can tell somebody you're sick and where it hurts—just in case.

Table 20.1 Parts of the Body

Body Part	Spanish Translation	Pronunciation
ankle	el tobillo	ehl toh-bee-yoh
arm	el brazo	ehl brah-soh
back	la espalda	lah ehs-pahl-dah
body	el cuerpo	ehl kwehr-poh
brain	el cerebro	ehl seh-reh-broh
chest	el pecho	ehl peh-choh
chin	la barbilla	lah bahr-bee-yah
ear	la oreja	lah oh-reh-hah
eye	el ojo	ehl oh-hoh
face	la cara	lah kah-rah
finger	el dedo	ehl deh-doh
foot	el pie	ehl pee-yeh
hand	la mano	lah mah-noh
head	la cabeza	lah kah-beh-sah
heart	el corazón	ehl koh-rah-sohn
knee	la rodilla	lah rroh-dee-yah
leg	la pierna	lah pee-yehr-nah
mouth	la boca	lah boh-kah

Body Part	Spanish Translation	Pronunciation
nail	la uña	lah oo-nyah
neck	el cuello	ehl kweh-yoh
nose	la nariz	lah nah-rees
skin	la piel	lah pee-yehl
shoulder	el hombro	ehl ohm-broh
spine	la espina	lah ehs-pee-nah
stomach	el estómago	ehl ehs-toh-mah-goh
throat	la garganta	lah gahr-gahn-tah
toe	el dedo del pie	ehl deh-doh dehl pee-yeh
tongue	la lengua	lah lehn-gwah
tooth	el diente	ehl dee-yehn-teh
wrist	la muñeca	lah moo-nyeh-kah

I Have a Headache

Jet lag is no joke. In the 1970s, when it was popular to backpack around Europe on five dollars a day, my husband and I decided to do just that before we started our family. We arrived in England during an extremely hot spell, and we spent our first three nights in an unbearably hot trailer—that's what happens when you go without reservations. We hardly slept a wink. When the sun came up, we were exhausted, but we'd still go out sight-seeing.

In a Flash

Keep a picture of yourself nearby. Point to the parts of your body and practice naming them in Spanish.

Our next stop was Paris. We had another hot room without a bath in the red-light district. Sleep still wouldn't come. At the end of a week and a half of traveling, when we were delirious from lack of sleep, we finally went to the doctor. The kind man prescribed a sleep aid. Finally, we were able to resume a normal life.

If you run into a problem and have to seek medical help, the obvious first question will be: "What's the matter with you?" "*¿Qué le pasa?*" (keh leh pah-sah). To say what hurts or bothers you, use the expression *tener dolor de (en)* + the part that hurts.

Tengo dolor de cabeza.
tehn-goh doh-lohr deh kah-beh-sah.
I have a headache.

Tiene dolor en el brazo.
tee-yeh-neh doh-lohr ehn ehl brah-soh
He has pain in his arm.

Memory Master

Remember to conjugate the verb *tener* (to have) so it agrees with the subject. Although the Spanish use *tener* to express what's bothering them, the English translation might not include the word "have."

¿Tienes dolor en los pies?
Do your feet hurt?

Memory Master

Remember that *de* contracts with *el* to become *del* with masculine singular nouns.

It Hurts

You can also choose to talk about your symptoms using the shoe verb *doler* (doh-lehr), to hurt. *Doler* is a stem-changing verb and is used in the same way as the verb *gustar*. This means you'll only have to use two verb forms: *duele* (dweh-leh) and *duelen* (dweh-lehn). Why is that? *Doler* means something is hurting (to) you; therefore, an indirect object pronoun is used to refer to the person in pain.

The indirect object pronouns include *me* (to me), *te* (to you), *le* (to him, her, or you), *nos* (to us), *os* (to you), and *les* (to them or you). The subject of the sentence is the body part causing the pain:

Me duele el pie.	Me duelen los pies.
My foot hurts.	*My feet hurt.*

To be specific you may say:

Le duele a ella el pie.	Les duelen a ellos los pies.
Her foot hurts.	Their feet hurt.

Let's take a closer look at how this works. Let's say you've been playing volleyball for the first time in a long while. At the end of the day, your whole body aches. You might say the following to a friend:

Me duele la cabeza.	Me duelen los dedos.
My head hurts.	*My fingers hurt.*
(My head is hurting	(My fingers are hurting
to me.)	to me.)

What about the other members of your volleyball team? Once again, don't let the reverse word order fool you. Remember to choose an indirect object pronoun that refers to the person in pain. The subject will follow the verb *doler* and must, therefore, agree with it. Let's see how this works:

¿Te duele el brazo?
teh dweh-leh ehl brah-soh
Does your arm hurt?

Nos duelen las piernas.
nohs dweh-lehn lahs pee-yehr-nahs
Our legs hurt.

No les duelen las manos.
noh lehs dweh-lehn lahs mah-nohs
Their (Your) hands don't hurt.

¿Le duele el estómago?
leh dweh-leh ehl ehs-toh-mah-goh
Does his (her, your) stomach hurt?

¿Os duelen los dedos?
ohs dweh-lehn lohs deh-dohs
Do your fingers hurt?

If you want to emphasize who is in pain, you can add the preposition *a* + a name or prepositional pronoun.

A Julio le duelen las espaldas.   A ellos le duele la garganta.
Julio's shoulders hurt.   *Their throats hurt.*

Notice that it is unnecessary to use a possessive adjective before the name of the body part because the indirect object pronoun states to whom the pain is occurring.

What's the Matter?

Perhaps your symptoms are indicative of something a bit more complicated than aches or pains. Maybe there's a problem that requires further medical attention. A list of possible symptoms and conditions is provided in Table 20.2. These words will come in handy when you need to provide a more detailed description of your aches and pains. Use the word *tengo* (tehn-goh), *I have*, to preface your complaint.

Table 20.2   Other Symptoms and Conditions

Symptoms and Conditions	Spanish Translation	Pronunciation
abscess	un absceso	oon ahb-seh-soh
blister	una ampolla	oo-nah ahm-poh-yah
broken bone	un hueso roto	oon weh-soh rroh-toh
bruise	una contusión	oo-nah kohn-too-see-yohn
bump	una hinchazón	oo-nah een-chah-sohn
burn	una quemadura	oo-nah keh-mah-doo-rah
chills	un escalofrío	oon ehs-kah-loh-free-yoh
cough	una tos	oo-nah tohs
cramps	un calambre	oon kah-lahm-breh
diarrhea	una diarrea	oo-nah dee-yah-rreh-yah
fever	una fiebre	oo-nah fee-yeh-breh
indigestion	una indigestión	oo-nah een-dee-hehs-tee-yohn
lump	un bulto	oon bool-toh
migraine	una jaqueca	oo-nah hah-keh-kah
pain	un dolor	oon doh-lohr
rash	una erupción	oo-nah eh-roop-see-yohn
sprain	una torcedura	oo-nah tohr-seh-doo-rah
swelling	una inflamación	oo-nah een-flah-mah-see-yohn
wound	una herido	oo-nah eh-ree-doh

Other useful phrases to help describe your illness include:

Yo toso.   Yo estoy agotado(a).
yoh toh-soh   yoh ehs-toy ah-goh-tah-doh(dah)
I'm coughing.   *I'm exhausted.*

Yo no puedo dormir.   Yo tengo náuseas.
yoh noh pweh-doh   yoh tehn-goh
dohr-meer   now-seh-yahs
I can't sleep.   *I'm nauseous.*

Yo estornudo.   Yo estoy sangrando.
yoh ehs-tohr-noo-doh   yoh ehs-toy sahn-grahn-
I'm sneezing.   doh
                                  I'm bleeding.

Me duele todo el cuerpo.   Me siento mal.
meh dweh-leh toh-doh   meh see-yehn-toh mahl
ehl kwehr-poh   *I feel bad.*
I hurt everywhere.

¡Atención!

Be sure you really mean it before you tell anyone that you are *embarazada (ehm-bah-rah-sah-dah)*. There's no masculine form because the word means "pregnant."

It Hurts Right Here

Now use all you've learned so far to describe your symptoms and complaints to a doctor. Pretend you have the following health problems. (Sample responses can be found on page 420, in Appendix A.)

flu-like symptoms _____

an allergy _____

a sprained ankle _____

a migraine _____

This Is What's Wrong

Obviously, you won't be the only one doing the talking when you visit the doctor. You will be asked to fill out forms, to tell about any medications you're taking, and to answer other questions about your symptoms and general health. The doctor or nurse might ask whether you have some of the symptoms or illnesses listed Table 20.3.

Table 20.3 Symptoms and Illnesses

Symptom/Illness	Spanish Translation	Pronunciation
allergic reaction	una reacción alérgica	oo-nah rreh-ahk-see-yohn ah-lehr-hee-kah
angina	la angina	lah ahn-hee-nah
appendicitis	la apendicitis	lah ah-pehn-dee-see-tees
asthma	el asma	ehl ahs-mah
bronchitis	la bronquitis	lah brohn-kee-tees
cancer	el cáncer	ehl kahn-sehr
cold	un resfriado, un catarro	oon rrehs-free-yah-doh, oon kah-tah-rroh
diabetes	la diabetes	lah dee-yah-beh-tehs
dizziness	el vértigo	ehl behr-tee-goh
dysentery	la disentería	lah dee-sehn-teh-ree-yah
exhaustion	la fatiga	lah fah-tee-gah
flu	la gripe	lah gree-peh
German measles	la rubeola	lah rroo-beh-yoh-lah
gout	la gota	lah goh-tah
heart attack	un ataque al corazón	oon ah-tah-keh ahl koh-rah-sohn
hepatitis	la hepatitis	lah eh-pah-tee-tees
measles	el sarampión	ehl sah-rahm-pee-yohn
mumps	las paperas	lahs pah-peh-rahs
pneumonia	la pulmonía	lah pool-moh-nee-yah
polio	la poliomielitis	lah poh-lee-oh-mee-yeh-lee-tees
smallpox	la viruela	lah bee-roo-weh-lah
stroke	un ataque de apoplejía	oon ah-tah-keh deh ah-poh-pleh-hee-yah
sunstroke	una insolación	oo-nah een-soh-lah-see-yohn
tetanus	el tétano	ehl teh-tah-noh
tuberculosis	la tuberculosis	lah too-behr-koo-loh-sees
whooping cough	la tosferina	lah tohs-feh-ree-nah

How Long Have You Felt This Way?

One of the most frequent questions a doctor asks is, "How long have you been feeling this way?" There are two ways this question can be asked and two ways for you to give an appropriate answer. The first question and answer pair is the most common and probably is the easiest to use.

In a Flash

For every day for a week think of three things you like to do and tell how long you've been doing them.

¿Cuánto tiempo hace que + present tense verb?
kwahn-toh tee-yehm-poh ah-seh keh
(For) how long (has) have + present tense verb?

You would answer this question with the following:

Hace + time + *que* + present tense verb

The following is the second way you might be asked how long you've been sick:

¿Desde cuándo + present tense?
dehs-deh kwahn-doh
(For) How long has (have) + present tense.

You would answer this question with the following:

present tense of verb + *desde hace* + time

Here are some examples of what you might be asked and how you might respond to the questions.

¿Cuánto tiempo hace que sufre?
kwahn-toh tee-yehm-poh ah-seh
keh soo-freh
(For) How long have you been suffering?

¿Desde cuándo sufre?
dehs-deh kwahn-doh soo-freh
(For) How long have you been suffering?

Hace dos días (que sufro).
ah-seh dohs dee-yahs (keh soo-froh)
(I've been suffering) For two days.

(Sufro) desde hace ayer.
soo-froh dehs-deh ah-seh ah-yehr
(I've been suffering) Since yesterday.

In a Flash

Describe in Spanish how you feel today.

Keep the Doctor Informed

Look at the following sample of an actual medical form you might have to fill out. Practice what you've learned by giving the most up-to-date information about yourself.

FEDERICO A. PEREIRA
Calle Fortaleza 168
San Juan, P.R.
Tel: 555-3468
Fax: 555-9084

TARJETA MÉDICA

Fecha _____

Apellido _____ Nombre _____

Dirección _____

N° de teléfono _____

Fecha de nacimiento _____ edad _____

Profesión _____

Situación de familia   soltero(a)   _____

casado(a)   _____

divorciado(a)   _____

viudo(a)   _____

Síntomas

_____

_____

_____

_____

Antecedentes Médicos

Enfermedades sufridos

❑ la reacción alérgica
❑ la angina
❑ la apendicitis
❑ la asma
❑ la bronquitis
❑ el cáncer
❑ el resfriado, el catarro del pecho
❑ la diabetes
❑ el vértigo
❑ la disentería
❑ la fatiga
❑ la rubéola
❑ la gota
❑ el ataque de corazón
❑ la hepatitis
❑ el sarampión
❑ las paperas
❑ la pulmonía
❑ la poliomielitis
❑ la viruela

❑ el apoplejía
❑ la insolación
❑ el tétanos
❑ la tuberculosis
❑ la tos ferina

Alergias

❑ a la penicilina
❑ a los antibióticos
❑ otros _____

Vacunas

❑ la tos ferina
❑ las paperas
❑ la poliomielitis
❑ el sarampión
❑ la viruela
❑ el tétanos
❑ la tuberculosis

¡Atención!

Just in case you decide to take a boat trip or go scuba diving, bring along some dramamine or the wrist bands that prevent seasickness.

I'm Not a Hypochondriac

Now use what you have learned to explain how long you've been suffering. Talk about a cough you've had for two weeks, a headache that's stuck around for three days, or the stomach ache that's been bugging you for nearly a month. (Sample responses can be found on page 421, in Appendix A.)

1. cough _____.
2. headache _____.
3. stomach ache _____.

Memory Master

To say "that" after *decir,* use *que:*

Él dice que no estoy muy enfermo.
ehl dee-seh keh noh ehs-toy mwee ehn-fehr-moh
He says that I'm not very sick.

What Do You Tell the Doctor?

When something is really bothering you and you're somewhat frightened, what do you tell the doctor? Do you tell him what is truly bothering you? Or are you afraid to enumerate all your symptoms? To discuss what you say or tell someone, use the irregular verb *decir* (to tell, to say). You will notice that *decir* is a go-go shoe verb. The *yo* form ends in *-go,* and the *e* from the stem changes to *i* in all forms except *nosotros* and *vosotros*.

decir (to tell, to say)

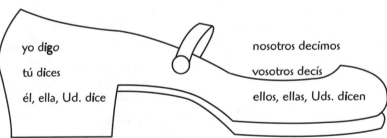

yo digo
tú dices
él, ella, Ud. dice

nosotros decimos
vosotros decís
ellos, ellas, Uds. dicen

Me, Myself, and I

Use the irregular, stem-changing shoe verb *sentirse* (sehn-teer-seh) to express how you feel. Do you notice something strange about this verb, something that just doesn't look right? Besides the *ie* stem-change, this verb does not end like most others—*-se* is attached to the infinitive ending. This actually is a special pronoun, called a reflexive pronoun, that can serve as either a direct or indirect object pronoun.

Quite simply, a reflexive pronoun shows that the subject is performing an action upon itself. The subject and the reflexive pronoun refer to the same person(s) or thing(s). (She washes herself. They enjoy themselves.) Don't panic about these verbs. They are quite easy to use and will be explained more fully in the next section. For the time being, here's how to conjugate a reflexive verb using the correct reflexive pronouns:

Memory Master

Sentirse (used reflexively) tells about a person's state of health—how he or she feels.

Me siento bien.
I feel well.

The verb *sentir* (used non-reflexively) refers to our sense of touch.

Siento algo en mi espalda.
I feel something on my shoulder.

sentirse (to feel)

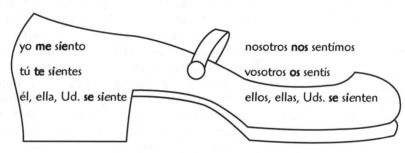

yo **me** siento

tú **te** sientes

él, ella, Ud. **se** siente

nosotros **nos** sentimos

vosotros **os** sentís

ellos, ellas, Uds. **se** sienten

The following sentences will help you express how you feel:

Me siento bien.
meh see-yehn-toh bee-yehn
I feel well.

Me siento mal.
meh see-yehn-toh mahl
I feel bad.

Me siento mejor.
meh see-yehn-toh meh-hohr
I feel better.

Me siento peor.
meh see-yehn-toh peh-yohr
I feel worse.

You've seen the doctor and have gotten a prescription, *una receta* (oo-nah reh-seh-tah). You're now ready to leave the doctor's office. Wait! Not so fast! Don't forget this very important question that might save you some money:

¿Puede darme un recibo para mi seguro médico?
pweh-deh dahr-meh oon rreh-see-boh pah-rah mee seh-goo-roh meh-dee-koh
May I please have a receipt for my medical insurance?

295

10 minutos al día

Reflexive pronouns show that the action of the verb is reflected back to the subject. In other words, the subject is acting upon itself. When conjugated, the subject and the reflexive pronoun must refer to the same person or thing.

yo *me*	nosotros *nos*
tú *te*	vosotros *os*
él, ella, Ud. *se*	ellos, ellas, Uds. *se*

Is It Reflexive?

Memory Master

Here's a refresher on direct and indirect objects:

Direct Objects **Indirect Objects**

la *her*
le *him (Spain)* le *to him, to her*

lo *him (Spanish America), it*

los (m.) *them* les *to them*

las (f.) *them*

Me, te, nos, and os are both direct and indirect object pronouns.

Are you the type of person who is always doing favors for someone else and generally tends to put yourself last? Or do you think of yourself first because, after all, who else will do that if you don't? Are you *generoso* or *egoísta* when it comes to yourself and others? In Spanish, when you perform an action upon or for yourself, that action (verb) is reflexive and requires a reflexive pronoun. In many instances, you can use the same verb without the reflexive pronoun when performing the action upon or for someone else. In these cases, an object pronoun—direct or indirect—is used.

Yo me lavo.
yoh meh lah-boh
I wash myself.

Lavo a mi niño.
lah-boh ah mee nee-nyoh
I wash my son.

Yo lo lavo.
yoh loh lah-boh
I wash him.

In the last example, the direct object pronoun *lo* expresses "him."

Me compro un libro.
I buy myself a book.

Le compro un libro.
I buy her a book.

Le compro un libro a Ana.
I buy Ann a book.

In the preceding example, the indirect object pronoun *le* expresses "for her."

Some verbs are always or almost always used reflexively. Table 20.4 provides a list of the most common reflexive verbs. The verbs followed by an asterisk (*) are shoe verbs.

Table 20.4   Common Reflexive Verbs

Reflexive Verb	Pronunciation	Meaning
acordarse (ue)*[de]	ah-kohr-dahr-seh [deh]	to remember
acostarse (ue)*	ah-kohs-tahr-seh	to go to bed
afeitarse	ah-feh-yee-tahr-seh	to shave
alegrarse	ah-leh-grahr-seh	to be glad
apresurarse	ah-preh-soo-rahr-seh	to hurry
apurarse	ah-poo-rahr-seh	to hurry
bañarse	bah-nyahr-seh	to bathe oneself
callarse	kah-yahr-seh	to be silent
cepillarse	seh-pee-yahr-seh	to brush (hair, teeth)
despertarse (ie)*	dehs-pehr-tahr-seh	to wake up
desvestirse (i)*	dehs-behs-teer-seh	to undress
divertirse (ie)*	dee-behr-teer-seh	to have fun
ducharse	doo-chahr-seh	to take a shower
engañarse	ehn-gah-nyahr-seh	to be mistaken
enojarse	eh-noh-hahr-seh	to become angry
equivocarse	eh-kee-boh-kahr-seh	to be mistaken
fiarse [de]	fee-yahr-seh [deh]	to trust
fijarse [en]	fee-hahr-seh [ehn]	to notice
irse	eer-seh	to go away
lavarse	lah-bahr-seh	to wash oneself
levantarse	leh-bahn-tahr-seh	to get up
llamarse	yah-mahr-seh	to be called, to be named
maquillarse	mah-kee-yahr-seh	to put on make-up
olvidarse [de]	ohl-bee-dahr-seh [deh]	to forget
pararse	pah-rah-seh	to stop oneself
peinarse	peh-yee-nahr-seh	to comb one's hair
ponerse	poh-nehr-seh	to put on, to become, to place oneself
quedarse	keh-dahr-seh	to remain
quejarse	keh-hahr-seh	to complain
quitarse	kee-tahr-seh	to remove

continues

Table 20.4 Continued

Reflexive Verb	Pronunciation	Meaning
reírse [de]	rreh-yeer-seh [deh]	to laugh [at]
sentarse (ie)*	sehn-tahr-seh	to sit down
sentirse (ie)*	sehn-teer-seh	to feel
vestirse (i)*	behs-teer-seh	to get dressed

Remember that shoe verbs require appropriate spelling changes. (Refer to Chapter 12, "Settling In," to refresh your memory.) Here are some examples of conjugated shoe verbs in sample sentences:

Yo me acuesto.   Yo me divierto.   Yo me visto.
I go to bed.   *I have fun.*   *I get dressed.*

Verbs followed by *a*, *de*, or *en* require those prepositions to make their intentions understood.

Yo me apresuro a partir.
I hurry to leave.

Yo no me olvido de nada.
I don't forget anything.

Yo me fío de él.
I trust him.

In a Flash

Practice those reflexive verbs with spelling changes. Every day select two from the list and use them in complete Spanish sentences.

Who's Doing What to Whom?

My husband is a very fortunate man. He only has about three things to do in the morning before leaving for work, and he can fly out the door in 10 to 15 minutes. Before I leave in the morning, it seems I do at least 100 things: I wash myself, I dry my hair, I get dressed, I eat breakfast, I brush my teeth, and so on. That's why I need an hour and fifteen minutes between the time I wake up and when I walk out the door.

When a reflexive verb is used in Spanish, it is understood that the subject is performing the action for or upon itself because the reflexive pronoun says so. It then becomes unnecessary to use the possessives adjectives "my" (*mi, mis*), "your" (*tu, tus*), and so on, because it is obvious upon whom the action is being performed. The definite article is used instead.

Yo me cepillo los dientes.
yoh meh seh-pee-yoh lohs dee-yehn-tehs
I brush my teeth.

Ella se pinta las uñas.
eh-yah seh peen-tah lahs oo-nyahs
She polishes her nails.

What Are They Doing?

Tell what each person is doing in these pictures.
(Check your answers on page 421, in Appendix A.)

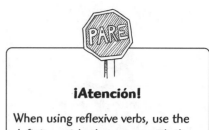

¡Atención!

When using reflexive verbs, use the definite article that agrees with the part of the body being discussed.

1. yo _____

2. nosotros _____

3. Uds. _____

4. tú _____

5. ella _____

6. vosotros _____

7. él _____

8. Ud. _____

The Position of the Reflexive Pronoun

By now, you know word order in Spanish differs greatly from what we are accustomed to in English. To us, word order seems to be backwards in Spanish. In English, we tend to put reflexive pronouns after verbs. You might tell a friend, "I always look at myself in the mirror before I go out." In Spanish this may or may not be the case. Fortunately, the rules for placement of pronouns in Spanish are quite consistent. Reflexive pronouns are placed in the same position as the direct and indirect object pronouns you already studied in Chapter 15, "A Shopping Spree."

Yo me divierto.	*I have fun.*
Yo no me divierto.	*I don't have fun.*
Voy a divertirme.	*I'm going to have fun.*
or	
Me voy a divertir.	
Estoy divirtiéndome.	*I'm having fun.*
or	
Me estoy divirtiendo	

In an affirmative command, reflexive pronouns change position. They are placed immediately after and joined to the verb.

¡Levántese!	but	¡No se levante!		¡Apúrense!	but	¡No se apuren!
Get up!		*Don't get up!*		*Hurry up!*		*Don't hurry!*

When using the present progressive (the -ing form) and attaching the pronoun to the present participle (*estar* + present participle + pronoun) or when forming an affirmative command, remember to count back three vowels from the end and add an accent.

Estamos peinándonos.
ehs-tah-mohs peh-yee-nahn-doh-nos
We're combing our hair.

¡Quédese aquí!
keh-deh-seh ah-kee
Stay here!

Están cepillándose el pelo.
ehs-tahn seh-pee-yahn-doh-seh
ehl peh-loh
They're brushing their hair.

¡Siéntese, por favor!
see-yehn-teh-seh pohr fah-bohr
Please sit!

10 minutos al día

Reflexive pronouns are placed in the same location as object pronouns—before the conjugated verb. With an infinitive or a gerund, the reflexive pronoun can be placed after and attached to the infinitive or the gerund. In an affirmative command, reflexive pronouns are placed after and attached to the verb. Count back three vowels and add an accent.

Practicing Reflexive Verbs

Use what you've learned so far to describe four things you do before leaving the house in the morning. Then describe four things you are going to do before going to bed. (Sample responses can be found on page 421, in Appendix A.)

Example: Yo me despierto.
　　　　　Yo voy a cepillarme los dientes.

1. _____ .
2. _____ .
3. _____ .
4. _____ .
5. _____ .
6. _____ .
7. _____ .
8. _____ .

Hurry Up!

You're traveling in a group with some of your best friends. *Siesta* time is over, and you've decided to go out and have some fun. In your haste to get ready, everyone is telling everyone else what to do. Practice forming reflexive commands by telling your friends to do and not do the following. (Check your answers on page 421, in Appendix A.)

Example: brush your hair
            Cepíllense el pelo.
            No se cepillen el pelo.

1. wake up _____ .
2. get up _____ .
3. take a bath _____ .
4. hurry up _____ .
5. get dressed _____ .
6. comb your hair _____ .
7. brush your teeth _____ .
8. have fun _____ .

The Least You Need to Know

➤ Know how to describe the different parts of the body as well as your symptoms and feelings. This will help you should you fall ill while on vacation.

➤ To ask how long something has been going on, use "*¿Cuánto tiempo hace que* + present tense?" or "*¿Desde cuándo* + present tense?" To answer, use "*Hace* + time + *que* + present tense" or "present tense + *desde hace* + time."

➤ Reflexive verbs, identified by the reflexive pronouns that accompany them, are used to show that the subject is acting upon itself.

Chapter 21

Did I Pack the Toothpaste?

In This Chapter

➤ Health care items large and small

➤ The verb *venir* (to come)

➤ Speaking in the past

In Chapter 20, "Is There a Doctor in the House?," you learned how to talk about any medical problems you might encounter. Perhaps you're experiencing some minor aches and pains or signs and symptoms that are bothersome but don't require a visit to the doctor. Whether you want to simply purchase a box of cough drops or you need a prescription filled, you'll want to make a quick stop at *una farmacia* (oo-nah fahr-mah-see-yah), a drugstore.

On our last trip, I inadvertently left our toiletry case at home. My husband, who always remains undaunted by life's small unpleasantries, gently reminded me that toothbrushes, toothpaste, razors, shaving cream, hairbrushes, combs, and so on are rather universal items. My blunder was only a minor inconvenience and certainly was not a reason to spoil a delightful vacation. This chapter can help you replenish your supplies and shows you how to talk about the past using the preterite (past) tense.

Finding What You Need

So you've run out of an essential item. If it's medicine you need, look for a green cross, the universal symbol for pharmacies (*farmacias*). If you are looking for a tube of lipstick or a bottle of your favorite perfume, you must go to *una perfumería* (oo-nah pehr-foo-meh-ree-yah), which specializes in toiletries. When you need to have a prescription filled, you can use the following question to ask for the nearest pharmacy:

¿Dónde está la farmacia (de guardia) más cercana?
dohn-deh ehs-tah lah fahr-mah-see-yah (deh gwahr-dee-yah) mahs sehr-kah-nah
Where's the nearest (all-night) pharmacy?

You can then speak to the druggist, as follows:

Necesito medicina.
neh-seh-see-toh meh-dee-see-nah
I need medication.

¿Podría preparar esta receta (en seguida)?
poh-dree-yah preh-pah-rahr ehs-tah reh-seh-tah (ehn seh-gee-dah)
Could you please fill this prescription (immediately)?

¿Cuánto tiempo tardará?
kwahn-toh tee-yehm-poh tahr-dah-rah
How long will it take?

Culture Corner

In the Spanish–speaking world, pharmacies are specifically health–related and may dispense medicines and drugs over the counter that would normally require a prescription in the States. It is not unusual for someone who is ill to consult his pharmacist for proper medication. Only when a person is seriously ill does he go to a doctor.

If you're simply looking for something over-the-counter, Table 21.1 can help you find it in the *farmacia*, the *perfumería*, or even the *supermercado*. Begin by saying to a clerk, "*Busco...*" (boos-koh), "I'm looking for...," or "*Necesito...*" (neh-seh-see-toh), "I need."

Table 21.1 Drugstore Items

Item	SpanishTranslation	Pronunciation
alcohol	el alcohol	ehl ahl-koh-ohl
antacid	el antiácido	ehl ahn-tee-yah-see-doh
antihistamine	el antistamínico	ehl ahn-tee-stah-mee-nee-koh
antiseptic	el antiséptico	ehl ahn-tee-sehp-tee-koh
aspirin	la aspirina	lah ahs-pee-ree-nah

Item	SpanishTranslation	Pronunciation
band-aid	la curita	lah koo-ree-tah
brush	el cepillo	ehl seh-pee-yoh
condoms	los condones	lohs kohn-doh-nehs
cotton absorbent	el algodón hidrófilo	ehl ahl-goh-dohn ee-droh-fee-loh
cough drops	las pastillas para la tos	lahs pahs-tee-yahs pah-rah lah tohs
cough syrup	el jarabe para la tos	ehl hah-rah-beh pah-rah lah tohs
deodorant	el desodorante	ehl deh-soh-doh-rahn-teh
depilatory	el depilatorio	ehl deh-pee-lah-toh-ree-yoh
eye drops	las gotas para los ojos	lahs goh-tahs pah-rah lohs oh-hohs
first-aid kit	el botiquín de primeros auxilios	ehl boh-tee-keen deh pree-meh-rohs owk-see- lee-yohs
gauze	la gasa	lah gah-sah
heating pad	la almohadilla de calefacción	lah ahl-moh-ah-dee-yah deh kah-leh-fahk-see-yohn
ice pack	la bolsa de hielo	lah bohl-sah deh ee-yeh-loh
laxative mild	el laxante ligero	ehl lahk-sahn-teh lee-heh-roh
mirror	el espejo	ehl ehs-peh-hoh
moisturizer	la crema hidratante	lah kreh-mah ee-drah-tahn-teh
mouthwash	el enjuagador bucal	ehl ehn-hwah-gah-dohr boo-kahl
nail file	la lima	lah lee-mah
nose drops	las gotas para la nariz	lahs goh-tahs pah-rah lah nah-rees
perfume	el perfume	ehl pehr-foo-meh
razor electric	la rasuradora eléctrica	lah rrah-soo-rah-doh-rah eh-lehk-tree-kah
razor blade	la hoja de afeitar	lah oh-hah deh ah-feh-yee-tahr
safety pin	el seguro, el imperdible	ehl seh-goo-roh, ehl eem-pehr-dee-bleh
scissors	las tijeras	lahs tee-heh-rahs
shampoo anti-dandruff	el champú anti-caspa	ehl chahm-poo ahn-tee kahs-pah

continues

Table 21.1 Continued

Item	SpanishTranslation	Pronunciation
shaving cream	la crema de afeitar	lah kreh-mah deh ah-feh-yee-tahr
sleeping pills	las pastillas para dormir	lahs pah-stee-yahs pah-rah dohr-meer
talcum powder	el polvo de talco	ehl pohl-boh deh tahl-koh
thermometer	un termómetro	oon tehr-moh-meh-troh
tissues	los pañuelos de papel	lohs pah-nyoo-weh-lohs deh pah-pehl
toothbrush	el cepillo de dientes	ehl seh-pee-yoh deh dee-yehn-tehs
toothpaste	la pasta dentífrica	lah pahs-tah dehn-tee-free-kah
tweezers	las pinzas	lahs peen-sahs
vitamins	las vitaminas	lahs bee-tah-mee-nahs

For Babies		
Item	**Spanish Translation**	**Pronunciation**
bottle	un biberón	oon bee-beh-rohn
diapers disposable	los pañales desechables	lohs pah-nyah-lehs deh-seh-chah-blehs
pacifier	un chupete	oon choo-peh-teh

In a Flash

Put Spanish labels on all the items in your medicine cabinet. Learn their names by heart. Remove the labels and try to name everything you see.

What's on Sale

You're vacationing in Puerto Rico and, believe it or not, there's a huge Walgreen's across the street from your fancy hotel. Why pay exorbitant mini-bar prices when everything you'd ever want or need is just a few feet away? Check out the following ad and ask for some of the items you might want to pick up. (Sample responses can be found on page 421, in Appendix A.)

Curitas
Plásticas. Pqte. doble de 60 curitas
de 3/4" x 3" c/u. Total 120 curitas.

1. _____

Champú anti-caspa.
Varias fórmulas, con o sin
acondicionador. De 15 oz.

2. _____

Aspirina
Genérica. Para aliviar el dolor,
y bajar la fiebre. Frasco trae
100 tabletas, de 325 mgs.

3. _____

Fragancias Florales
Refrescantes. Escoja entre aromas de lila o
rosa. Colonia con atomizador, 2oz.
humectante, 12 oz.; o
talco, 4 oz.

5. _____

Anti-Plaque
Enjuague bucal para antes
del cepillado. Anti-Placa.
Sabor regular o menta.
De 16 oz. c/u.

4. _____

Special Needs

The items in Table 21.2 could be bought from or located by special organizations that cater to the needs of the physically challenged or pharmacies that specialize in *el alquiler de aparatos médicos* (ehl ahl-kee-lehr deh ah-pah-rah-tohs meh-dee-kohs), the rental of medical appliances.

> ¿Dónde puedo obtener...?
> dohn-deh pweh-doh ohb-teh-nehr
> *Where can I get...?*

Table 21.2 Special Needs

Medical Appliance	Spanish Translation	Pronunciation
cane	el bastón	ehl bahs-tohn
crutches	las muletas	lahs moo-leh-tahs
hearing aid	el aparato para sordos	ehl ah-pah-rah-toh pah-rah sohr-dohs
seeing eye dog	el perro guía	ehl peh-rroh gee-yah
walker	el andador	ehl ahn-dah-dohr
wheelchair	la silla de ruedas	la see-yah deh rroo-weh-dahs

Culture Corner

Many large cities and towns have at least one all–night pharmacy called una farmacia de guardia (oo-nah fahr-mah-see-yah day gwahr-dee-yah). If you find that a drug store is closed, look on the door for a sign listing the nearest stores that are open.

Come Along with Me

You've decided to call the pharmacy ahead of time to order or locate a certain product. If you want to tell the pharmacist when you will be coming by to pick it up, use the verb *venir* (to come). The following diagram provides the forms of this irregular verb. Note that *venir* is a go-go verb because its *yo* form ends in *-go*. *Venir* is also similar to a shoe verb in that the *nosotros* and *vosotros* forms look like the infinitive, while the forms for the other subject pronouns do not.

To tell the phramacist when you'll be stopping by say:

Yo vengo a las dos
Yoh behn-goh ah lahs dohs
I'm coming at 2 o'clock

venir (to come)

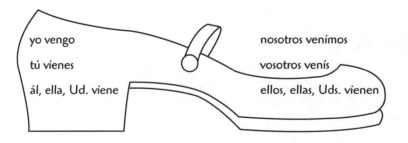

yo vengo
tú vienes
ál, ella, Ud. viene

nosotros venimos
vosotros venís
ellos, ellas, Uds. vienen

Living in the Past

No matter how much time I put aside to pack or how many times I run to add items to my packing list, I invariably forget something important. This year, it was the special shampoo and conditioner I need to achieve that unique look. The hotel brand was a generic disaster. I also left my hair dryer at home because the hotel brochure promised one in every room. They didn't lie, but it was the slowest hair dryer I've ever used, and I was sorry I didn't pack my own. To discuss what you did or did not do, you must use the past tense. In Spanish, this tense is called the *pretárito*, the preterite.

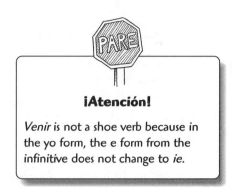

¡Atención!

Venir is not a shoe verb because in the yo form, the e form from the infinitive does not change to *ie*.

The Preterite of Regular Verbs

Forming the preterite of regular verbs is quite easy because all the verbs follow their family's rules. Verbs that have spelling and stem changes and verbs that are totally irregular require a little more attention.

To form the preterite of regular verbs, drop the infinitive ending (-*ar*, -*er*, or -*ir*) and add the following endings:

Memory Master

The preterite is used to express an action that was completed at a specific time in the past.

-ar Verbs	Preterite Stem	Pronoun(s)	Preterite Endings
hablar	habl-	yo	-é,
		tú	-aste
		él, ella, Ud.	-ó
		nosotros	-amos
		vosotros	-asteis
		ellos, ellas, Uds.	-aron
-er and *-ir* Verbs	Preterite Stem	Pronoun(s)	Preterite Endings
vender	vend-	yo	-í
abrir	abr-	tú	-iste
		él, ella, Ud.	-ió
		nosotros	-imos
		vosotros	-isteis
		ellos, ellas, Uds.	-ieron

Verbs ending in -*car*, -*gar*, and -*zar* drop the -*ar* infinitive ending to form the preterite and have a spelling change only in the *yo* form. All other forms are regular.

-*car* Verbs	Change	Yo Form	Other Forms
buscar	c changes to qu	yo busqué	buscaste, buscó, buscamos, buscasteis, buscaron

You might find the following common -*car* verbs useful:

Verb	Pronunciation	Meaning
aplicar	ah-plee-kahr	to apply
buscar	boos-kahr	to look for
colocar	koh-loh-kahr	to place, to put
comunicar	koh-moo-nee-kahr	to communicate
equivocarse	eh-kee-boh-kahr-seh	to be mistaken
explicar	ehks-plee-kahr	to explain
fabricar	fah-bree-kahr	to manufacture, to make
indicar	een-dee-kahr	to indicate
marcar	mahr-kahr	to mark, to designate
pescar	pehs-kahr	to fish
sacar	sah-kahr	to take out
significar	seeg-nee-fee-kahr	to mean
tocar	toh-kahr	to touch, to play (musical instrument)

-*gar* Verbs	Change	Yo Form	Other Forms
pagar	g changes to gu	yo pagué	pagaste, pagó, pagamos, pagasteis, pagaron

You might find the following common -*gar* verbs useful:

Verb	Pronunciation	Meaning
apagar	ah-pah-gahr	to put out, to turn off, to extinguish
colgar *ue	kohl-gahr	to hang
encargar	ehn-kahr-gahr	to put in charge, to entrust

Verb	Pronunciation	Meaning
entregar *ie	ehn-treh-gahr	to deliver
jugar *u	hoo-gahr	to play (sports, games)
llegar	yeh-gahr	to arrive
negar *ie	neh-gahr	to deny
pagar	pah-gahr	to pay

-zar Verbs	Change	Yo Form	Other Forms
gozar	z changes to c	yo gocé	gozaste, gozó, gozamos, gozasteis, gozaron

You might find the following common *-zar* verbs useful:

Verb	Pronunciation	Meaning
abrazar	ah-brah-sahr	to hug, to embrace
almorzar *ue	ahl-mohr-sahr	to eat lunch
avanzar	ah-bahn-sahr	to advance, to hurry
comenzar *ie	koh-mehn-sahr	to begin, to commence
cruzar	kroo-sahr	to cross
empezar	ehm-peh-sahr	to begin
gozar	goh-sahr	to enjoy
lanzar	lahn-sahr	to throw

Any *-ir* verbs that have a stem change in the present tense also have a stem change in the preterite. In the present, an *e* in the stem could change to *ie* or *i*. In the preterite, *e* only changes to *i* and *o* changes to *u* only in the third person singular (*él, ella, Ud.*) and third person plural forms (*ellos, ellas, Uds.*). For a list of common verbs with these changes, refer to Chapter 12, "Settling In." For all *-ir* verbs in which the endings are regular in the present, the endings are also regular in the past.

The following are some *-ir* verbs that are irregular in the past tense:

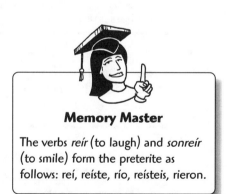

Memory Master

The verbs *reír* (to laugh) and *sonreír* (to smile) form the preterite as follows: reí, reíste, río, reísteis, rieron.

Infinitive	Yo, Tú, Nosotros, Vosotros	Third Person Singular	Third Person Plural
preferir (to prefer)	preferí, preferiste, preferimos, preferisteis	prefirió	prefirieron
pedir (to ask)	pedí, pediste, pedimos, pedisteis	pidió	pidieron
dormir (to sleep)	dormí, dormiste, dormimos, dormisteis	durmió	durmieron

Verbs that end in *-er* or *-ir* with a vowel immediately preceding the infinitive ending (except *traer*, to bring, and *atraer*, to attract, which are irregular and are explained later in the chapter) change *i* to *y* in the third person singular (*él, ella, Ud.*) and third person plural (*ellos, ellas, Uds.*) forms in the preterite. In all other forms, the *i* has an accent mark, as follows:

Infinitive	Yo, Tú, Nosotros, Vosotros	Third Person Singular	Third Person Plural
caer (to fall)	caí, caíste, caímos, caísteis	cayó	cayeron
creer (to believe)	creí, creíste, creímos, creísteis	creyó	creyeron
leer (to read)	leí, leíste, leímos, leísteis	leyó	leyeron
oír (to hear)	oí, oíste, oímos, oísteis	oyó	oyeron
poseer (to possess)	poseí, poseíste, poseímos, poseísteis	poseyó	poseyeron

Verbs ending in *-uir* also follow this rule, except an accent appears on the *i* only in the *yo* form. See Chapter 12, "Settling In," for other verbs that fit this category.

Infinitive	Yo, Tú, Nosotros, Vosotros	Third Person Singular	Third Person Plural
incluir (to include)	incluí, incluiste, incluimos, incluisteis	incluyó	incluyeron

10 minutos al día

To form the preterite of regular verbs, drop the infinitive ending (*-ar, -er, -ir*) and add the following endings:

-ar Verbs

	Preterite Stem	Pronoun(s)	Preterite Endings
hab<u>lar</u>	habl–	yo	-é,
		tú	-aste
		él, ella, Ud.	-ó
		nosotros	-amos
		vosotros	-asteis
		ellos, ellas, Uds.	-aron

-er and *-ir* Verbs

	Preterite Stem	Pronoun(s)	Preterite Endings
vend<u>er</u>	vend–	yo	-í
abr<u>ir</u>	abr–	tú	-iste
		él, ella, Ud.	-ió
		nosotros	-imos
		vosotros	-isteis
		ellos, ellas, Uds.	-ieron

The Preterite of Irregular Verbs

Some verbs are irregular in the preterite; their stems must be memorized. That's the bad news. The good news is that all irregular verbs in the preterite have the same endings, regardless of their infinitive endings. The endings are as follows:

Pronoun	Verb Ending	Pronoun	Verb Ending
yo	-e	nosotros	-imos
tú	-iste	vosotros	-isteis
él, ella, Ud.	-o	ellos, ellas, Uds.	-ieron

Table 21.3 lists the most common irregular verbs.

Table 21.3   Irregular Verbs in the Preterite

Infinitive	Preterite Stem	Preterite Forms
andar (to walk)	anduv-	anduve, anduviste, anduvo, anduvimos, anduvisteis, anduvieron
caber (to fit)	cup-	cupe, cupiste, cupo, cupimos, cupisteis, cupieron
estar (to be)	estuv-	estuve, estuviste, estuvo, estuvimos, estuvisteis, estuvieron
hacer (to make, to do)	hic-, hiz-	hice, hiciste, hizo, hicimos, hicisteis, hicieron
poder (to be able to)	pud-	pude, pudiste, pudo, pudimos, pudisteis, pudieron
poner (to put)	pus-	puse, pusiste, puso, pusimos, pusisteis, pusieron
querer (to want)	quis-	quise, quisiste, quiso, quisimos, quisisteis, quisieron
saber (to know)	sup-	supe, supiste, supo, supimos, supisteis, supieron
tener (to have)	tuv-	tuve, tuviste, tuvo, tuvimos, tuvisteis, tuvieron
venir (to come)	vin-	vine, viniste, vino, vinimos, vinisteis, vinieron

Of course, there's an exception to every rule. For the following verbs that are irregular in the preterite, the *-ieron* ending for the third person plural forms (*ellos, ellas, Uds.*) becomes *-eron* before the letter *j*:

Infinitive	Preterite Stem	Preterite Forms
decir (to say)	dij-	dije, dijiste, dijo, dijimos, dijisteis, dijeron
producir (to produce)	produj-	produje, produjiste, produjo, produjimos, produjisteis, produjeron
traer (to bring)	traj-	traje, trajiste, trajo, trajimos, trajisteis, trajeron

Three high-frequency irregular verbs are *dar* (to give), *ir* (to go), and *ser* (to be). In the following conjugations, note that accent marks are not used with these verbs, just as with the verb *ver* (to see).

Dar, although an *-ar* verb, uses the preterite endings for *-er* and *-ir* verbs:

yo di	nosotros dimos
tú diste	vosotros disteis
él, ella, Ud. dio	ellos, ellas, Uds. dieron

Ir and *ser* have the same preterite forms, so you have to follow the conversation to know which one is being used. For both verbs use these conjugations:

yo fui	nosotros fuimos
tú fuiste	vosotros fuisteis
él, ella, Ud. fue	ellos, ellas, Uds. fueron

The verb *ver* is conjugated in a regular fashion without the accents:

yo vi	nosotros vimos
tú viste	vosotros visteis
él, ella, Ud. vio	ellos, ellas, Uds. vieron

¡Atención!

Since *ir* and *ser* have the same preterite forms, pay careful attention to any conversation so you know which verb is being used.

Memory Master

When using reflexive verbs in the preterite, remember to include the reflexive pronoun.

Nos levantamos temprano.
We got up early.

Me equivoqué.
I made a mistake.

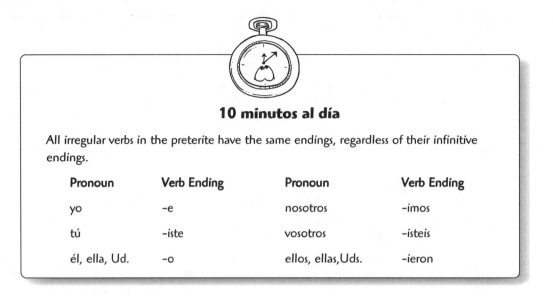

10 minutos al día

All irregular verbs in the preterite have the same endings, regardless of their infinitive endings.

Pronoun	Verb Ending	Pronoun	Verb Ending
yo	-e	nosotros	-imos
tú	-iste	vosotros	-isteis
él, ella, Ud.	-o	ellos, ellas, Uds.	-ieron

Talking About Your Past

You're sitting in a cafe with some friends, and the conversation turns to what you each did yesterday. Express what each person did in the past by giving the correct preterite form for the infinitive in parentheses. (Answers can be found on page 422, in Appendix A.)

1. Ud. (trabajar) _____ mucho.
2. Carlota (comer) _____ en el café.
3. Tú (escribir) _____ un poema.
4. Yo (leer) _____ un libro.
5. Nosotros (andar) _____ por el parque.
6. Yo (jugar) _____ al tenis.
7. Ellos (tener) _____ una cita.
8. Yo (equivocarse) _____.
9. Uds. (oír) _____ las noticias.
10. Vosotros (decir) _____ la verdad.
11. Ellas (dormir) _____ hasta la una.
12. Yo (pagar) _____ todas mis cuentas.

Questions in the Past

A yes or no question about the past can be formed using intonation, the tags *¿verdad?* or *¿no?*, or inversion. This is exactly the same way you wouldask a question about the present.

In a Flash

Make a list in Spanish of everything you did yesterday.

¿Tú fuiste al cine?
too fwees-teh ahl see-neh
Did you go to the movies?

Tú fuiste al cine, ¿verdad? (¿no?)
too fwees-teh ahl see-neh behr-dahd (noh)
You went to the movies, didn't you?

¿Fuiste tú al cine?
fwees-teh too ahl see-neh
Did you go to the movies?

To ask for information, simply put the question word at the beginning of the sentence.

In a Flash

Practice asking a friend questions in the past. Vary them by asking for yes-no answers and for specific information.

¿Cuándo fuiste (tú) al cine?
kwahn-doh fwees-teh ahl see-neh
When did you go to the movies?

¿Con quién fuiste al cine?
kohn kee-yehn fwees-teh ahl see-neh
With whom did you go to the movies?

¿Cómo fuiste al cine?
koh-moh fwees-teh ahl see-neh
How did you go to the movies?

To answer yes or no or to give more information, follow the pattern used for the present tense.

Sí, fui al cine.
see fwee ahl see-neh
Yes, I went to the movies.

No, no fui al cine.
noh, noh fwee ahl see-neh
No, I didn't go to the movies.

Fui al cine con Ana.
fwee ahl see-neh kohn ah-nah
I went to the movies with Ana.

Fui al cine en coche.
fwee ahl see-neh ehn koh-cheh
I went to the movies by car.

317

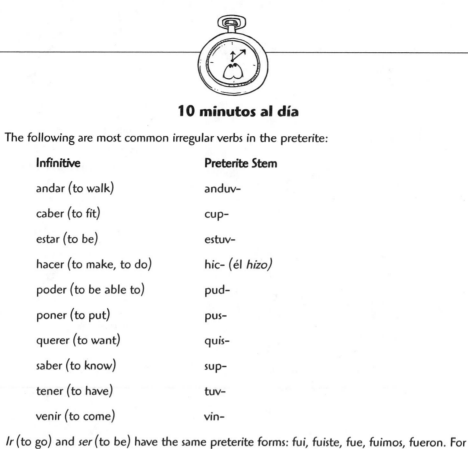

10 minutos al día

The following are most common irregular verbs in the preterite:

Infinitive	Preterite Stem
andar (to walk)	anduv–
caber (to fit)	cup–
estar (to be)	estuv–
hacer (to make, to do)	hic– (él *hizo*)
poder (to be able to)	pud–
poner (to put)	pus–
querer (to want)	quis–
saber (to know)	sup–
tener (to have)	tuv–
venir (to come)	vin–

Ir (to go) and *ser* (to be) have the same preterite forms: fui, fuiste, fue, fuimos, fueron. For the rest, just add *-e, -iste, -o, -imos, -isteis, -ieron*.

May I Question Your Past?

Yesterday was a holiday, the weather was beautiful, and everyone was free to do as he or she wanted. Some people relax on their day off, others do chores, still others go out and have a good time. Ask about your acquaintances and record the answers given to you as indicated in parentheses. (Answers can be found on page 422, in Appendix A.)

Example: Ana/ir al parque (no).
Ud.: ¿Ana, fuiste al parque?
Ana: No, no fui al parque.

Paco y Josá/jugar al tenis (sí).
Ud.: ¿Jugaron Uds. al tenis?
Paco y Jose: Sí, jugamos al tenis.

1. Carlos/hacer una visita al museo (sí).

   _____

   _____

2. Pablo y Jorge/dar un paseo (no).

   _____

   _____

3. María/pescar en el mar (no).

   _____

   _____

4. Isabel y Pilar/almorzar en el centro (sí).

   _____

   _____

5. Adela/traer regalos a sus primos (sí).

   _____

   _____

6. Francisco y Rafael/servir refrescos a sus amigos (no).

   _____

   _____

What Didn't Get Done?

Have you ever made a list of chores, only to find at the end of the day that your list was completely unrealistic? Let's say you made a list for today, and now your day has come to an end. Tell what you did and did not accomplish. (Sample responses can be found on page 422, in Appendix A.)

_____

_____

_____

_____

In a Flash

Use the preterite in the negative and express what you didn't do yesterday that you should have.

The Least You Need to Know

➤ To get prescription drugs, you must go to *una farmacia*. Toiletries can be purchased at *una perfumería*.

➤ Use the irregular verb *venir* to express "to come."

➤ The preterite (past tense) of regular verbs in Spanish can be formed by dropping the infinitive endings and adding the appropriate past tense ending for the verb's family.

➤ Irregular preterite stems must be memorized, but they all have the same ending. Just add *-e, -iste, -o, -imos, -isteis, -ieron* (*-eron* after *j*).

Chapter 22

Making a Phone Call

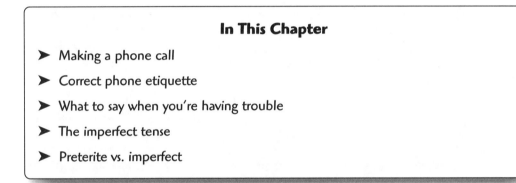

In This Chapter

➤ Making a phone call

➤ Correct phone etiquette

➤ What to say when you're having trouble

➤ The imperfect tense

➤ Preterite vs. imperfect

You're feeling rather chipper now that you've taken care of all your personal and medical needs. Chapter 21, "Did I Pack the Toothpaste?," really helped you put yourself back on course. Now you'd like to let the friends you left behind know how great everything is going. It's time to phone home.

Most Americans don't sufficiently acknowledge our superior phone system. To truly appreciate our excellent telecommunications network, a person needs only to make a phone call in a foreign country. In many instances, a simple local call creates quite a challenge, and long distance can be a nightmare. Operator assistance often is necessary for even the most mundane tasks.

To make things worse, imagine how difficult it can be to communicate with a foreign speaker when you cannot read lips or observe body language for clues. This chapter can help you in this situation. You'll learn how to place a local or international call from a foreign country and how to deal with wrong numbers and other calling problems. You'll also learn how to describe a continuous action in the past using the imperfect tense.

Placing the Call

Making a long distance call from afar usually requires a complicated explanation of the phone system, some operator assistance, and a lot of patience—there can be an awful lot of numbers to punch in. In some countries, you might have to use special tokens and push certain buttons just to complete a local call. When learning how to use the phone, consult Table 22.1 so you can correctly describe the type of call you'd like to make.

Table 22.1 Types of Phone Calls

Type of Phone Call	Spanish Translation	Pronunciation
collect call	la llamada por cobrar, la llamada con cargo	lah yah-mah-dah pohr koh-brahr, lah yah-mah-dah kohn kahr-goh
credit-card call	la llamada con tarjeta de crédito	lah yah-mah-dah kohn tahr-heh-tah deh kreh-dee-toh
local call	la llamada local	lah yah-mah-dah loh-kahl
long-distance call	la llamada de larga distancia	lah yah-mah-dah deh lahr-gah dees-tahn-see-yah
out-of-the-country call	la llamada internacional	lah yah-mah-dah een-tehr-nah-see-yoh-nahl
person-to-person call	la llamada de persona a persona	lah yah-mah-dah deh pehr-soh-nah ah pehr-soh-nah

The different parts of the telephone are featured in Table 22.2.

Table 22.2 The Telephone

Telephone Parts	Spanish Translation	Pronunciation
booth	la cabina (casilla) telefónica	lah kah-bee-nah (kah-see-yah) teh-leh-foh-nee-kah
button	el botón	ehl boh-tohn
coin-return button	el botón de recobrar	ehl boh-tohn deh rreh-koh-brahr
cordless phone (portable phone)	el teléfono inalámbrico	ehl teh-leh-foh-noh een-ah-lahm-bree-koh

Telephone Parts	Spanish Translation	Pronunciation
dial	el disco	ehl dees-koh
keypad	las teclas	lahs teh-klahs
phone card	la tarjeta telefónica	lah tahr-heh-tah teh-leh-foh-nee-kah
public phone	el teléfono público	ehl teh-leh-foh-noh poo-blee-koh
receiver	el auricular	ehl ow-ree-koo-lahr
slot	la ranura	lah rrah-noo-rah
speaker telephone	el teléfono altavoz	ehl teh-leh-foh-noh ahl-tah-bohs
telephone	el teléfono	ehl teh-leh-foh-noh
telephone book	la guía telefónica	lah gee-yah teh-leh-foh-nee-kah
telephone number	el número de teléfono	ehl noo-meh-roh deh teh-leh-foh-noh
token	la ficha	lah fee-chah
touch-tone phone	el teléfono de botónes	ehl teh-leh-foh-noh deh boh-toh-nehs

Now you are ready to phone home. Table 22.3 provides the words you'll need to understand the Spanish directions for placing a phone call.

Table 22.3   How to Make a Phone Call

Telephone Term	Spanish Translation	Pronunciation
to call back	volver* a llamar	bohl-behr ah yah-mahr
to dial	marcar	mahr-kahr
to hang up (the receiver)	colgar*	kohl-gahr
to insert the card	introducir la tarjeta	een-troh-doo-seer lah tahr-heh-tah
to know the area code	saber la clave de área	sah-behr lah klah-beh deh ah-reh-yah
to leave a message	dejar un mensaje	de-hahr oon mehn-sah-heh
to pick up (the receiver)	descolgar*	dehs-kohl-gahr

continues

323

Table 22.3   Continued

Telephone Term	Spanish Translation	Pronunciation
to telephone	telefonear	teh-leh-foh-neh-yahr
to wait for the dial tone	esperar el tono, la señal	ehs-peh-rahr ehl toh-noh, lah seh-nyahl

* These verbs are stem-changing shoe verbs. The o will change to ue in the present tense for all forms except nosotros and vosotros.

Calling from Your Hotel Room

Imagine that you're sitting in your hotel room and find that you need some information regarding hotel services. Look carefully at this card provided for your convenience. Which number would you dial for the following? (Answers can be found on page 422, in Appendix A.)

PARA TELEFONEAR

Club de recreo y gimnasia	32	Médicos	0
Correo	39	Piscina	49
Lavado de ropa	51	Servicio de equipaje	54
Llamadas para despertarse	16	Servicio de transporte	61

To get in touch with the doctor?_____   To place a wake-up call?_____

To get your laundry done?_____   To contact the pool?_____

To find out about your mail?_____   To make transportation plans?_____

To have your bags picked up?_____   To make an appointment for a massage?_____

Using a Public Phone

For practice, read the following directions explaining how to use money or a credit card to place a call. Continue with the instructions for how to place calls that are local, long distance, and international. Use your dictionary for help if you need it.

Como llamar por teléfono en una cabina:

1. Descuelga el auricular del teléfono.

2. Deposita las monedas necesarias o introduce la tarjeta de crédito para pagar la tarifa indicada.

3. Espera hasta escuchar la señal de marcar.

4. Marca el número.

5. Habla con la persona.

6. Después de terminar, cuelga el auricular y saca la tarjeta.

Culture Corner

To place a long distance call in Spain, dial the city code, *el indicativo* (ehl een-dee-kah-tee-boh), before you dial the number. In Spain, bigger cities like Madrid have seven-digit numbers (such as 2 10 48 23, which is read "*dos, diez, cuarenta y ocho, veintitrés*"); smaller cities have six-digit numbers. In the rest of the Spanish-speaking world, telephone numbers have five or six digits.

INSTRUCCIONES PARA EL USO
DEL TELEFONO DURANTE SU ESTANCIA
EN ESPAÑA

SERVICIO AUTOMATICO

1. Descuelgue el microteléfono y espere la señal para marcar.

2. LLAMADAS URBANAS E INTERURBANAS DENTRO DE LA MISMA PROVINCIA Marque el número deseado.

3. LLAMADAS INTERURBANAS. Marque el código interurbano de la ciudad a la cual va destinada la llamada, y a continuación el número del abonado deseado.

4. LLAMADAS INTERNACIONALES Marque el 07. Espere un segundo tono más agudo que el normal. A continuación el indicativo del país(*) hacia el cual va encaminada la llamada, seguido del de la ciudad (**), y del número del abonado deseado.

(*) Consulte los indicativos de países en la última página.

(**) Recuerde que no debe marcar el prefijo de acceso al servicio automático interurbano del país de destino, que generalmente es un 0 (cero).

NOTA: Para conferencias no automáticas llame a la operadora. Marque el 003 para información general

Culture Corner

Public pay phones, *cabinas telefónicas,* with instructions in several languages, are widely available. A call can also be placed from the telephone exchange, *la central telefónica,* or from your hotel, which will probably impose a heavy surcharge. In important cities, special telephone offices are open all day and enable you to call anywhere.

If you need the area code for the country you want to call, consult the telephone directory, *la guía telefónica* (lah gee-yah teh-leh-foh-nee-kah). If you want to call home to the U.S. or Canada, do the following:

1. Wait for the dial tone.
2. Dial 07 and then wait for a second tone.
3. Dial the country code, *el código territorial* (ehl koh-dee-goh teh-rree-toh-ree-ahl), which is 1 for both the United States and Canada + the area code of the city + the phone number you desire.

You should be connected with little trouble.

Special Needs

Many telephone products are available for people with limited visual, auditory, and motor skills. Read the following description of what is available to the physically challenged. Can you figure out what services are provided?

Ahora las personas con impedimentos de audición o del habla pueden comunicarse por teléfono con personas oyentes a cualquier hora y día del año. La Autoridad de Teléfonos comenzó a ofrecer el Servicio de Relevo de Telecomunicaciones (SRT) para llamadas. El personal del Centro de Relevo, llamado Asistente de Comunicaciones (AC), recibirá el mensaje en texto enviado por el audioimpedido y lo leerá en voz alta al oyente a través de otra línea, y viceversa.

Toda llamada es manejada con la más estricta confidencialidad y sin límite de tiempo.

Did you understand that there are special operators who will take messages from and receive messages for people who are hearing impaired or who cannot speak? Did you notice that this service is strictly confidential and is available at any time? If you did, you're really becoming a pro!

Who Is It?

Did you ever notice it is more difficult to understand people over the telephone than in person? This is especially true if they are speaking a different language. Body language, facial expressions, and gestures can help us understand the message a speaker is conveying. Without those clues, your best bet is to become familiar with the Spanish expressions used for making and answering a phone call. Table 22.4 shows you how to begin a typical telephone conversation.

Table 22.4   Making a Phone Call

Expressions Used When Making a Call	Meaning	Expressions Used When Answering a Call	Meaning
Diga. Oiga. Bueno.	Hello.	Diga. Oiga. Bueno.	Hello.
...por favor Soy... Habla...	...please It's...	¿De parte de quién? ¿Quién habla? Soy...	Who's calling? This is...
¿Está...?	Is...in (there)?	No cuelgue, por favor.	Hold on.
Quisiera hablar con...	I would like to speak to...	Un momento. Él/Ella no está.	Just a moment He/She is not in
¿Cuándo regresará?	When will he (she) be back?	¿Quiere dejar un mensaje?	Do you want to leave a message?
Volveré a llamar más tarde.	I'll call back later.		

Sorry, Wrong Number

You can run into many problems when making a phone call: a wrong number, a busy signal, a hang up, and so on. Here are some examples of phrases you might say or hear if you run into any difficulties:

> ¿Qué número está llamando?
> keh noo-meh-roh ehs-tah yah-mahn-doh
> *What number are you calling?*

> Es un error. (Yo tengo) Ud. tiene un número equivocado.
> ehs oon eh-rrohr. (yoh tehn-goh) oo-stehd tee-yeh-neh oon noo-meh-roh eh-kee-boh-kah-doh
> *It's a mistake. (I have) You have the wrong number.*

¡Atención!

Some Spanish telephone booths are primarily for local calls. If you want to call another city or country, you will have to locate a *cabina* that has a green stripe across the top and that is marked *interurbano* (een-tehr-oor-bah-noh), interurban or long distance.

Memory Master

In English, when we want to express that someone is going to do something again, we generally use the prefix *re–*, as in *retry, recall, recycle, redo*. In Spanish, the idiomatic expression *volver (ue)* + *a* + infinitive gets this meaning across. The verb *volver* must be conjugated.

Vuelva a llamar más tarde.
Call back later.

Se nos cortó la línea.
seh nohs kohr-toh lah lee-neh-yah
We got cut off (disconnected).

La línea está ocupada.
la lee-neh-yah ehs-tah oh-koo-pah-dah
The line is busy.

Remarque Ud. el número, por favor.
rreh-mahr-keh oo-stehd ehl noo-meh-roh, pohr fah-bohr
Please redial the number.

El teléfono está descompuesto (dañado, fuera de servicio).
ehl teh-leh-foh-noh ehs-tah dehs-kohm-pwehs-toh (dah-nyah-doh, fweh-rah deh sehr-bee-see-yoh)
The telephone is out of order.

No puedo oír nada.
noh pweh-doh oh-yeer nah-dah
I can't hear you.

Vuelva a llamarme más tarde.
bwehl-bah ah yah-mahr-meh mahs tahr-deh
Call me back later.

While You Were Out

While you were out sight-seeing, the receptionist at the front desk took a message for you from a colleague. What information does the message slip give you? (See page 422 in Appendix A for a translation.)

PARA _Miguel_
FECHA _11/7/95_ HORA _4:25_ A.M./P.M.

MIENTRAS UD. NO ESTUVO
SR
SRA _Roberta Cruz_
SRTA
DE _Aerolíneas México_
NUMERO DE TELEFONO _12-34-56_

○ LLAMO POR TELEFONO   ⊗ FAVOR DE LLAMARLO
○ LLAMO PARA UNA CITA   ○ VOLVERA A LLAMARLO
○ DESEA VERLO   ○ VENGA A VERME

RECADO _Quiere hablarle. lo_
más pronto posible

RECADO TOMADO POR _Ana_

The Imperfect

We *shopped* till we *dropped*. When we *returned* to our cozy hotel room, my husband *decided* to take a nap. I **was sitting** in a chair reading a book when all of a sudden the lights *went out*. I *wondered* what *happened*. I *looked* out the window, and I *saw* that everything **was** dark. I didn't **know** what to do. Night **was falling** and I **was getting** hungry. I *woke* my husband, and we *decided* to find our way out in the darkness. It **was** so hard to walk. We **couldn't** see two feet in front of us. When we *got* to the stairs, we **were** relieved to see that someone from the hotel **was guiding** the guests with flashlights from the fifth floor to the lobby. We *made* the best of it and *ate* at a charming restaurant nearby.

Memory Master

Use the imperfect for times in the past when you would record the continuous events on a video camera. Use the preterite when you would point and shoot an event that occurred at a specific moment in time.

This really happened to us, in the not-so-distant past in a luxury hotel in Puerto Rico. In English, we speak or write easily in the past without giving much thought to what we are saying. In Spanish, however, it's not that simple. There are two different simple past tenses: the *preterite* (*italicized in the preceding paragraph*) and the **imperfect** (**shown in bold**). This tends to make speaking in the past a bit confusing. Just remember that, even if you mistake one for the other, you'll still be understood. Sometimes either tense is correct. What's the difference? The preterite expresses specific actions or events that were completed in the past; the imperfect expresses continuous or repeated actions, events, situations, or states in the past.

Formation of the Imperfect

Before going into a more detailed explanation, let's see how the imperfect is formed. There are only three irregular verbs in the imperfect tense, and no changes are necessary for verbs with spelling and stem changes.

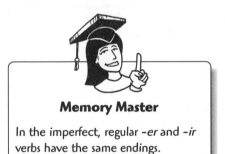

Memory Master

In the imperfect, regular *-er* and *-ir* verbs have the same endings.

➤ To form the imperfect of regular verbs, drop the infinitive ending (*-ar*, *-er*, or *-ir*) and add the proper endings.

-ar Verbs	Imperfect Stem	Conjugation
hablar	habl-	yo habl**aba**
		tú habl**abas**
		él, ella, Ud. habl**aba**

continues

continued

-ar Verbs	Imperfect Stem	Conjugation
		nosotros habl**ábamos**
		vosotros habl**abais**
		ellos, ellas, Uds. habl**aban**

-er and *-ir* Verbs	Imperfect Stem	Conjugation
vender	vend-	yo vend**ía**
		tú vend**ías**
		él, ella, Ud. vend**ía**
		nosotros vend**íamos**
		vosotros vend**íais**
		ellos, ellas, Uds. vend**ían**
abrir	abr-	yo abr**ía**
		tú abr**ías**
		él, ella, Ud. abr**ía**
		nosotros abr**íamos**
		vosotros abr**íais**
		ellos, ellas, Uds. abr**ían**

➤ The following are the three irregular verbs in the imperfect:

Infinitive	Meaning	Imperfect Endings
ir	to go	iba, ibas, iba, íbamos, ibais, iban
ser	to be	era, eras, era, éramos, erais, eran
ver	to see	veía, veías, veía, veíamos, veíais, veían

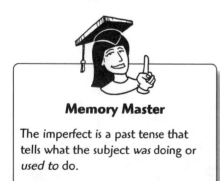

Memory Master

The imperfect is a past tense that tells what the subject *was* doing or *used to* do.

The Preterite vs. the Imperfect

Which tense should you use? And when? The preterite expresses an action that was completed at a specific time in the past. Thinking of a camera might help you understand this concept. The preterite represents an action that could be captured by a snapshot—the action happened and was completed.

Yo fui al cine ayer.
yoh fwee ahl see-neh ah-yehr
I went to the movies yesterday.

330

The imperfect expresses an action that continued in the past over an indefinite period of time. Think again of a camera. The imperfect represents an action that could be captured by a video camera—the action continued to flow. It *was* happening, *used to* happen or *would* (meaning *used to*) happen. The imperfect is a descriptive tense.

Memory Master

Think of the imperfect as a continuous wavy line traveling through the past. The preterite is simply a dot, one moment in past time.

> Yo iba al cine con mi abuelo.
> yoh ee-bah ahl see-neh kohn mee ah-bweh-loh
> *I used to go the movies with my grandfather.*

The two lists that follow provide a more in-depth look at the differences between the two tenses.

Preterite

1. Expresses specific actions or events that were started and completed at a definite time in the past (even if the time isn't mentioned).

   Viajé con mi amigo.
   bee-yah-heh kohn mee ah-mee-goh
   I traveled with my friend.

2. Expresses a specific action or event that occurred at a specific point in time.

   Ayer yo salí a la una.
   ah-yehr yoh sah-lee ah lah oo-nah
   Yesterday I went out at 1 o'clock.

3. Expresses a specific action or event that was repeated a stated number of times.

   Fuimos al cine tres veces.
   fwee-mohs ahl see-neh trehs beh-sehs
   We went to the movies three times.

Imperfect

1. Describes ongoing or continuous actions in the past (which might or might not have been completed).

   Yo viajaba con mi amigo.
   yoh bee-yah-hah-bah kohn mee ah-mee-goh
   I was traveling with my friend.

2. Describes repeated or habitual actions that took place in the past.

   Generalmente yo salía a la una.
   heh-neh-rahl-mehn-teh yoh sah-lee-yah ah lah oo-nah
   I usually went out at 1 o'clock.

331

3. Describes a person, place, thing, or state of mind.

Estábamos contentos.
ehs-tah-bah-mohs kohn-tehn-tohs
We were happy.

Quería salir.
keh-ree-yah sah-leer
I wanted to go out.

El mar estaba peligroso.
ehl mahr ehs-tah-bah
peh-lee-groh-soh
The sea was dangerous.

La puerta estaba abierta.
lah pwehr-tah ehs-tah-bah
ah-bee-yehr-tah
The door was open.

In a Flash

Make a list in Spanish of things you did as a child. Use a mixture of the imperfect and preterite tenses.

What Happened?

It was a day like any other, or so I thought. Little did I know what was in store for me. Complete my story with the correct form of the verbs provided, using either the preterite or imperfect tense. (Check your answers on page 423, in Appendix A.)

(1. Ser)_____ las cinco de la tarde. (2. Estar)_____ lloviendo cuando yo
(3. salir)_____ de mi oficina para regresar a casa. (4. Tomar)_____ el autobús.
(5. Llegar)_____ delante de mi casa media hora más tarde. (6. Entrar)_____ y
(7. subir)_____ a mi apartamento. (8. Sacar)_____ mis llaves pero no las
(9. necesitar)_____. (10. Observar)_____ que mi puerta (11. estar)_____
abierta. Yo no (12. saber)_____ por qué. (13. Tener)_____ mucho miedo.
(14. Estar)_____ convencido de que alguien me (15. robar)_____.
(16. Empujar)_____ la puerta con cuidado y (17. entrar) _____lentamente. No
(18. escuchar)_____ nada. (19. Marchar)_____ hacia el teléfono, cuando de
repente todos mis amigos (20. gritar)_____ en voz alta: ¡Feliz cumpleaños! ¡Qué
sorpresa!

10 minutos al día

To form the imperfect, drop the infinitive endings (*-ar, -er, -ir*) from the verb and add the following endings:

> *-ar* verbs: *-aba, -abas, -aba, -ábamos, -abais, -aban*

> *-er* and *-ir* verbs: *-ía, -ías, -ía, -íamos, -íais, -ían*

Three verbs are irregular in the imperfect:

> *ir: iba, ibas, iba, íbamos, ibais, iban*

> *ser: era, eras, era, éramos, erais, eran*

> *ver: veía, veías, veía, veíamos, veíais, veían*

The Least You Need to Know

➤ Master the vocabulary you need and follow directions to make phone calls in a foreign country.

➤ The imperfect is formed by adding the endings *-aba, -abas, -aba, -ábamos, -abais,* and *-aban* to *-ar* verbs. The endings *-ía, -ías, -ía, -íamos, -íais,* and *-ían* are added to *-er* and *-ir* verbs.

➤ The three irregular verbs in the imperfect—*ir, ser,* and *ver*—must be memorized.

➤ The imperfect is used to describe what the subject *was* doing. The preterite states what the subject *did*.

Chapter 23

Where's the Nearest Post Office?

In This Chapter

➤ Receiving and sending mail

➤ The difference between *saber* and *conocer*

➤ The present perfect tense

In the preceding chapter, you learned how to successfully complete a phone call, how to carry on a polite conversation using proper phone etiquette, and how to deal with typical, everyday telephone problems. You've looked at your hotel telephone bill and have decided it's too costly to phone home as often as you'd like. Writing letters is the simplest solution, so now we're off to the local post office.

Your friends will be deeply offended if you don't send them postcards, and you don't want to see the look in your mom's eyes if she doesn't receive a letter. Let's say you bought a great souvenir, but it's too heavy to lug on the plane. Shipping it sounds like a great idea. If you follow directions, fill out the proper forms, and apply the correct postage, you can rest assured your mail will get to its destination. This chapter shows you how to send air, registered, and special-delivery mail. You'll also learn how to write letters that describe your past and present activities and acquaintances.

Culture Corner

If all you need is stamps, you can pick them up at *estancos* (ehs-tahn–kohs), shops that sell tobacco, stamps, and seals. When you're ready to send a letter home, look for the red and yellow mailboxes.

Please, Mr. Postman

There's so much to write about, you hardly know where to begin. You've seen the Prado, run with the bulls in Pamplona, and basked in the sun on the Costa del Sol. You can't wait for your family and friends to read about your wonderful adventures. You don't want your postcards and letters to arrive home after you do. You want speedy delivery, and you're prepared to pay the extra price for airmail service. Naturally, you'll want to keep a few essentials on hand such as envelopes and stamps. Table 23.1 provides the vocabulary you need to send your mail.

Table 23.1   Mail and Post Office Terms

Postal Terms	Spanish Translation	Pronunciation
address	la dirección	lah dee-rehk-see-yohn
addressee	el destinatario	ehl dehs-tee-nah-tah-ree-yoh
air letter	el correo aéreo	ehl koh-rreh-yoh ah-yee-reh-yoh
commemorative stamp	el sello conmemorativo	ehl seh-yoh kohn-meh-moh-rah-tee-boh
envelope	el sobre	ehl soh-breh
letter	la carta	lah kahr-tah
mailbox	el buzón	ehl boo-sohn
money order	el giro postal	ehl hee-roh pohs-tahl
package	el paquete	ehl pah-keh-teh
parcel	el paquete	ehl pah-keh-teh
postcard	la tarjeta postal	lah tahr-heh-tah pohs-tahl
postage	el franqueo	ehl frahn-keh-yoh
postal code	el código postal	ehl koh-dee-goh pohs-tahl
postal meter	la franqueadora postal	lah frahn-keh-yah-doh-rah pohs-tahl
postal worker	el cartero (la cartera)	ehl kahr-teh-roh (lah kahr-teh-rah)
postmark	el matasellos	ehl mah-tah-seh-yohs

Postal Terms	Spanish Translation	Pronunciation
rate	la tarifa de franqueo	lah tah-ree-fah deh frahn-keh-yoh
sender	el remitiente	ehl rreh-mee-tee-yehn-teh
sheet of stamps	la hoja de sellos	lah oh-hah deh seh-yohs
slot	la ranura	lah rrah-noo-rah
stamp	el sello	ehl seh-yoh
window	la ventanilla	lah behn-tah-nee-yah

The services provided by the Spanish Postal Service are two-fold in nature. They include the following:

➤ Services pertaining strictly to different types of correspondence such as letters, postcards, and packages.

➤ Services dealing with postal banking services such as postal and telegraphic money orders. Unlike in other European cities, post offices in Spain do not normally handle telephone calls.

Getting Postal Service

You've written some postcards to your friends, dashed off a letter to your closest relatives, and even managed some business correspondence. If you need directions to the nearest post office or mailbox simply ask the following question:

¿Dónde está el correo (buzón) más próximo?
dohn-deh ehs-tah ehl koh-rreh-yoh (boo-sohn) mahs prohk-see-moh
Where is the nearest post office (mailbox)?

You'll find that, just like back home, you might have to fill out special forms and paperwork depending on the types of letters and packages you've decided to send. Postage rates depend on how quickly you want your mail delivered. It's important to be able to correctly identify the type of service you need.

¿Cuál es la tarifa de franqueo de...?
kwahl ehs lah tah-ree-fah deh frahn-keh-yoh deh
What is the postage rate for...?

Type of Delivery	Spanish Translation	Pronunciation
an insured letter	una carta asegurada	oo-nah kahr-tah ah-seh-goo-rah-dah
a letter to the United States	~~una carta a los~~ Estados Unidos	oo-nah kahr-tah ah lohs ehs-tah-dohs oo-nee-dohs
an airmail letter	una carta por correo aéreo	oo-nah kahr-tah pohr koh-rreh-yoh ah-yee-reh-yoh
a registered letter	una carta certificada	oo-nah kahr-tah sehr-tee-fee-kah-dah
a special delivery letter	una carta urgente	oo-nah kahr-tah oor-hehn-teh

Culture Corner

If you don't know in advance where you'll be staying but would like to pick up your mail personally (you'll need to show your passport as ID and pay a nominal fee for each item received), or if you want to have your mail forwarded to a certain address, you can register at the *Lista de Correos* (lees-tah deh koh-rreh-ohs), the general delivery window.

Here are some other useful phrases:

Quisiera mandar esta carta (este paquete) por correo regular (aéreo, urgente).
kee-see-yeh-rah mahn-dahr ehs-tah kahr-tah (ehs-teh pah-keh-teh) pohr koh-rreh-yoh rreh-goo-lahr (ah-yee-reh-yoh, oor-hehn-teh)
I would like to send this letter (this package) by regular mail (by airmail, by special delivery).

Quisiera mandar este paquete contra reembolso.
kee-see-yeh-rah mahn-dahr ehs-teh pah-keh-teh kohn-trah rreh-ehm-bohl-soh
I would like to send this package C.O.D.

¿Cuánto pesa esta carta (este paquete)?
kwahn-toh peh-sah ehs-tah kahr-tah (ehs-teh pah-keh-teh)
How much does this letter (package) weigh?

¿Cuándo llegará (llegarán)?
kwahn-doh yeh-gah-rah (yeh-gah-rahn)
When will it arrive?

Sending a Telegram

People generally send telegrams when there's important news to announce or to acknowledge: your oldest son is finally getting married, the birth of a child or grand-child, a fabulous business deal, or your best friend got an exciting promotion. When you want to send a telegram, the following phrases will prove helpful:

Quisiera mandar un telegrama (a cobro revertido).
kee-see-yeh-rah mahn-dahr oon teh-leh-grah-mah (ah koh-broh rreh-behr-tee-doh)
I would like to send a telegram (collect).

¿Cuánto cuesta por palabra?
kwahn-toh kwehs-tah pohr pah-lah-brah
How much is it per word?

¿Puede darme un formulario (un impreso), por favor?
pweh-deh dahr-meh oon fohr-moo-lah-ree-yoh (oon eem-preh-soh) pohr fah-bohr
May I please have a form?

¿Dónde están los formularios?
dohn-deh ehs-tahn lohs fohr-moo-lah-ree-yohs
Where are the forms?

Culture Corner

With over 600 offices all over the country, the Spanish Postal Service provides a wide range of modern and efficient services. The main offices located in Madrid, Barcelona, and Bilbao, as well as those in the international airports, are open 24 hours a day. You can also expect to find post offices, *Correos y Telégrafos* (koh-rreh-ohs ee teh-leh-grah-fohs), in railway stations, small villages, and ports.

Can You Read This?

Looking for something to read while you wait in line at the post office? Perhaps you're interested in the local news and your hotel provides a complimentary newspaper each morning. Wherever you go, there might be important signs you need to read. If you see the word *aviso* (ah-bee-soh), you know there is some kind of warning such as *agua no potable* (undrinkable water). Table 23.2 features items you might read while visiting a Spanish-speaking country.

Table 23.2 Things to Read

Item to Be Read	Spanish Translation	Pronunciation
ad	un anuncio	oon ah-noon-see-yoh
book	un libro	oon lee-broh
magazine	una revista	oo-nah rreh-bees-tah
menu	una carta, un menú	oo-nah kahr-tah, oon meh-noo
newspaper	un periódico	oon peh-ree-yoh-dee-koh
novel	una novela	oo-nah noh-beh-lah
pamphlet	un folleto	oon foh-yeh-toh
receipt	un recibo	oon rreh-see-boh
sign	un letrero	oon leh-treh-roh
warning	un aviso	oon ah-bee-soh

¡Atención!

Note the irregular yo forms for both *saber, yo sé,* and *conocer, yo conozco.* For all other subjects, these verbs follow the rules for the conjugation of regular *-er verbs.*

Did You Know That...?

Do you know the name of a great Spanish restaurant? You do? What is its address? How about its phone number? You know the owner? She's your second cousin and really knows how to prepare a mean *paella*? That's great. To express certain facts, information, relationships, and abilities, you need the two Spanish verbs that express "to know," *saber* and *conocer.* Study the verbs first and then read the paragraphs that follow for an explanation of how to use each verb properly.

saber (to know)

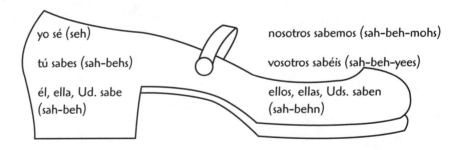

yo sé (seh)   nosotros sabemos (sah-beh-mohs)

tú sabes (sah-behs)   vosotros sabéis (sah-beh-yees)

él, ella, Ud. sabe   ellos, ellas, Uds. saben
(sah-beh)   (sah-behn)

conocer (to know)

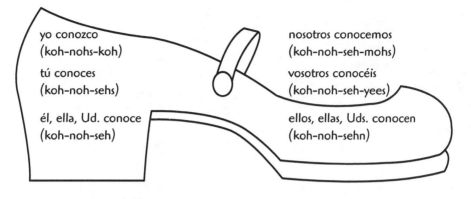

yo conozco
(koh-nohs-koh)

nosotros conocemos
(koh-noh-seh-mohs)

tú conoces
(koh-noh-sehs)

vosotros conocéis
(koh-noh-seh-yees)

él, ella, Ud. conoce
(koh-noh-seh)

ellos, ellas, Uds. conocen
(koh-noh-sehn)

What's the Difference?

If there are two ways to express "to know," how are you supposed to know when to use each one? It is important to remember that the Spanish differentiate between knowing facts and how to do things (*saber*) and knowing (being acquainted with) people, places, things, and ideas (*conocer*).

The verb *saber* shows knowledge gained through learning or experience. It expresses that someone knows a fact or has memorized something. *Saber* means "to know how" when it is followed by an infinitive.

¿Sabe la dirección?
sah-beh lah dee-rehk-see-yohn
Do you know the address?

Yo sé donde está.
yoh seh dohn-deh ehs-tah
I know where it is.

¿Él sabe nadar?
ehl sah-beh nah-dahr
Does he know how to swim?

The verb *conocer* shows familiarity with a person, a place, or a thing. If you can replace "to know" with "to be acquainted with," you know to use the verb *conocer*.

Memory Master

Remember to use the personal *a* (which has no translation) before a direct object noun or pronoun.

Yo conozco a Juan.   *I know Juan.*

¿No conoces
a ella?   *Don't you
know her?*

In a Flash

Make a list of people you know and things you know how to do.

¿Conoce a Marta?
koh-noh-seh ah mahr-tah
Do you know Martha? (Are you acquainted with her?)

¿Conoces este poema?
koh-noh-sehs ehs-teh poh-eh-mah
Do you know that poem? (Have you heard it but you don't know the words?)

Notice the difference between the following sentences:

Yo sé la canción.
I know the song (by heart).

Yo conozco la canción.
I know the song (I'm familiar with it).

10 minutos al día

The two Spanish verbs that express to know, *saber* and *conocer*, are used in different contexts.

Use *saber* in the following situations:

➤ To show knowledge gained through learning and experience

➤ To state a fact

➤ To express knowledge that has been memorized

➤ To express knowing how to do something

Use *conocer* in the following situation:

➤ To show familiarity with a person, a place, or a thing. You should be able to substitute the words "to be acquainted with" for "to know."

Using Saber and Conocer

If you keep the differences between the two verbs in mind, you will quickly learn to use them properly. Show that you've gotten the hang of it by filling in the blanks with the correct form of *saber* or *conocer*. (Answers can be found on page 423, in Appendix A.)

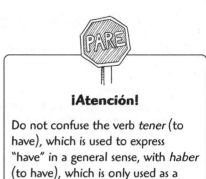

¡Atención!

Do not confuse the verb *tener* (to have), which is used to express "have" in a general sense, with *haber* (to have), which is only used as a helping verb in compound tenses.

Yo tengo muchos amigos.
I have many friends.

Yo he telefoneado a mis amigos.
I have called my friends.

1. Ellos _____ donde está el correo.

2. Yo no _____ su número de teléfono.

3. ¿_____ Ud. al señor Castro?

4. Nosotros _____ esquiar.

5. ¿_____ tú a esa mujer?

6. Ella _____ Madrid.

7. ¿_____ Uds. que yo soy cubana?

8. Vosotros _____ este monumento.

What Have You Done?

"Good grief!" you exclaim as you realize you've forgotten to call your loved ones to tell them you've arrived safely. You have promised in the past to do the very same thing, and you always seem to let it slip your mind. It's probably because you've gotten so caught up in the excitement of your trip.

To express what you have or have not done, you must use the present perfect tense in Spanish. This tense refers to an action that has already happened, either in the general past or quite recently in relation to now. ("I've started to study Spanish.") It can also be used to speak about past events that carry over into the present. ("I've always wanted to study that language [and I still want to now].")

The present perfect is a compound tense, which means it is made up of more than one part. Two elements are needed to form the present perfect—the helping verb *haber* (ah-behr, to have) which expresses that something has taken place, and a past participle, which expresses exactly what the action was.

The present perfect tense is formed as follows:

    subject noun or pronoun + helping verb + past participle

The Helping Verb Haber

Because *haber* follows the subject of the sentence, it must be conjugated. Table 23.3 gives the present tense of this helping verb.

Table 23.3 The Helping Verb *Haber* (to Have)

Conjugation of Haber	Pronunciation	Meaning
yo he	yoh eh	I have
tú has	too ahs	you have
él, ella, Ud. ha	ehl, eh-yah, oo-stehd ah	he, she, it has; you have
nosotros hemos	nohs-oh-trohs eh-mohs	we have
vosotros habéis	bohs-oh-trohs ah-beh-yees	you have
ellos, ellas, Uds. han	eh-yohs, eh-yahs, oo-steh-dehs ahn	they, you have

Forming Past Participles

To this helping verb, you must now add a past participle. The helping verb is always conjugated because it is the first verb. The past participle remains the same, no matter what the subject might be.

➤ To form the past participles of regular verbs, drop the infinitive ending (*-ar*, *-er*, or *-ir*) and add the following endings:

-ar Verb	Past Participle Stem	Past Participle Ending
hablar	habl-	-ado

-er and *-ir* Verbs	Past Participle Stem	Past Participle Ending
vender	vend-	-ido
decidir	decid-	-ido

➤ For verbs ending in *-er* or *-ir* in which a vowel immediately precedes the infinitive
ending, add an accent mark on the *i* as follows:

Infinitive	Past Participle Stem	Past Participle
caer (to fall)	ca-	caído
creer (to believe)	cre-	creído
leer (to read)	le-	leído
oír (to hear)	o-	oído
reír (to laugh)	re-	reído
traer (to bring)	tra-	traído

10 minutos al día

You probably will use the following irregular past participles often:

Infinitive	Past Participle
abrir (to open)	abierto
cubrir (to cover)	cubierto
decir (to say, to tell)	dicho
escribir (to write)	escrito
hacer (to do, to make)	hecho
morir (to die)	muerto
poner (to put)	puesto
resolver (to resolve)	resuelto
romper (to break)	roto
ver (to see)	visto
volver (to return)	vuelto

Memory Master

The present perfect tense is used to express an action that began in the past and continues to the present, or is some way connected to the present: I have eaten here often.

The preterite is used to express an action that was completed in the past: I ate here once.

The imperfect is used to express a continuous action in the past: I used to eat here.

In a Flash

Make a list of everything you have and haven't done today.

Presently Perfect

Now let's take this formula and put the present perfect to use.

Yo he hablado con mi familia.
yoh heh ah-blah-doh kohn mee fah-meel-yah
I have spoken with my family.

Nosotros hemos comido demasiado.
noh-soh-trohs eh-mohs koh-mee-doh deh-mah-see-yah-doh
We've eaten too much.

Ud. ha recibido una carta.
oo-stehd ah rreh-see-bee-doh oo-nah kahr-tah
You have received a letter.

Él ha hecho el trabajo.
ehl ah eh-choh ehl trah-bah-hoh
He has done the work.

Ellos han visto El Prado.
eh-yohs ahn bees-toh ehl prah-doh
They have seen El Prado.

The past participle cannot be separated from the helping verb. This is the case even when using the word "no," an adverb, or a subject noun or pronoun in a question.

Jaime no ha dicho la verdad.
James didn't tell the truth.

Nosotros siempre hemos llegado puntualmente.
We've always arrived on time.

¿Han llamado los muchachos?
Have the boys called?

¿No he comprendido ella?
Didn't she understand?

Using the Present Perfect

It's a holiday weekend and most people have some spare time to themselves. Describe what each person has or has not done to make the most of this opportunity. Use the correct forms of the helping verb *haber* and the past participle of the indicated infinitive. (Answers can be found on page 423, in Appendix A.)

Example: (yo/mirar) la televisión
Yo he mirado la televisión.

(Ud./no poner) la mesa
Ud. no ha puesto la mesa.

1. (nosotros/ir) al cine _____ .
2. (ellos/jugar) al fútbol _____ .
3. (tú/no) trabajar _____ .
4. (yo/leer) una novela _____ .
5. (Ud./no escribir) cartas _____ .
6. (vosotros/no correr) al centro _____ .
7. (Uds./no traer) su ropa a la lavandería _____ .
8. (ella/volver) a casa temprano _____ .

10 minutos al día

The present perfect is a compound tense. This means it contains two parts:

1. The helping verb *haber*. *Haber* is conjugated and indicates that something has taken place: *he, has, ha, hemos, habéis, han*

2. The past participle. The past participle tells what the action was. To form the past participle of regular verbs, drop the infinitive ending (*-ar, -er, -ir*) and add *-ado* for *-ar* verbs and *-ido* for *-er* and *-ir* verbs.

The Least You Need to Know

➤ Go to a Spanish post office to mail letters and packages or to send money.

➤ *Saber* means to know a fact or to know how to do something. *Conocer* means to be acquainted with a person, a place, or a thing.

➤ The present perfect tense expresses what has happened in the general past or quite recently. It is made up of the conjugated form of the helping verb *haber* and a past participle.

Part 5
Taking Care of Business

It's a small world after all, especially today where business is concerned. Knowledge of a foreign language is becoming increasingly important in all walks of life in an ever-expanding, multicultural world.

Part 5 is dedicated to readers whose jobs and businesses require more than a cursory knowledge of Spanish. In our high-tech society, all the modern and essential computer terms and phrases—as well as the vocabulary necessary to fax and to photocopy— are a must. Banking and business expressions will also certainly come in handy. For people who must travel extensively or who would like to combine business with pleasure, alternatives to the traditional hotel stay are presented.

By the time you've finished Part 5, if you've worked seriously, steadfastly, and conscientiously, you'll be well equipped and ready to handle just about any situation that might arise—in Spanish. Good luck! I feel confident that you can do it on your own.

Chapter 24

Doing Business

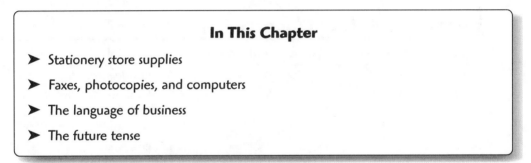

In This Chapter

➤ Stationery store supplies

➤ Faxes, photocopies, and computers

➤ The language of business

➤ The future tense

Chapter 23, "Where's the Nearest Post Office?," ensured that your family and friends would be able to read all about your exploits. What if you need to do business in a Spanish-speaking country? Writing an intelligent, well-worded letter is a valuable skill. You should also be able to talk about the faxes, photocopies, and computers that are so important in business today. This chapter presents key phrases used in business and teaches you how to describe your plans for your company's future.

Culture Corner

Spanish–speaking countries offer a wealth of business opportunities. Because Spanish is the fourth most-widely spoken language in the world, it's no wonder it is studied and used in business by so many people today.

I Need Supplies

To successfully conduct any type of business, you need to keep certain basic supplies on hand. No doubt, you'll want to stop at the stationery store, *la papelería* (lah pah-pehl-eh-ree-yah), to stock up on the business items listed in Table 24.1. You can start by saying the following:

Quisiera comprar...
kee-see-yeh-rah kohm-prahr
I would like to buy...

Table 24.1   At the Stationery Store

Business Supply	Spanish Translation	Pronunciation
ball-point pen	el bolígrafo	ehl boh-lee-grah-foh
calculator (solar)	la calculadora (solar)	lah kahl-koo-lah-doh-rah (soh-lahr)
envelopes	los sobres	lohs soh-brehs
eraser	la goma	lah goh-mah
glue	el pegamento	ehl peh-gah-mehn-toh
notebook	el cuaderno	ehl kwah-dehr-noh
paper	el papel	ehl pah-pehl
paper clips	los sujetapapeles	lohs soo-heh-tah-pah-peh-lehs
pencils	los lápices	lohs lah-pee-shehs
pencil sharpener	el sacapuntas	ehl sah-kah-poon-tahs
post-its	las notas autoadhesivas desprendibles	lahs noh-tahs ow-toh-ahd-eh-see-bahs dehs-prehn-dee-blehs
ruler	la regla	lah rreh-glah
scotch tape	la cinta adhesiva	lah seen-tah ahd-eh-see-bah
stapler	la grapadora	lah grah-pah-doh-rah
stationery	los objetos de escritorio	lohs ohb-heh-tohs deh ehs-kree-toh-ree-yoh

Business Supply	Spanish Translation	Pronunciation
string	la cuerda	lah kwehr-dah
wrapping paper	el papel del envoltorio	ehl pah-pehl dehl ehn-bol-toh-ree-yoh
writing pad	el bloc	ehl blohk

Photocopies, Faxes, and Computers

If you want your business to run smoothly, you can't do without three items: faxes, photocopies, and computers. Use the sections that follow to help you keep them running smoothly.

Making Photocopies

I recently left the country to get some materials for this book. I pestered a lot of people, but I got just about everything I needed. As luck would have it, when I went to the business center to have photocopies made, all the machines were out of order. Off I trudged to the nearest photocopy store, where I used the following phrases:

> Quisiera hacer una fotocopia de este papel (este documento).
> kee-see-yeh-rah ah-sehr oo-nah foh-toh-koh-pee-yah deh ehs-teh pah-pehl (ehs-teh doh-koo-mehn-toh)
> *I would like to make a photocopy of this paper (this document).*

> Quisiera mandar hacer una fotocopia de este documento.
> kee-see-yeh-rah mahn-dahr ah-sehr oo-nah foh-toh-koh-pee-yah deh ehs-teh doh-koo-mehn-toh
> *I would like to have a photocopy made of this document.*

In a Flash

Label in Spanish all the stationery items you keep on your desk. Don't remove the labels until you have all the names memorized. Then test your knowledge.

Memory Master

Remember to put the correct form of the demonstrative adjective (*este, esta, estos, estas*) before the noun you are using.

¿Cuánto cuestan estas fotocopias? How much do these photocopies cost?

¿Cuánto cuesta por página?
kwahn-toh kwehs-tah pohr pah-hee-nah
What is the cost per page?

¿Puede Ud. agrandarlo (cincuenta por ciento)?
pweh-deh oo-stehd ah-grahn-dahr-loh (seen-kwehn-tah pohr see-yehn-toh)
Can you enlarge it (by 50 percent)?

¿Puede Ud. reducirlo (veinticinco por ciento)?
pweh-deh oo-steh rreh-doo-seer-loh (beh-yeen-teh ee seen-koh pohr see-yehn-toh)
Can you reduce it (by 25 percent)?

¿Puede Ud. hacer una copia en color?
pweh-deh oo-stehd ah-sehr oo-nah koh-pee-yah ehn koh-lohr
Can you make a color copy?

Memory Master

Use the following pronouns after prepositions:

mí (me); ti (you—familiar); él (him, it); ella (her, it); Ud. (you—polite); nosotros (us); vosotros (you—familiar); ellos (them—masculine); ellas (them— feminine); Uds. (you—polite).

Let Me Take Care of That

Mandar (conjugated) + *hacer* (the infinitive form) describes having something done for someone. Use the indirect object (*le* or *les*, meaning "for him," "for her," or "for them") + *mandar* + *hacer* + noun. You also can use *mandar* + *hacer* + noun + the preposition *para* + the name of the person (or the prepositional pronoun referring to the person) for whom the work is being done, as in the following examples:

Yo les mando hacer una fotocopia.
yoh lehs mahn-doh ah-sehr oo-nah foh-toh-koh-pee-yah
I'm having a photocopy made for them.

Yo mando hacer una fotocopia para mi jefe.
yoh mahn-doh ah-sehr oo-nah foh-toh-koh-pee-yah pah-rah mee heh-feh
I'm having a photocopy made for my boss.

Yo mando hacer una fotocopia para él.
yoh mahn-doh ah-sehr oo-nah foh-toh-koh-pee-yah pah-rah ehl
I'm having a photocopy made for him.

Fax It

Let's face it, a fax machine has become almost as important as a telephone in many households. My son went to visit a college in Pittsburgh, and we gave him cash to pay for his hotel room. Imagine our surprise when he called and informed us that they wouldn't accept his money. They threatened to cancel his room unless he could provide a credit card (which he didn't have at the time). So off we went at 10 p.m. to find a fax machine and send a photocopy of our credit card.

When you are able to transmit and receive messages and information in a matter of minutes, you can speed up the time it takes to transact business. That translates into extra cash. If you are conducting business in a Spanish-speaking country, it's a must to be fax-literate.

¿Tiene Ud. un fax?
tee-yeh-neh oo-stehd oon fahks
Do you have a fax machine?

¿Cuál es su número de fax?
kwahl ehs soo noo-meh-roh deh fahks
What is your fax number?

Quisiera mandar un fax.
kee-see-yeh-rah mahn-dahr oon fahks
I'd like to send a fax.

¡Atención!

Use *quisiera* (*kee-see-yeh-rah*) "I would like," which is far more polite than *quiero* (*kee-yeh-roh*) "I want."

¿Puedo enviar por fax este documento, por favor?
pweh-doh ehn-bee-yahr pohr fahk ehs-teh doh-koo-mehn-toh, pohr fah-bohr
May I fax this, please?

¿Puedo enviarle a Ud. por fax (este documento)?
pweh-doh ehn-bee-yahr-leh ah oo-stehd pohr fahks (ehs-teh doh-koo-mehn-toh)
May I fax this letter (document) to you?

Enviémelo por fax.
ehn-bee-yeh-meh-loh pohr fahks
Fax it to me.

Yo no recibí (Yo no he recibido) su fax.
yoh noh rreh-see-bee (yoh noh eh rreh-see-bee-doh) soo fahks
I didn't get your fax.

¿Recibió Ud. (¿Ha recibido Ud.) mi fax?
rreh-see-bee-yoh (ah rreh-see-bee-doh oo-stehd) mee fahks
Did you receive my fax?

Su fax es ilegible.
soo fahks ehs ee-leh-hee-bleh
Your fax is illegible.

¿Puede Ud. enviármelo otra vez?
pweh-deh oo-stehd ehn-bee-yahr-meh-loh oh-trah behs
Please send it again.

Favor de confirmar que Ud. recibió (Ud. ha recibido) mi fax.
fah-bohr deh kohn-feer-mahr keh oo-stehd rreh-see-bee-yoh (oo-stehd ah rreh-see-bee-doh) mee fahks
Please confirm that you've received my fax.

Memory Master

You can politely ask someone to write to you as follows:

por favor (*poh fah-bohr*): Ecríbame, por favor.

Hágame el favor de + infinitive: Hágame el favor de escribirme.

Favor de + infinitive: Favor de escribirme.

I Love My Computer

I have a friend who runs a business without a computer. As a result, his accountant threatens to walk off the job on a daily basis. Today, a computer is an absolute necessity. Not only do you have to know how to operate one, you also must know about the industry standards and programs for your field and for the system you are using. The phrases that follow will help you conduct business using computers, even if you're not a computer geek. Table 24.2 will have you sounding like a pro in no time.

¿Qué sistema (tipo, género) de computadora tiene Ud.?
keh sees-teh-mah (tee-poh, heh-neh-roh) deh kohm-poo-tah-doh-rah tee-yeh-neh oo-stehd
What kind of computer do you have?

¿Qué sistema operador usa Ud. (está Ud. usando)?
keh sees-teh-mah oh-peh-rah-dohr oo-sah oo-stehd (ehs-tah oo-stehd oo-sahn-doh)
What operating system are you using?

¿Qué procesador de textos usa Ud. (está Ud. usando)?
keh proh-seh-sah-dohr deh tehks-tohs oo-sah oo-stehd (ehs-tah oo-stehd oo-sahn-doh)
What word processing program are you using?

¿Qué hoja de cálculo electrónico usa Ud. (está Ud. usando)?
keh oh-hah deh kahl-koo-loh eh-lehk-troh-nee-koh oo-sah oo-stehd (ehs-tah oo-stehd oo-sahn-doh)
What spreadsheet program are you using?

¿Qué periféricos usa Ud. (está Ud. usando)?
keh peh-ree-feh-ree-kohs oo-sah oo-stehd (ehs-tah oo-stehd oo-sahn-doh)
What peripherals do you have?

¿Son compatibles nuestros sistemas?
sohn kohm-pah-tee-blehs nwehs-trohs sees-teh-mahs
Are our systems compatible?

¿Tiene Ud…?
tee-yeh-neh oo-stehd
Do you have…?

¿Usa Ud. (Está Ud. usando)…?
oo-sah oo-stehd (ehs-tah oo-stehd oo-sahn-doh)
Do you use…?

¡Atención!

When conducting business and speaking to associates, always use the polite Ud. form.

Memory Master

Use the present progressive tense to express what you are doing now. Conjugate the verb *estar* and add the present participle: drop the infinitive ending and add *-ando* for *-ar* verbs and *-iendo* for *-er* and *-ir* verbs.

Table 24.2   Mini-Dictionary for Computer Users

Computer Term	Spanish Translation	Pronunciation
access (to access)	el acceso (accesar)	ehl ahk-seh-soh (ahk-seh-sahr)
accessibility	la accesibilidad	lah ahk-seh-see-bee-lee-dahd
bar graph	el histograma	ehl ees-toh-grah-mah
baud	el baudio	ehl bow-dee-yoh
bookmark	la marca	lah mahr-kah
boot	arrancar	ah-rrahn-kahr

continues

357

Table 24.2   Continued

Computer Term	Spanish Translation	Pronunciation
brand name	la marca	lah mahr-kah
bug	el error	ehl eh-rrohr
byte	el byte, el octeto	ehl bee-teh, ehl ohk-teh-toh
cable	el cable	ehl kah-bleh
cartridge	el cartucho	ehl kahr-too-choh
laser	de laser	deh lah-sehr
ink jet	de tinta	deh teen-tah
CD-ROM disk	el disco optinúmerico	ehl dees-koh ohp-tee-noo-meh-ree-koh
chip	el chip	ehl cheep
click	chascar	chahs-kahr
clipboard	el tabloncillo	ehl tah-blohn-see-yoh
clone	el clone	ehl kloh-neh
compatible	compatible	kohm-pah-tee-bleh
computer	la computadora	lah kohm-poo-tah-doh-rah
computer science	la informática	lah een-fohr-mah-tee-kah
connection	la conexión	lah koh-nehk-see-yohn
connector	el conector	ehl koh-nehk-tohr
CPU	la unidad central	lah oo-nee-dahd sehn-trahl
cursor	el cursor	ehl koor-sohr
cyberspace	el ciberespacio	ehl see-behr-ehs-pah-see-yoh
DOS	el sistema disco operante	ehl sees-teh-mah dees-koh oh-peh-rahn-teh
data base	la base de data	lah bah-seh deh dah-tah
debug	suprimir fallos de	soo-pree-meer fah-yohs deh
debugger (software)	la supresión de fallos	lah soo-preh-see-yohn deh fah-yohs
desk top computer	el ordenador	ehl ohr-deh-nah-dohr
diskette	el disquete	ehl dees-keh-teh
$3^1/_2$ in.	de tres y media pulgadas	deh trehs ee meh-dee-yah pool-gah-dahs
$5^1/_4$ in.	de cinco y cuarto pulgadas	deh seen-koh ee kwahr-toh pool-gah-dahs
8 in.	de ocho pulgadas	deh oh-choh pool-gah-dahs
disk drive	la disquetera	lah dees-keh-teh-rah
download	bajar, descargar	bah-hahr, dehs-kahr-gahr
driver	el piloto	ehl pee-loh-toh
drop-down menu	el menúderrama	ehl meh-noo-deh-rrah-mah

Computer Term	Spanish Translation	Pronunciation
e-mail	el mensaje eléctrico, el correo electrónico	ehl mehn-sah-heh eh-lehk-tree-koh, ehl koh-rreh-yoh eh-lehk-troh-nee-koh
e-mail address	la dirrección de correo electrónico	lah dee-rehk-see-yohn deh koh-reeh-yoh eh-lehk-troh-nee-koh
field	el campo	ehl kahm-poh
filter	el filtro	ehl feel-troh
floppy disk	el disco flexible	ehl dees-koh flehk-see-bleh
freenet	la red libre	lah rrehd lee-breh
freeware	los programas de libre distribución, dominio público	lohs proh-grah-mahs deh lee-breh dees-tree-boo-see-yohn, doh-mee-nee-yoh poob-lee-koh
function key	la tecla de función	lah tehk-lah deh foon-see-yohn
furniture	los muebles	lohs mweh-blehs
graphics card (high resolution)	la carta gráfica (de alta resolución)	lah kahr-tah grah-fee-kah (deh ahl-tah rreh-soh-loo-see-yohn)
hacker	el/la pirata	ehl/lah pee-rah-tah
hard disk	el disco duro	ehl dees-koh doo-roh
hardware	el hardware	ehl hard-wahr
home computer use	el doméstico	ehl doh-mehs-tee-koh
home page	la página inicial	lah pah-hee-nah ee-nee-see-yahl
host	el sistema central	ehl sees-teh-mah sehn-trahl
icon	el icono	ehl ee-koh-noh
information superhighway	la carretera electrónica	lah kah-rreh-teh-rah eh-lehk-troh-nee-kah
insert	insertar	een-sehr-tahr
interface	la interfaz	lah een-tehr-fahs
Internet	el internet	ehl een-tehr-neht
joystick	el joystick, el control	ehl johy-steek, ehl kohn-trohl
key	la tecla	lah tehk-lah
keyboard	el teclado	ehl tehk-lah-doh
laptop computer	la computadora portátil	lah kohm-poo-tah-doh-rah pohr-tah-teel
line graph	el gráfico curvilíneo	ehl grah-fee-koh koor-bee-lee-neh-yoh

continues

Table 24.2   Continued

Computer Term	Spanish Translation	Pronunciation
link (to link)	el enlace (enlazar)	ehl ehn-lah-seh (ehn-lah-sahr)
mainframe	el sistema grande	ehl sees-teh-mah grahn-deh
memory	la memoria	lah meh-moh-ree-yah
memory card	la carta de extensión de memoria	lah kahr-tah deh ehks-tehn-see-yohn deh meh-moh-ree-yah
merge	fusionar	foo-see-yoh-nahr
microcomputer	el micro ordenador	ehl mee-kroh ohr-deh-nah-dohr
modem	el modem	ehl moh-dehm
monitor black and white color	el monitor blanco y negro color	ehl moh-nee-tohr blahn-koh ee neh-groh koh-lohr
motherboard	la carta-madre	lah kahr-tah mah-dreh
mouse	el ratón	ehl rrah-ton
network	la red	lah rrehd
online service	los servicios en línea	lohs sehr-bee-see-yohs ehn lee-neh-yah
operating system	el sistema operador	ehl sees-teh-mah oh-peh-rah-dohr
peripherals	los periféricos	lohs peh-ree-feh-ree-kohs
pie graph	el gráfico circular	ehl grah-fee-koh seer-koo-lahr
power surge	el parasito violento	ehl pah-rah-see-toh bee-yoh-lehn-toh
public domain	el domano público	ehl doh-mah-noh poo-blee-koh
reboot	volver a arrancar	bohl-behr ah ah-rrahn-kahr
scan	barrer	bah-rrehr
scanner	el scanner	ehl skah-nehr
scanning	el barrido	ehl bah-rree-doh
screen	la pantalla	lah pahn-tah-yah
search engine	el buscador	ehl boos-kah-dohr
server	el servidor	ehl sehr-bee-dohr
shareware	los programas compartidos	lohs proh-grah-mahs kohm-pahr-tee-dohs
sleeve	la manga	lah mahn-gah
software	el software	ehl sohft-wehr
spell checker	el verificador de ortografía	ehl beh-ree-fee-kah-dohr deh ohr-toh-grah-fee-yah

Computer Term	Spanish Translation	Pronunciation
spreadsheet	la hoja de cálculo electrónica	lah oh-hah deh kahl-koo-loh eh-lehk-troh-nee-kah
system	el sistema	ehl sees-teh-mah
tape back-up	la cinta de seguridad	lah seen-tah deh seh-goo-ree-dahd
terminal	el terminal	ehl tehr-mee-nahl
thesaurus	el diccionario de sinónimos	ehl deek-see-yoh-nah-ree-yoh deh see-noh-nee-mohs
training	la formación	lah fohr-mah-see-yohn
upload	subir, cargar	soo-beer, kahr-gahr
user	el utilisador	ehl oo-tee-lee-sah-dohr
web	la malla, la telaraña	lah mah-lah, lah teh-lah-rah-nyah
webmaster	el administrador de red	ehl ahd-mee-nee-strah-dohr deh rrehd
word processor	el procesador de textos	ehl proh-seh-sah-dohr deh tehks-tohs
worksheet	la hoja de cálculo	lah oh-hah deh kahl-koo-loh
workstation	la estación de trabajo	lah ehs-tah-see-yohn deh trah-bah-hoh

Surfing the Net

Whenever I can't seem to find my husband, I just go down to the den. Chances are excellent that he's right there, face glued to the computer screen, eyes glued to the monitor, fingers poised on the keyboard. Although his first love is golf, his newest passion is surfing the net. He spends hours traveling to different countries and collecting information about every subject imaginable. If you care to join him, you can do so in Spanish! It's so simple that I did it myself in a matter of minutes. Here's what you do:

1. Go to the location box on your Web browser.

2. Type **http://www.altavista.digital.com**.

¡Atención!

To say "Internet" in Spanish, use *el internet* and pronounce it exactly as you would in English.

To say "e-mail" in Spanish, use *el correo electrónico* (ehl koh-rreh-yoh eh-lehk-troh-nee-koh).

In a Flash

Need a word in Spanish? Can't find your dictionary? Try the following location:

http://www.telefonica.es/fat/elex.html

You'll be amazed at what is available in cyberspanglish.

3. Click Enter.

4. You will see a search screen.

5. Click on any language.

6. Then select Spanish.

7. You can search for any subject you like and can practice everything you've learned so far!

Do You Know Your Computer?

Let's say you want to communicate via computer with a business associate in a Spanish-speaking country. You need to be able to provide certain facts about your system to facilitate transmission. Can you answer these questions about your computer? (Translations and sample responses appear on page 423, in Appendix A.)

1. ¿Qué sistema de computadora usa Ud.?

   _____

2. ¿Qué periféricos usa Ud.?

   _____

3. ¿Su sistema tiene cuántos megaoctetos de memoria?

   _____

4. ¿Cuál es la velocidad de su modem?

   _____

5. ¿Qué software usa Ud.?

   _____

Send Your Business This Way

If you are planning to import or export merchandise to a firm that uses Spanish as its primary language, knowledge of a few key shipping phrases ought to help you expedite matters:

Ud. paga (Nosotros pagamos) los cargos de transporte.
oo-stehd pah-gah (nohs-oh-trohs pah-gah-mohs) lohs kahr-gohs deh trahns-pohr-teh
You (We) pay the shipping.

Le damos a Ud. la opción o por camionera o
por avión
leh dah-mohs ah oo-stehd lah ohp-see-yohn
oh pohr kah-mee-yoh-neh-rah oh pahr ah-
bee-yohn
*We give you the choice of (having the merchan-
dise shipped) by truck or by plane.*

Le mandaremos una nota de entrega además
de una copia de la factura con cada entrega.
leh mahn-dah-reh-mohs oo-nah noh-tah deh
ehn-treh-gah ah-deh-mahs deh oo-nah koh-
pee-yah deh lah fahk-too-rah kohn kah-dah
ehn-treh-gah
*We will send you a delivery slip as well as a copy
of the invoice with each delivery.*

Culture Corner

Did you know that...

- Colombia is the world's second largest exporter of coffee?

- Mexico is the largest producer of silver and one of the largest producers of natural gas and petroleum?

- Argentina is the fourth largest exporter of corn and the fifth largest exporter of wheat?

A Heck of a Deal

Everybody loves a good price or, better yet, a
discount. If you want to seal a deal, try the following phrases:

Nuestros precios son muy competitivos.
nwehs-trohs preh-see-yohs sohn mwee kohm-peh-tee-tee-bohs
Our prices are very competitive.

Podemos reducir los gastos.
poh-deh-mohs rreh-doo-seer lohs gahs-tohs
We can reduce the cost (sell you the merchandise at a better price).

Podemos hacerle a Ud. un descuento de diez por ciento.
poh-deh-mohs ah-sehr-leh ah oo-stehd oon dehs-kwehn-toh deh dee-yehs pohr-
see-yehn-toh
We can give you a 10 percent discount on the merchandise.

Si Ud. paga dentro de treinta días, podemos darle a Ud. un descuento de cinco
por ciento.
see oo-stehd pah-gah dehn-troh deh treh-een-tah dee-yahs, poh-deh-mohs dahr-
leh ah oo-stehd oon dehs-kwehn-toh deh seen-koh pohr-see-yehn-toh
If you pay within 30 days, we can give you a discount of 5 percent.

A Quality Job

Remember, if you can make the person feel comfortable and confident, you've probably got a done deal. In the business world, no one likes to feel taken advantage of, especially if there is a language barrier.

Ud. encontrará que nuestras mercancías sean de calidad superior.
oo-stehd ehn-kohn-trah-rah keh nwehs-trahs mehr-kahn-see-yahs seh-yahn deh kah-lee-dahd soo-peh-ree-yohr
You will find our merchandise to be high quality.

Hay algo más que le puedo hacer?
ah-yee ahl-goh mahs keh leh pweh-doh ah-sehr
Is there anything else I can do for you?

Ud. puede devolver las mercancías si no está completamente satisfecho.
oo-stehd pweh-deh deh-bohl-behr lahs mehr-kahn-see-yahs see noh ehs-tah kohm-pleh-tah-mehn-teh sah-tees-feh-choh
You can return the merchandise if you are not completely satified.

Es un placer hacer negocios con Ud.
ehs oon plah-sehr ah-sehr neh-goh-see-yohs kohn oo-stehd.
It's a pleasure doing business with you.

Es un placer servirle a Ud.
ehs oon plah-sehr sehr-beer-leh ah oo-stehd.
It's a pleasure to serve you.

Now you've got a feel for the types of phrases you might need to do business in Spanish. If you plan to pursue further business ventures, the mini-dictionary in Table 24.3 provides all the terms the average businessperson might need.

Table 24.3 Mini–Dictionary for Business People

Business Term	Spanish Translation	Pronunciation
accountant	el contador	ehl kohn-tah-dohr
activity	la actividad	lah ahk-tee-bee-dahd
amount	el importe	ehl eem-pohr-teh
appraise	valuar	bah-loo-wahr
assets	el activo, los bienes	ehl ahk-tee-boh, lohs bee-yeh-nehs
authorize	autorizar	ow-toh-ree-sahr
balance sheet	la hoja de saldo	lah oh-hah deh sahl-doh
bankruptcy	la bancarrota	lah bahn-kah-rroh-tah
bill	la factura	lah fahk-too-rah
bill of exchange	la letra de cambio	lah leh-trah deh kahm-bee-yoh
bill of lading	el conocimiento de embarque	ehl koh-noh-see-mee-yehn-toh deh ehm-bahr-keh
bill of sale	el contrato de venta, la escritura de venta	ehl kohn-trah-toh deh behn-tah, lah ehs-kree-too-rah deh behn-tah
bookkeeping	la contabilidad	lah kohn-tah-bee-lee-dahd
business	los negocios	lohs neh-goh-see-yohs
buy	comprar	kohm-prahr
buy for cash	pagar al contado	pah-gahr ahl kohn-tah-doh
cash	el dinero	ehl dee-neh-roh
cash a check	cobrar un cheque	koh-brahr oon cheh-keh
compensation for damage	la indemnización de daños personales	lah een-dehm-nee-sah-see-yohn deh dahn-yohs pehr-soh-nah-lehs
competitive price	el precio competidor	ehl preh-see-yoh kohm-peh-tee-dohr
consignee	el cosignador	ehl koh-seeg-nah-dohr
consumer	el consumidor	ehl kohn-soo-mee-dohr
contract	el contrato	ehl kohn-trah-toh
contractual obligations	las obligaciones contractuales	lahs ohb-lee-gah-see-yoh-nehs kohn-trahk-too-wah-lehs
cost price	el precio de costo	ehl preh-see-yoh deh kohs-toh
credit	el crédito	ehl kreh-dee-toh
date of maturity	el día de madurez	ehl dee-yah deh mah-doo-rehs
debit	el débito	ehl deh-bee-toh

continues

Table 24.3 Continued

Business Term	Spanish Translation	Pronunciation
deliver	entregar	ehn-treh-gahr
discount	el descuento, la rebaja	ehl dehs-kwehn-toh, lah rreh-bah-hah
due	vencido	ben-see-doh
expenditures	los gastos	lohs gahs-tohs
expenses	los gastos	lohs gahs-tohs
export	exportar	ehks-pohr-tahr
foreign trade	el comercio exterior	ehl koh-mehr-see-yoh ehks-teh-ree-yohr
goods	los productos, los bienes	lohs proh-dook-tohs, lohs bee-yeh-nehs
home trade	el intercambio doméstico	ehl een-tehr-kahm-bee-yoh doh-mehs-tee-koh
import	importar	eem-pohr-tahr
interest rates	los tipos de interés	lohs tee-pohs deh een-teh-rehs
invoice	la factura	lah fahk-too-rah
lawsuit	el pleito	ehl pleh-yee-toh
lawyer	el abogado	ehl ah-boh-gah-doh
liabilities	los pasivos	lohs pah-see-bohs
mail-order business	el negocio de ventas por correo	ehl neh-goh-see-yoh deh behn-tahs pohr koh-rreh-yoh
maintenance expenses	los gastos de mantenimiento	lohs gahs-tohs deh mahn-teh-nee-mee-yehn-toh
management	la gestión	lah hehs-tee-yohn
manager	el gerente	ehl heh-rehn-teh
merchandise	la mercancía	lah mehr-kahn-see-yah
middleman	el intermediario	ehl een-teh-meh-dee-yah-ree-yoh
money	el dinero	ehl dee-neh-roh
office	la oficina	lah oh-fee-see-nah
outlay	los gastos iniciales	lohs gahs-tohs ee-nee-see-yah-lehs
overhead expenses	los gastos generales	lohs gahs-tohs heh-neh-rah-lehs
owner	el propietario	ehl proh-pee-yeh-tah-ree-yoh
package	el paquete	ehl pah-keh-teh

Business Term	Spanish Translation	Pronunciation
partner	el socio	ehl soh-see-yoh
pay	pagar	pah-gahr
payment	el pago	ehl pah-goh
percent	por ciento	pohr see-yehn-toh
producer	el productor	ehl proh-dook-tohr
property	la propiedad	lah pro-pee-yeh-dahd
purchase	la compra	lah kohm-prah
recession	la recesión, la crisis	lah rreh-seh-see-yohn, lah kree-sees
retailer	el minorista	ehl mee-noh-rees-tah
running expenses	los gastos de funcionamiento	lohs gahs-tohs deh foon-see-yoh-nah-mee-yehn-toh
sale	la venta	lah behn-tah
sample	la muestra	lah mwehs-trah
sell	vender	behn-dehr
sell for cash	vender al contado	behn-dehr ahl kohn-tah-doh
selling price	el precio de venta	ehl preh-see-yoh deh behn-tah
send	mandar	mahn-dahr
send back	devolver	deh-bohl-behr
send C.O.D.	mandar contra reembolso	mahn-dahr kohn-trah rreh-yehm-bohl-soh
settle	arreglar	ah-rreh-glahr
shipment	el envío	ehl ehn-bee-yoh
shipper	el enviador	ehl ehn-bee-yah-dohr
slump	la crisis económica	lah kree-sees eh-koh-noh-mee-kah
supply and demand	la oferta y la demanda	lah oh-fehr-tah ee lah deh-mahn-dah
tax	el impuesto	ehl eem-pwehs-toh
tax-exempt	libre de impuestos	lee-breh deh eem-pwehs-tohs
trade	el comercio	ehl koh-mehr-see-yoh
transact business	hacer negocios	ah-sehr neh-goh-see-yohs
transfer	transferir	trahns-feh-reer
transportation charges	los gastos de transporte	lohs gahs-tohs deh trahns-pohr-teh
value added tax	el impuesto sobre el valor añadido	ehl eem-pwehs-toh soh-breh ehl bah-lohr ah-nyah-dee-doh

continues

Table 24.3   Continued

Business Term	Spanish Translation	Pronunciation
wholesaler	el mayorista	ehl mah-yoh-rees-tah
wrap	envolver	ehn-bohl-behr
yield a profit	producir un beneficio	proh-doo-seer oon beh-neh-fee-see-yoh

What's in Store for the Future

A successful business person looks towards the future and prepares for it wisely. In Spanish, the future can be expressed in one of these three ways:

➤ Use a present tense form of the verb, usually in conjunction with other words that show the future is implied:

¿Qué vuelo llega esta noche?
keh bweh-loh yeh-gah ehs-tah noh-cheh
What flight is arriving tonight?

➤ Use the irregular verb *ir* + *a* + infinitive. Because the verb *ir* means "to go," it is understandable that it is used to express what the speaker is going to do. Because "to go" is the first verb, it must be conjugated. The action that the speaker is going to perform is expressed by the infinitive of the verb.

Voy a ir al centro.
boy ah eer ahl sehn-troh

I'm going to go to the city.

Ellos van a echar (mandar) la carta al correo.
eh-yohs bahn ah eh-chahr (mahn-dahr) lah kahr-tah ahl koh-rreh-yoh
They are going to send the letter.

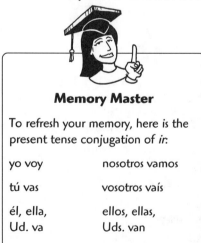

Memory Master

To refresh your memory, here is the present tense conjugation of *ir*:

yo voy	nosotros vamos
tú vas	vosotros vaís
él, ella, Ud. va	ellos, ellas, Uds. van

The Future Tense

The future also can be expressed by changing the verb to the future tense. The future tense tells what the subject will do or what action will take place in the future. The future tense of regular verbs can be formed by adding the future endings to the infinitive of the verb.

Verb	Future Stem	Conjugation	Verb Pronunciation
hablar	hablar	yo hablaré	ah-blah-reh
		tú hablarás	ah-blah-rahs
		él, ella, Ud. hablará	ah-blah-rah
		nosotros hablaremos	ah-blah-reh-mohs
		vosotros hablaréis	ah-blah-rah-yees
		ellos, ellas, Uds. hablarán	ah-blah-rahn
vender	vender	yo venderé	behn-deh-reh
		tú venderás	behn-deh-rahs
		él, ella, Ud. venderá	behn-deh-rah
		nosotros venderemos	behn-deh-reh-mohs
		vosotros venderéis	behn-deh-reh-yees
		ellos, ellas, Uds. venderán	behn-deh-rahn
abrir	abrir	yo abriré	ah-bree-reh
		tú abrirás	ah-bree-rahs
		él, ella, Ud. abrirá	ah-bree-rah
		nosotros abriremos	ah-bree-reh-mohs
		vosotros abriréis	ah-bree-reh-yees
		ellos, ellas, Uds. abrirán	ah-bree-rahn

Yo hablaré con mis amigos mañana.
yoh ah-blah-reh kohn mees ah-mee-gohs mah-nyah-nah
I will speak with my friends tomorrow.

Nosotros no venderemos nuestra casa.
noh-soh-trohs noh behn-deh-reh-mohs nwehs-trah kah-sah
We will not sell our house.

Abrirán Uds. una cuenta?
ah-bree-rahn oo-steh-dehs oo-nah kwehn-tah
Will you open an account?

The Future Tense of Irregular Verbs

Some verbs form the future tense by dropping the *e* from the infinitive ending and adding the future endings previously mentioned.

Infinitive	Future Stem	Future Endings
caber (to fit)	cabr-	-é, -ás, -á, -emos, -éis, -án
poder (to be able)	podr-	
querer (to want)	querr-	
saber (to know)	sabr-	

For some verbs, the *e* or *i* is dropped from the infinitive ending and is replaced by a *d*. The future endings are then added.

Infinitive	Future Stem	Future Endings
poner (to put)	pondr-	-é, -ás, -á, -emos, -éis, -án
salir (to leave)	saldr-	
tener (to have)	tendr-	
valer (to be worth)	valdr-	
venir (to come)	vendr-	

The verbs *decir* and *hacer* also are irregular, as follows:

Infinitive	Future Stem	Future Endings
decir (to say)	dir-	-é, -ás, -á, -emos, -éis, -án
hacer (to make, to do)	har-	

Plans for the Day

Your Spanish hosts are sleeping in today, and you feel like going out on your own to take care of some personal business. Make a list of five activities you plan to do using the future tense. (Sample responses can be found on page 423, in Appendix A.)

1. _____ .
2. _____ .
3. _____ .
4. _____ .
5. _____ .

10 minutos al día

All verbs have the same future endings: *-é, -ás, -á, -emos, -éis, -án.* The future of regular verbs can be formed by adding these endings to the infinitive of the verb.

Some irregular verbs form the future by dropping the *e* from the infinitive and adding the future endings: *cab<u>e</u>r* (to fit) *cabr-*, *pod<u>e</u>r* (to be able) *podr-*, *quer<u>e</u>r* (to want) *querr-*, *sab<u>e</u>r* (to know) *sabr-*.

Some verbs replace the *e* or *i* with *d*. The future endings are then added: *pon<u>e</u>r* (to put) *pondr-*, *sal<u>i</u>r* (to leave) *saldr-*, *ten<u>e</u>r* (to have) *tendr-*, *ven<u>i</u>r* (to come) *vendr-*.

The verbs *decir* and *hacer* are irregular: *decir* (to say) *dir-*, *hacer* (to make, to do) *har-*.

Predicting the Future

Do you wish you owned a crystal ball so you could look into the future? If you're curious about your fate, consult your horoscope to see what's in store for you. What does this horoscope predict for each sign? (Translations can be found on page 424, in Appendix A.)

ARIES (marzo 21–abril 19)
Oportunidades financieras excelentes se presentarán.

TAURO (abril 20–mayo 20)
Ud. pasará un mes agradable.

GEMINIS (mayo 21–junio 21)
Ud. tendrá tensiones y disputas con sus colegas.

CANCER (junio 22–julio 21)
Ud. estará en buena forma.

LEO (julio 22–agosto 21)
Ud. se concentrará en sus asuntos financieros.

VIRGO (agosto 22–septiembre 22)
Ud. tomará una decisión importante acerca de su futuro profesional.

continues

continued

LIBRA (septiembre 23–octubre 22)
Ud. estará en armonía con sus amigos.

ESCORPION (octubre 23–noviembre 21)
Sus ambiciones le servirán.

SAGITARIO (noviembre 22–diciembre 21)
Ud. tendrá discusiones importantes con miembros de su familia.

CAPRICORNIO (diciembre 22–enero 20)
Todo irá bien para Ud.

ACUARIO (enero 21–febrero 19)
Ud. conocerá a una persona importante.

PISCIS (febrero 20–marzo 20)
Su horario estará lleno todas las noches y Ud. tendrá muchos planes para el fin de semana.

The Least You Need to Know

➤ To conduct business in a Spanish-speaking country, you need to know the business lingo. You should be especially familiar with terms used to discuss photocopying, faxing, and computers.

➤ To express that someone is going to do something, use the correct form of the verb *ir* + *a* + the infinitive of the verb.

➤ The future usually is formed by adding the following endings to the infinitive: *-é, -ás, -á, -emos, -éis, -án*. A few irregular verbs must be memorized.

Chapter 25

Renting a Villa

In This Chapter

➤ Apartments and houses

➤ Rooms, furnishings, amenities, and appliances

➤ Using the conditional tense

Although you love the luxury of a well-appointed hotel, it might not prove to be cost-effective for you in the long run. You might want to purchase or rent a place to stay instead. Why not consider an apartment, a house, a condominium, or even a piece of time-share property? Should you make this decision, this chapter will teach you how to get the furnishings, appliances, and amenities you want and need. You'll also learn how to express what you would do in certain circumstances by using the conditional.

I Want to Live in a Castle

Renting or buying a piece of real estate in a Spanish-speaking country is becoming more and more popular. If you've decided you're ready to escape the rat race and are looking for a change of scenery, you'll want to be able to pick up the real estate section of a Spanish newspaper and understand what the ads offer. You'll also want to be able to discuss the ad with the owner or real estate agent. Do you want cathedral ceilings? A two-car garage? A fireplace? What makes your home your castle? Table 24.1, which lists the various features people look for in a home, will prepare you for your big move. Use the verb *necesito* (neh-seh-see-toh), "I need," to express what you want.

Table 24.1   The House, the Apartment, the Rooms

Stuff for Your Home	Spanish Translation	Pronunciation
air conditioning (central)	el aire acondicionado (central)	ehl ah-yee-reh ah-kohn-dee-see-yoh-nah-doh (sehn-trahl)
apartment	el apartamento	ehl ah-pahr-tah-mehn-toh
attic	el ático, el entretecho	ehl ah-tee-koh, ehl ehn-treh-teh-choh
backyard	el jardín	ehl hahr-deen
balcony	el balcón	ehl bahl-kohn
basement	el sótano	ehl soh-tah-noh
bathroom	el cuarto de baño	ehl kwahr-toh deh bah-nyoh
bedroom	el dormitorio	ehl dohr-mee-toh-ree-yoh
cathedral ceiling	el vacío catedral	ehl bah-see-yoh kah-teh-drahl
ceiling	el techo	ehl teh-choh
closet	el armario	ehl ahr-mah-ree-yoh
courtyard	el patio	ehl pah-tee-yoh

Stuff for Your Home	Spanish Translation	Pronunciation
den	el estudio	ehl ehs-too-dee-yoh
dining room	el comedor	ehl koh-meh-dohr
elevator	el ascensor	ehl ah-sehn-sohr
family room	la sala de estar	lah sah-lah deh ehs-tahr
fireplace	la chimenea	lah chee-meh-neh-yah
floor	el suelo	ehl sweh-loh
floor (story)	el piso	ehl pee-soh
garage	el garaje	ehl gah-rah-heh
ground floor	la planta baja	lah plahn-tah bah-hah
hallway	el pasillo	ehl pah-see-yoh
heating electric gas	la calefacción eléctrica a gas	lah kah-leh-fahk-see-yohn eh-lehk-tree-kah ah gahs
kitchen	la cocina	lah koh-see-nah
laundry room	la lavandería	lah lah-bahn-deh-ree-yah
lease	el contrato de arrendamiento	ehl kohn-trah-toh deh ah-rrehn-dah-mee-yehn-toh
living room	la sala	lah sah-lah
maintenance	el mantenimiento	ehl mahn-teh-nee-mee-yehn-toh
owner	el dueño	ehl dweh-nyoh
rent	el alquiler	ehl ahl-kee-lehr
roof	el techo	ehl teh-choh
room	el cuarto, la habitación	ehl kwahr-toh, lah ah-bee-tah-see-yohn
security deposit	la fianza, la garantía	lah fee-yahn-sah, lah gah-rahn-tee-yah
shower	la ducha	lah doo-chah
staircase	la escalera	lah ehs-kah-leh-rah
storage room	la despensa	lah dehs-pehn-sah
tenant	el arrendatario	ehl ah-rrehn-dah-tah-ree-yoh
terrace	la terraza	lah teh-rrah-sah
window	la ventana	lah behn-tah-nah

Culture Corner

Homes in Spanish–speaking countries often face inward to a courtyard, which protects the privacy of the family.

Be It Ever So Humble

You don't cook, so a microwave is a must. How else will you be able to heat up all those delectable leftovers? You're not in the habit of hanging laundry out on a line—a washer/dryer combination must be available to you. Can you live without a television? What furniture do you need? Before you rent or buy a piece of property, it's always wise to find out what is included. Consult Table 24.2 for the names of pieces of furniture you might want. Use *Hay...?* (ah-yee), "Is (Are) there...?," to ask your questions.

Table 24.2   Furniture and Accessories

Furniture and Accessories	Spanish Translation	Pronunciation
armchair	el sillón	ehl see-yohn
bed	la cama	lah kah-mah
bookcase	la estantería	lah ehs-tahn-teh-ree-yah
carpet	la moqueta	lah moh-keh-tah
chair	la silla	lah see-yah
clock	el reloj	ehl rreh-loh
curtains	las cortinas	lahs kohr-tee-nahs
dishwasher	el lavaplatos	ehl lah-bah-plah-tohs
dresser	la cómoda	lah koh-moh-dah
dryer	la secadora	lah seh-kah-doh-rah
food processor	el procesador de cocina	ehl proh-seh-sah-dohr deh koh-see-nah
freezer	el congelador	ehl kohn-heh-lah-dohr
furniture	los muebles	lohs mweh-blehs
home appliances	los aparatos eléctricos	lohs ah-pah-rah-tohs eh-lehk-tree-kohs
lamp	la lámpara	lah lahm-pah-rah
microwave oven	el microondas	ehl mee-kroh-ohn-dahs
mirror	el espejo	ehl ehs-peh-hoh
oven	el horno	ehl ohr-noh

Furniture and Accessories	Spanish Translation	Pronunciation
refrigerator	el refrigerador	ehl rreh-free-heh-rah-dohr
rug	la alfombra	lah ahl-fohm-brah
sofa	el sofá	ehl soh-fah
stereo	el estéreo	ehl ehs-teh-reh-yoh
stove	la estufa	lah ehs-too-fah
table	la mesa	lah meh-sah

television
  large screen
	el televisor
	  con pantalla grande
		ehl teh-leh-bee-sohr
		  kohn pahn-tah-yah grahn-deh

VCR	el VCR, la video casete de grabadora	ehl bee-cee-ahr, lah bee-deh-yoh kah- seht-teh deh grah-bah-doh-rah
washing machine	la lavadora	lah lah-bah-doh-rah

Purchasing Furniture

If your place is unfurnished, you'll surely have to pick up some furniture. We all have in mind the services, help, and guarantees we expect from a store. Read the following ad to find out what attractive offers you could expect from this company. (See page 424 in Appendix A for a translation.)

MUEBLERÍA DE MADRID

Un valor seguro

Nosotros le garantizamos gratuitamente (free) sus muebles por 5 años y los cojines de las sillas por 2 años contra todo defecto de fabricación.

Nosotros venimos gratuitamente a su casa para tomar medidas, hacer estimados y para aconsejarle.

Nosotros le ofrecemos una garantía sin riesgos, gratuitamente, por un año.

Nosotros nos llevaremos sus muebles viejos despues de que compre muebles nuevos.

Nosotros garantizamos estos servicios y estas garantías sin incremento de precio, en todas nuestras tiendas, en todas partes de España.

Are You Buying or Renting?

Do you have any questions? Of course you do. That's normal when you rent or buy a piece of property. To express your preferences or questions, use the following phrases to help you get exactly what you want:

Culture Corner

Many homes in Spanish–speaking countries have an inner courtyard called *un patio* (oon pah-tee-yoh), which is often surrounded by a high adobe wall. Most rooms face the patio, which is adorned with potted plants, flowers, and perhaps even a fountain. To get from the street to the inner patio, take a special path known as the *zaguán* (sah-gwahn).

In a Flash

Read the ads for apartments and houses in a Spanish newspaper. Select the one that appeals to you most.

Busco…
boos-koh
I'm looking for…

> los anuncios clasificados
> lohs ah-noon-see-yohs klah-see-fee-kah-dohs
> *the classified ads*

> los bienes raíces
> lohs bee-yeh-nehs rrah-yee-sehs
> *the real estate advertising section*

> una agencia inmobiliaria
> oo-nah ah-hehn-see-yah
> een-moh-bee-lee-yah-ree-yah
> *a real estate agency*

Quisiera alquilar (comprar)…
kee-see-yeh-rah ahl-kee-lahr (kohm-prahr)
I would like to rent (buy)…

> un apartmento
> oon ah-pahr-tah-mehn-toh
> *an apartment*

> una casa
> oo-nah kah-sah
> *a house*

> un condominio
> oon kohn-doh-mee-nee-yoh
> *a condominium*

¿Es lujoso (lujosa)?
ehs loo-hoh-soh (sah)
Is it luxurious?

¿Cuánto es el alquiler?
kwahn-toh ehs ehl ahl-kee-lehr
What is the rent?

¿Hay robos?
Ah-yee rroh-bohs
Are there break-ins?

¿Hay copropiedad?
Ah-yee koh-proh-pee-yeh-dahd
Is there time-sharing?

Culture Corner

Almost every home in a Spanish-speaking country has wrought-iron window and balcony grills called *rejas* (reh-hahs). These bars allow the owner to safely leave his windows open and get a nice cool breeze.

¿Cuántos son los gastos de mantenimiento
del apartamento (de la casa)?
kwahn-tohs sohn lohs gahs-tohs deh mahn-teh-nee-mee-yehn-toh dehl ah-pahr-
tah-mehn-toh (deh lah kah-sah)
How much is the maintenance of the apartment (house)?

¿Está incluído(a)_____?
ehs-tah een-kloo-wee-doh(dah)
Is _____ included?

   la calefacción
   lah kah-leh-fahk-see-yohn
   the heat

   la electricidad
   lah eh-lehk-tree-see-dahd
   the electricity

   la climatización
   lah klee-mah-tee-sah-see-yohn
   the air-conditioning

   el gas
   ehl gahs
   the gas

Culture Corner

The front walls of many houses in Spanish-speaking countries border the sidewalk, so do not be surprised that there often is no front yard. If someone wants to sit in the front, he puts a chair outside on the sidewalk.

¿De cuántos son las mensualidades?
deh kwahn-tohs sohn lahs mehn-soo-wah-lee-dah-dehs
How much are the monthly payments?

Quisiera pedir una hipoteca.
kee-see-yeh-rah peh-deer oo-nah ee-poh-teh-kah
I'd like to apply for a mortgage.

¿Tengo que dejar un depósito?
tehn-goh keh deh-hahr oon deh-poh-see-toh
Do I have to leave a deposit?

Voy al banco.
boy al bahn-koh
I'm going to the bank.

What Are Your Needs?

Suppose you are looking for a permanent place to stay in a Spanish-speaking country. Are the number of bathrooms and bedrooms important to you? Do you plan to cook and require a modern kitchen? Do you need a two-car garage? Tell the real estate agent exactly what would make you happy. (Sample responses can be found on page 424, in Appendix A.)

I Can't Decide

Armed with a marker and a cup of coffee, you've decided to begin scanning the real estate ads in search of your dream getaway. There are many places to choose from in many different price ranges. Your friend cut this ad out from the paper, and she thinks it fits your criteria. What does this property offer you? (See page 424 in Appendix A for a translation.)

LA CASA GRANDE
3ra SECCION
Un Hagar Segura y a su Alcance...
DESDE $80,000*

A sólo pasos del centro del pueblo áreas recreativas, restaurantes, centros comerciales, carreteras principales, playa y las más bellas vistas del áreas este de Puerto Rico.

- Modernas residencias con dos elegantes fachadas
- 3 dormitorios, baño y marquesina
- Solar básico de 300.30 m.c.
- SEPARELA CON $600

Making a Choice

You've found a wonderful listing in the paper, and you've even gone to look at the property. Look at the floor plan you were given and answer the following questions. (Sample responses can be found on page 425, in Appendix A.)

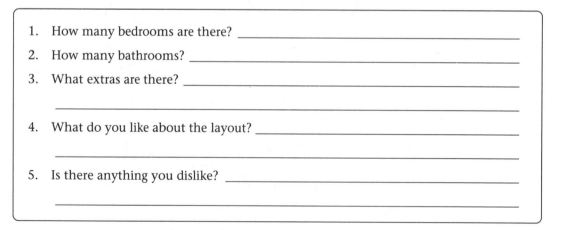

1. How many bedrooms are there? _____

2. How many bathrooms? _____

3. What extras are there? _____

   _____

4. What do you like about the layout? _____

   _____

5. Is there anything you dislike? _____

   _____

These Are the Conditions

Would you prefer to live in the city or on the beach? Would you rather take possession of a furnished or unfurnished property? How about a swimming pool? The conditional is a mood in Spanish that expresses what the speaker would do or what would happen under certain circumstances. The conditional of the verb *querer* or *gustar* is frequently used to express what the speaker would like.

¡Atención!

Pay attention to the different endings so you can determine whether the future (expressing "will") or the conditional (expressing "would") is being used.

> Quisiera (Me gustaría) alquilar una casa.
> kee-see-yeh-rah (meh goos-tah-ree-yah) ahl-kee-lahr oo-nah kah-sah
> *I would like to rent a house.*

Forming the Conditional

The conditional is formed with the same stem used to form the future tense, whether you are using a regular or irregular verb. The endings for the conditional, however, are different. They are exactly the same as the *-er* and *-ir* verb endings for the imperfect tense. To form the conditional, start with the future stem and add the imperfect endings shown in the following table.

Memory Master

The conditional endings are the same for all verbs whether they belong to the *-ar, -er,* or *-ir* family or are irregular. You will also notice that all of the conditional endings have accents.

Verb	Conditional Stem	Conditional Endings	Pronunciation
hablar	hablar	-ía	ee-yah
vender	vender	-ías	ee-yahs
abrir	abrir	-ía	ee-yah
		-íamos	ee-yah-mohs
		-íais	ee-ah-yees
		-ían	ee-yahn

Yo le hablaría.
yoh leh ah-blah-ree-yah
I would speak to him (her).

Nosotros no venderíamos nuestro coche a ningún precio.
noh-soh-trohs noh behn-deh-ree-yah-mohs nwehs-troh koh-cheh ah neen-goon
preh-see-yoh.
We would not sell our car at any price.

¿Abrirían Uds. una cuenta conjunta?
ah-bree-ree-yahn oo-steh-dehs oo-nah kwehn-tah kohn-hoon-tah
Would you open a joint account?

The Conditional of Irregular Verbs

Some verbs form the conditional by dropping the *e* from the infinitive ending and adding the conditional endings just shown.

Infinitive	Conditional Stem	Conditional Endings
caber (to fit)	cabr-	-ía
poder (to be able)	podr-	-ías
querer (to want)	querr-	-ía
saber (to know)	sabr-	-íamos
		-íais
		-ían

For some verbs, the *e* or *i* is dropped from the infinitive ending and is replaced with a *d*. The conditional endings are then added.

Infinitive	Conditional Stem	Conditional Endings
poner (to put)	pondr-	-ía
salir (to leave)	saldr-	-ías
tener (to have)	tendr-	-ía
valer (to be worth)	valdr-	-íamos
venir (to come)	vendr-	-íais
		-ían

The verbs *decir* and *hacer* are irregular, as follows:

Infinitive	Conditional Stem	Conditional Endings
decir (to say)	dir-	-ía
hacer (to make, to do)	har-	-ías
		-ía
		-íamos
		-íais
		-ían

10 minutos al día

The conditional tells what the subject of the sentence would do or what action would take place. It is formed using the same stem as the future tense. The infinitive is used for regular verbs; various special stems are used for irregular verbs. You then add the conditional endings: *-ía, -ías, -ía, -íamos, -íais, -ían.*

What Would You Do?

I think everyone dreams of winning the lottery, especially when the stakes are high. What would you do with 25 million dollars? I bet you can rattle off a list of things immediately. Do you have visions of a fancy sports car, luxurious worldwide travel, and a beautiful home with every possible amenity? Make a list of everything you would do if you won *la lotería* (lah loh-teh-ree-ah) tomorrow. (Sample responses can be found on page 425, in Appendix A.)

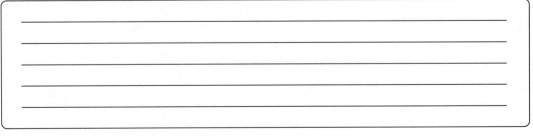

The Least You Need to Know

➤ Spanish homes are built to protect the privacy of the family and are laid out differently than homes in the United States.

➤ Learning the correct vocabulary will help you get the living space you want.

➤ The conditional is formed using the future stem (usually the infinitive) and the *-er* and *-ir* verb families' imperfect endings. A few irregular verbs must be memorized.

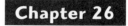

Chapter 26

It's a Question of Money

In This Chapter

➤ Banking terms

➤ The subjunctive

You're now prepared for an extended stay in a Spanish-speaking country. In the preceding chapter, you learned the necessary words to buy or rent new living quarters and to get the facilities you want to live the good life. This could mean a dining area to accommodate all your business staff or a backyard with an in-ground pool.

This chapter will appeal to anyone who has to make a trip to the bank: tourists who want to change money, a businessperson seeking financial assistance, an investor in foreign affairs, or a potential home buyer. You will also learn how to use the subjunctive to express your special wants, needs, and desires.

Remember to bring along your passport; it's the only acceptable form of identification in banks.

At the Bank

People visiting a foreign country might stop in a bank for many reasons. Because banks reputedly give good exchange rates, they often attract tourists who want to change their money to local currency. People with more far-reaching goals might want to establish credit and set up savings and checking accounts. Others might seek to purchase land, real estate, or a business. If you fit into any of these categories, you'll find the phrases in Table 26.1 quite useful.

Table 26.1   Mini-Dictionary of Banking Terms

Banking Term	Spanish Translation	Pronunciation
advance payment	el pago adelantado	ehl pah-goh ah-deh-lahn-tah-doh
automatic teller machine	el cajero automático	ehl kah-heh-roh ow-toh-mah-tee-koh
balance	el saldo	ehl sahl-doh
bank	el banco	ehl bahn-koh
bank account	la cuenta bancaria	lah kwehn-tah bahn-kah-ree-yah
bankbook	la cartilla de ahorros, la libreta de ahorros	lah kahr-tee-yah deh ah-oh-rrohs, lah lee-breh-tah deh ah-oh-rrohs
banknote	el billete de banco	ehl bee-yeh-teh deh bahn-koh
bill	la factura	lah fahk-too-rah
borrow	prestar	prehs-tahr
branch	la sucursal	lah soo-koor-sahl
cash	el dinero en efectivo	ehl dee-neh-roh ehn eh-fehk-tee-boh
to cash	cobrar	koh-brahr
cash flow	la corriente en efectivo, los movimientos en efectivos, el flujo de efectivo	lah koh-rree-yehn-teh ehn eh-fehk-tee-boh, lohs moh-bee-mee-yehn-tohs ehn eh-fehk-tee-bohs, ehl floo-hoh deh eh-fehk-tee-boh
cashier	el cajero	ehl kah-heh-roh
change (transaction)	el cambio	ehl kahm-bee-yoh

Banking Term	Spanish Translation	Pronunciation
change (coins)	la moneda	lah moh-neh-dah
check	el cheque	ehl cheh-keh
checkbook	la chequera	lah cheh-keh-rah
checking account	la cuenta corriente	lah kwehn-tah koh-rree-yehn-teh
coin	la moneda	lah moh-neh-dah
credit	el crédito	ehl kreh-dee-toh
currency (foreign)	el dinero (la divisa)	ehl dee-neh-roh (lah dee-bee-sah)
customer	el cliente	ehl klee-yehn-teh
debt	la deuda	lah deh-yoo-dah
deposit	el depósito, el ingreso	ehl deh-poh-see-toh, ehl een-greh-soh
to deposit	depositar, ingresar	deh-poh-see-tahr, een-greh-sahr
down payment	el desembolso inicial	ehl deh-sehm-bohl-soh ee-nee-see-yahl
employee	el empleado	ehl ehm-pleh-yah-doh
endorse	endosar	ehn-doh-sahr
exchange rate	el tipo de cambio	ehl tee-poh deh kahm-bee-yoh
fill out	llenar	yeh-nahr
final payment	el pago final	ehl pah-goh fee-nahl
guarantee	la garantía	lah gah-rahn-tee-yah
holder	el titular, el portador, el tenedor	ehl tee-too-lahr, ehl pohr-tah-dohr, ehl teh-neh-dohr
installment payment	el pago (el abono) a plazos	ehl pah-goh (ehl ah-boh-noh) ah plah-sohs
installment plan	las facilidades de pago	lahs fah-see-lee-dah-dehs deh pah-goh
interest	el interés	ehl een-teh-rehs
simple	simple	seem-pleh
compound	compuesto	kohm-pwehs-toh
interest rate	la tasa (el tipo) de interés	lah tah-sah (ehl tee-poh) deh een-teh-rehs
invest	investir	een-behs-teer
investment	la inversión	lah een-behr-see-yohn
loan	el préstamo	ehl preh-stah-moh
take out a loan	hacer un préstamo	ah-sehr oon preh-stah- moh
long term	a largo plazo	ah lahr-goh plah-soh

continues

Table 26.1 Continued

Banking Term	Spanish Translation	Pronunciation
manage	administrar, manejar	ahd-mee-nees-trahr, mah-neh-hahr
money exchange bureau	el departamento de intercambio	ehl deh-pahr-tah-mehn-toh deh een-tehr-kahm-bee-yoh
monthly statement	el extracto de cuenta, el estado de cuenta, el mensual	ehl ehks-trahk-toh deh kwehn-tah, ehl ehs-tah-doh deh kwehn-tah, ehl mehn-soo-wahl
mortgage	la hipoteca	lah ee-poh-teh-kah
open account	la cuenta corriente	lah kwehn-tah koh-rree-yehn-teh
overdrawn check	el cheque sin fondos	ehl cheh-keh seen fohn-dohs
overdraft	el giro en descubierto, el saldo deudor	ehl hee-roh ehn dehs-koo-bee-yehr-toh, ehl sahl-doh deh-yoo-dohr
pay cash	pagar en efectivo	pah-gahr ehn eh-fehk-tee-boh
payment	el pago	ehl pah-goh
percentage	el porcentaje	ehl pohr-sehn-tah-heh
promissory note	el pagaré	ehl pah-gah-reh
purchase	comprar	kohm-prahr
quarter	el trimestre	ehl tree-mehs-treh
receipt	el recibo	ehl rreh-see-boh
revenue	los ingresos	lohs een-greh-sohs
safe	la caja fuerte	lah kah-hah fwehr-teh
sale	la venta	lah behn-tah
save	ahorrar	ah-oh-rrahr
savings account	la cuenta de ahorros	lah kwehn-tah deh ah-oh-rrohs
short term	a corto plazo	ah kohr-toh plah-soh
sign (to)	firmar	feer-mahr
signature	la firma	lah feer-mah
sum	el monto, el total, la suma	ehl mohn-toh, ehl toh-tahl, lah soo-mah
teller	el cajero	ehl kah-heh-roh
total	el total, el monto	ehl toh-tahl, ehl mohn-toh
transfer	la transferencia	lah trahns-feh-rehn-see-yah
traveler's check	el cheque de viajero	ehl cheh-keh deh bee-yah-heh-roh

Banking Term	Spanish Translation	Pronunciation
void (adj.)	inválido	een-bah-lee-doh
void (v.)	anular	ah-noo-lahr
window	la ventanilla	lah behn-tah-nee-yah
withdraw	sacar, retirar	sah-kahr, rreh-tee-rahr
withdrawal	el retiro	ehl rreh-tee-roh

Things I Need to Do

If you're planning a trip to the bank, the phrases in this section will be helpful in common, everyday banking situations: making deposits and withdrawals, opening a checking account, or taking out a loan.

> ¿Cuál es el horario de trabajo?
> kwahl ehs ehl oh-rah-ree-yoh deh trah-bah-hoh
> *What are the banking hours?*

Express your wishes by using "*Quisiera...*" with any of the phrases that follow:

> Quisiera...
> kee-see-yeh-rah
> *I would like...*

> hacer un depósito
> ah-sehr oon deh-poh-see-toh
> *to make a deposit*

> cobrar un cheque
> koh-brahr oon cheh-keh
> *to cash a check*

> hacer un retiro
> ah-sehr oon rreh-tee-roh
> *to make a withdrawal*

> abrir una cuenta
> ah-breer oo-nah kwehn-tah
> *to open an account*

> hacer un pago
> ah-sehr oon pah-goh
> *to make a payment*

Culture Corner

Money can be exchanged at *una casa de cambio* (oo-nah kah-sah deh kahm-bee-yoh) as well as at banks. Some money exchanges offer excellent rates; others charge exorbitant commissions. It always is wise to investigate a few first. Remember that the worst exchange rates are given by hotels, airports, and railway stations, so avoid them whenever possible.

¡Atención!

If you travel with traveler's checks, make sure to keep the numbers of the checks in a separate place...just in case.

¡Atención!

It's a good idea to change $50 into foreign currency before leaving on your trip. It's wise to have some pocket change in case airport money exchanges are closed or have long lines. This might also allow you to leave the airport and get a better rate for your money.

liquidar una cuenta
lee-kee-dahr oo-nah kwehn-tah
to close an account

pedir un préstamo
peh-deer oon prehs-tah-moh
to apply for a loan

cambiar divisas
kahm-bee-yahr dee-bee-sahs
to change some foreign money

Other helpful phrases you can use at a bank include:

¿Recibiré un extracto de cuentas (un estado de cuentas) mensual?
rreh-see-bee-reh oon ehks-trahk-toh deh kwehn-tahs (oon ehs-tah-doh deh kwehn-tahs) mehn-soo-wahl
Will I get a monthly statement?

¿Cuál es la tasa (el tipo) de cambio del dólar hoy?
kwahl ehs lah tah-sah (ehl tee-poh) deh kahm-bee-yoh dehl doh-lahr oh-yee
What is today's exchange rate?

¿Tiene un cajero automático?
tee-yeh-neh oon kah-heh-roh ow-toh-mah-tee-koh
Do you have an automatic teller machine?

¿Cómo se usa?
koh-moh seh oo-sah
How does one use it?

Quisiera hacer un préstamo personal.
kee-see-yeh-rah ah-sehr oon prehs-tah-moh pehr-soh-nahl
I'd like to take out a personal loan.

Quisiera pedir una hipoteca.
kee-see-yeh-rah peh-deer oo-nah ee-poh-teh-kah
I'd like to apply for a mortgage.

¿Cuál es el plazo del préstamo?
kwahl ehs ehl plah-soh dehl prehs-tah-moh
What is the time period of the loan?

¿De cuánto son las mensualidades?
Deh kwahn-toh sohn lahs mehn-soo-wah-lee-dah-dehs
How much are the monthly payments?

¿Cuál es la tasa (el tipo) de interés?
kwahl ehs lah tah-sah (ehl tee-poh) deh een-teh-rehs
What is the interest rate?

Using the Bank

If you plan to spend any length of time in a Spanish-speaking country, you'll need the many services offered by a bank. Whether for business or pleasure, you'll certainly have to make deposits and withdrawals into your savings and checking accounts. Look at the slips below and answer the following questions with the appropriate letter. Check your answers on page 425, in Appendix A.

A

Depósito a Cuenta de Cheques

		$	¢
Fecha **E** _____ 19___	EFECTIVO		
Nombre	CHEQUES		
Letra de molde. Incluya sus dos apellidos/Please print.			
Sucursal	Asegúrese de endosar cada cheque.		
Número de Cuenta			
G			
Este depósito está sujeto a las condiciones estipuladas en las reglas y reglamentos aplicables a su cuenta.	**F** TOTAL		

Fondos depositados podrían no estar disponibles para retiro inmediato.

13

B

Depósito a Cuenta de Ahorros

		$	¢
Fecha **E** _____ 19___	EFECTIVO		
Nombre	CHEQUES		
Letra de molde. Incluya sus dos apellidos/			
Sucursal	Asegúrese de endosar cada cheque.		
Número de Cuenta			
G			
Este depósito está sujeto a las condiciones estipuladas en las reglas y reglamentos aplicables a su cuenta.	**F** TOTAL		

Fondos depositados podrían no estar disponibles para retiro inmediato.

17

C

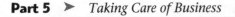**FirstBank**   **Hoja de Retiro**   **Fecha** E _____

Nombre _____   **Sucursal** _____

La cantidad de F _____

|____| |____G_____| **Cantidad** $ _____

Suc.   **Núm. de cuenta**

D _____   _____
   Firma del cliente   **Firma del cliente**

1. Which is for your savings account?_____
2. Which is for checking?_____
3. Which are for deposits?_____
4. Which one is for a withdrawal?_____
5. Where would you put your account number?_____
6. How about the amount to be deposited or withdrawn?_____
7. Which do you have to sign?_____
8. Where?_____
9. Where do you indicate the date of the transaction?_____

What Are Your Needs?

If you're like me, no matter how much money you have, you always need just a little bit more to tide you over. In Spanish, there are two ways to express need:

Need can be expressed using *tener* (conjugated) + *que* + verb (infinitive).

Yo tengo que ir al centro.	Nosotros tenemos que partir.
I have to go downtown.	*We have to leave.*

The Moody Subjunctive

You can also express need using the expression *Es necesario que…* (ehs neh-seh-sah-ree-yoh keh), "It is necessary that…." This and other expressions showing necessity are followed by a special verb form called the subjunctive.

The subjunctive is a mood, not a tense, and it expresses wishing, wanting, emotion, and doubt. It is used after many expressions showing uncertainty. Because the subjunctive is not a tense (a verb form indicating time), the present subjunctive can be used to refer to actions in the present or in the future. (The past subjunctive will not be treated in this book because its use is limited.)

To use the subjunctive, the following conditions must be met:

➤ Two different clauses must exist with two different subjects.

➤ The two clauses must be joined by *que*.

➤ One of the clauses must show need, necessity, emotion, or doubt.

> Es necesario que yo hable con mi amigo.
> ehs neh-seh-sah-ree-yoh keh yoh ah-bleh kohn mee ah-mee-goh
> *I (I'll) have to speak to my friend.*

> Es necesario que nosotros vendamos nuestra casa.
> ehs neh-seh-sah-ree-yoh keh noh-soh-trohs behn-dah-mohs nwehs-trah kah-sah
> *We (We'll) have to sell our house.*

> Es necesario que Uds. abran una cuenta de ahorros.
> ehs neh-seh-sah-ree-yoh keh oo-steh-dehs ah-brahn oo-nah kwehn-tah deh ah-oh-rrohs
> *You (You'll) have to open a savings account.*

Memory Master

Tener is an irregular verb. The following conjugation should help refresh your memory:

yo tengo	nosotros tenemos
tú tienes	vosotros tenéis
él, ella, Ud. tiene	ellos, ellas, Uds. tienen

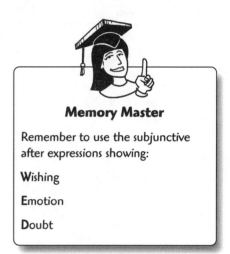

Memory Master

Remember to use the subjunctive after expressions showing:

Wishing

Emotion

Doubt

Forming the Regular Subjunctive

To form the present subjunctive of regular verbs, drop the *-o* ending from the *yo* form in the present tense and add the opposite endings. All *-ar* verbs change present tense *a* to *e*, and *-er* and *-ir* verbs change present tense *e* or *i* to *a*, as shown in Table 26.2. (This is just like the command form you learned in Chapter 10, "The Plane Has Landed.")

Table 26.2   The Present Subjunctive of Regular Verbs

-ar Verbs Hablar	
que yo hable	que nosotros hablemos
que tú hables	que vosotros habléis
que él (ella, Ud.,) hable	que ellos (ellas, Uds.) hablen

-er Verbs Vender	
que yo venda	que nosotros vendamos
que tú vendas	que vosotros vendáis
que él (ella, Ud.) venda	que ellos (ellas, Uds.) vendan

-ir Verbs Abrir	
que yo abra	que nosotros abramos
que tú abras	que vosotros abráis
que él (ella, Ud.) abra	que ellos (ellas, Uds.) abran

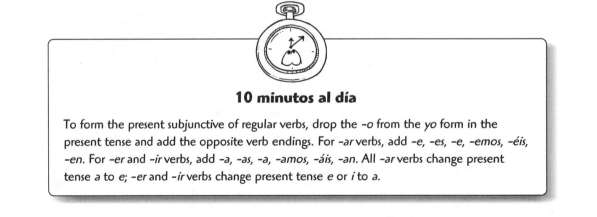

10 minutos al día

To form the present subjunctive of regular verbs, drop the *-o* from the *yo* form in the present tense and add the opposite verb endings. For *-ar* verbs, add *-e, -es, -e, -emos, -éis, -en*. For *-er* and *-ir* verbs, add *-a, -as, -a, -amos, -áis, -an*. All *-ar* verbs change present tense *a* to *e*; *-er* and *-ir* verbs change present tense *e* or *i* to *a*.

Irregular Verbs in the Subjunctive

Because the subjunctive is formed by dropping endings from the *yo* form of the verb, verbs whose *yo* form is irregular will also have irregular subjunctive forms, to which the proper subjunctive endings are then added.

Infinitive	Yo form	Subjunctive Stem	Subjunctive Endings (The Same for All)
conocer (to know)	conozco	conozc-	-a, -as, -a, -amos, -áis, -an
decir (to say)	digo	dig-	
hacer (to make, to do)	hago	hag-	
oír (to hear)	oigo	oig-	
poner (to put)	pongo	pong-	
salir (to go out)	salgo	salg-	
traer (to bring)	traigo	traig-	
venir (to come)	vengo	veng-	

Spelling Change Verbs in the Present Subjunctive

Verbs ending in *-car*, *-gar*, and *-zar* have the following changes in the present subjunctive to maintain the proper pronunciation:

➤ For *-car* verbs, *c* changes to *qu* in all forms of the subjunctive and *a* changes to *e* in the ending:

Buscar (to look for)	
que yo busque	que nosotros busquemos
que tú busques	que vosotros busquéis
que él (ella, Ud.) busque	que ellos (ellas, Uds.) busquen

➤ For *-gar* verbs, *g* changes to *gu* in all forms of the subjunctive and *a* changes to *e* in the ending:

Pagar (to pay)	
que yo pague	que nosotros paguemos
que tú pagues	que vosotros paguéis
que él (ella, Ud.) pague	que ellos (ellas, Uds.) paguen

➤ For *-zar* verbs, *z* changes to *c* in all forms of the subjunctive and *a* changes to *e* in the ending:

Cruzar (to cross)

que yo cruce	que nosotros crucemos
que tú cruces	que vosotros crucéis
que él (ella, Ud.) cruce	que ellos (ellas, Uds.) crucen

Stem-Changing Verbs in the Present Subjunctive

For verbs ending in *-ar* and *-er*, the same change occurs in the stem vowel in the subjunctive that occurs in the stem vowel in the present tense (refer to Chapter 12, "Settling In"). The stem vowel does not change in the *nosotros* and *vosotros* forms. To form the present subjunctive of regular verbs, drop *o* from the *yo* form of the present and add opposite verb endings: *-ar* verbs change present tense *a* to *e*; *-er* and *-ir* verbs change present tense *e* or *i* to *a*.

pensar (to think)

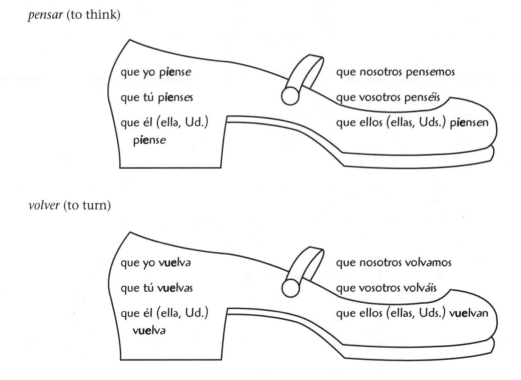

que yo piense   que nosotros pensemos

que tú pienses   que vosotros penséis

que él (ella, Ud.)   que ellos (ellas, Uds.) piensen
    piense

volver (to turn)

que yo vuelva   que nosotros volvamos

que tú vuelvas   que vosotros volváis

que él (ella, Ud.)   que ellos (ellas, Uds.) vuelvan
    vuelva

For verbs ending in *-ir*, the same change occurs in the stem vowel in the subjunctive that occurs in the stem vowel in the present tense (again, refer to Chapter 12). Additionally, the stem vowel changes from *e* to *i* or from *o* to *u* in the *nosotros* and *vosotros* forms. Remember to change to the opposite vowel in the ending for the subjunctive (*-ar* verbs change *a* to *e*; *-er* verbs change *e* to *a*):

sentir (to feel)

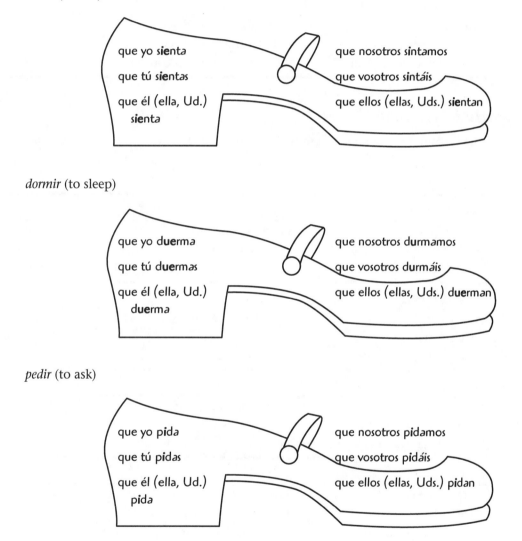

que yo sienta   que nosotros sintamos

que tú sientas   que vosotros sintáis

que él (ella, Ud.) sienta   que ellos (ellas, Uds.) sientan

dormir (to sleep)

que yo duerma   que nosotros durmamos

que tú duermas   que vosotros durmáis

que él (ella, Ud.) duerma   que ellos (ellas, Uds.) duerman

pedir (to ask)

que yo pida   que nosotros pidamos

que tú pidas   que vosotros pidáis

que él (ella, Ud.) pida   que ellos (ellas, Uds.) pidan

Some verbs ending in *-iar* and *-uar* (refer to Chapter 12) require an accent on the *i* (*í*) and the *u* (*ú*) in all forms of the subjunctive except *nosotros* and *vosotros*. In the *vosotros* form, the *e* of the subjunctive ending takes the accent.

Guiar (to guide)

que yo guíe	que nosotros guiemos
que tú guíes	que vosotros guiéis
que él (ella, Ud.) guíe	que ellos (ellas, Uds.) guíen

Continuar (to continue)

que yo continúe	que nosotros continuemos
que tú continúes	que vosotros continuéis
que él (ella, Ud.) continúe	que ellos (ellas, Uds.) continúen

---

Highly Irregular Verbs

Some verbs follow no rules and must be memorized. The verbs of this type that are most useful include:

Dar (to give)

que yo dé	que nosotros demos
que tú des	que vosotros deis
que él (ella, Ud.) dé	que ellos (ellas, Uds.) den

Estar (to be)

que yo esté	que nosotros estemos
que tú estés	que vosotros estéis
que él (ella, Ud.) esté	que ellos (ellas, Uds.) estén

Ir (to go)

que yo vaya	que nosotros vayamos
que tú vayas	que vosotros vayáis
que él (ella, Ud.) vaya	que ellos (ellas, Uds.) vayan

Saber (to know)

que yo sepa	que nosotros sepamos
que tú sepas	que vosotros sepáis
que él (ella, Ud.) sepa	que ellos (ellas, Uds.) sepan

Ser (to be)

que yo sea	que nosotros seamos
que tú seas	que vosotros seáis
que él (ella, Ud.) sea	que ellos (ellas, Uds.) sean

So Much to Do, So Little Time

I have a million things to do today; I bet you do, too. A great way to escape the hassles and obligations of your daily routine is to go on vacation. When you return, however, it's back to the grind. Describe what the following people have to do using *tener que* + infinitive and then *es necesario que* + subjunctive. Check your answers on page 425, in Appendix A.

Example: él/trabajar
Él tiene que trabajar.
Es necesario que él trabaje.

1. nosotros/preparar la cena _____

_____

2. ella/aprender español _____

_____

3. ellos/vivir en Puerto Rico _____

_____

4. yo/cerrar esa cuenta _____

_____

5. vosotros/no perder su cartera _____

_____

6. tú/no mentir _____

_____

7. Ud./no dormir tarde _____

_____

8. él/pedir la cuenta _____

_____

9. Uds./continuar a estudiar _____

_____

continues

continued

10. tú/graduarse _____

_____

11. ellas/dar un paseo _____

_____

12. nosotros/estar a tiempo _____

_____

13. yo/ir al centro _____

_____

14. vosotros/saber jugar al tenis _____

_____

15. Ud./ser más responsable _____

_____

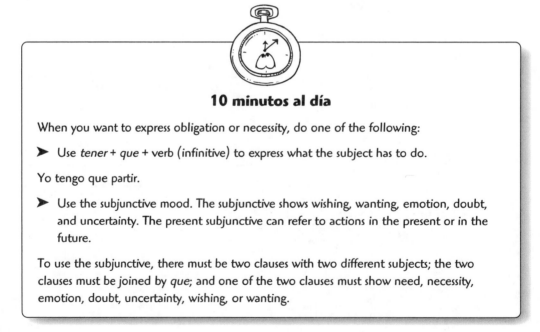

10 minutos al día

When you want to express obligation or necessity, do one of the following:

➤ Use *tener* + *que* + verb (infinitive) to express what the subject has to do.

Yo tengo que partir.

➤ Use the subjunctive mood. The subjunctive shows wishing, wanting, emotion, doubt, and uncertainty. The present subjunctive can refer to actions in the present or in the future.

To use the subjunctive, there must be two clauses with two different subjects; the two clauses must be joined by *que*; and one of the two clauses must show need, necessity, emotion, doubt, uncertainty, wishing, or wanting.

Impersonal Expressions

Es necesario que is a common expression used with the subjunctive. The following are some other common impersonal expressions that require the subjunctive:

Phrase	Pronunciation	Meaning
Es aconsejable que	ehs ah-kohn-seh-hah-bleh keh	It is advisable that
Es bueno que	ehs bweh-noh keh	It is good that
Es difícil que	ehs dee-fee-seel keh	It is difficult that
Es dudoso que	ehs doo-doh-soh keh	It is doubtful that
Es fácil que	ehs fah-seel keh	It is easy that
Es importante que	ehs eem-pohr-tahn-teh keh	It is important that
Es imposible que	ehs eem-poh-see-bleh keh	It is impossible that
Es increíble que	ehs een-kreh-yee-bleh keh	It is incredible that
Es indispensable que	ehs een-dees-pehn-sah-bleh keh	It is indispensable that
Es malo que	ehs mah-loh keh	It is bad that
Es mejor que	ehs meh-hohr keh	It is better that
Es posible que	ehs poh-see-bleh keh	It is possible that
Es preciso que	ehs preh-see-soh keh	It is essential that
Es probable que	ehs proh-bah-bleh keh	It is probable that
Es una lástima que	ehs oo-nah lahs-tee-mah keh	It is a pity that
Más vale que	mahs bah-leh keh	It is better that

Obligations

We all have many obligations to fulfill. Combine the following elements to express the obligations of the subjects. See page 426 in Appendix A for the answers.

> Example: necesario/vosotros/volver a las dos
> Es necesario que vosotros vuelvan a las dos.

In a Flash

Using the subjunctive and *tener que,* make a list of things you have to do this week.

1. aconsejable/tú/decir la verdad

   _____

2. importante/nosotros/ir a la biblioteca

   _____

3. indispensable/yo/venir a tiempo

   _____

4. necesario/Uds./buscar esta carta

   _____

5. preciso/ella/pagar

   _____

6. bueno/ellos/saber prepararlo

   _____

The Least You Need to Know

➤ Spanish banks are modern and efficient and provide the same services as ours.

➤ Use *tener* (conjugated) + *que* + verb (infinitive) to express that the subject needs or has to do something.

➤ The subjunctive is used to express need, wishing, emotion, and doubt. To form the present subjunctive of most verbs, drop the *-o* from the *yo* form and add the appropriate subjunctive ending. Spelling-change verbs, stem-changing verbs, and irregular verbs require special changes.

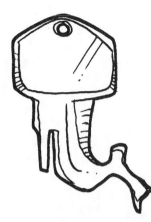

Answer Key

Chapter 3

Practice Makes Perfect?

1. The piano is big.
2. The actor is horrible.
3. The information is terrible.
4. The teacher is sincere.
5. The tiger is cruel.
6. The cereal is delicious.

It's Easy to Write!

1. El presidente es elegante.
2. La computadora es interesante.
3. La información es importante.
4. El hotel es grande.
5. El color es magnífico.

You've Got the Swing of It!

1. Juan prepares the menu.
2. The mechanic repairs the car.
3. The tourist uses the information.
4. The program ends.
5. Marta celebrates her birthday.
6. José adores the program.

Give Your Opinions

1. El programa es excelente.
2. El parque es popular.
3. El plato es famoso.
4. El restaurante es grande.
5. El teatro es moderno.
6. El programa es magnífico.
7. El actor es dinámico.
8. El hotel es confortable.

Now You're a Pro!

Sports: Bogotá defends her title.

Economy: A report confirms the vitality of the economy.

International: China shows an interest in fast-food restaurants.

Information: There is a solution to arteriosclerosis.

Chapter 4

Bilingual Dictionaries—A Crash Course

1. bien
2. el pozo
3. el grito
4. llorar
5. solamente
6. justo
7. verificar
8. cheque

Chapter 5

On the Go (sample responses)

1. en coche
2. en metro
3. en coche
4. en autobús
5. en avión
6. a pie
7. en barco
8. en barco
9. en coche
10. en metro

What Time Is It? (sample responses)

1. adiós
2. inmediatamente, en seguida
3. tarde
4. temprano

Following Directions

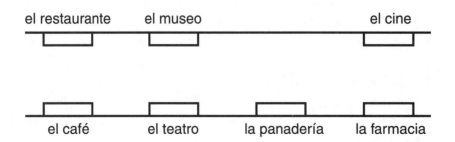

el restaurante   el museo   el cine

el café   el teatro   la panadería   la farmacia

Sure, I'll Go!

1. por supuesto   2. claro   3. de acuerdo   4. está bien

Is Everything Okay?

1. tengo   3. calor.   5. sed.   7. razón.
2. sueño.   4. hambre.   6. miedo.

What's Happening in the World?

1. En Madrid hace calor.
2. En Sevilla hace frío y nieva.
3. En Córdoba hace mal tiempo.
4. En México llueve.
5. En Panamá hace buen tiempo.

6. En Argentina hace viento.
7. En Columbia hace sol.
8. En Peru hace frío.
9. En Barcelona hace buen tiempo.

Chapter 6

El or La?

Definite article:

1. el   3. la   5. el   7. la   9. la
2. el   4. la   6. el   8. el   10. el

Indefinite article:

1. un   3. una   5. un   7. una   9. una
2. un   4. una   6. en   8. un   10. un

Identifying More Nouns

1. una   3. un   5. un   7. un   9. un
2. una   4. un   6. una   8. una   10. un

More Than One

1. las tiendas
2. las actrices
3. los restaurantes
4. los palacios
5. los automóviles
6. las flores
7. los reyes
8. los monumentos
9. los franceses
10. los autores

Practice with Plurals

1. el lápiz
2. el regalo
3. el collar
4. el paquete
5. la revista
6. la loción

Chapter 7

Formal or Informal?

1. A doctor? Ud.
2. Your cousin? tú
3. Your friend? tú
4. A salesman? Ud.
5. A woman? Ud.
6. Two female friends? vosotras
7. Two male friends? vosotros
8. A policeman? Ud.
9. Your friends? vosotros

Who's Who?

1. Eduardo? él
2. Anita? ella
3. Sara y Beatriz? ellas
4. Gloria? ella
5. Arturo? él
6. Juan y Miguel? ellos
7. Roberto y Lupita? ellos
8. Alba? ella
9. Blanca? ella
10. Cristina y Manuel? ellos
11. Paco? él
12. Julio y Amalia? ellos

Conjugation 101

1. anuncia
2. buscan
3. observamos
4. ando
5. nadáis

Conjugation 102

1. corres
2. comen
3. bebemos
4. responde
5. aprende
6. debo

Conjugation 103

1. vivís
2. aplaude
3. escriben
4. omites
5. asiste
6. abro
7. descubrimos
8. reciben

Ask Away (sample responses)

1. ¿Nosotros hablamos demasiado? ¿no? ¿verdad?
   ¿Está bien? ¿Hablamos nosotros demasiado?
2. ¿Él asiste...? ¿no? ¿verdad? ¿Está bien? ¿Asiste él...?
3. ¿Uds. comprenden mucho? ¿no? ¿verdad? ¿Está bien? ¿Comprenden Uds. mucho?
4. ¿María escribe...? ¿no? ¿verdad? ¿Está bien?
   ¿Escribe María...?

Tell Us About Yourself (sample responses)

1. Yo no fumo.
2. Yo grito mucho.
3. Yo bailo bien.
4. Yo cocino bien.
5. Yo hablo español.
6. Yo charlo con mis amigos.
7. Yo no leo muchas revistas.
8. Yo no escribo muchas cartas.

Chapter 8

Ser vs. Estar

1. somos   2. es   3. están   4. son   5. está

What's Happening?

1. Yo estoy leyendo.
2. Yo estoy escuchando música.
3. Yo estoy comiendo.
4. Yo estoy cantando.
5. Yo estoy hablando español.
6. Yo estoy mirando una película.
7. Yo estoy durmiendo.

Having a Conversation (sample responses)

1. Buenas tardes.
2. Me llamo…
3. Estoy bien, gracias. Y Ud.?
4. Soy de Nueva York.
5. Soy abogado.

Tell Me More (sample responses)

1. ¿De dónde es Roberto? ¿Con quién viaja? ¿Dónde viaja con su familia? ¿Cómo viaja? ¿Cuánto tiempo pasan en España? ¿Dónde pasan un mes? ¿Qué desean visitar? ¿Cuándo regresan?

2. ¿Cómo te llamas? ¿De dónde eres? ¿A quién buscas? ¿Por qué? ¿Qué deseas practicar? ¿Cuándo hablas inglés? ¿Cómo es el inglés? ¿Cómo eres tú?

Chapter 9

A Sense of Belonging

1. la tía de Miguel
2. el padre de los muchachos
3. los abuelos de las muchachas
4. el tío de Lupe
5. los primos de la familia
6. la novia del nieto

What's in an Apellido?

1. Vega
2. Fernández
3. Pérez
4. Rueda
5. Ana Fernández de Vega
6. Rueda
7. Diego Vega Fernández
8. María Vega Fernández

What Are Your Preferences? (sample responses)

1. Mis actrices favoritas son…
2. Mi canción favorita es…
3. Mis restaurantes favoritos son…
4. Mi deporte favorito es…
5. Mi color favorito es…
6. Mi película favorita es…

You're on Your Own (sample responses)

1. Buenos días. Me llamo…
2. ¿Ud. conoce a mi hermano, Jorge?
3. Le presento a mi hijo, Miguel.
4. Mucho gusto en conocerle.
5. El gusto es mío.

Using Tener

1. tenemos cuidado
2. tiene lugar
3. tiene éxito
4. tienen dolor del estómago
5. tengo suerte
6. tienes prisa

Give Your Own Descriptions (sample responses)

1. importante 2. buenas 3. inteligente 4. magníficas 5. divertidas

Check Out the Personal Ads

1. A 47-year-old North American lawyer and art gallery director who is tall, attractive, and sophisticated seeks a loving, young, educated, English-speaking 28- to 42-year-old woman with long hair for romance, matrimony, and a family.

2. A 6',166 lb., 28-year-old Chilean man who likes romantic music, dancing, sports, and studying seeks a 25- to 35-year-old woman who is understanding, happy, intelligent, and honest, for friendship.

3. A 40-year-old working woman who is nice and caring seeks a Brazilian man with same qualities for friendship and a serious relationship.

4. A 37-year-old divorced Dominican woman with two children seeks a 35- to 40-year-old 5'10" or taller, nonsmoking, hard-working, fun man with a good sense of humor.

410

Chapter 10

Airline Advice

➤ Hand luggage must be kept in special compartments or under the passenger's seat during takeoff and landing. Many compartments are available to travelers.

➤ Don't keep valuable things in your luggage: money, jewels, or your passport.

➤ Don't put fragile items or those that can deteriorate in your luggage. They are not protected in case of damage.

Filling Out Forms

1. your name (printed) + your maiden name
2. your complete address
3. your date of birth
4. your place of birth
5. your profession
6. the airport you left from
7. your airline
8. your flight number
9. where your passport was issued
10. your signature

Signigicant Signs

1. c   2. e   3. a   4. f   5. b   6. d

What's the Message?

You may not bring dangerous items aboard such as certain gases—butane, oxygen, propane, corrosives, acids, dry cell batteries, flammable liquids and solids, radioactive materials, explosives, weapons, pyrotechnical materials, mercury, and magnetic materials.

Where To?

1. vamos   2. va   3. vas   4. van   5. voy   6. vais

Ask for It (sample answers)

1. Los baños, por favor.
2. ¿Dónde está el control de pasaportes?
3. La aduana, por favor.
4. ¿Hay asecenores por aquí?
5. Los taxis, por favor.
6. ¿Dónde está el cambio de dinero, por favor?
7. La parada de autobús, por favor.
8. ¿Hay una oficina de objetos perdidos por aquí?
9. La salida, por favor.
10. El alquiler de carros, por favor.

Giving Commands

Verb	Ud.	Uds.	Meaning
ir	vaya	vayan	go
continuar	continue	continuen	continue
seguir*	siga	sigan	continue
bajar	baje	bajen	go down
caminar	camine	caminen	walk
subir	suba	suban	go up
pasar	pase	pasen	pass
tomar	tome	tomen	take
doblar	doble	doblen	turn
cruzar*	cruce	crucen	cross

Chapter 11

Using ¿Qué? and ¿Cuál?

1. ¿Cuál es su nombre?
2. ¿Cuál es su dirección?
3. ¿Qué lee Ud.?
4. ¿Cuál es su nacionalidad?
5. ¿Qué metro va a la Ciudad de México?

Off You Go

Make reservations 24 hours in advance; you must rent for 1 day and rental is based on a 24 hour period; you have unlimited kilometers; you can drop your car off at a sister agency; you are only liable for 1,500 pesos in case of damage; there is an additional small fee in case of theft; there's 24 hour road service; you must pay for your own gas; prices are subject to change.

What Did You Rent?

This car comes with air-conditioning, front and rear seat belts, an air bag on the driver's side, electric windows, inside door locks, and an AM/FM radio.

Your Number's Up

cuarenta y cinco	sesenta y siete	ochenta y nueve
trescientos veinticinco	once	setenta y dos

It's Movie Time

1. Mi querido presidente empieza a las tres y diez, a las seis menos veinticinco, a las ocho, y a las diez y veinticinco.

2. Casino empieza a las tres menos diez, a las cinco menos veinticinco, a las seis y veinte, y a las ocho y cinco.

3. Mi primo Vinnie empieza a la una y media, a las cuatro y cuarto, a las siete menos cuarto, y a las diez menos veinte.

Chapter 12

Just in Case

WHAT TO DO IN CASE OF A FIRE

If the fire is in your room: Go to the exit and close the door to your room. Follow the lights along the floor. Tell the reception desk.

If you hear the fire alarm: Go to the exit and close the door to your room. Follow the lights along the floor.

If there is smoke in the corridors or the stairway is impassable: Stay in your room. Go to the window and make yourself visible while awaiting the arrival of the firemen.

Which Offers the Most?

España	La Capilla	Plaza Central	Hotel
bar	x		x
color TV	x	x	
music	x	x	
laundry service			
dry cleaning service			
air conditioning	x	x	x
in-room safe	x	x	
gym			
restaurant	x		x
sauna	x		
Jacuzzi	x		
fitness center	x		
VIP room	x		
parking			x
hair dryer in room		x	

continues

continued

España	La Capilla	Plaza Central	Hotel
terrace		x	
nonsmoking room		x	
room service	x	x	
in the city	x		

Using Ordinal Numbers

tobacco—planta baja

flowers—planta 1

records—sótano 1

toys—planta 2

travel items—planta 3

park—sótano 2, 3, & 4

interpreter—planta baja

travel agency—planta 3

photos—sótano 1, planta 2

keys—planta 1

Using -ar and -er Verbs

1. piensas
2. almorzamos
3. entiendo
4. vuelven
5. pensáis
6. cuesta
7. descendemos
8. cerráis

Using -ir Verbs

1. prefiero
2. dormimos
3. repiten
4. mentís
5. muere
6. reís

Using -uir, -iar, and -uar Verbs

1. envio
2. incluimos
3. continúa
4. contribuyen
5. actúas
6. guiáis
7. continúa

Chapter 13

What's the Date?

1. el cinco de agosto
2. el ocho de agosto
3. el veintidós de agosto
4. el quince de agosto
5. el seis de agosto
6. el treinta y uno de julio

Using Dar

1. dan un paseo
2. dáis gritos
3. damos gracias
4. doy un abrazo
5. das con

Chapter 14

Take Me to the Zoo!

Parque Zoológico de Madrid

Parque Zoológico del Bosque

Parque Zoológico del Castillo

Parque Zoológico del Bosque

all of them

Parque Zoológico de Madrid

Parque Zoológico del Castillo

Making Suggestions (sample responses)

Quiero ir a la corrida de toros. ¿Qué piensas?

Vamos a ir al carnaval.

Partamos para el castillo.

¿Por qué no vamos al circo?

Your Sentiments, Exactly (sample responses)

1. No me encantan las corridas de toros.
2. Me gusta ir al cine.
3. Me encanta ir a los castillos.
4. Me encanta el circo.
5. No me gusta ir al acuario
6. Me gustan los museos.
7. No me encantan los parques de atracciones.

Where Are You Going?

1. Voy a España.
2. Voy a China.
3. Voy a México.
4. Voy a Rusia
5. Voy a Italia.
6. Voy a Inglaterra.
7. Voy a Francia.
8. Voy a los Estados Unidos.

Chapter 15

You're Putting Me On (sample responses)

1. Yo llevo un vestido, medias, zapatos, un reloj, un collar, dos pulseras y dos anillos.
2. Yo llevo un bikini y sandalias.
3. Yo llevo un traje, una camisa, calcetines, zapatos y un reloj.
4. Yo llevo una camisa, jeans, calcetines, tenis, un reloj y dos anillos.
5. Yo llevo un pantalón, un suéter, calcetines, zapatos, un abrigo, una bufanda y guantes.

I've Got It!

1. encantan
2. gusta
3. gustan
4. encanta
5. gustan
6. gusta

Putting Gustar to Work

1. (No) me gusta el sombrero rojo.
2. (No) me gusta la camisa pequeña.
3. (No) me gusta la camiseta grande.
4. (No) me gustan los zapatos verdes.

Using Direct Object Pronouns

1. (No) Lo compro.
2. (No) Los quiero.
3. (No) La escojo.
4. (No) Las tomo.
5. (No) Lo considero.
6. (No) Los detesto.

Using Indirect Object Pronouns

1. Cómprele un abrigo. No le compre una chaqueta.
2. Cómpreles vestidos. No les compre faldas.
3. Cómpreles sombreros. No les compre guantes.
4. Cómprele una camiseta. No le compre una bolsa.
5. Cómpreles casetes. No les compre discos.
6. Cómprele una pulsera. No le compre un reloj.

What Do You Think? (sample responses)

Esta corbata larga de rayas es horrible.

Estos pantalones cortos de tartán son prácticos.

Esta camisa de lunares es demasiado chillona.

Esta pequeña camiseta de rayas es elegante.

Chapter 16

Going Places

1. Voy a la abacería.
2. Voy a la pastelería.
3. Voy a la carnicería.
4. Voy a la frutería.
5. Voy a la pescadería.
6. Voy a la tienda de licores.
7. Voy a la confitería.
8. Voy a la lechería.

Serious Shopping

1. A la lechería
2. A la carnicería
3. A la panadería
4. A la frutería
5. A la pescadería

Your Likes and Dislikes (sample responses)

1. Me encanta el pescado.
2. No me gusta la carne.
3. Me encantan los productos lácteos.
4. No me gustan las frutas.
5. Me encantan las legumbres.
6. Me gustan las bebidas.
7. Me encantan los postres.

What's in the Fridge? (sample responses)

una botella de agua mineral
un saco de galletas
una caja de dulces

un pan
panecillos
una botella de gaseosa

Getting What You Want

1. Deseo una libra de jamón.
2. ¿Podría darme un litro de gaseosa?
3. Una barra de chocolate, por favor.
4. Deseo una caja de galletitas.
5. Un sace de dulces, por favor.
6. ¿Podría darme una media libra de pavo.

Chapter 17

Which Restaurant Do You Prefer?

La Casita—grilled meats
La Princesa—seafood
Restaurante de Madrid—private rooms, music
Cena Romántica—romantic dinner for 2 with wine, music, and a complimentary rose

El Rincón—good selection of dishes at reasonable prices, live music

La Cava—private rooms, fish, meat dishes, and roasts

Let's Eat Out

Quiero hacer una reservación para viernes para dos personas en la terraza para las nueve y media.

Oh, Waiter!

1. Necesito un salero.
2. Me falta una servilleta.
3. Necesito un tenedor.
4. Me falta un cuchillo.
5. Necesito un plato.
6. Me falta una cucharita.

Muchas Gracias (sample responses)

1. ¡Qué sopa tan excelente!
2. ¡Qué bistec tan delicioso!
3. ¡Qué vino más sabroso!
4. ¡Qué ensalada tan magnífica!
5. ¡Qué postre tan rico!

Chapter 18

Shall We Play? (sample responses)

1. Me gusta la equitación.
2. Detesto la navegación.
3. Me encanta la natación.
4. No me gusta esquiar.
5. Me gusta el fútbol.
6. Me encanta el golf.
7. Me gusta el tenis.

See You There!

1. Tú puedes jugar al tenis. Tú quieres ir a la cancha.
2. Nosotros podemos jugar al golf. Nosotros queremos ir al campo.
3. Uds. pueden ir de pesca. Uds. quieren ir al mar.
4. Ella puede jugar al baloncesto. Ella quiere ir a la cancha.
5. Yo puedo patinar. Yo quiero ir a la pista.

Invite Your Friends Along

1. ¿Quieres ir al parque?
2. ¿Puedes acompañarme a la pista?
3. ¿No quieres acompañarme a la piscina? a la playa?
4. ¿No puedes ir a la pista?
5. ¿Queres ir a la montaña?
6. ¿Puedes acompañarme al campo?

Won't You Join Us? (sample responses)

1. Con mucho gusto.
2. No estoy libre.
3. Por supuesto.
4. Tal vez.
5. ¿Por qué no?

I Think... (sample responses)

Me encanta una película de amor.

Una película de ciencia ficción es un desastre.

Let's Play

1. jugamos
2. tocan
3. toco
4. juegas
5. juega
6. tocan

Do You Do It Well? (sample responses)

1. Hablo español rápidamente.
2. Cocino bien.
3. Pienso inteligentemente.
4. Trabajo cuidadosamente.
5. Bailo lentamente.
6. Nado bastante mal.

Chapter 19

No Starch

They are not responsible for buttons or other adornments on clothing. In case of loss or damage, the hotel will give up to 10 times the cost of the service. They are not responsible for synthetic materials or items left for more than 3 months. They are closed Saturdays, Sundays, and holidays. Emergency service will cost 50% more.

Traveling Shoes

It will pick up and deliver your shoes to your address.

Seeing About Glasses

Translation: same day service; sunglasses with/without prescription; competitive prices; large selection; adjustments and repairs; contact lenses; courteous, good service; expert treatment by professionals.

Time for Repairs (sample responses)

Mi reloj no funciona. Está parado. Necesito una batería. ¿La tiene Ud.? Necesito mi reloj en seguida.

Getting the Picture

The photo shop makes your vacation pictures more beautiful, 25% larger, and develops them more quickly at a better price. They take credit cards and give discounts and a free album.

Using These Pronouns

1. contigo
2. Uds.
3. mí
4. ellos
5. nosotros
6. él

How Do You Measure Up? (sample responses)

Soy menos grande que mi hermano.

Soy más gorda que mi madre.

Soy tan encantadora como mi hermana.

Bailo mejor que mi esposo.

Trabajo tan diligentemente como mi amiga.

Escucho más pacientemente que mi hijo.

Chapter 20

It Hurts Right Here (sample responses)

Flu: Tengo dolor de cabeza. Me duele todo el cuerpo. Yo toso y estoy agotado. Me siento mal.

Allergy: Yo toso y estornudo. Yo no puedo dormir.

Sprained ankle: Me duele el tobillo. Tengo una torcedura y una inflamación. No puedo caminar.

Migraine: Tengo dolor de cabeza. Tengo náuseas. Me siento mal.

I'm Not a Hypochondriac

1. Hace dos semanas que yo toso. Toso desde hace dos semanas.
2. Hace tres días que tengo dolor de cabeza. Tengo dolor de cabeza desde hace tres días.
3. Hace un mes que me duele el estómago. Me duele el estómago desde hace un mes.

What Are They Doing?

1. me cepillo los dientes
2. nos vestimos
3. se despiertan
4. te acuestas
5. se maquilla
6. os afeitáis
7. se peina
8. se lava

Practicing Reflexive Verbs (sample responses)

1. Yo me despierto.
2. Yo me levanto.
3. Yo me desvisto.
4. Yo me baño.
5. Yo me visto.
6. Yo me preparo el desayuno.
7. Yo me cepillo los dientes.
8. Yo me peino.

Hurry Up!

1. Despiértense Uds. No se despierten Uds.
2. Levántense Uds. No se levanten Uds.
3. Báñense Uds. No se bañen Uds.
4. Apúrense Uds. No se apuren Uds.
5. Vístanse Uds. No se vistan Uds.
6. Péinense Uds. No se peinen Uds.
7. Cepíllense Uds. los dientes. No se cepillen Uds. los dientes.
8. Diviértanse Uds. No se diviertan Uds.

Chapter 21

What's on Sale

1. ¿Dónde están las curitas?
2. Busco el champú anti-caspa.
3. Quiero comprar aspirinas.
4. ¿Tiene Ud. enjuagor bucal?
5. Quiero comprar perfume.

Talking About Your Past

1. trabajó
2. comió
3. escribiste
4. leí
5. anduvimos
6. jugué
7. tuvieron
8. me equivoqué
9. oyeron
10. dijisteis
11. durmieron
12. pagué

May I Question Your Past?

1. ¿Carlos, hiciste una visita al museo?
   Sí, hice una visita al museo.

2. ¿Pablo y Jorge, dieron Uds. un paseo?
   No, no dimos un paseo.

3. ¿María, pescaste en el mar?
   No, no pesqué en el mar.

4. ¿Isabel y Pilar, almorzaron Uds. en el centro?
   Sí, almorzamos en el centro.

5. ¿Adela, les trajiste regalos a tus primos?
   Sí les traje regalos a mis primos.

6. ¿Francisco y Rafael, les sirvieron Uds. refrescos a sus amigos?
   No, no les servimos refrescos a nuestros amigos.

What Didn't Get Done? (sample responses)

No comí el almuerzo.

Fui al centro.

No estudié mucho.

Hice mucho trabajo.

Me levanté temprano.

No oí las noticias.

No telefoneé a mis padres.

Busqué un nuevo apartamento.

Chapter 22

Calling from Your Hotel Room

1. 0
2. 51
3. 39
4. 54
5. 16
6. 49
7. 61
8. 32

While You Were Out

On July 11th, 1975, at 4:25 P.M., Roberta Cruz from Aerolíneas, México called. Her number is 12-34-56. She wants you to call her back as soon as possible. Ana took the message for you.

What Happened?

1. Eran	6. Entré	11. estaba	16. Empujé
2. Estaba	7. subí	12. sabía	17. entré
3. salí	8. Saqué	13. Tenía	18. escuché
4. Tomé	9. necesité	14. Estaba	19. marchaba
5. llegué	10. observé	15. robó	20. gritaron

Chapter 23

Using Saber and Conocer

1. saben	3. conoce	5. conoces	7. saben
2. sé	4. sabemos	6. conoce	8. conocéis

Using the Present Perfect

1. Nosotros hemos ido…
2. Ellos han jugado…
3. Tú no has trabajado…
4. Yo he leído…
5. Ud. no ha escrito…
6. Vosotros no habéis corrido…
7. Uds. no han traído…
8. Ella no ha vuelto…

Chapter 24

Do You Know Your Computer?

1. What computer system do you use? Uso una sistema…

2. What peripherals do you use? Uso un disco optinúmerico, dos disqueteras, y una cinta de seguridad.

3. How many megabytes of memory does your system have? Tiene cuarenta y ocho megaoctetos de memoria.

4. What is the speed of your modem? La velocidad es veintiocho coma ocho.

5. What software do you use? Uso un procesador de textos.

Plans for the Day (sample responses)

1. Iré al centro comercial.
2. Telefonearé a mi familia.
3. Saldré con mis amigos.
4. Haré un viage.
5. Abriré una cuenta.

Predicting the Future

Aries—Excellent financial opportunites will present themselves to you.

Taurus—You will have a very nice month.

Gemini—You will have tension and disputes with your colleagues.

Cancer—You will be in good shape.

Leo—You will concentrate on your financial affairs.

Virgo—You will make an important decision about your professional future.

Libra—You will be in harmony with your friends.

Scorpio—Your ambitions will serve you.

Sagittarius—You will have important discussions with members of your family.

Capricorn—Everything will go well for you.

Aquarius—You will become acquainted with an important person.

Pisces—Your nightly schedule will be full and you will have many weekend plans.

Chapter 25

Purchasing Furniture

Your furniture will be guaranteed for 5 years and seat covers for 2 years should there be any problem with the manufacturing.

They will give free decorating consultation and will come to give free estimates and take measurements.

You will be given a risk-free guarantee for one year.

Your old furniture will be removed after you buy new furniture.

All services are guaranteed (against a price increase) in all of their stores throughout Spain.

What Are Your Needs? (sample responses)

Quisiera una casa amueblada grande con tres habitaciones, una terraza, un garaje, y una piscina. ¿Qué aparatos elécticos hay? Necesitamos un refrigerador, un microondas, una lavadora y una secadora.

I Can't Decide

A safe place to live within your price range. It's near downtown, recreational facilities, restaurants, malls, main highways, beaches, and has a wonderful view of Puerto Rico. The residences are modern, have elegant facades, three bedrooms, and a bathroom.

Making a Choice

1. Four bedrooms
2. Four-and-a-half bathrooms
3. Maid's quarters, separate entrance for family and workers, an office, 2 fireplaces, a terrace off the master bedroom, and private layout
4. I like the big kitchen: Me gusta la cocina grande.
5. I don't like where the dining room is situated: No me gusta donde está situado el comedor.

What Would You Do? (sample responses)

Yo me compraría un nuevo coche deportivo y una casa muy grande. Yo daría mucho dinero a los pobres. Yo viajaría por todo el mundo. Yo iría en España con toda mi familia. Yo no trabajaría.

Chapter 26

Using the Bank

1. B
2. A
3. A and B
4. C
5. G
6. F
7. C
8. D
9. E

So Much to Do, So Little Time

1. Nosotros tenemos que preparar…
   Es necesario que preparemos…

2. Ella tiene que aprender…
   Es necesario que aprenda…

3. Ellos tienen que vivir…
   Es necesario que vivan…

4. Yo tengo que cerrar…
   Es necesario que cierre…

5. Vosotros no tenéis que perder…
   Es necesario que no perdáis…

6. Tú no tienes que mentir.
   Es necesario que no mientas.

7. Ud. no tiene que dormir…
   Es necesario que no duerma…

8. El tiene que pedir…
   Es necesario que no pida…

9. Uds. tienen que continuar…
   Es necesario que continúen…

10. Tú tienes que graduarte.
    Es necesario que te gradues.

11. Ellas tienen que dar…
    Es necesario que den…

12. Nosotros tenemos que estar…
    Es necesario que estemos…

13. Yo tengo que ir…
    Es necesario que vaya…

14. Vosotros tienen que saber…
    Es necesario que sepáis…

15. Ud. tiene que ser…
    Es necesario que sea…

Obligations

1. Es aconsejabe que tú digas....
2. Es importante que nosotros vayamos...
3. Es indispensable que yo vengo...
4. Es necesario que Uds. busquen...
5. Es preciso que ella pague.
6. Es bueno que ellos sepan...

Verb Charts

Regular Verbs

-ar Verbs USAR—to use Gerund: usando **Past participle:** usado
Commands: ¡Use Ud.! ¡Usen Uds.! ¡Usemos!

Present (do)	Preterite (did)	Imperfect (was)	Future (will)	Conditional (would)
uso	usé	usaba	usaré	usaría
usas	usaste	usabas	usarás	usarías
usa	usó	usaba	usará	usaría
usamos	usamos	usábamos	usaremos	usaríamos
usáis	usasteis	usábais	usaréis	usaríais
usan	usaron	usaban	usarán	usarían

-er Verbs COMER—to eat Gerund: comiendo **Past participle:** comido
Commands: ¡Coma Ud.! ¡Coman Uds.! ¡Comamos!

Present	Preterite	Imperfect	Future	Conditional
como	comí	comía	comeré	comería
comes	comiste	comías	comerás	comerías
come	comió	comía	comerá	comería
comemos	comimos	comíamos	comeremos	comeríamos
coméis	comisteis	comíais	comeréis	comeríais
comen	comieron	comían	comerán	comerían

-ir Verbs VIVIR—to live Gerund: viviendo **Past participle:** vivido
Commands: ¡Viva Ud.! ¡Vivan Uds.! ¡Vivamos!

Present	Preterite	Imperfect	Future	Conditional
vivo	viví	vivía	viviré	viviría
vives	viviste	vivías	vivirás	vivirías
vive	vivió	vivía	vivirá	viviría
vivimos	vivimos	vivíamos	viviremos	viviríamos
vivís	vivisteis	vivíais	viviréis	viviríais
viven	vivieron	vivían	vivirán	vivirían

Stem-Changing Verbs

-ar Verbs

PENSAR (e to ie)—to think
Present: pienso, piensas, piensa, pensamos, pensáis, piensan
Other verbs like pensar include cerrar (to close), comenzar (to begin), and empezar (to begin).

MOSTRAR (o to ue)—to show
Present: muestro, muestras, muestra, mostramos, mostráis, muestran
Other verbs like mostrar include almorzar (to eat lunch), contar (to tell), costar (to cost), encontrar (to find), recordar (to remember), and volver (to return).

JUGAR—to play (a sport or game)
Present: juego, juegas, juega, jugamos, jugáis, juegan
Preterite: jugué, jugaste, jugó, jugamos, jugasteis, jugaron

-er Verbs

DEFENDER (e to ie)—to defend, to forbid
Present: defiendo, defiendes, defiende, defendemos, defendéis, defienden
Other verbs like defender include descender (to descend), entender (to understand, to hear), perder (to lose), and querer (to want).

VOLVER (o to ue)—to return
Present: vuelvo, vuelves, vuelve, volvemos, volvéis, vuelven
Another verb like volver is poder (to be able to, can).

-ir Verbs

PEDIR (e to i)—to ask for Gerund: pidiendo
Present: pido, pides, pide, pedimos, pedís, piden
Preterite: pedí, pediste, pidió, pedimos, pedisteis, pidieron
Other verbs like pedir include impedir (to prevent), medir (to measure), repetir (to repeat), and servir (to serve).

SENTIR (e to ie, i)—to feel Gerund: sintiendo
Present: siento, sientes, siente, sentimos, sentís, sienten
Preterite: sentí, sentiste, sintió, sentimos, sentisteis, sintieron
Other verbs like sentir include advertir (to warn, to notify), consentir (to consent), mentir (to lie), preferir (to prefer), and referir (to refer).

DORMIR (o to ue, u)—to sleep Gerund: durmiendo
Present: duermo, duermes, duerme, dormimos, dormís, duermen
Preterite: dormí, dormiste, durmió, dormimos, dormisteis, durmieron
Another verb like dormir is morir (to die).

-uir Verbs (except *-guir*)

INCLUIR (y)—to include Gerund: incluyendo
Present: incluyo, incluyes, incluye, incluimos, incluís, incluyen
Preterite: incluí, incluiste, incluyó, incluimos, incluisteis, incluyeron
Other verbs like incluir include concluir (to conclude, to end), construir (to construct), contribuir (to contribute), destruir (to destroy), and sustituir (to substitue).

-eer Verbs

LEER (i to y)—to read
Preterite: leí, leíste, leyó, leímos, leísteis, leyeron

-iar Verbs

ENVIAR (i to í)—to send
Present: envío, envías, envía, enviamos, enviáis, envían
Other verbs like enviar include confiar + en (to confide in), guiar (to guide), and variar (to vary).

-uar Verbs

ACTUAR (u to ú)—to act
Present: actúo, actúas, actúa, actuamos, actuáis, actúan
Another verb like actuar is continuar (to continue).

Spelling-Change Verbs

-cer or *-cir* Verbs

CONVENCER (c to z)—to convince
Present: convenzo, convences, convence, convencemos, onvencéis, convencen

CONOCER (c to zc)—to know
Present: conozco, conoces, conoce, conocemos, conocéis, conocen

-ger or *-gir* Verbs

EXIGIR (g to j)—to demand
Present: exijo, exiges, exige, exigimos, exigís, exigen

429

-uir Verbs

DISTINGUIR (gu to g)—to distinguish
Present: distingo, distingues, distingue, distinguimos, distinguís, distinguen

-car Verbs

BUSCAR (c to qu)—to look for
Preterite: busqué, buscaste, buscó, buscamos, buscasteis, buscaron

-gar Verbs

PAGAR (g to gu)—to pay
Preterite: pagué, pagaste, pagó, pagamos, pagasteis, pagaron

-zar Verbs

GOZAR (z to c)—to enjoy
Preterite: gocé, gozaste, gozó, gozamos, gozasteis, gozaron

Irregular Verbs

DAR—to give
Present: doy, das, da, damos, dáis, dan
Preterite: di, diste, dio, dimos, disteis, **dieron**

DECIR—to say **Gerund:** diciendo **Past participle:** dicho
Present: digo, dices, dice, decimos, decís, **dicen**
Preterite: dije, dijiste, dijó, dijmos, dijisteis, dijeron
Future: diré, dirás, dirá, diremos, diréis, dirán
Conditional: diría, dirías, diría, diríamos, diríais, dirían

ESTAR—to be
Present: estoy, estás, está, estamos, estáis, **están**
Preterite: estuve, estuviste, estuvo, estuvimos, estuvisteis, estuvieron

HACER—to make, to do **Past participle:** hecho
Present: hago, haces, hace, hacemos, hacéis, hacen
Preterite: hice, hiciste, hizo, hicimos, hicisteis, hicieron
Future: haré, harás, hará, haremos, haréis, harán
Conditional: haría, harías, haría, haríamos, haríais, harían

IR—to go **Gerund:** yendo
Present: voy, vas, va, vamos, vais, van
Preterite: fui, fuiste, fue, fuimos, fuisteis, fueron
Imperfect: iba, ibas, iba, íbamos, ibais, iban

430

OÍR—to hear Gerund: oyendo

Present: oigo, oyes, oye, oímos, oís, oyen
Preterite: oí, oíste, oyó, oímos, oísteis, oyeron

PODER (o to ue)—to be able to, can Gerund: pudiendo

Present: puedo, puedes, puede, podemos, podéis, pueden
Preterite: pude, pudiste, pudo, pudimos, pudisteis, pudieron
Future: podré, podrás, podrá, podremos, podréis, podrán
Conditional: podría, podrías, podría, podríamos, podríais, podrían

PONER—to put Past participle: puesto

Present: pongo, pones, pone, ponemos, ponéis, ponen
Preterite: puse, pusiste, puso, pusimos, pusisteis, pusieron
Future: pondré, pondrás, pondrá, pondremos, pondréis, pondrán
Conditional: pondría, pondrías, pondría, pondríamos, pondríais, pondrían

QUERER—to want

Present: quiero, quieres, quiere, queremos, queréis, quieren
Preterite: quise, quisiste, quiso, quisimos, quisisteis, quisieron
Future: querré, querrás, querrá, querremos, querréis, querrán
Conditional: querría, querrías, querría, querríamos, querríais, querrían

SABER—to know

Present: sé, sabes, sabe, sabemos, sabéis, saben
Preterite: supe, supiste, supo, supimos, supisteis, supieron
Future: sabré, sabrás, sabrá, sabremos, sabréis, sabrán
Conditional: sabría, sabrías, sabría, sabríamos, sabríais, sabrían

SALIR—to go out, to leave

Present: salgo, sales, sale, salemos, saléis, salen
Future: saldré, saldrás, saldrá, saldremos, saldréis, saldrán
Conditional: saldría, saldrías, saldría, saldríamos, saldríais, saldrían

SER—to be

Present: soy, eres, es, somos, sois, son
Preterite: fui, fuiste, fue, fuimos, fuisteis, fueron
Imperfect: era, eras, era, éramos, erais, eran

TENER—to have

Present: tengo, tienes, tiene, tenemos, tenéis, tienen
Preterite: tuve, tuviste, tuvo, tuvimos, tuvisteis, tuvieron
Future: tendré, tendrás, tendrá, tendremos, tendréis, tendrán
Conditional: tendría, tendrías, tendría, tendríamos, tendríais, tendrían

TRAER—to bring Past participle: traído

Present: traigo, traes, trae, traemos, traéis, traen
Preterite: traje, trajiste, trajo, trajimos, trajisteis, trajeron

VENIR—to come Gerund: viniendo

Present: vengo, vienes, viene, venimos, **venís, vienen**
Preterite: vine, viniste, vino, vinimos, vinisteis, vinieron
Future: vendré, vendrás, vendrá, vendremos, vendréis, vendrán
Conditional: vendría, vendrías, vendría, vendríamos, vendríais, vendrían

VER—to see Past participle: visto

Present: veo, ves, ve, vemos, veis, ven
Preterite: vi, viste, **vio,** vimos, visteis, vieron
Imperfect: veía, veías, veía, veíamos, veíais, veían

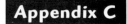

Dictionaries

Spanish to English

This dictionary follows international alphabetical order. The Spanish letter combination ch and ll are not treated as separate letters; therefore, ch will follow cg instead of being at the end of c, and ll will appear after lk and not at the end of l. Note that ñ is treated as a separate letter and follows n in alphabetical order.

a at, to

abogado *m.* lawyer

abordar to board

abrazar to embrace, to hug

abrigo *m.* overcoat

abril April

abrir to open

aceite *m.* oil

acompañar to accompany

aconsejable advisable

adiós good-bye

aduana *f.* customs

advertir *ie warn

aeromozo(a) steward(ess)

aeropuerto *m.* airport

agosto August

agua *m.* water

ahora now

ahorrar to save

ajo *m.* garlic

al to the

al centro downtown

alegre happy

Alemania Germany

algodón *m.* cotton

allá there

almacén *m.* department store

alquilar to rent

alrededor de around

alto tall

amarillo yellow

anaranjado orange

andar to walk

antes (de) before

aprender to learn

aquí here

arreglar to adjust, to fix

arroz *m.* rice

asado baked, roasted

ascensor *m.* elevator

asegurar to guarantee

así so, thus

asiento *m.* seat

aterrizar to land

avión *m.* airplane

aviso *m.* warning

ayer yesterday

ayudar to help

azúcar *m.* sugar

azul blue

bajar to go down

bajo short

banco *m.* bank

baño *m.* bathroom

barbero *m.* hairdresser

bastante enough, quite, rather

beber to drink

bien well

bienvenido welcome

bistec *m.* beef steak

bizcocho *m.* biscuit, sponge cake

blanco white

boca *f.* mouth

boleto *m.* ticket

bolígrafo *m.* ball-point pen

bolsa *f.* pocketbook

bonito pretty

botella *f.* bottle

brazo *m.* arm

bueno good

buscar to look for

buzón *m.* mailbox

caja *f.* box

caja fuerte *f.* safe, safe-deposit box

cajero *m.* automatic teller machine

cama *f.* bed

camarero (a) waiter(ress)

cambiar to change

cambio de dinero *m.* money exchange

camisa *f.* shirt, man-tailored

carne *f.* meat

carta *f.* letter, menu, card

cartera *f.* briefcase, wallet

casa *f.* house

casi almost

centro comercial *m.* mall

cerca (de) near

cerrar *ie to close

cerveza *f.* beer

césped *m.* lawn

chaleco salvavidas *m.* life vest

champiñon *m.* mushroom

champú *m.* shampoo

cheque *m.* check

cheque de viajero *m.* traveler's check

ciento hundred

cinco five

cincuenta fifty

cine *m.* movies

cinturón *m.* belt

cinturón de seguridad *m.* seat belt

claro light, of course

cobrar to cash

coche *m.* car

comenzar *ie to begin

comer to eat

comisaria de policia *f.* police station

cómo how

comprar to buy, to purchase

comprender to understand

con with

contestar to answer

contra against

correo electrónico *m.* E-mail

corto short

creer to believe

cruzar to cross

cuál which

cuándo when

cuánto how much, many

cuarenta forty

cuarto *m.* room, quarter

cuarto de baño *m.* bathroom

cuatro four

cucharita *f.* teaspoon

cuchillo *m.* knife

dar to give

de about, from, of

de nada you're welcome

de nuevo again

debajo de below, beneath, under

deber to owe

deber + infinitive to have to + infinitive

decir to say, to tell

dejar delante de to allow, to leave in front of

demasiado too much

descuento *m.* discount

desde from, since

después (de) after

detrás de behind

día *m.* day

diciembre December

diente *m.* tooth

diez ten

dinero *m.* currency, money

doce twelve

dolor *m.* pain

domingo Sunday

dónde where

dos two

durante during

durar to last

empezar *ie to begin

en in

encontrar *ue to find, to meet

enero January

enfermo sick

enfrente de in front of

entre among, between

escala *f.* stop-over

escribir to write

escuchar   to listen to

esperar   to hope, to wait

Estados Unidos *m./pl.*   United States

estar   to be

este *m.*   East

estudiar   to study

evitar   to avoid

fácil   easy

factura *f.*   bill, invoice

faltar   to lack, to miss

febrero   February

feo   ugly

firmar   to sign

flaco   thin

folleto *m.*   pamphlet

fresa *f.*   strawberry

frito   fried

fumar   to smoke

gerente *m.*   manager

gobernanta *f.*   maid service

grande   big

gustar   to like

habitación *f.*   room

hablar   to speak, to talk

hacer   to do, to make

hacia   toward

hasta   until

helado *m.*   ice cream

hijo(a)   child, son (daughter)

hora *f.*   hour, time

hoy   today

huevo   egg

iglesia *f.*   church

impermeable *m.*   raincoat

ir   to go

joven   young

joya *f.*   jewel

jueves   Thursday

jugar   to play

jugo *m.*   juice

juguete *m.*   toy

julio   July

junio   June

lápiz *m.*   pencil

lavandería *f.*   laundry

lavar (se)   to wash (oneself)

leche *f.*   milk

leer   to read

librería *f.*   bookstore

libro *m.*   book

llave *f.*   key

llegar   to arrive

llevar   to carry, to wear

lugar *m.*   place

lunes   Monday

madre *f.*   mother

mandar   to order, to send

mano *f.*   hand

mantequilla *f.*   butter

manzana *f.*   apple

mañana   tomorrow, morning

marroquinería *f.*   leather goods store

martes   Tuesday

marzo   March

más   more

mayo   May

mejor   better

menos   less

mensaje *m.*   message

mercado *m.*   market

mes *m.*   month

mesa *f.*   table

metro *m.*   subway

mezclar   to mix

miércoles   Wednesday

mil   thousand

mirar   to look at, to watch

montar   to go up, to ride

monto *m.*   sum, total

mostrar *ue   to show

mucho   much, many

muebles *m./pl.*   furniture

museo *m.*   museum

muy   very

nadie   nobody

naipes *m./pl.*   cards

negro   black

noche *f.*   evening

norte *m.*   north

noventa   ninety

noviembre   November

nueve   nine

nuevo   new

nuez *f.*   nut, walnut

ochenta   eighty

ocho   eight

octeto *m.*   byte

octubre   October

oeste *m.*   west

oír   to hear

once   eleven

otoño *m.*   autumn

padre *m.*   father

pagar   to pay

país *m.*   country

pan *m.*   bread

panadería *f.*   bakery

pantalones *m./pl.*   pants

papa *f.*   potato

papel *m.*   paper

para   for

parada *f.* stop

partir to divide, to share

pasado last

pasar to pass, to spend time

pastel *m.* cake, pie

pastilla *f.* pill

pato *m.* duck

pavo *m.* turkey

película *f.* film, movie, roll (film)

pelo *m.* hair

pensar to think

pequeño small

perder *ie to lose, to miss

periódico *m.* newspaper

pez *m.* fish

piscina *f.* swimming pool

piso *m.* floor (story)

planta baja *f.* ground floor

playa *f.* beach

poco little, few

poder *ue to be able

pollo *m.* chicken

poner to put

por along, by, per, through

por favor please

por qué why

portero *m.* bellman

postre *m.* dessert

precio *m.* price

preguntar to ask

prestar to borrow, to lend

primavera *f.* spring

primero first

pronóstico *m.* weather forecast

pronto soon

próximo next

qué what

querer *ie to want

queso *m.* cheese

quién who, whom

quince fifteen

quitar to leave

recibir to receive

recibo *m.* receipt

recordar *ue to remember

regresar to return

reloj *m.* clock, watch

revista *f.* magazine

rojo red

ropa *f.* clothing

roto broken

sábado Saturday

sacar to take out

sal *f.* salt

sala *f.* living room

salida *f.* departure, exit, gate

salir to go out, to leave, to deboard, to exit

seguir *i to follow, continue

seis six

sello *m.* stamp

semana *f.* week

señor *m.* sir

señora *f.* Mrs.

señorita *f.* Miss

septiembre September

ser to be

sesenta sixty

setenta seventy

siempre always

siete seven

sin without

sobre on, upon

subir to climb, to go up

sucio *m.* dirty

sucursal *f.* branch

sur *m.* South

tabaquería *f.* tobacco store

también also, too

tan as, so

tarde late

tarde *f.* afternoon

tarifa rate

tasa *f.* rate

temprano early

tenedor *m.* fork, holder

tener to have

tener que + infinitive to have to + infinitive

tiempo *m.* time, weather

tienda *f.* store

tirar to pull, to shoot

toalla *f.* towel

tocar to touch

todavía still, yet

todo all

tomar to take

traer to bring

traje *m.* suit

trece thirteen

treinta thirty

tren *m.* train

tres three

último last

uno one

valer to be worth

vaso *m.* glass

veinte twenty

vender to sell

venir to come

venta *f.* sale

ventana *f.* window

ver to see

verano *m.* summer

verde green

viaje *m.* trip

viernes Friday

vivir to live

volver*ue to return

vuelo *m.* flight

ya already

zapato *m.* shoe

English to Spanish

able (to be) poder

about de

above encima de

to accompany acompañar

ad anuncio *m.*

address dirección *f.*

to adjust arreglar

advisable aconsejable

afraid (to be afraid [of]) tener miedo [de]

after después (de)

afternoon tarde *f.*

again de nuevo

against contra

ago hace

to agree with estar de acuerdo con

air-conditioning aire acondicionado *m.*

airline aerolínea *f.*

airport aeropuerto *m.*

all todo

almost casi

already ya

also también

always

American consulate consulado americano *m.*

American embassy embajada americana *f.*

to answer contestar

April abril

around alrededor (de)

to arrive llegar

ashtray cenicero *m.*

to ask preguntar, pedir

August agosto

automatic teller machine cajero automático *m.*

autumn otoño *m.*

to avoid evitar

bad malo

bag saco *m.*

bagage claim area reclamo de equipage *m.*

bakery panadería *f.*

ball-point pen bolígrafo *m.*

band-aid curita *f.*

bank banco *m.*

bathing suit traje de baño *m.*

bathrooms baño *m.*

to be estar, ser

beach playa *f.*

beer cerveza *f.*

before antes (de)

to begin comenzar, empezar *ie

behind detrás (de)

to believe creer

bellman portero *m.*

below debajo de

beneath debajo de

better mejor

between entre

big grande

bill factura *f.*

black negro

blanket manta *f.*

blue azul

to board abordar

book libro *m.*

bookstore librería *f.*

booth (phone) cabina telefónica *f.*

to borrow prestar

bottle botella *f.*

box caja *f.*

boyfriend novio *m.*

branch (office) sucursal *f.*

brand name marca *f.*

bread pan *m.*

briefcase cartera *f.*

to bring traer

broiled a la parrilla

brown pardo, marrón

butter mantequilla *f.*

to buy comprar

by por

to call telefonear

can lata *f.*

candy dulces *m./pl.*

candy store confitería *f.*

cane bastón *m.*

car coche *m.*, automóvil *m.*, carro *m.*

cart carrito *m.*

to cash a check cobrar un cheque

cashier cajero *m.*

chair silla *f.*

to change cambiar

change (coins) moneda *f.*

check   cheque *m.*

checkbook   chequera *f.*

cheese   queso *m.*

chicken   pollo *m.*

child   hijo *m.*

church   iglesia *f.*

to close   cerrar *ie

clothing   ropa *f.*

coffee   café *m.*

comb   peine *m.*

to come   venir

to continue   continuar, seguir *i

corner   rincón *m.*

to cost   costar *ue

cup   taza *f.*, copa *f.*

customer   cliente *m.*

customs   aduana *f.*

daughter   hija *f.*

day   día *m.*

December   diciembre

to decide   decidir

to declare   declarar

delicatessen   tienda de ultramarinos *f.*

to deliver   entregar

dentist   dentista *m.*

department store   almacén *m.*

departure   salida *f.*

dessert   postre *m.*

to dial   marcar

diaper (disposable)   pañal desechable *m.*

difficult   difícil

dirty   sucio *m.*

discount   descuento *m.*, rabaja *f.*

to do   hacer

doctor   doctor *m.*, médico *m.*

door   puerta *f.*

doorman   portero *m.*

dozen   docena *f.*

to drink   beber

duck   pato *m.*

during   durante

E-mail   correo electrónico *m.*

early   temprano

to earn   ganar

East   este *m.*

easy   fácil

to eat   comer

egg   huevo *m.*

eight   ocho

eighteen   diez y ocho

eighty   ochenta

elevator   ascensor *m.*

eleven   once

employee   empleado *m.*

to end   terminar

to enjoy   gozar

enough   bastante

entrance   entrada *f.*

envelope   sobre *m.*

exhange rate   tasa de cambio *f.*

exit   salida *f.*

to explain   explicar

to express   expresar

facing   frente a

far (from)   lejos (de)

father   padre *m.*

February   febrero

to feel   sentirse *ie

fifteen   quince

fifty   cincuenta

to fill (out)   llenar

film   película *f.*

to find   hallar, encontrar *ue

fish   pez *m.*, pescado *m.*

five   cinco *m.*

to fix   arreglar

flight   vuelo *m.*

to follow   seguir *i

for   para, por

to forget   olvidarse (de)

fork   tenedor *m.*

forty   cuarenta

four   cuatro

fourteen   catorce

Friday   viernes

from   de, desde

front, in front (of)   delante (de)

front desk   recepción *f.*

fruit   fruta *f.*

gasoline   gasolina *f.*

gate   salida *f.*, puerta *f.*

girlfriend   novia *f.*

to give   dar

glass   vaso *m.*

to go   ir

to go down   bajar

to go out   salir

gold   oro *m.*

good   bueno

good-bye   adiós

gray   gris

green   verde

grocery store   abacería *f.*

hair   pelo *m.*

ham   jamón *m.*

hamburger   hamburguesa *f.*

hanger   percha *f.*

happy   alegre

hat   sombrero *m.*

to have   tener

to have to… tener que + infinitive, deber + infinitive

to hear oír

hello buenos días

to help ayudar

here aquí

holiday fiesta *f.*

to hope esperar

hour hora *f.*

house casa *f.*

how cómo

how much, many cuánto

hundred ciento

hungry (to be hungry) tener hambre

hurry (to be in a hurry) tener prisa

ice cream helado *m.*

ice cubes cubitos de hielo *m./pl.*

immediately en seguida

in en

instead of en vez de

acket chaqueta *f.*

jam mermelada *f.*

January enero

jar pomo *m.*

jelly mermelada *f.*

jewelry store joyería *f.*

juice jugo *m.*

July julio

June junio

to keep guardar

ketchup salsa de tomate *f.*

key llave *f.*, tecla *f.*

knife cuchillo *m.*

to land aterrizar

to last durar

last pasado, último

late tarde

late in arriving en retraso

laundry lavandería *f.*

to learn aprender

leather cuero *m.*

to leave dejar, salir

to lend prestar

less menos

letter carta *f.*

life vest chaleco salvavidas *m.*

to like gustar

liquor store tienda de licores *f.*

to listen to escuchar

little poco

to live vivir

lobster langosta *f.*

to look at mirar

to look for buscar

to lose perder *ie

magazine revista *f.*

maid criada *f.*

maid service gobernanta *f.*

mailbox buzón *m.*

to make hacer

mall centro comercial *m.*

management gestión *f.*

manager gerente *m.*

March marzo

May mayo

to mean significar

mechanic mecánico *m.*

to meet encontrar *ue

menu carta *f.*, menú *m.*

message mensaje *m.*

milk leche *f.*

to miss perder *ie

Monday lunes

money dinero *m.*

money exchange cambio de dinero *m.*

month mes *m.*

more más

morning mañana *f.*

mother madre *f.*

movie película *f.*

movies cine *m.*

Mrs. señora *f.*

museum museo *m.*

mustard mostaza *f.*

napkin servilleta *f.*

near cerca (de)

necessary necesario

to need necesitar

new nuevo

news noticias *f./pl.*

newspaper periódico *m.*

next próximo

next to al lado de

nice simpático

nine nueve

nineteen diez y nueve

ninety noventa

nobody nadie

north norte *m.*

to notify, to warn advertir *ie

November noviembre

now ahora

O.K. de acuerdo

October octubre

of de

of course por supuesto, claro

often a menudo

on sobre

one uno

439

onion   cebolla *f.*

to open   abrir

opposite   frente a

orange   anaranjado

orange   naranja *f.*

to order   mandar

out of order   fuera de servicio

to owe   deber

owner   propietario *m.*

package   paquete *m.*

pain   dolor *m.*

pamphlet   folleto *m.*

pants   pantalones *m./pl.*

paper   papel *m.*

parents   padres *m./pl.*

park   parque *m.*

passport   pasaporte *m.*

to pay   pagar

pencil   lápiz *m.*

pepper   pimienta *f.*

percent   por ciento

phone (public)   teléfono público *m.*

phone card   tarjeta telefónica *f.*

pie   pastel *m.*

piece   pedazo *m.*

pill   pastilla *f.*

pillow   almohada *f.*

pineapple   piña *f.*

place   lugar *m.*

plate   plato *m.*

to play games   jugar

to play an instrument   tocar

please   por favor

pocketbook   bolsa *f.*

police officer   agente de policia *m.*

police station   comisaria de policia *f.*

pool   piscina *f.*

porter   portero *m.*

postcard   tarjeta postal *f.*

postage   franqueo *m.*

potato   papa *f.*, patata *f.*

pound   libra *f.*

pretty   bonito

price   precio *m.*

problem   problema *m.*

to put   poner, colocar

quickly   rápidamente

raincoat   impermeable *m.*

rate   tarifa *f.*

rather   bastante

to read   leer

ready   listo

receipt   recibo *m.*

to receive   recibir

red   rojo

relatives   parientes *m./pl.*

to remember   recordar *ue

to rent   alquilar

to repair   reparar

to repeat   repetir *i

to return   regresar, volver *ue

rice   arroz *m.*

roll (film)   película *f.*

room   cuarto *m.*

safe   caja fuerte *f.*

safety pin   seguro *m.*, imperdible *m.*

sale   venta *f.*

salesperson   vendedor *m.*

salt   sal *f.*

salt shaker   salero *m.*

Saturday   sábado

to say   decir

scissors   tijeras *f./pl.*

seafood   mariscos *m./pl.*

seat   asiento *m.*

seat belt   cinturón de seguridad *m.*

to see   ver

to sell   vender

to send   mandar, enviar

to send back   devolver *ue

September   septiembre

to serve   servir *i

to settle   arreglar

seven   siete

seventeen   diez y siete

seventy   setenta

shampoo   champú *m.*

shirt   camisa *f.*

shoe   zapato *m.*

short   bajo, corto

to show   enseñar

sick   enfermo

since   desde

sir   señor *m.*

sister   hermana *f.*

six   seis

sixteen   diez y seis

sixty   sesenta

skirt   falda *f.*

slice   trozo *m.*

small   pequeño

to smoke   fumar

sneakers   tenis *m./pl.*

soap   jabón *m.*

soap opera   telenovela *f.*

soda   gaseosa *f.*, soda *f.*

son   hijo *m.*

soon   pronto

South   sur *m.*

South America   Sud América *f.*, América del Sur *f.*

Spain   España

to speak   hablar

to spend money   gastar

to spend time   pasar

spicy   picante

spoon   cuchara *f.*

spring   primavera *f.*

stadium   estadio *m.*

stain   mancha *f.*

staircase   escalera *f.*

stamp   sello *m.*

stapler   grapadora *f.*

still   todavía

stop   parada *f.*

stop-over   escala *f.*

store   tienda *f.*

string   cuerda *f.*

student   estudiante (*m.* or *f.*)

to study   estudiar

to substitute   sustituir

subway   metro *m.*

suddenly   de repente

sugar   azúcar *m.*

suit   traje *m.*, sastre *m.*

suitcase   maleta *f.*

summer   verano *m.*

Sunday   domingo

sunglasses   gafas de sol *f./pl.*

suntan lotion   loción de sol *f.*

supermarket   supermercado *m.*

sweater   suéter *m.*

to swim   nadar

swimming pool   piscina *f.*

T-shirt   camiseta *f.*

table   mesa *f.*

tailor   sastre *m.*

to take   tomar

take off   despegue *m.*

to take out   sacar

to take place   tener lugar

to talk   hablar

tall   alto

tax   impuesto *m.*

tea   té *m.*

to teach   enseñar

teacher   profesor *m.*

telephone   teléfono *m.*

telephone book   guía telefónica *f.*

telephone number   número de teléfono *m.*

television   televisor *m.*

to tell   decir, contar *ue

ten   diez

thank you   muchas gracias

theater   teatro *m.*

then   pues

there   allá

to think   pensar *ie

thirsty (to be thirsty)   tener sed

thirteen   trece

thirty   treinta

thousand   mil

three   tres

through   por

Thursday   jueves

ticket   boleto *m.*

tie   corbata *f.*

time   tiempo *m.*, hora *f.*

time (at the same time)   al mismo tiempo

time (at what time?)   a qué hora

time (on time)   a tiempo

tip   propina *f.*

tire   goma *f.*, llanta *f.*

tissue   pañuelo de papel *m.*

to   a

tobacco store   tabaquería *f.*

today   hoy

tomorrow   mañana

too   también

too much   demasiado

tooth   diente *m.*

toothbrush   cepillo de los dientes *m.*

toothpaste   pasta dentifrica *f.*

toward   hacia

towel   toalla *f.*

toy   juguete *m.*

train   tren *m.*

to travel   viajar

traveler's check   cheque de viajero *m.*

trip   viaje *m.*

Tuesday   martes

turkey   pavo *m.*

to turn   doblar

to turn off   apagar

to turn on   encender *ie

twelve   doce

twenty   veinte

two   dos

umbrella   paraguas *m.*

under   debajo de

to understand   comprender, entender *ie

United States   Estados Unidos *m./pl.*

until   hasta

upon   sobre

value   valor *m.*

vegetable   legumbre *f.*

very   muy

to visit   visitar

to wait for   esperar

441

waiter   camarero *m.*

wallet   cartera *f.*

to want   querer *ie

warning   aviso *m.*

to watch   mirar, guardar

to wear   llevar, usar

weather   tiempo *m.*

Wednesday   miércoles

week   semana *f.*

welcome   bienvenido

well   bien

west   oeste *m.*

what   qué

wheelchair   silla de ruedas *f.*

when   cuándo

where   dónde

which   cuál

white   blanco

who(m)   quién

why   por qué

window   ventana *f.*

window (ticket)   ventanilla *f.*

wine   vino *m.*

winter   invierno *m.*

without   sin

wool   lana *f.*

to work   funcionar, trabajar

worth (to be)   valer

to wrap   envolver *ue

to write   escribir

yellow   amarillo

yesterday   ayer

yet   todavía

young   joven

you're welcome   de nada

zero   cero

Index

U

V